DEDICATION
▼ ▼ ▼ ▼ ▼

To my son Spyros.

ACKNOWLEDGMENTS
▼ ▼ ▼ ▼ ▼

This book has come into being because my friend, William Adams, was doggedly determined that it do so. Kathleen Griffin in kind devotion brought it to fruition.

The Emergence of the Western World

▼ ▼ ▼ ▼ ▼

Harold E. Lurier
Pace University

KENDALL/HUNT PUBLISHING COMPANY
4050 Westmark Drive Dubuque, Iowa 52002

CONTENTS

▼ ▼ ▼ ▼ ▼

FOREWORD

History is a humanistic art, the telling of a story of men and the world they create, whether singly or in social groups. The historian, to be sure, must be well-grounded in all the skills needed to gather his facts and to weave them into a dramatic narrative. He must appreciate the disciplines of archeology, economics, anthropology, literature, etc., but it is not necessary that the techniques of these disciplines be portrayed as such to the reader. It is more important that the story be enriched by them. In short, the tale must be accurate, coherent, and must give a reasonable picture of how men have acted in the past so as to produce the world of today. Above all, the tale must not only catch his attention, but it must please, satisfy and even stimulate the reader to seek a deeper understanding of man and his ways.

Also, I believe a story demands a theme and that a theme can be found in the history of Western Civilization. This theme is profoundly humanistic. Man is best viewed as a creature of will as well as of reason. He focuses his life on goals, some of his own choosing, others he merely finds thrust upon him, and he attempts to construct his life so as to attain them. The fascination of the study of man is to analyze how he chooses the goals that he does, whether alone or in close harmony with his fellows, his successes, his failures, and the manner in which he settles for alternatives. Man, furthermore, follows the same basic pattern when acting in social groups. A society also has aims, a picture of the good life, and the

institutions that emerge to attain them. As they succeed, the whole society may be said to succeed; as they fail, the whole society may be said to fail. In any case, society, as man himself, may be said always to be directing itself towards goals, even though at times it may appear to be dormant. It is always an extension of man and it is always striving to realize goals, modifying, discarding, creating institutions in the process. Only in this light can societies be said to rise, mature, decline and fail. But always the basic life-force of man and his society persists.

This book has been written to follow these broad philosophical lines. It is the story of Western Civilization in its origins and early development from the Hellenic world through the Middle Ages. The drama of the story will be the emergence of societies that have successively striven to attain certain goals, the tensions that have arisen as these goals were not attained, the sense of decay and even crisis that mark such transitions, and then the emergence of new institutions designed to attain better the old goals, or new goals better suited to some new condition of man.

As to why I begin the story with the Hellenic world, I can only say that it is a conviction of mine that Western civilization is exactly that, the civilization of the Western world. I prefer to follow the course of Western society and describe its encounters with the East, ancient or otherwise, so as to bring into the narrative appropriately and as it actually happened such elements as were absorbed or that caused changes. If the theme of the book is developed properly, then the Eastern cultures ought to be presented as they became, and to the extent that they did indeed become, a part of the Western culture. My views must not be taken to imply any particular superiority of the Western experience over any other, but I do believe that the culture of the West does have its distinctive personality, and I have chosen to describe it, for I believe it is a distinct and important culture of the world today.

This book, then, is intended to be the history of Western Civilization as it emerged within the setting of the ancient Eastern Mediterranean world, developed its own character and dynamism primarily under the guidance of the Greeks, who invented *Historia* after all, and produced eventually the structure of the society in which Western man and, to the extent that he has influenced them, all men live today.

THE WORLD OF HELLAS

▼ ▼ ▼ ▼ ▼

▶ **Silenus from the Theater of Dionysos in Athens.** The figure helps support the Roman stage added after the era when the works of the great Greek tragedians were staged for the first time in this theater. Silenus was a creature associated with the god Dionysos.

▶ **Acropolis of Athens.** The walls are those of Cimon and Pericles. To the left are the Propylaea and the temple of Athena Nike. To the right is the Roman theater of Herod Atticus.

▶ **Theater of Dionysos beside the acropolis of Athens.** The theater was in continuous use in classical, Hellenistic and Roman periods, with each age adding renovations. Originally it must have held at most 20,000 spectators, far less than the 30,000 Plato estimates in the *Symposium*.

Early History

The history of Europe begins with the appearance of the Greeks in the rocky southern extremities of the Balkan peninsula. The more ancient Near Eastern peoples contributed much to European history, to be sure, but their contribution was only assimilated as it was understood and transmitted by the Greeks. They were the first to break with obscure mythological explanations of the world around them. They asked lucid questions and sought rational explanations of all that affects the life of man. They perceived the aesthetic meaning of the world, and as an ideal they saw man living in that world, in dignified harmony with his fellow man. The Greek view of life, then, their sense of aesthetics, and their humanism gave voice to a culture that has remained the basis of European civilization ever after.

But who were the Greeks? As recently as the mid-Nineteenth Century the study of the history of Greece began with the *Iliad* and *Odyssey* of Homer, then thought to be the earliest description of the entrance of the Greeks into the Mediterranean world. The work of Heinrich Schliemann, who excavated Troy after 1870 and then the mainland cities of Mycenae and Tiryns, and Sir Arthur Evans, who uncovered the city of Knossos in Crete in the years after 1900, changed this situation drastically. Their discoveries disclosed many centuries of complicated history preceding the Homeric wars. It is now clear that as early as 6000 B.C. Neolithic man began to inhabit the Aegean world. At first cave dwellers, these primitives slowly learned to build huts, cultivate grains, domesticate sheep and cattle, spin fibers, and weave rough clothing. They lived in an orderly family and social structure and had developed a crude religion focused on the worship of female fertility figures.

The Minoans

Around 3000 B.C. a series of peoples began to invade Crete, the Aegean islands, and the mainland of Greece. Coming from the Near East, these peoples brought with them a sophisticated commercial civilization which they adapted to their new homes. The Cretan city of Knossos became the focus of a sea empire which is called Minoan after the legendary Cretan king Minos. The Minoans developed highly skilled crafts, and produced pottery, gold and silver artifacts, and highly efficient ships. Powerful fleets spread a web of trade throughout a complex of subject cities, and wealth poured into Knossos from all over the European and Near Eastern worlds. The Minoan civilization attained extraordinary heights. Graceful and elegant palaces, sometimes three stories high; well-stocked warehouses; theatres and sports arenas filled cities of paved roads and efficient drainage systems. The Minoans developed art forms of great beauty. Brilliantly-colored frescos, stucco reliefs, and mosaics covered the walls of their buildings inside and out. Skillfully executed vases and statues, as well as the most advanced architecture of the ancient world, show the good taste and intelligence of the Minoans. Their religion was based on a Near Eastern mother-goddess figure whose snake-embracing image has been found in many versions. The government seems to have taken the form of a widespread confederation led by a god-king, whose power was limited by an aristocratic council.

Around 2000 B.C. a new group of invaders began to move southward through the Balkan mountains into the Minoan world. These were the Achaeans, a Greek-speaking Indo-European people. Rapidly assimilating themselves to the higher culture they found in the Minoan cities, the Achaeans soon became independent of Cretan rule, though they eagerly adopted Cretan commercial and artistic techniques. About 1700 B.C. Knossos was devastated by a great earthquake, and the Minoan world began to fall apart. Cities in eastern Crete rose to power and ushered in a new phase of Minoan history. They developed a more democratic form of government, and a new cursive script (Linear A). On the mainland the Achaeans continued to prosper, and soon they began to compete with the cities of Crete, establishing direct commercial contact with Egypt and the Near East. Soon they began to attack Crete and on at least one occasion successfully established themselves in Knossos, where they began to write in archaic Greek, using the letters of the Cretan cursive script (Linear B). In the last centuries of its history (1600–1200 B.C.), Minoan Crete slowly faded into insignificance. The catastrophic eruption of the volcanic island Thera, just north of Crete, must have played some role in these developments. The scene shifted to the Greek world on the mainland.

The Early Greeks

Greece is a small country of about 50,000 square miles. It is covered with rugged mountains that make land travel extremely difficult. But the sea is everywhere in Greece, no point being more than 70 miles from the coast. The Greeks, then, are divided by the mountains, but they are bound together by the sea. A system of city states with no political unity emerged, while at the same time there developed a strong sense of Hellenic cultural unity. The soils of Greece are poor and rocky and it is a constant struggle to eke out a meager, frugal living. The climate is harsh in its extremes, yet it is usually mild enough to permit out-of-door living throughout most of the year, and the air is marvelously clear and invigorating. The geography of the country, then, went far in molding the frugal, simple character of the Greeks, their restless pursuit of the horizons of the sea and mind, their inventive experiments in the art of living, and their obstinate refusal to admit their faults.

The Greeks entered Greece in successive waves of Achaeans, Aolians, Ionians, Dorians and the like, who moved southward through the mountains, settling first in the north around Epirus, then moving into city states in central and southern Greece, and finally crossing over to the Aegean islands and the coast of Asia Minor. The Achaeans brought with them the Greek language and a new type of pottery, but their culture for many centuries was basically the Minoan one they found in their new homes. Warlike in nature, this vigorous young people quickly surpassed their Minoan teachers and developed their own skills and weapons. A coalition of their cities led by the prince of Mycenae attacked Crete in about 1450 B.C. and destroyed Knossos. On the ruins of the Minoan empire the Achaean princes established a confederation behind the leadership of Mycenae. They built cities surrounded by massive stone walls and protected by lofty citadels. Each prince considered himself quite independent and aggressively sought for spoils wherever he could find them. Political institutions were primitive, and society was organized around the family, the clan (a number of families descended from one ancestor), and the tribes (a collection of clans). Men were regulated by their clan rather than by a state government, and throughout the history of Greece a man's first loyalty was to his clan and to his brotherhood (*phratris*), the group of clans to which his own clan belonged.

Achaeans developed into a farming and pastoral people. They also became skillful craftsmen and traded widely around the Aegean world. Above all, however, they were booty-seekers, and they concentrated their military prowess on eliminating commercial rivals and on expanding their territories. It was for this reason that they attacked and destroyed the ancient and prosperous city of Troy in about 1180 B.C.

The war with Troy had been a long and difficult one, and it left the Achaeans exhausted. The Dorians, who had been slowly moving southward into Thrace and Thessaly, now attacked the Achaean cities with a violence that caused the Achaean survivors to flee before the storm. The Dorians were relatives of the Achaeans, speaking a special dialect of Greek, but they launched the first destructive invasion of Greece. They destroyed the Minoan-Mycenaean world and plunged Greece into the 300 year period often described as the "Dark Ages" of Greek history. The Dorians were copiers, rather than innovators, but they did introduce iron to the Greek world, and it was out of their society that classical Greece arose.

Homeric Greece (1100–800 B.C.)

The *Iliad* and the *Odyssey* of Homer, written in the 8th Century, gather together a cycle of songs or lays that kept alive the legends of the vanished Achaeans and added to them new ones that illuminate the world of the Dorians. As we have seen, Greece was divided into distinct states, each one separated from the other by high mountains. In each city-state, or *polis*, the head of the clan ruled as a priest-king, chief judge, and commander-in-chief. He lived in a palace built on an acropolis, around which the city clustered. The office of the king became a hereditary one, and the king usually claimed descent from a god. The community was composed of various clans, and the king had absolute power only over his own clan. The heads of the other clans, the princelings and chieftains, formed an aristocracy which sat in a council under the leadership of the king. Among the clan chiefs, the king was the only one who would act in the interests of the whole community, and the clans allowed him the power to act in this area while they retained their ancient freedoms. Thus the king appeared to be progressive, became more popular, and eventually grew in power while the chieftains became weaker. The common people met in a popular assembly to hear what their leader planned for them, but they had no power, no prestige, no voice in government. The three elements, the kingly, the aristocratic, and the popular or democratic, remained always the basic components of the Greek city-state governments.

The city states were almost always at war, for the Dorians spent most of their time at war, or athletics, which were a substitute for war. The armies reflected the social structure of the tribes. The better soldiers were the clan leaders, and battles were largely duels between them, each seeking to slay the other so as to strip him of his arms and armor. The Dorian economy was basically agrarian. The land was divided up between the clans, and the clan members all worked together on the land.

The religion of the Homeric world was a collection of beliefs that reflected the rustic simplicity of the people. The Greeks accepted the Minoan earth goddess and transformed her into the mother-goddess of fertility, Demeter, but they brought their own gods with them. These were gods of the sky, a collection of boisterous, anthropomorphic deities that differed from men only in their immortality and their great power. They ruled the universe and the destinies of men. Since there was no revealed dogma connected with their worship, men created an unending series of stories to describe the gods and their activities. Worship was a clan affair, conducted by the clan chief, so that there did not arise an organized priesthood. The gods were usually considered as protectors of whole communities and though they did concern themselves with the fate of individuals, their concern was with the way in which the individual related to the group as a whole.

The Age of Colonization

As the Dorian states developed, they tended to form alliances to seek better security. The result was a lessening of the amount of war. As this happened, each government tended to seek more stability within itself. The king attempted to bring under his control the heads of the aristocratic families. A political contest between them broke out throughout Greece. By the middle of the 8th Century, every Greek city-state had passed into the hands of an aristocracy, descendants of the old clan-chieftains. These aristocracies took the lion's share of the land in the state and ran the government to serve their own interests, but so long as the state remained agrarian and their interest remained mainly in land, no tension arose. However, slowly each state developed a class structure. The aristocrats had the greatest power, wealth and prestige. Beneath them the small farmers and agricultural workers lived under almost slave-like conditions. In the cities a class of artisans began to emerge as the state turned from war to peace.

Economic conditions for the lower classes were very bad. Food supplies were always low because of inadequate farming techniques and poor soil. Population tended to rise as warfare diminished. The lower classes were too numerous, too hungry, too poor to remain at home. Furthermore, acting first as pirates, then as traders, certain adventuresome members of the state had built ships, become seafarers, and had explored the Aegean world. They brought back knowledge of distant places, and wealth that indicated the opportunities that awaited overseas. The introduction of the use of money, and the rise in the standard of living, opened an ever increasing gap between the rich and poor. Encouraged by their leaders, then forced by necessity, led by dreams of advancement, great numbers of Greeks set out from their mother states to establish colonies all over the Mediterranean and Black Sea coasts.

The colonists remained citizens of the mother country and maintained close ties.

They developed a lively trade with their new neighbors and developed industries to produce goods for exchange. Mother countries had to develop cash crops (olives, wine, etc.) and new industries to produce the goods necessary to maintain trade with the colonies. The result was that there began to emerge a much more complicated social structure in the state. Rich aristocratic landowners, lording it over a depressed farmer class, now found competition in a class of rich merchants, shipbuilders, and manufacturers, who invested their money in land and profit-yielding crops. The skilled artisans of the cities formed a distinct group. Social tension led to bitter class antagonism which ultimately led to the overthrow of the aristocracies and the establishment of oligarchies maintained by precariously poised minorities. As the Greeks had spread around the Mediterranean, they had come into contact with new opportunities and new ideas. In Asia Minor, for instance, not only did the Greeks find great wealth and a sharp rise in their standard of living, but they also began to hear the teachings of the Ionian philosophers that offered explanations of the world that struck at the roots of aristocratic rule. They also learned a new alphabet there which made the language much more accessible to the common man. In Italy they heard from Pythagoras and others of the innate dignity of man. A clamor for more democratic government arose which first led to anarchy and to the rule of tyrants who came to power on a wave of popular enthusiasm to destroy the rule of vested interests and to usher in the rule of the lower classes. The tyrants ruled absolutely and though they occasionally ruled well, understanding the problems and aspirations of the lower classes, nonetheless they were more often corrupted by their

power. They did not last long in Greece, nor did their rule lead to some form of dictatorship. Rather, democratic government followed the tyrants, for the lower classes learned from them how much power they had, and they chose to support instead with religious patriotism the small, integrated, secular community, the city-state.

The classic pattern of political development in the Greek community, then, was the emergence of the city-state first as a monarchy, then as an aristocracy, that encouraged colonialism and trade, then as an oligarchy that dissolved in class war and chaos, and finally as a democracy, which dissolved in its turn into mob rule and foreign conquest.

The City-State

The typical city-state (*polis*) of Greece was a small city clustered around a "high city" (*acropolis*) on which were built a citadel, markets, temples and public buildings. Around the city stretched the farm lands dotted by tiny rural villages. All public activity of the whole region took place in the city itself. The population was small and the citizens lived, worked, worshipped and played in a sort of public intimacy. Within the *polis* there was always the atmosphere of a small town family. On the other hand, the government had the sophistication that is associated with a national state. Defense, law and order, public finances and foreign policy were all provided for on a large scale. The government, moreover, felt it a duty to control education, maintain the state religion, and sponsor the arts. Indeed, all three tended to merge. Each *polis* had an official state cult that focused on a patron god who was the protector of the community. The state cult fostered patriotism and civic unity, and its morality taught the individual to serve the common good. And this provided the themes of art and literature. The citizens competed vigorously for control over the government, for it was the only instrument for public change. Furthermore, all Greeks were convinced that a political community was a living organism, from within which all social or political improvement had to arise. Thus, they lived in close cooperation within the society, and were expected to be always ready to submerge personal interest in the general welfare. They believed a community could only improve from within. The tightly integrated *polis* could focus the creative energies of its citizens to an astonishing degree to produce in breathless speed great works of art, science, and philosophy. But the Greeks suffered from the prejudice that they could never learn from the outside. Too inbred, the Greeks were often cut off from new ideas. They never lent themselves to another system. Thus, each *polis* remained an isolated entity, and fratricidal war eventually left Greece a power vacuum that invited conquest from the outside. When this happened, it was too late for the Greek city-states to unite against the common enemy.

Sparta

There were many city-states in Greece. Each reflected its own special geography and historical development, but they all went through the classic political pattern described above. Some stopped early in their growth and, like Sparta, are examples of arrested development. Others, like Athens,

went through the whole pattern. A study of the two extremes, then, affords a good idea of what all the states were like. It is easy to emphasize the differences between Athens and Sparta, but it is more important to keep in mind that they were both examples of the same system, strove to achieve the same objectives, and that their similarities far outweigh their differences.

The Spartans were Dorians who had conquered Laconia in southern Greece in the 11th Century B.C. and who had installed themselves in five villages as conquerors over the Achaeans, whom they enslaved. During the age of colonization, Sparta began the classic development, expanding outward into the Peloponnesus, especially to the southwest into Messenia. Trade and manufacturing began to transform the agrarian appearance of the state, and a class of merchants began to emerge. The arts were cultivated, and at least one major poet, Alcman, flourished. The growth of the state came to an abrupt halt in 640 B.C. as the result of a revolt of Messenia. For twenty years Sparta had to use every resource at her command to put down the revolt. By 620 B.C. she was successful, but she was determined that her rule in southern Greece would never again be so threatened. Always a harsh government, the Spartan state now became an armed camp dedicated to the maintenance of Spartan control throughout the Peloponnesus. The society was divided up into three castes: the citizens, the *perioekoi*, the *helots*.

The citizens numbered from five to ten per cent of the population. They were the rulers and soldiers, and all the resources of the state were organized to provide the means for their function. The *perioekoi* were a caste of conquered neighbors, perhaps descended from Achaeans who had escaped the original conquest, who were allowed personal freedom as farmers and merchants, but who had no rights as citizens. The *helots* were the slaves that did all the work of the community either directly for the state or as assigned to serve on citizens' farms.

The community was kept in a constant state of war alert. The government was in the hands of two figurehead kings and five *ephors,* executive overseers, elected annually by the citizens. They were assisted by a council of the heads of the leading clans and a general assembly of all the citizens over thirty years of age. The government was a dictatorship of the council working through the *ephors*, and it exerted the power of life and death over all inhabitants.

Commercial life was severely restricted to a few *perioekoi*, who were not allowed to introduce luxuries to soften the lives of the warrior citizens. The arts were totally repressed for the same reason, and contacts with the outside world was discouraged so as to keep out artistic and intellectual contamination. The atmosphere of the state was dour, cheerless, disciplined, frugal.

The daily lives of the citizens were under the control of the state. All infants were inspected at birth so that weaklings could be exposed to die. From the age of seven, young boys were housed in barracks where they were trained in the harsh life of soldiers. Inadequately dressed, underfed, severely disciplined, the boys grew up tough, ruthless, resourceful campaigners. After thirty, young men married, lived at home, but continued to eat at the common mess and to keep in military trim. The girls were also given a rigorous training, less harsh than that given to the boys, to be sure, but one that was designed to instill in the moth-

ers of Sparta the desire to produce hero sons who would willingly die for their country.

The Spartan system produced an army that in the end conquered Greece. The Spartan citizens were intensely patriotic, but they were also devoid of all intellectual and artistic creativity. Fear, dullness, unthinking militarism, the very antithesis of the Greek spirit at its best, were the characteristics of Sparta. Most Greeks were repelled by the system and derided the Spartans. Yet in times of stress Sparta always remained, as it still does, the ideal of those who would integrate individual citizens into a tightly-controlled community to achieve collective security.

Athens

The Athenian city-state also originated at the time of the Dorian conquest, when a fusion of the Attic towns into a *polis* took place. Here, however, the citizen class was mainly pre-Dorian in nature. The government began as a monarchy, but soon became an aristocracy under the control of nine executives *(archons)* assisted by the Council of the Areopagus, composed of the heads of the leading families in the state and the customary general assembly of citizens. During the 7th Century, as colonization was undertaken, the city was agitated by a good deal of unrest. In 621 B.C. a law code was introduced by Draco, according to tradition, which was marked by an unusually severe system of penalties. But written laws were a big improvement over the older oral traditions, for they put the law into the hands of the lower classes. A generation later, in the 590's, Solon, a popular, though aristocratic, politician put an end to periods of

One of the maidens of the eastern portico of the Erechtheion. This one, carried off by Lord Elgin, is now in the British Museum. She is one of six maidens in procession, illustrating the Greek concept of stasis. They are in motion, but seem at the same time to be at rest.

Kouros **from the Acropolis Museum in Athens.** The figure is early 5th Century and shows the emergence of the classic Attic style freed from the stiffness of the Archaic style. The figure is introspective, with an inner life of its own, which illuminates the best of Hellenic sculpture.

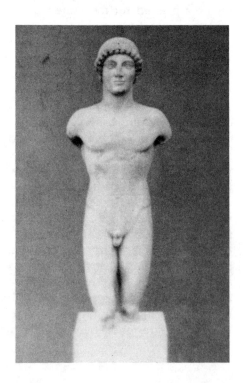

extreme tension by introducing a general legal reform, whose tone betrays a commercial background. Debts were cancelled, imprisonment for debt was outlawed, the currency was stabilized, new industries were introduced—all measures to relieve the economic plight of the lower classes. A new constitution divided the society into classes according to wealth. Taxes and privileges were tied proportionately to wealth. The assembly was strengthened and the courts were made more democratic by introducing large juries picked at random from the general citizenry.

The Age of the Tyrants brought Pisistratus (560 B.C.) and Cleisthenes (508–502 B.C.) to power. The one strengthened the economy of the state by improving the supply of wheat, wine, and olives and by issuing new silver coinage. The other introduced the first democracy in Athenian history. The population was divided into ten tribes composed of smaller units called *demes,* which were self-governing and open to naturalized as well as native-born citizens. Each tribe annually elected fifty citizens to sit in a council of five hundred, which governed the state. This council acted as a steering committee for the general assembly, which had the power to pass legislation. The Council of the Areopagus became a high court, while the lower courts were put into the hands of large juries selected by lot by the tribes. Public office was restricted to the wealthy, who were elected by popular vote.

Even more important than the specific institutions, the general tone of the government was one of genuine democracy. The general assembly met out in the open at least ten times a year. The council of five hundred met in rotating groups of fifty that sat for one of the ten months in the Athenian calendar. Since a different citizen presided each month, the chances were good that a citizen would be president of his state at least once in his lifetime. The juries that heard court cases were very large (201 in minor cases, but 501 or 1501 were common in important trials) on the principle that there is safety in numbers, a principle that explains the five hundred men in the steering committee. In a typical trial the jury acted as judge and district attorney as well as jury, while all actions were initiated by private citizens who had to plead the case in person in court. The defendant conducted his own defense in person.

The whole system was thus in the hands of amateurs who were expected to know the laws, human nature, and affairs of state so well they could, without special training, play the role of legislator, executive, judge and juror. Never has democracy been so directly in the hands of the public, who could upon the vote of a simple majority exile anyone they wished for ten years as a danger to the state (ostracism). On the other hand, many citizens simply did not respond to the invitation to freedom. Women were excluded from public life, and *metics* (resident aliens) and slaves had no role in the state whatsoever.

The Persian Wars

The greatest period in Greek history was ushered in by the Persian Wars. The Persian Empire in the 6th Century was a vast conglomerate state stretching from the Mediterranean to the Indus River in India. It incorporated vast numbers of people and supplies. However, its very size was its weakness. Dozens of peoples with their own customs, languages, governments were held together loosely under the governorships of imperial satraps. The army was composed of a polyglot collection of independent units fighting under competing generals. There was no unity of command, no unity of tactics.

During the reign of Darius the Empire had expanded into Greek territory in Asia Minor. In 499–94 B.C. some of the Ionian coastal cities revolted with Athenian aid. Darius decided to destroy Athens in revenge. He landed in 490 B.C. at Marathon, some 26 miles from Athens, with a large army of light-armed infantry. Heavy-armed Greek *phalanxes* fighting with inspired discipline under Athenian leaders won a great victory.

The *phalanx* was an example of the Greek mind at its best. An army is organized into units of different sizes, each one of which is trained in what is today called close army drill so that at a command the whole unit acts as one man, going forward or to the rear. The men in the front ranks use swords, those behind use spears, and upon all sides arrows extend the fire power. The army fights in units that have the discipline of one man and is the answer to the great but disorganized power of the Persian army. It is no accident that the *phalanx* was introduced early in the Spartan conquest of the Peloponnesus.

Xerxes, son of Darius, swore to avenge his father's humiliation and launched a massive invasion of Greece in 480 B.C. Tradition relates that over a million men crossed the Hellespont and rolled across northern Greece like an avalanche. The number is certainly much exaggerated, but surely it was a huge army, and the crisis for Greece was mortal. At the same time, Xerxes send a fleet to cut Athens off from help, and

to provide him with a means of getting his army out of Greece when Athens was defeated.

While a small Spartan army of three hundred men sacrificed itself valiantly at Thermopylae to gain time for Greece, the united Greek armies under Themistocles evacuated Attica, built fleets, and waited for the Persians in the Saronic Gulf. The Persians quickly overran Attica and reached the shore, opposite the island of Salamis, from where Xerxes watched in a rage as his superior fleet was trapped, out-maneuvered, and finally destroyed by the wily Greeks. As the Persians streamed northward to escape the trap they had fallen into, they were met at Platea (479 B.C.) by the Greeks, who won another resounding victory. A small nation on the frontier of civilization had decisively defeated the greatest empire in the world. A wave of pride and exhilaration swept across the Greek world bearing with it a great artistic outburst. Furthermore, the Greeks now undertook the liberation of the Asiatic coast. But more important, the Persian Wars proved to be a turning point in European history. The West had been saved from Asiatic domination and had been assured of an independent development of its own institutions.

The Athenian Empire and the Peloponnesian War

To meet the Persian menace the Greek states had pooled their resources under Athenian leadership. In 478 B.C. Athens organized the Delian League, which was a confederation of most Greek states, who placed money, supplies, troops, and ships on the sacred island of Delos where representatives met under Athenian control to direct the defense of Greece. In 454 B.C. Athens moved the funds to her Acropolis. Pericles (d. 429 B.C.) turned the member states into provinces, made Athenian currency their official medium of exchange, gave Athenian courts jurisdiction over all cases in all the states, and denied the members the right to withdraw from trade and political agreements with Athens. In fact the League itself had become an Empire!

On the whole, the member states benefitted from Athenian leadership. However, Athens intervened constantly in local affairs. Throughout Greece she sponsored democratic governments of her type and she founded many new colonies. Pericles' dream of a united Greek world in the form of an Athenian Empire inspired him to encourage Athenian merchants to adopt aggressive imperialism to achieve this end. Wealth was produced throughout the Greek world, but everywhere aristocratic parties became hostile and fearful of Athenian power. This opinion was carefully cultivated by Sparta, who felt an antipathy for the Athenian system, a natural jealousy and an understandable fear of Athenian domination and absorption.

A Peloponnesian League was formed to counter the Delian League and in 431 B.C. Greece was plunged into the Peloponnesian War, which raged until 404 B.C. During the fratricidal conflict the best elements of the Greek spirit, selfless sacrifice, patriotism, and bravery, commingled with the failures of the democratic process, deceit, betrayal, senseless arrogance, and mob prejudice, to bring Greece to the point of exhaustion. Racked by plague, betrayed by her leaders, terrorized by fear-crazed angry mobs, Athens was forced to sue for peace, and Sparta was the conqueror of Greece. Everywhere

she hastened to implant her rule through parties and governments favorable to her. Civil war swept over Greece. A mood of pessimism and disillusion paralyzed the minds of Greek statesmen. Everywhere men turned to the hope of deliverance, even at the hands of an invader. The invader was waiting impatiently to the north.

Greek Civilization in the Golden Age

During the period of the Athenian domination over the Greek world and lasting until the Macedonian conquest Greece experienced a Golden Age. Rarely have the religious spirit of a people, their plastic arts, their intellectual ability fused so perfectly into a single expression of the human condition. Ever since, the tone of this age has been called "classic," and has served as a model for any penetrating and serious probing of human problems that is presented in a lucid, balanced and stimulating form.

Greek Religion

The Greek religion was basically an attempt to identify the mysterious implacable forces that control the universe and man's situation within it and to discover the means of placating them, if hostile, enlisting their support, if reasonable, or gaining power over them, if controllable, so as to ensure the fertility of men and the fields and to obtain a happy issue for human endeavors. The Greeks believed that the universe contained great energy which could become a benign or sinister power in the lives of men. Like all primitive peoples, the Greeks originally located the source of this power in natural phenomena—thunder, lightening, sun, earthquakes—and its dynamic quality was suggested by ascribing to the natural world a role in human affairs. Eventually this led to an anthropomorphic collection of gods that represented the dynamic power of the universe in all of its varied forms.

The Greek gods were a collection, then, of the pre-Dorian sea- and earth-gods and the later Indo-European sky-gods. Though there was an official pantheon and hierarchy of gods including Zeus, the king; Hera, the queen; Athena, goddess of wisdom; Aphrodite, goddess of love and beauty; Apollo, god of light, music, and healing, every natural feature was represented by some god, and the major gods themselves were fusions of many of these local gods. The gods were understood in human form. They lived, fought, loved, quarreled as men do. They were petty, jealous, noble, sublime as men are. But, unlike men, the gods had great power and lived forever. Men needed to come to terms with that power by sacrificial offerings, service, loyalty to the gods. If man satisfied the gods, he would receive their favor; if he angered them, he would be punished. So simple a religion as this did not require a priesthood, and since no revealed religious truths were involved, simple descriptive myths arose, but no speculative theology.

The Greeks also believed that gods and men both were controlled by a mysterious fate or chance (*tyche*) which was the real motivating energy of the universe. Each man had assigned to him his particular destiny or place in the movement of the universe through time (*moira*) and his role in life was to accept this with human dignity and good will.

The Greeks were almost completely involved with life on this earth and had only the vaguest speculations about life after death, which they abhorred. In general, the dead lived on as they had when alive, except that they no longer lived in the light, only in shadow, and had no inspiration, no hope, no growth. The Greeks had no real concept of the soul and personal salvation, though there arose an important group of mystery cults that might suggest some such notion. Near Eastern fertility rituals surrounding the gods Adonis, Bacchus, Dionysius, Demeter, Persephone, and the like, spread widely across the Greek world. In each case, the worshippers formed a mystic cult whose membership was private. Initiation ceremonies and highly emotional annual festivals prepared the worshippers for a descent of the ever-living god into their midst. As the god entered into each celebrant, he brought with him his eternal life so that, filled with the god, the worshipper was literally outside himself, greater than himself, god-like and as such assured of eternal life.

Religion gave to the Greeks a means of coming to terms with the world around them. It gave them an ethical system and an ideal way of life. It also provided an important outlet for the repressed emotions of certain citizens who did not participate fully in the intimate city-state. Religion also provided one of the few instances of Greek unity. The cult of Apollo at Delphi, for instance, brought Greeks from every part of Greece to seek advice of the oracle. The worship of Zeus at Olympia gave rise in 776 B.C. to the famous Olympic games to which every Greek state sent contestants. The Mysteries at Eleusis in honor of Demeter and Persephone was a pan-Hellenic cult, and on the sacred island of Delos every Greek state had its headquarters. Finally, Greek religion remained a constant source of inspiration for the artistic and philosophic life of Greece.

The Arts

The Greeks always believed that art was a form of education. Its purpose was to instruct men in the art of living. A Greek building, for instance, and this is particularly true of the Parthenon on the Acropolis of Athens, was a study in the conquest of the discordant elements in the world by intelligent order. The tensions of the stresses and thrusts of the heavy roof, the shifting sight lines of the perspective, the unyielding heaviness of stone, all these are meticulously balanced in a miracle of harmony and proportion that transforms the building into a serene victory of order over chaos. So, too, might man conquer with his mind the seething disorder of his emotions, and the Greeks believed that this could be better achieved in the presence of a perfect example.

Greek sculpture illustrates the same principle. The archaic Apollos of the 6th Century, even the more accomplished marbles of Myron and Praxiteles in the 5th and 4th centuries are fine examples of serene poise. The body, caught in the instance of launching the discus, or scraping the limbs after a bath, or carrying an infant child, is transformed from a powerful mechanical machine into a poetic and lyrical statement of what man is ideally and ought to strive to become in reality. Greek sculpture rarely concerned itself with pictorial literalness in the superficial appearance of things, but with the significance of the underlying reality of things as we understand and absorb them.

The drama was a totally engrossing experience for the Greeks. It originated in the annual festivals in honor of the god Dionysius, where it was customary to act out in song and dance certain episodes in the life of the god. A priest and chorus of men dressed as goats to represent followers of the god (*tragos*, goat; *oidia*, song; *tragoidia*, goat-song) carried on a dialogue which explored lofty moral themes. Aeschylus (525–456 B.C.) introduced a second actor and the technique of telling a dramatic story through dialogue. His plays, only seven of which survive, probe deeply the spiritual nature of the universe. In the *Oresteia*, for instance, he portrays in profoundly universal terms the basic problem of man's wrongdoing, his sense of guilt, his attempt to do justice by vengeance, the retribution that befalls him, and his final understanding that justice is a transcendent quality in the hands of the gods.

Sophocles (496–406 B.C.) added more actors and used more complicated plot structures. He accepted the approach of his older contemporary, but he focused on the human response to the fact of a transcendent justice. In his *Oedipus Tyrannus* he portrayed a man caught in an inexorable web of circumstance. He thinks he is free, strives mightily to be a good king and a just man, but because he forgets the limits of man's role in the universe, he is guilty of overweening pride (*hybris*) and the extent of his crimes is slowly brought home to him. He has fulfilled his destiny, he is a parricide, and he has committed incest with his mother. In horror, he plucks out his eyes and spends the rest of his days seeking an understanding of his fate. When finally it comes, and he realizes that man must accept with dignity whatever fate life bestows upon him and still believe in the gods and the rightness of things as they are, he is released from his torment.

Euripides (480–406 B.C.) turned away from the lofty themes of his predecessors and tried to probe more deeply into the inner personality of his protagonists. He was interested in the problems of motivation, frustration, adjustment. He concentrated mainly on women, graphically portraying some of the most repelling, yet memorable, heroines of all literature. Unpopular in his own day and accused of immorality and impiety, he has proved to be the Greek tragedian of most enduring popularity in subsequent centuries.

If tragedy probed lofty themes to elevate and purify the emotions of its audiences, as Aristotle once stated, comedy had quite different aims. Raucous and bawdy, the comic plays arose from another aspect of the Dionysian festivals, the revelries that were intended to amuse the worshippers and remind them of the fertility significance of the god and his companions. Gross obscenities, pungent language and unseemly conduct filled the plays, but at the same time they became a form of social criticism. The eleven plays of Aristophanes (450–385 B.C.) that have survived, for example, have outrageous plots that are filled with biting comments on politics, famous men, human foibles. In them, the Greeks could laugh at themselves, their pretentions and their leaders. Used with sensitivity, they provide a wonderful insight into the everyday life of the ancient Greeks.

The drama was always written in poetic form and apparently the poets of the Golden Age concentrated their talents on writing plays, for there is only one poet in this period who can match Homer, Hesiod,

Sappho and the other poets of the Archaic period. He was Pindar (518–438 B.C.), who invented the ode. His poetry had less importance for its content that for its form that was adopted by the Latin poet Horace and through him passed into European literature. Again man imposes order over discordant elements, and the result is beauty.

The humanistic interests of the Greeks gave rise to the first histories in the modern sense of the word. Herodotus (484–428 B.C.), "the father of history," wrote a broad panoramic history of the Persian Wars. He drew the classic portraits of its heros and their deeds, but he was interested in far more than a panegyric of his countrymen. He had travelled widely throughout the civilized world. He had studied men, heard their tales, examined their customs. His curiosity was insatiable, but he never lost a sense of humorous skepticism and balance even when reporting in straightforward manner outrageous superstitions and folktales.

Thucydides (460–400 B.C.) has usually been more carefully studied by historians than Herodotus. His account of the Peloponnesian War has always been accepted as the first modern or scientific history. He believed that history was controlled by a dispassionate operation of cause and effect. The war had causes, it followed its course because men acted in certain ways, and ended as it did because these causes and acts led to specific results. He attempted to be objective and accurate, and he believed that the human situation being a universal one, all men could learn how to improve their own affairs by studying the experience of the Greeks. His work is rather self-conscious and calculated, if thoughtful and scholarly. It lacks the lively humanity of Herodotus.

Xenophon (430–354 B.C.), a contemporary and friend of Plato, and like him a youthful admirer of Socrates, was a remarkable example of a Greek gentleman of letters. He was a student of philosophy in his younger years, a soldier, adventurer, aristocratic conservative in politics, and he left behind a wide range of important works. His *Anabasis* was an excellent job of war-reporting, while his biographical sketches of Socrates and Cyrus of Persia show a sensitive, if somewhat romantic, appreciation of the qualities of greatness. He also wrote lively studies of day to day politics and gentlemanly life.

The Philosophy of Greece

Greek philosophy begins with the writings of a group of thinkers who lived in the 6th Century in Ionia, around the city of Miletus. Though these teachers were thoroughly imbued with the religious attitudes of their day toward the nature of the universe and the roles played in it by gods and men, nevertheless they attempted to find some rational pattern that would explain the origin and functioning of the universe in naturalistic terms. These pre-Socratic philosophers led by Thales of Miletus and his student, Anaximander, interpreted the universe as a basic organic unity. All its diverse components were actually manifestations of a primal substance—water, according to Thales; air, according to Anoximenes; and basic mass itself, according to Anaximander—in various stages of change and form. They believed that the religious myths of the Homeric world were useless in explaining the natural forces of this world and that the method of science ought to be the careful, pragmatic observation of things as they are in order to relate all observable phenomena

to one basic principle, or first cause. Thus Greek thinkers for the first time in history were able to break with mythological explanations of the world and to embark on a rational, scientific search for natural hypotheses to explain the apparent disconnectedness of the world. Xenophanes, for instance, taught that the whole universe was One and that plurality only existed in man's mind. There was only one god, he believed, that rules over all. Lesser gods were fictitious representations of natural forces. Parmenides established Western rationalism in its basic form by insisting that what appears to man's senses as change, or differentiation, is really an illusion. The senses cannot convey truth, only opinion. Therefore, if man would seek truth, he must rely on his reason. The mind alone can perceive the unchanging reality of all being.

Psychology and the study of ethics were added to Greek philosophy by Pythagoras (c.582–507 B.C.), who founded a monastic brotherhood at Croton in southern Italy. A profound student of music and musical theory, Pythagoras experimented with lyre strings of various lengths and became convinced that there exists a law that governs the relationships between the tonal pitch and the physical property of the string. He also came to the conclusion that numbers are realities, not symbols, and that the universe is composed of numbers arranged in harmonious groupings. He believed that man could determine the basic harmony of the universe and could become somehow absorbed in it. To do this, man must realize that his body contains within it, as does the physical, phenomenal world, a soul of non-material essence. By a rigorous training of diet and exercise and discipline of the will, man can subdue his flesh, achieve harmony within the soul and release it so that it can achieve a life everlasting in the harmony of the mathematical universe. The influence of Pythagoras has been profound in that he drew for the first time the distinction between an "evil" world of the flesh and a "good" world of the spirit. His work also suggested to Plato his doctrine of the immortality of the "soul."

The next phase of Greek philosophy unfolded in Athens during the course of the 5th Century. The ages was one of strife and social ferment in which old values gave way to new, traditional aristocracies to restless democracies. It was a time when man turned his attention away from cosmic, transcendent philosophies to an examination of his own self and role in the world around him. Heraclitus (500 B.C.) rejected the views of Parmenides and taught that the world is in a constant state of change. As one steps into a river, the one foot is placed in the water, but the second foot enters different water. That the river appears one and unchanging is an illusion of the senses. But he did hypothesize that the substance of the universe is a sort of fire that in its dynamic aspect (*Logos*) shapes and creates the universe in a constant process of conflict, change and growth. Empedocles (c.493–433 B.C.) sharpened these suggestions by stating that the universe is alive and consists of four forces: fire, air, water, earth. These are led by the force of love (*eros*, an inherent attraction for the appropriate) to combine in various ways and by the force of antipathy to break up and withdraw from each other. Thus, disconnected phenomena are the result of the one influence, whereas the basic unity and harmony of the universe result from the other.

Zeno (b.c.490 B.C.) argued with his teacher Parmenides that sense-perceived change was illusory and went on to deny even the existence of motion and space. By applying Pythagorean mathematics and logic to carefully selected speculative problems (Does Achilles catch the tortoise? Is an arrow in flight in place?) he tried to demonstrate that separate place and the movement of an object in time are both illusions of the senses. Anaxagoras (500 B.C.) sharpened the dispute by postulating a divine, transcendent and incorporeal Mind (*nous*) which creates and sets into turbulent motion all the phenomena of the universe. The senses perceive the eternally changing combinations, but the mind alone can make contact with the unchanging Mind. The ordinary man is content to live within the limitations of the senses; the wise man seeks the freedom that results from the pursuit of the Mind.

Democritus (c.460–c.370 B.C.) suggested an interesting compromise to the apparent contradiction between a world of change and one of permanence. He decided that all matter was composed of basic, irreducible particles (atoms) that move eternally in an infinite void. All atoms are identical with each other except that some are larger or heavier, but as to essential nature, there is no difference. These particles have always been in existence, and their differing weights set up a falling or swirling motion in the primeval void which will last forever. In motion, the atoms temporarily interlock to produce the material phenomena of the universe, but at last they break away, rearrange their combinations, and present the appearance of new phenomena. The universe is controlled by laws of attraction, combination, the indestructibility of matter which are eternal, unchanging. Men do not need gods to explain it, but by using reason they can see in perspective the moving, changing aspect of matter. The wise man will avoid the world of sense-perceived change, but will follow the lead of his own atom-composed soul and will seek a balanced, measured contact with the rational underlying structure of all things.

The ideas of this whole period in Greek philosophy had a profound effect on Plato and Aristotle and through them all subsequent Western though, but their most immediate effect was on the men of their own time. The democratic forces of the 5th Century were bringing into being new classes and new men of talent. Their problems were practical in nature. How does one succeed in life? How does one adapt oneself to society? What is the responsible life for a moral but ambitious man? Teachers were sought out to describe the world as it is, to instruct man in how to come to terms with it, and to discover moral principles that would be at once practical and true. The Sophists followed the lead of Protagoras (c.481–411 B.C.) who had proclaimed, "Man is the measure of all things," by which he suggested that all truth is relative to a particular stage in man's knowledge and that man's needs determine his view of the universe. Man tries to manipulate the universe so as to achieve what he feels at any given moment is happiness. At the same time Protogoras suggested that while the gods do not exist, there is a moral force in the world that governs men's relationships and which transcends man-made law as a sort of Mind that determines the true order of the universe. Sophocles apparently heard Protagoras' lectures and developed them in the theme of his *Antigone*.

The Sophists have been severely condemned as opportunistic money-makers who sold knowledge to the ambitious, to be used as a technique for political or social advancement. It is true that they were practical men who were involved in preparing men for the lives they would have to lead.

Thus they taught rhetoric, argumentation, and the art of persuasion. But at the same time the best of them, such as Hippias and Gorgias, taught that since truth is relative to individual men, it is their responsibility as individuals to improve their character and conduct so as to maintain just and ordered relationships between men. Ethics, psychology, politics, and education are fields that begin with these "wise-guys." Common men were attracted by their practical teachings and the elevated moral tone they gave to democracy, but traditionalists objected to their atheism and their lack of respect for traditional moral codes. It is ironic that Socrates, who stood for all the Sophists condemned, was himself thought of as a Sophist.

Socrates (469–399 B.C.) called himself a gadfly come to goad the Athenians to examine themselves and improve their condition. He spent his life seeking knowledge, attacking prejudice, and proclaiming with great courage the fundamental goodness of man. He believed that the good exists and that it is man's nature to seek it, for what man would willingly do evil, when he can just as easily do good? Evil is ignorance and misjudgment. The evil man is deluded that his act will bring him some good. Therefore, man needs careful education and constant encouragement to use his essential nature to find the good. Also, Socrates believed that man possesses an immortal "soul," that links him to the eternal universe, the knowledge of which fact ought to give man a calm courage in the face of an often threatening, ignorant world. His condemnation as an atheistic perverter of the young men who flocked to his side and his enforced suicide so movingly described in the works of his finest pupil Plato attest to the consistency and integrity of the man.

Plato (c. 429–347 B.C.) saw in the death of his master Socrates a living symbol of the evils of his day. The Athenian democracy had disintegrated into mob rule in which any determined schemer could plot his way to success and in which quality, virtue, talent were swallowed up by a vulgar commonality. His bias was in favor of an aristocratic ordering of society under an intellectual elite that would direct men of spirit to organize the productive capacities of common men to achieve an ideal for the society as a whole. He further believed that men are locked in a world of their sense perceptions, which distort and alter according to transitory points of view. This is the world of opinion. Men of intellect, led on by a desire for truth and the good, go beyond their senses. By the use of their intellect they perceive and make contact with a world of pure forms that are eternal, unchanging and which underlay their shadowy copies that are in the material world, objects of man's senses. Plato believed that the role of the true philosopher is to teach man by a rational inductive dialectic the good life, based on the world of real forms that culminate in the ultimate form, the good. He opened a school in 387 B.C., the Academy, where he and his successors expounded his teachings until its eventual close in the 6th Century A.D. In the last analysis, Plato's view of the state is that of his times. The unsettled conditions of the 4th Century, he thought, could be cured by the establishment of a well-ordered community in which each citizen played a specified role. Each man was to be judged by how well he played his role. Each individual knows his role as he knows the good, by an intuitive flash or insight. By discipline, by self-analysis, by a willingness to strive for the good, each man achieves the good life and ultimately, by the contact of his soul with the Ideal Form, eternal life.

Plato's most important student was Aristotle (384–322 B.C.). A Macedonian, the young Aristotle came to the Academy and remained for twenty years, absorbing as much of his master's thought as he was able. He then opened his own school, the Lyceum, where he taught a type of Platonism that was precise, practical and closely tied to the observable world. Aristotle was himself a man of scientific temperament. He believed the thoughtful man ought to observe carefully the world around him. Even though he accepted Plato's suggestion of the existence of a permanent form behind the apparent object in the sense-perceived world, he could never separate the two, suggesting instead that every phenomenon in the physical world had attached to it a material, an image imposed upon it by its creator, energy necessary to produce it and finally the purpose for which it was brought into being. Aristotle believed that all growth and movement was the realization of an implicit potential, much as it is an acorn's predestined end, if it develops, to become an oak tree. All life is moving, he thought, to an ultimate end which causes all movement, though it in itself does not move. It is the Prime Mover, a magnet that draws all life toward itself. Each man ought to arrange his life in a balanced, temperate way to achieve the detachment necessary to contemplate his ultimate good. This good is attached to the common good of the whole society, and the individual's good can be achieved only when the general good is realized. Thus, a well-ordered balanced state in which all interests are served in a collective compromise is the state best suited to the needs of man. Aristotle left behind an encyclopedic collection of all the knowledge of his day which passed on to later ages the finest expression of the Greek genius.

ALEXANDER AND THE HELLENISTIC WORLD
▼ ▼ ▼ ▼ ▼

▶ The Hellenistic style with its emphasis on movement and agitation is for this reason very different from the serenity and stasis of the Classical age.

◄ **Hellenistic head.** The style has changed significantly from the Classical avoidance of literal portraiture. The boy seems to be alive and involved with, and not contemplating, the world around him.

► **The Tower of the Winds in the Roman *agora* in Athens.** Built in the 1st Century B.C. by the Hellenistic astronomer Andronicus of Kyrrhos, the building contains a *klepsydra,* a water clock, that counted drops of water to measure time, and it acted as a sundial and weathervane at the same time, a typical example of the ingenuity of Hellenistic science. A tradition, probably untrue, says that it was a gift from Julius Caesar to Athens.

The Failure of the City-State System

In the years that followed the Peloponnesian War the Greek city-state system inexorably crumbled. Sparta attempted to replace Athenian hegemony with her own. In every Greek state she forced the ouster of democratic governments and replaced them with Spartan-type oligarchies under the control of Spartan governors. Thebes and Athens raised a coalition of the frightened Greeks, and war spread throughout central Greece. Civil war within each state, bands of restless mercenaries and ambitious war leaders turned Greece into chaos. The Persian world fell into the same condition as rival claimants fought over the throne of the Great Xerxes. Sparta fought to establish herself in the Ionian cities of the Persian empire. The coalition fought her at home. The Great King of Persia invaded Greece, and in the end all factions went down to defeat. Sparta was defeated by Thebes at Leuctra in 371 B.C. But Theban sponsorship of a Greek revival failed with the death of her great leader Epaminondas in 362 B.C. All attempts at settling Greek and Persian rivalries had failed, and the Greco-Persian world became a power-vacuum awaiting deliverance from its exhaustion. The city-state system had failed because the city-state itself had proved inadequate as a political technique to handle the affairs of the Greek world. It was economically too small a unit to support policies it undertook. Overpopulation always remained a problem, and the low standard of daily living kept up a relentless pressure. Furthermore, the very virtues of the city-state became its vices. Too committed to the idea that it was perfectible only by the vigilant attention of its citizens,

the city-state closed itself off from outside influences and ideas. City patriotism easily turned to blind prejudice. Thus it was that every attempt at a federal union of the Greek world was doomed to fail. Too small to survive singly, too prejudiced to enter a federal system, the Greek states collapsed. Thoughtful men, such as Plato, easily turned to the hope of deliverance from their agony at the hands of a strong ruler who would bring peace, even if at the price of a liberty that had failed to bring security. The Thirty Tyrants of Athens, Lysander of Sparta, the Theban Epaminondas, Dionysias of Syracuse, the Great King of Persia, among others, each in turn presented himself as such a deliverer, but all failed until Philip II marched south at the head of a barbaric Macedonian army.

Philip the Macedonian

Macedonia until the 5th Century had been peopled by a race of farmers and horse breeders who were related distantly to the Greeks, but who were much closer in blood and culture to more barbaric Balkan strains. The government was nominally a monarchy, but a socially mobile aristocracy fought bitterly over local holdings, and the country remained weak until organized by the power of the king. The early Macedonian kings had been weak, though they had established contact with the Greek world and had begun to move southward into Thessaly.

Philip began his career as regent for his infant nephew, who was left King in 359 B.C. upon the death in battle of his father King Perdiccas III. Philip was a brutal man, an excellent leader of soldiers, and a man of inordinate bodily appetites. But he was also a shrewd politician, and an avid student of the superior Greek culture to his south. In fact, it seems that Philip was a sincere admirer of Greece. He introduced Greek institutions, particularly in military affairs, and he surrounded himself with a new aristocracy of fanatically devoted followers. Philip ruthlessly exterminated barbarism among his people. He brought Aristotle to his capitol at Pela to be tutor to his young son, and it is probable that his invasion reflected a genuine desire to bring release to the Greeks as much as internal Macedonian policy. Soon after becoming King in 359 B.C., Philip began his expansion. He moved eastward across Thrace and southward into Thessaly.

When he was ready, he provoked an occasion to enter Greek affairs. The Greek states were as usual engaged in a series of petty wars. Invited in as an ally, Philip kept the pot boiling by clever diplomatic manoeuverings while he took city after city in the north. Athens under the proddings of Demosthenes desperately sought to surround him with a coalition of Greek states, including Thebes and others, but in vain. For six years, Philip bought support among the enemies of Demosthenes with gold, egged on internecine Greek rivalries, then when all Greece was demoralized, he struck across Thrace and captured Byzantium. Open war with Athens followed. Invading boldly, he met a combined Athenian-Boeotian army at Chaeronea in 338 B.C. It was a savage battle and a disaster for Greece. Over 3,000 Athenians were lost, the Theban Sacred Band was sacrificed, and Philip was master of Greece. He established a league of all the Greek states to send representatives to a council at Corinth. There he dominated this first successful federation of the Greek world, and requisitioned moneys and ships from the politically neutralized states of Greece. With these, Philip planned to undertake a war of liberation against the Great King of Persia to unite the Greek world behind him. But it was at this moment that he was mysteriously murdered in a palace revolt in 336 B.C.

Alexander (356–323 B.C.)

Alexander inherited from his father a strong, violent, often savage personality. He was a born general, a leader of men. Restless, he fought at the side of his men in battle. He seemed always positive, dynamic, and he inspired confidence and devotion. It was easy to think of him as a god. At the same time he inherited the mystical qualities of the personality of his mother, Olympias. She was a member of the cult of Dionysius and delved in magic. Emotionally unbalanced, ambitious, she lived in a state of semi-hysteria. Alexander was deeply involved with her, and undoubtedly his frequent rages, moods of depression and irrational conduct reflect this. These two violent sides of his character were blended by the Hellenizing influence of his great teacher, Aristotle, and Alexander became interested in Greek philosophy, science, religion and, believing himself to be the descendent of Achilles and Hercules, he undertook to become the champion of Greek civilization.

Alexander came to power at the age of twenty. In rapid measure, he fought down all opposition in Macedonia and seated himself firmly on the throne. He then dashed across the Danube to attack and pacify the threatening barbarian Getae to the north. Turning southward to Greece, he put down revolts that had sprung up upon Philip's death. In spectacular haste he captured Thebes (335 B.C.) and ordered it destroyed. He spared Athens, but he took charge of the League of Corinth, cowed all the Greek states into submission, and left his trusted adviser Antipates in charge as viceroy of Macedonia and tyrant over Greek affairs, as he took up his father's mission to carry on a Greek *ravanche* against Persia.

The Persian Campaign

Alexander crossed the Hellespont with an excellently-trained army of about 32,000 infantry and 5,000 cavalry, organized into the sturdy *phalanx* and light, mobile auxiliary cavalry units. In addition, he had a corps of engineers, a commissary, a medical and a communications corps. Above all, it was an army led by an inspired general that felt it had a mission of great import to accomplish. Alexander fought alongside his men, saw to their needs, grieved over their wounds. He surrounded himself with a circle of devoted aides.

Persia, meanwhile, though potentially the greatest power of the day, suffered from fatal weaknesses. Her very size worked against her. A collection of dozens of nations, all following different customs, speaking various languages, held loosely together by ambitious Persian governors, the empire was in a state of constant turmoil. The army itself reflected this, as all contingents fought under their own leaders and followed no central command. The government itself was torn apart by rivalries within the royal house. From the death of Darius II (405 B.C.) to the murder of Artaxerxes in 336 B.C., the crown had passed

back and forth between rivals who used intrigue, assassination, civil war, and Greek mercenaries to rise to power, only to plunge the country into chaos and be replaced by the next claimant to the throne. Egypt was lost, the Jews of Palestine were aroused to furious revolt, the Greek cities were in helpless apathy, the rest of the empire was crumbling into separatist states. It was this Persian internal decay that explains in part the great success of Alexander's campaign.

He began his invasion with a rapid march through the Greek states of Ionia. Here he was acclaimed a liberator, and his task was fairly easy. He defeated the Persians at the Granicus River near Troy (334 B.C.) and replaced their satraps with Macedonian governors. Leaving behind small guards as he went, and keeping open his lines of communications with his fleet and patrols, he decided to go on into the Middle East. At the battle of Issus (333 B.C.) he defeated the Persians led by Darius in person, captured Darius' mother, wife, and daughters, and a huge amount of booty, which settled his worries about financing his campaign. From Issus Alexander marched southward along the coast, meeting little opposition except at Tyre, that fell only after a long spectacular assault in which he used war-ships and siege-engines. After taking Gaza, he marched into Egypt.

In Egypt he underwent a mystical experience that had interesting overtones as an indication of Alexander's intentions in the campaign. Leaving behind the urgent press of war and the laying out of the city of Alexandria, he rode almost 300 miles out into the Libyan Desert to visit the shrine of Ammon Re at the Oasis of Siwa. He had a private interview with the oracle there and let it be known that he had been hailed as the son of Ammon, whom the Greeks already identified with Zeus. The Egyptians easily accepted him as a god, for he was the pharaoh, who had always been acknowledged as divine. But the Greeks and the Persians no longer accepted the divinity of their kings, though their legends did include many god-hero figures. It is clear that Alexander, himself, was only too pleased to foster the idea of his divine origins.

From Egypt he struck at the heart of the empire by invading Mesopotamia itself. Darius fled in terror from the decisive battle of Gaugamela (331 B.C.), and Alexander was free to destroy the great capitol cities of the empire and to appropriate the enormous royal treasure, which has been estimated to have a buying power of billions of dollars. Shortly after, Darius was killed by his own body guard, and Alexander became Great King of Persia.

The next seven years saw Alexander and his shrinking army fighting across Afghanistan to pacify wild mountain tribesmen, who had never accepted Persian control. He then crossed into the Hindu Kush mountains through 14,000 foot high passes, and came down into the plains of northern India. For two years he struggled to control that region, and finally in 326 B.C. he crossed the Indus River and prepared to enter the turbulent affairs of the Indian subcontinent. Half-starved, exhausted, terrified at finding themselves at the very ends of the earth, meeting armies led by ranks of war elephants, his troops finally called a halt to the war. They demanded that he turn back. It was time to go home. Having reached the uttermost boundaries of the Persian Empire, Alexander was ready to return. So he sent off his armies in three parts, to explore the lands between India and Persia and to *rendez-vous* in Mesopotamia. He also sent his ad-

miral Nearchus with the fleet to map the coastline and plot the best routes by sea between the Malabar Coast and the Persian Gulf. Finally, in 323 B.C., the armies reached Persepolis. The adventure was over.

Alexander the Empire Builder

Having conquered a world, Alexander now had to face the problem of ruling it. One aspect of his problem was as obvious as it was universal. The vast territory stretching from Greece to India included dozens of peoples, governments, cultures. To rule it, one would have to find some means to put an end to the internecine wars among the Greek states, the Greek-Persian enmity, the religious and political tensions among the Near Eastern states, the jealousies among the Persian satraps. Alexander set himself the task of seeking out elements of unity. For one thing, he understood the role of symbolism in establishing centralizing governments. This undoubtedly explains why he went to such pains to present himself to Greek and Persian alike as a god-king. He insisted that suppliants prostrate themselves before him. He took to wearing the crown and robes of a king. He fostered countless legends about his birth and life that emphasized the miraculous. All of this was to give him the image of authority that would be necessary to forge the unity he desired. He cut across Greek animosities and ordered the Greek cities to take back all political exiles. He then moved toward a blending of Greek and Persian cultures. He married Barsine, the daughter of the Persian King, and he ordered his officers and thousands of his soldiers to marry Persian

The Lion of *Chaeroneia* raised over the bodies of the Theban Band killed at the battle. The battle fought here with Philip of Macedon ended Hellenic independence and marked the beginning of the Hellenistic Age.

Temple of Athena on the acropolis of Lindos on the island of Rhoses. Hellenic temples were always built in close association with the natural setting.

women. He hoped that a union of the two cultures would follow a union of the two races. He trained Persians for service in his army, while he founded scores of new Greek cities all over the empire from which he expected Greek civilization to spread and Hellenize all the peoples of Asia.

He was careful to lay out trade routes, encourage new industries, and foster economic ties throughout the empire, knowing full well the value of economic interest in drawing peoples together. There seems to be a suggestion that Alexander learned from Aristotle the concept of the one-world, the *oikonomia,* in which all peoples would live in harmony and like-mindedness *(homonoia).* If this is so, he was certainly a man of great vision pointing in the directions Rome would move centuries later. His fate, however, was to die of malaria on June 13, 323 B.C., after a reign of thirteen short years.

The Hellenistic World

Alexander's inopportune death took his followers by surprise. A bitter struggle for power broke out between the great generals of the army. Eventually three of them established great empires that dominated the Eurasian territories until Rome inexorably swallowed them piecemeal. In Egypt Ptolemy established an absolute kingdom in which all the land belonged to the king. Half was worked by private owners who lived in semi-starvation, sharing their production with the king. The other half was given out to priests, Greek mercenaries, and Near Eastern immigrants, ordered to develop the land and to share their profits with the king. Holding monopolistic control

over the economy of the whole country in the cities and countryside, the king became immensely wealthy. Surrounded by a Hellenized aristocracy, he waged aggressive wars, made laws, and directed the affairs of his people as arbitrarily as the god-king that he was.

In the Near Eastern portion of the empire Seleucus established one of the greatest empires ever known, stretching from the Black Sea to the Red and from the Mediterranean to India, including over 40 million subjects of every nationality, religion, culture known in the civilized world at the time. Under the Seleucids Greek Macedonian masters joined Hellenized native collaborators to form a new aristocracy that suppressed local institutions by force. The land was taken away from its former ecclesiastic and baronial owners and redistributed to new small land owners, mostly Greek immigrants, who slowly Hellenized the whole region. Scores of cities were founded in which new industries were established and trade encouraged. Everywhere native languages, urban proletariates and small farmers worked side by side with Hellenized elements that held superior positions. The temptation to join the Greek culture was strong for it meant a rise in status. However, the situation produced tensions, particularly among the Jews, who retained by war their cultural freedom under the Maccabees. A deep chasm began to open between the lower classes speaking the native language and reflecting a growing national spirit, and the upper classes, who were Greek-speaking, collaborating aristocracies.

The situation in Macedonia and Greece was utterly chaotic after Alexander's death. A series of ineffective tyrants ruled Macedonia itself, while with the Greek states total confusion reigned. Government followed government as the Spartan and Athenian institutions slowly crumbled. Two leagues emerged, the Achaean and the Aetolian, and Greece was torn apart as the powers kept up senseless rivalries, no one of them strong enough to dominate the whole country. Rising neighbors began to meddle, as did King Pyrrhus of Epirus, but no stability emerged until the conquest of the area by Rome.

Hellenistic Civilization

The emergence of the vast world-empires during the Hellenistic period brought about the final collapse of the city-state system. The intimacy of the city-state with its ideals of citizen participation had afforded men a focus for their lives for centuries. Each man sought his goals in terms of the community. His art, his literature, his religion, as well as his personal ethics were all determined by and directed toward the transcendent needs of the state. This had given him a sense of belonging, a sense of individual importance which produced a self-confidence that bordered on arrogance. In fact, it was this very emphasis on the individual state that had brought about political chaos in Greece. But the city-state mentality made no room for an individual's private inner world. Greeks lived in the open, their lives were almost totally public. There was no concept of secrecy or privacy. An individual seldom turned to personal problems of internal growth or spiritual crisis. When the close familial atmosphere of the states disappeared in the Hellenistic kingdoms, the common citizen was confronted with a shattering spiritual crisis. No longer did he participate in government as a free citizen; he was now a subject in an empire whose king sat in a distant capitol, making laws, collecting taxes. The citizen had become a subject, and the focus of his life was gone. With the emergence of a stratified class structure with an ever-widening gap opening between the rich and poor, the Hellenized and the national classes, the feeling of belonging in one family, one homogeneous enterprise was gone. Now the individual was forced back on his own resources to find some means of adjusting his life to the threatening painful world around him. War, crushing taxes, unpredictable tyranny, a life without public context, these forced man to seek within himself a definition of his life, an explanation of the universe and his role in it that would make life bearable, if not desirable.

The Arts and Sciences

The turbulence of the age is best seen in its art forms. The balance and restraint of the earlier age seemed inadequate to describe the mood of a world constantly in change. Thus, the theatrical flamboyance of the famous *Laocoon* seems natural to the period. Individual portraiture replaced the idealized types of the classic sculpture and individuals were portrayed in mannered poses which suggested superficial attitudes toward the ironies of life. (*Viz.* the Belvedere *Apollo* stands in a stage pose, the *Old Woman Going to Market* is a reminder that old age brings ugliness.) The mood is one of conceits and over-statement for effect. The *Venus de Milo* upon close examination reveals that the sculptor is more interested in the sensual quality of his model than her perfect beauty.

The period is one that has lost the inspiration for originality. Old themes are used over and over, each time in a contrived way to stimulate with a clever style, where depth has disappeared. The tendency toward exaggerated size is evidence of this. Statues, buildings, memorials make up for their lack of originality with hugeness, multiplication of elements, striking designs.

The age was also one of collecting. Writers compiled encyclopedic collections of all the literature of the past. Governments housed these in great libraries or museums. Writers tended more toward criticism than original statements. The drama languished as it lost its themes, and the new comedy emphasized mannerisms and situation farces. Poetry tended to become escapist (i.e., the *Idylls* of Theocritus), painting enticing nostalgic visions of the joyful life of secluded shepherds and shepherdesses living the simple life.

On the other hand, Greeks had come into contact with the world at large as never before. Exploration was fostered by the expanding states. New trade routes brought goods and knowledge from distant places. Men began to see the proportions of the world in truer perspective. Aristarchus (310–230 B.C.) understood the heliocentric movement of the universe, and Eratosthenes (275–194 B.C.) calculated to within 200 miles the actual circumference of the earth. He also drew up a map of the world which not only presupposed that the earth was round, but which correctly related the land masses of Asia, Africa, and Europe.

The turning away from theory toward the practicalities of everyday life produced a new interest in technology. Euclid wrote a fundamental textbook in plane geometry. Archimedes invented pulleys, the endless screw-type water pump, the windlass and new uses for levers. Other scientists of the day produced the water clock, machines powered by compressed air, and the steam engine.

The many wars and the new attention focused on the daily life of man stimulated great interest in medicine and therapy. Doctors practiced vivisection and gained an understanding of the basic organs of the body and their functions. The operation of the heart in relation to the blood was understood, the nerve system was examined and its interconnection with the brain was established. The use of drugs and medication, diet and post-operative care in clinics and hospitals ensured greater success for the improved surgery of the day than the Western world would see again for centuries.

Religion in the Hellenistic Age

The failure of the city-state, as has been pointed out by many authorities, was a frightening crisis for the ancient Greek. For centuries he had submerged his ego into the group-consciousness of his state. His gods, his laws, these had provided the framework for his life. Now they had all failed him, and he had to find a new basis for his life. At first, philosophers offered him solutions.

The world is evil, they said. The good life for man, then, cannot be found in the terms of the world. This life can only be found in his own nature. Furthermore, if the world around him no longer provides him with an opportunity to serve it, and in serving it to achieve a sense of personal importance, he must find within himself some quality that gives him importance, The Epicurians taught that the essence of good living lay in man's attitude to the world. Man's desires for the world give it importance and the power to give him pain. Hence, the good life is the withdrawal of desire. Seek nothing, value nothing, and there is no pain of failure, of loss.

The Cynics, on the other hand, taught that man must reject the evil world in all its manifestations, earthly possessions, institutions, ambitions. Only the intellect can lead to the good life, and that is within man. All men of intelligence belong to a world of their own that is universal, transcending the material world. The Cynics resembled certain types of Buddhist monks, though their tone was usually far more strident.

The Stoics approached the problem from a more metaphysical point of view. The universe, they taught, is meaningful. Every act that occurs is predetermined by a wise and purposeful God. Man cannot understand his purposes, but he must believe that they exist. Man cannot control the happenings of the universe, but he can control his reactions to them. One must train the will to have patience and fortitude in a world that, to man, seems to have gone mad. Furthermore, God has created all men and has placed them under his laws. These laws are all-pervasive in the world of nature and they operate equally for all men. Man has a spark of divinity within him, he has existence in an orderly universe governed by natural laws and he has a technique for adjusting to the evil world of men.

All three of these teachings enjoyed some popularity, but they were not real answers to the religious problems of the day. The average man could not accept the discipline that they demanded. Instead, men turned to religious ideas that stemmed from the more esoteric philosophies of Plato. There had always been a tendency toward

monotheism in Greece. Zeus had often been described by the poets as the king of the gods who had within himself the source of the power of all the other gods. Plato and Aristotle both end their philosophical postulations in a single deity, the Good or the Prime Mover. These ideas, however, were derived from pure logic and were quite beyond the comprehension of the average person. Nor were they religious in their application. Certain followers of Plato, however, undertook to reduce his system to the level of the average person and to transform it into a religion. This is essentially the origin of Neo-Platonism. The basic view of the universe that this religion presented was that the world consists of two elements, the material, which is perceived by man through his senses, and the intellectual, perceived by the mind. This world of the mind alone is perfect and eternal. The material world is subject to change and decay. The heavier the material substance of its composition, the more prone to decay it is. Hence, the further away from the earth a substance is, the less prone to decay. There exists, then, a hierarchy of matter from gross earth to ethereal heaven, the abode of the *daimones.*

In time this middle ground also became the area inhabited by the constellations of the Zodiac introduced from Mesopotamia. According to astrology the lives of men are influenced by the stars that happen to be above them at the time of their birth at other important moments.

All of these ideas, Epicureanism, Cynicism, Stoicism, and Neo-Platonism tended to merge by a syncretic process into a generally pessimistic view of life. Man seemed doomed by fatal powers over which he could exert no direct control. The usual escape from the situation was magic, and in this period every form of magic was practiced. At one level, attempts were made to control the *daimones* and the astral powers that existed in the spheres between men and the gods. On another level, an attempt was made to rise up to the very level of the powers, to become acquainted with them intimately, and to attain their knowledge, *gnosis*, of the essence of being. On still another level the *gnosis* might be attained by participation in the various mysteries, both old and new, that offered ecstatic contact with the transcendental.

An even more direct release for man could be found in the mystery cults of the day. A mystic union with an ever-living god who shared his eternal life with his worshippers as a reward for a sinless life or as a merciful gift was a guarantee that proved irresistible for most men of the age.

From very early times all over the Near East there was worshipped a fertility goddess in the form of the Great Mother *(Magna Mater)*. Her religion varied from place to place, but in general the myth was the same. She had a lover-consort Attys, and their love ended in disaster. Attys, for love of the goddess, castrated himself and died in agony. The priests of the cult of the Great Mother (often called Cybele) entered their office by castrating themselves as they dedicated themselves to the goddess. They then served her for life, dressed in women's clothing. The most important ceremony in the cult occurred once a year on March 15. At that time, after seven days of fasting by the worshippers, a newly-cut pine-tree, wrapped in linen and festooned with violets, was born into the temple of the goddess. The next day, the Day of Blood, saw a savage funeral ritual in which the priests slashed themselves with knives and initiates castrated themselves. After a further period of lamenting, the following was

chanted: "Be of good cheer, initiates, seeing that the god is saved; for we too, after our toils, shall find salvation."

Obviously, the cult was one in which the god of vegetation died, was buried, and was reborn. By re-enacting this cycle the initiate, by symbolic magic, was also assured of the same rebirth after death. Later this identity was intensified by the introduction of a ritual called the taurobolism. A bull was led onto a grate that covered a pit in which the initiate crouched. The bull was killed and the worshipper received the hot blood all over his body. When he emerged he was greeted as a reborn person and was venerated. The person had become one with the god and was assured of his immortality.

There had developed in Egypt over the centuries a cult associated with the goddess Isis. She and her two brothers, the good Osiris and the evil Set, were the figures of an ancient legend. Osiris and Isis were lovers who married and ruled Egypt. Set was jealous and killed Osiris. He cut the body up and buried the pieces all over Egypt. Isis, waiting and grieving, wandered from place to place until she had recovered them and given them decent burial.

Osiris became in Egypt a god of the dead, but the figure of Isis spread all over the Mediterranean. She became a loving, beautiful mother, who toiled ceaselessly to bring her children good fortune in this world and life in the world to come. Her priests served her with hymns, beautiful chants, the tinkling of bells. They had prescribed duties around the clock which were impressive to her worshippers who saw in them the sign of a perpetual *numen*. We have a touching description of how profoundly this religion moved its adherents in the famous passage in the *Golden Ass* of Apuleius, in which he described the rituals and the coming of the goddess in answer to the entreaties of her children.

The most important of these religions was the cult of Mithra. This god was first worshipped in Persia where he became associated with the dualism of Zoroastrianism. The world was considered a battleground on which the forces of light were locked in struggle with the forces of darkness. The outcome was known, but still the battle must be fought in order to achieve it. Mithra was born from a rock. He caught, tamed and killed a wild bull. From the bull came the medicines and plants helpful to mankind. Ahriman, the power of evil, tried to stop this, but Mithra joined forced with the sun-god. He is the Unconquered Sun, whose birthday is celebrated December 25. Mithra was good, truthful and holy and with Ahura Mazda, the power of good, he will be present when the forces of evil are finally consumed by fire at the end of the world.

Those who would serve the god, then, had to live chaste and abstentious lives. Step by step, they would rise up through seven grades of perfection, losing at each step some of the passions that trouble them on earth, until at last their souls would enter a perfect heaven of light.

Membership in this cult was restricted to men, who lived in accordance with a series of moral commandments. The figure of Mithra as an evil-conquering hero, and the severe discipline of the religion, made it very popular with soldiers. But it enjoyed a vast popularity in the period when Christianity was spreading into the Hellenistic world now under Roman control, and for a long time seemed destined to fills its place. This was probably due to the fact that it provided the only feasible answer to the problem of evil before Christianity. That evil existed, no one could question. But how to relate it to gods who were, themselves, perfectly good had been beyond the philosophies of all the ancient religions. Mithraism was also popular because it not only promised a life of perfect bliss in heaven, but offered a strict moral code to follow in this life.

All these religions offered hope to the people of the Hellenistic empires. All preached the good life and its reward in a future life of happiness. But Christianity offered the same things and in forms that were more deeply satisfying.

III
ROME: REPUBLIC AND EMPIRE
▼ ▼ ▼ ▼ ▼

▶ **The Flavian amphitheater in Rome** built by Vespasian and Titus in 72–80 A.D. The Colosseum held at least 50,000 spectators. During the Renaissance tons of stone were carted away to construct new buildings. It is the best preserved of ancient Roman structures.

▶ **Temple at Paestum near Naples.** Southern Italy was early colonized by Greeks. The temple has a Greek appearance, but there is already a Roman heaviness, squatness. Out of this will emerge a distinct Roman style based on Greek models, but merging Etruscan and native elements with them.

▶ **Home altar from Pompeii.** Roman religious practices centered on the family, those who had already lived and those who were yet to be born. The *paterfamilias* made contact with the family gods at altars like this.

The Monarchy

Rome was destined to face in unprecedented boldness and to solve the problems inherent in the ancient city-state system. The geography of Italy, like that of Greece, fostered the growth of a collection of city-states. Italy is a long peninsula jutting out from the "under-belly" of Europe. The coastline is one of the longest of any European country, but it is extremely regular, with few good harbors. Hence, with some spectacular exceptions, the peoples of Italy, especially the Romans, have taken to the sea only with great reluctance. The spine of Italy is a rugged chain of tall mountains, the Apennines, which is difficult to cross but is marked by well-protected valleys. The chain lies to the east of the peninsula, and to the west there lie fairly large well-water plains that can sustain sizable and stable groups. To the north lie the Alps, an overthrust type formation of mountains whose northern slopes rise gradually to many passes among the peaks, but whose southern scarp is abrupt and difficult to climb. Movement into Italy has always been easier than movement out. Furthermore, at the base of the Alps lies the great valley of the Po, always a fertile attraction to hungry northern nomads. The sunny temperate climate of Italy is proverbial and ensures the easy living that has acted like a magnet for centuries.

The earliest men in Italy date from the Old Stone Age. They had achieved a fair degree of civilization, marked by the custom of burying their dead in trenches. They lived in caves and later in crude huts. Around 1500 B.C. there began a series of invasions of Indo-European, bronze-working peoples who may have been connected with the Achaean tribes of Greece. Later the Villanovans, perhaps relatives of the Celts and Dorians, began moving in around 1000 B.C. Other peoples moved from the Balkans across the Adriatic, so that by the time the Etruscans, the Gauls and the Greeks had established themselves as the major powers in the peninsula, there was already a hodgepodge of Sabellian, Umbrian, and Volscian tribes settled throughout the heart of Italy.

The Etruscans

The Etruscans have remained an obscure people because their language has not yet been deciphered. The best scholarly theory suggests that they were in origin a seafaring people who left the Near Eastern coast of Lydia shortly after 1000 B.C. to sail westward seeking mineral deposits, which they found on Elba and in Tuscany. They settled in twelve cities that were held loosely together in a religious federation, grew wealthy, and spread northward into the Po Valley, and southward into the region around Naples. They captured the city of Rome in the course of the 6th Century B.C., and dominated Italian affairs until the 4th Century.

The Etruscan cities were held together for purposes of common religious rituals and games, but the league was dominated by whichever city was the strongest at the time. The society was aristocratic and wealthy, and the government consisted of a priest-king controlled by a senate and elected magistrates. Rome inherited these basic divisions of the public power from the Etruscans, as it did the patrician toga, the *fasces* (a bundle of sticks tied round an ax), and the idea of collegiate magistracies (at each level of government, power was held by a group of officials who had to act unanimously).

The best insight we have into the Etruscan way of life is gained from their temples and their tomb decorations. The Etruscans believed strongly in life, and they looked with dread on death. Their gods were sky-gods who governed the lives of men; their demons lived beneath the earth and they controlled the dead. The Etruscans believed that they could control the universe so as to prolong the life of the living, and by divination they expected to keep contact with the dead. They sacrificed to the gods, then, to ensure their good will and to obtain the good things of life. In their tombs lively paintings and life-like portrait sculptures kept the illusion of life. By reading meaning into the conformations of the livers of sacrificed animals, the flights of birds, or the flashes of lightening and rumblings of thunder, their augers could understand the will of the gods and could direct their actions accordingly. All in all, the Etruscan religion was a pragmatic attempt to control the forces of the universe so as to maintain life as long as possible this side of the tomb, and in the hereafter as well.

Etruscan art reflected this same attitude. They introduced the arch to replace the post and lintel form of architecture, making it possible to construct buildings large enough to bring government inside. Temples were solid, paintings and sculpture were lifelike and vital. Bronze work and pottery were modeled after Greek prototypes, but the Etruscans did not find the Greek mood congenial, and they soon expressed in fine workmanship their realistic attitudes toward life. Their culture was varied, rich, and left a lasting influence on Rome.

The Founding of Rome

The Greek states of southern Italy and Sicily early developed a brisk trade with the Etruscan cities of the north. In fact, these latter became middlemen through whose hands Greek goods flowed to the Gallic tribes of northern Europe. The principal trade routes from the south moved along the western coast and crossed the Tiber at a spot where an island and shallows offered a natural ford. At that spot the Alban Hills reached down to the river in long spurs. On these, as on several isolated hills in the river plain, primitive settlements were established by the Latins as early as 1000 B.C. From these easily-defended hilltops, some of the Latins dominated a complex of some 60 busy farm communities that were draining the swamp valley of the Tiber and dividing up the rich lands into innumerable small farms. These early settlements, according to tradition, in 753 B.C. were united into the city-state of Rome, and the inhabitants took the name Romans.

The Early Monarchy

The earliest form of government in Rome was the monarchy. Within the sacred boundary of the city (pomerium) the Roman tribes lived in peace. Until the end of the Republic, the injunction against military activity within the city was stringently enforced. The land was divided into twenty wards (tribus), and all was surrounded by a wall.

The sources for this period are very vague, but it seems certain that in the 7th Century B.C. a series of Etruscan kings replaced the native rulers. It is also certain that in this period was laid down the basic social and political structure of the Roman community.

The king held the chief sovereign power of the Roman people *(imperium)*. This gave him the power to lead armies, which he did in person. It also gave him the chief legislative position in the government. His decrees were law, though by custom he consulted with the Senate before declaring the law. He appointed boards of judges to hear cases in civil law *(quaestores)* and ecclesiastical law *(pontifices)*. He himself was the head of the public worship and was assisted by *fetiales*, priests expert in foreign affairs; *flamines*, heads of the official cults; the Vestal Virgins, who attended the sacred fire at the public hearth of Rome, and finally Augurs, who read the omens before any important business was undertaken.

The king was assisted also by the Senate. This body was made up by the noble patricians who had a monopoly of economic and social power in the state. These patricians alone could hold the higher posts in the army and in the religious cults. They had the right to elect the king, advise him in foreign policy, and to appoint a dictator *(interrex)* to call for the elections for a new king.

The commons of Rome, who represented about ninety percent of the people, were the *plebs*. These plebeians were by law prevented from rising to high public office either in the government or in the army. They served the nobility as serfs on the land usually, but even when they gained some degree of wealth as artisans or in trade, they were still barred by law from any social prominence.

The people of Rome, including both the *plebs* and the patricians, were organized into thirty *curiae*. The *curia* was a corporate body into which an individual had to be admitted as a condition of citizenship. The *curia* handled the legal problems of its membership. The *curiae* assembled to grant a new king his *imperium* and to furnish recruits for the army. The curiate assembly had no powers of initiative, and its opinions were dominated by the upper classes.

The society of Rome was held closely together by certain attitudes and customs that were not always explicitly stated by law. The basic unit was the household *(familia)* composed of the family proper, servants, slaves, clients, all those, in short, under the authority *(manus)* of the *paterfamilias*, the head of the household. All the property of the household, and the property of its members, were in his hands. It was up to him to keep peace with the household gods. He alone knew the formulae of sacrifice and prayers. This gave him great authority over everyone under his control. His authority, in fact, included the power of life and death, and he demanded absolute obedience.

All families descended from a common ancestor formed a clan *(gens)* and used in common the clan name *(nomen)*. The clan was held together by religious ties, and all the clans composed the *populous romanus* which lay obedient under the *manus* of its *paterfamilias*, the king, and later the consul.

Thus, Romans were held by discipline in various familial groupings. In addition to these and the patrician and plebeian states of mind, there was a customary relationship of a client to a patron, that was recognized by law. A man, his family, even his descendants were obliged to work for a patron family on the land, to vote for it in elections, to serve as armed retainers, or even as artists or members of a fawning entourage.

The social structure resulted from and was strengthened by the Roman state of mind. All Romans enjoyed freedom *(liber-*

tas), that is, as citizens they had the right to appeal a death sentence to the people as a whole *(provocatio)*, and they enjoyed equal rights to the benefits of the law. But there was also the concept that some men and some families had an inborn superiority *(dignitas)* that gave them a right to command, This power was respected with a reverential obedience *(pietas)*, but it was tempered by a sense of obligation on the part of its holder to act with responsibility and restraint worthy of his high position *(fides)*. Thus, the Romans were a sober, disciplined, responsible people who believed that life itself was a state of war *(vivere militare est)*.

Roman Religion

The religion of the Romans was at a much more primitive level throughout its history than the religions of Greece. Like all people at this stage, the Romans believed in what is generally called *mana*. The Romans called it *numen*, which has been defined as containing a sense of "result of action, sign of a force or power at work." Thus, a god contains *numen*, but a man of unusual personality may contain it as well. The senate had it, and the *populous romanus* had it.

Numen could be conferred by the gods. In other words, they could instill some of their power into an object, an act, or into a person. Men, themselves, often could infuse an object or act with *numen*. For instance, the boundary stones that were set up between pieces of property were infused with *numen* by the magical rites practiced by the farmers. In fact, they contained so much power that they became *tabu*. It was very dangerous to touch them and anyone who did so became himself *tabu*, or *sacer* in Latin, which

placed him beyond the protection of human rights. He could be killed on sight.

The Romans approached an object of *numen* to gain its power, but they were prudent enough to realize that it had to be replenished from time to time. Therefore, they sacrificed to the gods in a kind of sympathetic or homeopathic magic. A calf-bearing cow might be sacrificed to ensure abundant herds. The attitude was summed up in the phrase *do ut des,* I give so that you will give. The Romans were always shrewd bargainers, even with their gods. During the Second Punic War, for instance, the Senate actually drew up a formal contract between the gods and the Roman people, signed it, and expected both parties to live up to its terms.

The gods were served at their altars. The altar itself had *numen,* for we find the Romans often placed objects on the altar to increase its power, but most often it was *tabu* to touch an altar. An oath was made binding by touching the altar, however, because by so doing the oath-maker put himself in touch with the power that would harm him if he broke his oath. The altar was generally dedicated to some god, though this was not always the case. If the altar was so dedicated, it often bore the name of the god, so the *numen* and its container became the same object.

The early Romans were always quite vague about their gods. The gods obviously existed and they had great power. This power put them in a position of authority over men. Unlike the Greeks, the Romans were quite willing to leave it at this point. The personality of the god, its true name or sex, were of much less importance than its power. Vesta, goddess of the hearth; the Penates, protectors of the home; Ares, the goddess of growing things; these always remained forces rather than clear personalities. Some gods did emerge with human characteristics, to be sure. Jupiter, the sky-god, was the "father" of all the gods. But even he was more often seen in the rain, the thunder, or in certain sacred rocks than in his human form. The Romans never developed a mythology comparable to that of the Greeks.

The household was the area within which the Roman religion mainly operated. Every home was built around its hearth and the fire that burned upon it, which was sacred to Vesta. It was the duty of the woman of the house to tend this fire and to keep the hearth clean. In front of it was the table at which the family and the gods shared the daily meals. The gods always received their share of the food and drink.

The prosperity of the family was in the care of the Lares and Penates, ill-defined forces, often represented in little hominoid figurines, that had great power to protect the family possessions. These did not have as much power, however, as Janus, a name derived from *ianua*, an outer door of a house. The door of the house was especially charged with *numen* and to go through it, in or out, was always an act charged with great significance. All the luck of the family flowed through the door and careful ceremonies were needed to control this flow. Finally, the floor of the house, in contact with the powers of the earth, and the roof, in contact with the sky-gods, were sacred and required appropriate ritualistic care.

The work of the household was always surrounded by *numen*. Plowing, harvesting, the care of tools, building of sheds, in short every act of daily living had to be preceded by some act of magic that would ensure a good outcome. The drawing of the boundary around the property as a whole was an act of tremendous solemnity, since

the terminus, as it was called, was the magic circle that contained all that constituted the household. Terminus was also a god who, if he was served properly, would keep neighbors from quarreling with each other.

Most of his religion was centered within his household, but a Roman also worshipped in ceremonies connected with his clan, his tribe, certain associations or clubs, and finally the state itself. The state worship was carried on by a group of priests called the *Collegium Pontificum*, which included pontiffs (high priests), *flamens* (special priests), the Vestal Virgins, and the *rex sacrorum*, King of the Rites. They were organized under the Chief Pontiff (*Pontifex Maximus*). These priests and priestesses usually held no secular office, though only the *Pontifex Maximus* was expressly forbidden to do so. Yet they did not constitute a priestly caste. Their function was to advise men how they might serve the gods in order to get them to do what was needed. The priests over the years had collected many books of rituals and these were kept secret to protect their power. But this did not give the priests power as such. It just meant that they were needed to reach the gods. The priests also were needed to discover the will of the gods. Augurs were skilled in reading the signs (*auspicia*) with which the gods indicated their will. These were the flights of birds; the condition of the entrails, especially the liver of a sacrificial animal; thunder, or any unusual sign in the natural order.

The religious ceremonies that the priests performed took place on appointed feast-days or at the special request of the state, as when an unfriendly god had to be ejected from the state. A few descriptions will give an idea of their nature. The focus of the state, as with the household, was its hearth. This was originally viewed as the domestic fire of the king of the state and was tended by his daughters. After the establishment of the Republic, these daughters became a group of six maidens, the Vestal Virgins, chosen as children from patrician families. They served for thirty years, during which time they were not allowed to marry. They performed a variety of complicated rituals to gather wood, bless it, and with it keep the fire of Vesta burning constantly.

The state had its own Penates, which were stored in a room close to the home of the Vestal Virgins, and Lares, which were placed at important crossroads. There was also the state gateway. The *ianus* was the arch set up in the Forum that acted as the official gateway into the state. Roman armies always marched through it as they started out on a campaign. In later Roman history, many emperors set up such arches, through which they could re-enter the city with the fruits of their successful wars.

The Republic

The kings were expelled by popular revolt by the end of the 6th Century (509 B.C. is the traditional date). Their power was transferred to two officials called consuls. These two shared the one *imperium* conferred on the office by the people. They could lead the armies in war, could make law by edict and could impose the death penalty. They appointed the membership of the Senate, called into session the curiate assembly, and performed the religious obligations of the Roman people as a whole. They wore the royal toga and were always accompanied by the *fasces*, symbols of their power to beat

and kill, carried by the *lictors*. Their great power was limited by certain customary and practical considerations. They were bound by the traditions of ancient Rome *(mos maiorum)*, which included the right of appeal in death sentences to the clemency of the whole people. It also led them to consult in all weighty matters the views of the Senate. The consuls were elected to a term of one year in office; after this the consul, always in the early Republic from the patrician class, entered the Senate for the rest of his life. It was difficult indeed for a consul to go against the wishes of his class and future colleagues. His family often was in the Senate and it was impossible for him to ignore familial discipline. In short, the consuls were for the most part leaders of senatorial control over the government.

As the Republic developed, new magistrates emerged to assist the consul in his duties. *Praetors* emerged in the 4th Century B.C. to handle the affairs of the city while the consuls were away at war. They soon became important judges, and their guard was the most important fighting force within the *pomerium*. As the finances of the state became more elaborate, four *quaestors* emerged, two to guard the public treasury at home, and two to go into the field with the army and act as quartermasters. The supervision of the public works at Rome was given to four *aediles* who handled police matters, food supplies, and the regulation of the daily economic life of the community. They were also responsible for the public games. Finally there were the censors who took the public census every five years in order to assign the citizens to their proper classes, so that the lists of patrician senators could be kept up to date. They also assigned contracts for public construction, assigned the collection of state rents and taxes, and in general controlled the morals of the people in order to keep down excessive spending.

All these offices were elected usually for terms of one year. Each one was shared by a committee, unanimity being needed for effective action. The offices constituted a rising progression of service *(ordo)*, the candidate entering usually at the bottom (as *aedile)* and working his way up through increasingly difficult elections until he reached the top. Magistrates were considered to be under the power of the ranks above them *(maior potestas)*, all being under the authority of the consul. The collegiate system kept tyrants from emerging, and it place a premium on service to the community, but it depended on the sense of duty of the officers. Civil war inevitably followed a conflict between the consuls, just as serious tension resulted from disputes at any lower level.

The Senate was legally only an advisory body, but since it included in its ranks the patricians, wealthy plebeians, all ex-magistrates, it represented the strongest social forces in the state. Furthermore, its members sat for life and guarded a collected knowledge and experience in foreign and domestic affairs that stretched back farther than any other group in the Roman state. In the Senate the patricians were the patrons of society who felt they had the right to wield unlimited power. Few people felt strong enough to resist such an arrogance. Custom gave the Senate the power to declare states of emergency and to appoint dictators to take charge during these periods. It also assigned to each magistrate upon his election the area of his command and his duties. Because of its control over the magistracies, because it was consulted by the consuls on all laws passed, because it exerted a dominant role in the public assemblies, the Senate was the real government of Rome. It was conservative, wealthy, and hardworking. If its rule was oligarchic, nevertheless it served the Roman people well for many centuries.

The popular assembly of Rome was originally the curiate assembly described above. As the Republic developed, however, a change in its military organization took place. The army originally had consisted of patrician elements, but the military needs of the state became more pressing and the army came to be recruited from all the citizens who had sufficient property to qualify. Small land holders came to be the backbone of the new army. The censors assigned each citizen to a specific unit *(centuria)* according to his age and wealth. These units met to drill or to enter into actual fighting. The country had become a nation at arms. It often happened that the citizens met in the military units to discuss or vote on a legislative bill. When this happened they constituted the centuriate assembly. It became customary for the consuls to meet with the curiate assembly in restricted matters, while they dealt with the centuriate assembly more and more, for it was a truer cross-section of the society. This did not mean it was democratic. The units voted according to their wealth and contribution to the military effort. Thus the vote was heavily weighted in the direction of the patrician and merchant *(equites* or knights) classes. The plebs had little to say and had to turn elsewhere for a voice in the government.

Patrician vs. Plebeian

There were many reasons for discontent among the lower classes of Rome, and early in Republican history they began to agitate for legislative power to introduce reforms into the oligarchic government of the patrician Senate. First there was the problem of land reform. The Roman economy was mainly an agrarian one throughout its history. The land was divided into privately-owned holdings and the public lands conquered in war were owned by the Roman people in common. The mass of the poorer farmers owned tiny farms measuring a few hundred square feet. Barely able to support his family, his lands exposed to attack by raiders, the farmer was always in need of protection and economic aid. He tended to get into debt at high interest rates, and when he could not pay he lost his land and had to enter service as a semi-serf or sharecropper (*colonus*) on some rich man's estate. He also needed some use of the public lands, if not to expand his holdings, at least to graze his ox and other animals, if he had any. But the patrician class had the best portions of land, which they farmed profitably in large estates (*latifundia*). The small land-holder could not compete. The public land was always given over to these large estates because they produced more food for the state. The distribution of land after a successful war was also a way of rewarding the army, the patricians always getting the lion's share. Thus, the farmers gradually formed land reform programs which became the basis for their agitation for centuries.

The peasants made common cause with the urban proletariate. In fact, many lived in the city of Rome side by side with the artisans and merchants, usually on the Aventine hill. Rome had become a prosperous and productive community as early as Etruscan times. Many traders settled in the city, bringing in Greek and Etruscan wares

to exchange for the produce of many busy small shops that began to dot the city. By disciplined industry, the city dwellers began to build up a prosperous way of life and organized themselves into guilds (*collegia*). The *aediles* originally were officials elected by the people to handle the affairs of the various guilds. However, no matter how wealthy a plebeian might become, he was still barred by law from the rights and privileges of the patricians. The leading plebeians, living on an economic level rivalling that of the richest patricians, formed a program of legislative reform which absorbed into itself the peasants' program for land reform.

The path to success was opened by the reforms that had taken place in the army. In the formation of the *centuria* wealth was the criteria, and wealthy plebeians began to serve in the same units as patricians. A common interest developed, a friendship that could not be entirely ignored after the war was over. The plebeians began to hold higher offices in the army, and they were not willing to give up their officer status and slip back into an inferior class upon being mustered out. These are the men that gave the final spur to the general agitation of the lower classes.

The first victory of the plebs came with the election of the tribunes. Two officers (originally the *tribuni militum*) were elected by the plebes as their leaders (*tribuni plebis*). By the 3rd Century B.C. their number had grown to ten. These officials organized the commons into an assembly, the tribunate assembly, where popular problems could be discussed and political strategy developed. Every statement of this assembly was published with the opening formula *Plebi scita* . . . ("The Plebs lets it be known . . ."), hence our own word plebiscite. The tribunes led repeated general strikes in the city and often threatened to lead the lower classes into secession and the establishment of an independent rival community. Slowly the Senate made concessions. Offices in the state, the religious cults, and the army were opened to the Plebs (the first plebeian consul was elected in 362 B.C.). The laws forbidding intermarriage were rescinded. The tribunes were obvious targets for dangerous senatorial anger. They were protected by a solemn oath of the people that they would kill anyone that even laid a hand on a tribune in violence. This sacro-sanctity of person was strengthened by religious force and it could be extended to anyone who came to the tribune's home for sanctuary to escape patrician or even magisterial prosecution. The tribunes brought about the codification of Roman law and its publication in the famous Twelve Tables (449 B.C.). This brought the knowledge of the law to the people and protected them from arbitrary abuses by the patricians. Finally, by the terms of the Hortensian Law (287 B.C.) the tribunate assembly was freed of senatorial veto, and the ten tribunes, themselves, were recognized as having a veto over the Senate, for if they could protect the plebs from prosecution under a law, why not protect them from the passage of the law itself? Thus a tribune could walk into the Senate and stop deliberations at will. He could introduce legislative reforms in his own assembly and could agitate for their adoption by the Senate. By the end of the struggle, all legal differences between the patricians and the plebeians had disappeared. They had been replaced by differences between the rich and the poor. The state increasingly became a plutocracy, the basic economic problems were not solved. The tribunate became a powerful weapon, but it was potentially a two-edged sword to be used by anyone who could control a tribune, a fact the Senate was not slow to perceive.

The Italian Wars

For some 250 years until 265 B.C., Rome was at war almost constantly. It was this fact more than any other that stamped upon the Roman people their special characteristics and their peculiar institutions. Yet the Romans were not war-like enough to say that they actively sought out opportunities for aggression, though when war did come they always fought as if they were on the offensive and they never admitted defeat, fighting every war to victory. Rome's wars came primarily because of her position in the center of many competitive states. To protect her interests, to expand her territories to provide for an expanding population, and to support her allies, these were the causes of the wars.

The wars were fought in stages: The Etruscan wars 500–400 B.C.; the wars with the Gauls 400–343 B.C.; the Samite wars 343–290 B.C.; the war with Pyrrhus 281–275 B.C.; and finally the absorption of Greek southern Italy 275–265 B.C. The army was forged into a flexible instrument composed of legions (3600–4000 men each) divided up into well-trained, disciplined units (*maniples*) that could fight independently. The main weapon of the Romans, however, was their courage, their discipline and their stubborn determination always to be victorious. Perhaps no people has ever lived up to its own ideals as successfully as the Romans did in this period.

Each war came for specific causes, yet by the end a certain pattern had emerged that displayed Roman policy. Rome had, from the beginning, certain allies among her Latin neighbors. These were organized into a league under the domination of Rome, which recognized the sovereignty of the states in the league. Their troops fought independently, side by side with the Romans but under their own commanders. Furthermore, Rome offered two rights: *connubium*, the right to marry Roman citizens (the children of such marriages could adopt Roman citizenship); and *commercium*, the right to trade in Rome under the full protection of Roman law. The league stood firm throughout the wars, and new states entered it from time to time.

As each war ended, an agreement had to be reached. In each instance, in addition to the specific points of grievance, Rome always made certain provisions. Land was taken away from the loser (usually about one-third of its territories) to be offered to Roman citizens, veterans, speculators, farmers. The vanquished gave up all independent foreign policy, dealing with other states only through Rome, and they were obliged to send military units to Roman commanders whenever needed. Aside from these stipulations, the Romans respected the autonomy of the Italian states, and slowly an Italian League began to emerge.

In fact, by the middle of the 3rd Century B.C. Rome had pulled together a loose confederation of all the territory south of the Rubicon River. First, the peninsula was dotted with Roman colonies *(municipia)*. Roman immigrants forced out by overpopulation, retired veterans, and allies were organized into a defensive system of Roman outposts. Each state had a government copied after the government in Rome. Its citizens were full Roman citizens, but they were disenfranchised in the sense that they did not vote in Rome, but locally for their own officials. This actually represented a solution to the dilemma of the ancient city-state. Rome could now expand, establishing its citizens anywhere and keeping control over them while at the same time retaining the city-state concept of government.

Secondly, there were the Latin allies, those independent states who had opted to fight as allies of Rome because they felt tied very closely to Roman interests and sought rewards from Rome's successful wars. Finally, there were the Italian allies, those who had been the enemies of Rome. By the end of the period, while all the states of Italy remained independent, they were held together by Roman military and political domination of the peninsula. Rome had become an empire while it still remained a city-state. It had no concept of empire, no plan of conquest, no procedure prepared to organize new territories, no wish to become the arbiter of the affairs of the world, yet these were the very things that would be needed as circumstances pushed Rome into mastery of the Mediterranean world!

The Mediterranean Expansion

Carthage was originally founded in the 12th Century B.C. as a Phoenician colony by the mother city of Tyre. By 600 B.C. the colony had become independent and expanded into the central and western Mediterranean. Eventually Carthage controlled a widespread confederation of some fifty subject states in north Africa, along the Atlantic coast, in Sicily and islands of the central and western Mediterranean, and in Spain. Each state had to contribute military aid and taxes, while each was at the same time open to economic exploitation by Carthaginian merchants.

Carthage was a true aristocracy. The whole community was involved in the same general economic enterprise, manufacturing and trade. The society early formed itself into a tight-knit bourgeoisie led by the great merchants of the city. Two elected magistrates, the *suffetes*, headed the government. They presided over a senate of thirty aristocratic members elected for life, and a grand council of 300 ex-magistrates. These three elements made the laws of the community. There was no popular element in the government, but there was never any agitation for one, for economic prosperity and social mobility provided for the society's needs, so that it felt no desire to have a role in government. Even the courts were oligarchic, since there were no popular juries of the Greek type, only 104 judges appointed for life to keep down graft and lawlessness.

The armies were largely mercenary units recruited when needed. The main defense of the state was its fleets, which were also the main support of the whole Carthaginian system. With these fleets, Carthage maintained a close watch over the affairs of the Greek states in Sicily, which was the key to control of the central Mediterranean. In the 3rd Century B.C. Carthage (eager to oust Greek influence) decided to intervene in the turbulent politics of Sicily. One faction, a mercenary band called Mamertines, called on Rome for help. The Senate, traditionally conservative, refused. But the people of Rome hoped for new military allies that would

lessen their own commitments to the army and they voted to send an army to Sicily. Thus was launched the First Punic War (263–242 B.C.), a time of hysteria for Rome, of valiant effort and dogged determination to become the world's leading military power. Rome sent out its first overseas army and built its first fleets. By superior morale and skill, Rome finally defeated the Carthaginian fleets, took by assault her Sicilian fortresses, and defeated her armies in the field. Carthage withdrew from the army and sued for peace. Carthage lost Sicily, then four years later Sardinia, and had to pay indemnities that totaled 4,600 talents. Rome established friendship with the states of Sicily and absorbed the island into her alliance system. Under the guidance of a military *praetor* the island began to pay tribute and quickly became the first Roman province overseas.

Rome was now the dominant sea power in the central Mediterranean, and Carthage upon recovering from the war turned to Spain to recoup her losses. Under Hannibal, brilliant member of the Barcas, a leading military family in Carthage, the Carthaginian armies began to expand throughout the Iberian peninsula. Rome had no vital interest in Spain, but kept two armies there to watch developments. When the city of Saguntum under Carthaginian attack called on the Roman Senate for help, Rome demanded that Hannibal withdraw. When he refused to do so, the Second Punic War began (218–201 B.C.), and Rome sent an army under Scipio the Elder to fight at Saguntum. But Hannibal in a brilliant manoeuver led an army with cavalry and elephants around the Roman allies in southern Gaul, over the Alps and down into the plains of northern Italy. There he quickly made up for the staggering losses of his army by recruiting Celts and began to administer to Rome a series of stunning disasters. Army after army was smashed; consul after consul killed. At wits end, Rome rejected a policy of caution recommended by Fabius Maximus, and sent out 80,000 men to meet Hannibal at Cannae (216 B.C.). The result was total annihilation, the greatest disaster for the next 500 years of Roman history. The alliance system that had stood firmly up to this point, now began to crumble. But time was on the side of the Romans. All classes closed ranks in the crisis. Its large population made it possible to put more armies into the field. Hannibal did not have the means to take Rome by assault and his imposition of heavy levies on the allies of Rome turned them against him. Mistrusted at home, low on supplies and unable to bring in new troops from either Spain by land, or Africa by sea (Roman fleets controlled the waters), Hannibal raced against time. Rome, however, took the initiative by sending an invading army under Scipio the Younger, later called Africanus, into Africa against Carthage herself. In panic, Hannibal was recalled and at the battle of Zama (202 B.C.) he suffered a total defeat, an annihilation of the sort he, himself, had inflicted so often. The peace treaty spelled the end of Carthaginian power in the Mediterranean. Her fleets were destroyed, all her possessions were taken away from her, and the city herself became a small provincial municipality. An indemnity of 10,000 talents was levied to pay for the costly war, and Rome sought to vent its fury on its great enemy Hannibal, though he eventually escaped to the East, where Rome harried him, never forgetting nor forgiving, until in desperation he finally committed suicide in 183 B.C.

The Wars to 133 B.C.

During the course of the first two Punic Wars the Hellenistic states decided to take advantage of what they thought was Roman weakness and to interfere in the wars. Philip V of Macedonia and the Seleucid Antiochus III entered an uneasy alliance that frightened Rome's allies on the Adriatic and her friends in Pergamum and Rhodes. Rome decided to fight a preventive war and invaded the Balkans in the so-called Second Macedonian War. Philip was defeated at Cynoscephalae (197 B.C.) and Greece was at long last liberated from the Macedonians. But the Greek states had learned nothing from their history. The bitter rivalries continued. Complaints flowed to Rome against Philip's son and successor Perseus, and finally, led by the exasperated censor Cato, Rome again invaded the Greek world and put an end to the Macedonian kingdom at the battle of Pydna (168 B.C.). Yet Rome was reluctant to take firm control over Greece. She did not want the responsibility of protecting the Danubian frontier, her armies and people were war-weary, and the cultural glamour of Hellenism led Roman intellectuals to yearn for an independent Greece.

Meanwhile, Antiochus III had interfered in the Second Macedonian War and was preparing to take over all the Near East. Rome declared war and invaded the Selucid territories. The war ended in Roman victory at Magnesia (189 B.C.) and the peace treaty signed at Apamea (188 B.C.) opened a new problem for Rome. All the Roman allies in the area rushed in to divide the spoils. The collapse of Selucid power left a vacuum. Rome was called on more and more to decide Near Eastern affairs. Unable to be friendly with all, Rome began to exert an increasingly stern influence until finally, inexorably, Rome had to face the decision of whether or not to take on an empire.

The Senate was reluctant to get too involved in the affairs of other people. Yet Rome could not afford to stay aloof. Adventurers and usurpers rose up on every side. Egypt was invaded by Antiochus IV. Rhodes defied Roman troops. The Jews were threatened with extinction by Antiochus. Furthermore, there had emerged in Rome a new spirit. A new class of merchants led by the knights saw in the ruins of the Carthaginian and Hellenistic empires a splendid opportunity for enormous wealth and economic expansion. This imperialistic fervor, coupled with the real misery of the peoples of the area, abandoned by all orderly government, finally led to a policy of annexation. A war of extermination was launched against dying Carthage (149–146 B.C.) and the city passed out of existence. The citizens died in the defense of the city, the buildings were razed, and the land itself was sown with salt so nothing would ever grow on it again. The territory was annexed as the province of Africa.

Then Rome turned to Greece and put an end to the interminable squabbles. Corinth was destroyed (146 B.C.), while Macedonia and Greece were organized as a province (147 B.C.). Pergamum had been placed under the patronage of the Senate by the terms of the will of its last ruler, Attalus III, and became the province of Asia (129 B.C.). By 121, southern Gaul was organized as the province of Narbonensis. These provinces were treated as possessions of the Roman people, and their inhabitants were subjects of Rome.

Each province was established by a specific law which spelled out its rights and duties. A *praetor* elected by the centuriate assembly was sent as governor, though a consul was often sent if there was insurrection or war. The governor had *imperium* to handle all the judicial, political, and economic affairs of the province. Since he was far from home, his power was almost unrestricted. He was assisted by a small staff of legates and was maintained as a guest throughout the province by community contributions. The governor had many opportunities to become wealthy, and ruthless exploitation of the provinces quickly became characteristic of the system. A governor could be charged with malfeasance in office after his return to Rome, but political intrigue and the difficulty of conducting an investigation from Rome nullified the effect of this control. In fact, the provinces were exploited by the state at will. All communities paid taxes to Rome, while the province as a whole paid custom duties and tribute. In addition all the land taken over by the state at the time of annexation was rented out to economic exploiters to gain state revenue. Since Rome had no administrative machinery organized to handle these fiscal matters, corporations of Italian business men *(publicani)* bought for a specific sum the right to collect taxes and rents in the province. Of course, the state was assured of its income, but the publicani were out to make as large a profit as possible, so the provincials sank lower and lower into desperate straits.

The Transformation of the Republic

Throughout the Mediterranean world there now began to appear a group of Romans who had become powerful and wealthy as a result of the emergence of the empire. Often military commanders with privately-recruited armies of clients swept across provinces and eventually came to Rome, rich, powerful, and hungry for a role in the capitol. The rising plebeian classes often gained great wealth as provincial governors. Allied aristocracies joined the march on Rome. The older aristocracy was replaced by a new class, the *nobiles,* later called *optimates.* A mad scramble for power over the spoils transformed the government, and the old Senate was unable to keep control. New men were rising through the equestrian order, and social ferment added its leavening. The difficulty stemmed from the fact that a whole new way of life had come to the Romans. Never had such luxury as followed contact with the fabled Near East been seen in austere Rome. The upper classes amassed thousands, then millions of slaves, tribute flowed in with luxury goods from all over the world. The problem was one of distribution. By law and custom, the patricians could not engage in trade. Therefore, they had to resort to extra-legal business machinations or exploitation in the provinces to keep up with the freer, though more vulgar, "new men" *(novi homines).* The tension became unbearable.

At the same time, though there was much industrial production, little money was invested in technical development. Small-scale handicrafts were still the mainstay of the system. Slaves were used increasingly to replace free workers, and there grew up a large fluid proletariate in the city of Rome with no income, no industry to absorb it and no way to take part in the new luxurious way of life. On the land great wealth was invested, which was put to the intensive utilization of luxury crops, grapes, olives, beef. No investment was made in improving agricultural tools or techniques, so the small farms began to decline and thousands of farmers abandoned their lands to swell the crowds in Rome. Thus, while the state as a whole was being dramatically transformed, the masses of the lower classes were sinking into an ever more precarious existence. They were citizens, to be sure, and they could cast votes in the tribunate assembly. Politicians soon began to offer programs of reform in exchange for these votes, the more unscrupulous merely offering entertainment or handouts of food.

The Gracchi

Tiberius Gracchus was a member of a distinguished plebeian, but noble, family, well educated in Greek culture and Stoic philosophy, who had served well in the army during the siege of Carthage. When he was tribune in 133 B.C., he had already formed an important program of reform. He had seen a steady deterioration in the morale in the army at the same time that the Roman farmers were losing their holdings. He saw immediately the connection between the two events. As he became property-less, the farmer was no longer eligible for army service in the draft. Hanging around the city streets, these dispossessed loafers were instrumental in lowering the prestige of national service as they undermined public morale in general. Tiberius decided that by resettling the farmers on the land, he would restore the old morality, and thus be improving the quality of both the army and the government while at the same time be solving the basic economic problems of the state. To effect this, he proposed to take over the public lands that had been leased out to senatorial speculators, redistribute them cheaply to the small farmers who would be induced to leave Rome and return to the land. Unfortunately, the holders of the land had invested heavily in improvements and they balked at giving it up. To bypass opposition, Tiberius went straight to the people in the tribunate assembly. The Senate put up another tribune, Octavius, who vetoed the bill. Tiberius had him deposed by popular vote, a clearly unconstitutional move, and pushed through the legislation, when the Senate withheld funds to finance the land distribution. Tiberius used threats to force the Senate to his will. The Senate was frightened at the display of popular strength. They were jealous of their properties and refused to share their wealth. At the same time they felt that Tiberius was a demagogue leading a revolution. The Senate had served Rome well for centuries. Their rule was sanctioned by custom and tradition. Tiberius had acted largely within his constitutional rights as tribune, but he was breaking with tradition and seemed to be disturbing the balanced elements in the Roman system. Therefore, when he ran for re-election, again an unprecedented act, the Senate sent mobs against him that cut him down in the street. The assassination was a stupid move, for it announced the Senate's incapability of ruling by law. Also, once violence was introduced as the most effective way of settling political crises, the way was open to civil war and chaos.

The programs of Tiberius were passed on to his brother, Gaius, after his death. Gaius was elected tribune in 123 B.C. His program was even more radical than his brother's. He proposed laws whereby the people could dominate the magistrates and the Senate. He called for the establishment of a public dole to relieve the misery of the poor. He revived his brother's plan to redistribute the public lands and he sent out new colonies, while he made it possible for men without property to enter the army. To offset senatorial opposition to his strengthening of the plebeian classes, he made a bid for the support of the equestrian class which had begun to control the whole economic life of the empire. He offered them prestige second only to the senators themselves. He transferred from the Senate to them control over the Extortions Court, which controlled the activities of provincial governors. The Senate fought back, to be sure, introducing tribunate vetoes of every measure Gaius put forth. The crisis was reached when Gaius sought new support by enfranchising the Latin allies and moving the Italians to Latin status. Immediately, the *equites* and the Roman plebs cooled toward him, not wishing to share their privileges with the allies. Gaius in desperation seized the Aventine. The Senate sent the consuls against him, and Gaius fell in the ensuing battle. Again the Senate had to resort to force to solve a political crisis.

The Civil Wars (105–82 B.C.)

The Senate had demonstrated its political weakness. Soon the senatorial class as a whole would show its ineptness, its venality and its inability to create new institutions to meet new situations. The provinces were up in arms because of oppressive government. The allies were making a bid for a larger share in Roman success. The *equites* were hungry for larger profits. Frontier wars swept across the Empire as Rome came into contact with newly emerging peoples in northern Europe, Asia and Africa. All these

▶ **Colosseum at Rome, inside with subterranean passages exposed.** In the amphitheater gladiators fought each other, animal hunts were arranged, and often men fought animals. The floor could be flooded for mock sea battles. A huge net covering was used to protect spectators from the sun.

▶ **This bridge across the Tiber to the island Tiburtina is one of the oldest in Rome.** Rome was built near the shallow ford at this spot, just as nearby the Cloaca Maxima, the first sewer, was built to drain the marshy Forum. The superstructure of the bridge was added during the Renaissance.

problems called for imaginative leadership, and the Senate failed to provide it. Other forces rose to fill the gap.

The first crisis came in Numidia. There the king, Jugurtha, murdered his way to the throne, killed Italian settlers and seized Roman property. He rejected all offers of arbitration from the Senate and bribed all the army commanders sent against him. He went to Rome, bribed members of the Senate, murdered a rival in the city itself, and skipped back to Africa to the disgust and shame of the Senate that now declared serious war on him (110–108 B.C.). The war languished because of the difficult terrain and Jugurtha's wiliness, but the *Populares* (the reform party) accused the Senate of ineptness and corruption. They put up for the consulship Gaius Marius, himself an ignorant peasant, gruff, unpolished, but canny. His promise to bring Jugurtha home dead or alive, together with the obvious sneering condescension of the Senate, won him a landslide victory. He was elected, not for the customary one year, but for the duration of the war, a significant exception to the law and custom.

Marius reformed the social composition of the army. The property qualification had been gradually reduced until even the poor were eligible. However, the lowest classes, the proletariat, the most numerous in the state were still too poor to serve. Marius opened recruitment to all, regardless of property qualification. Immediately thousands of the poorest people of Rome had honorable jobs open to them. They became the backbone of the new army and produced a profound social revolution. Furthermore, their loyalty was immediately to Marius as Commander-in-Chief rather than to the state. They fought for him and he undertook to pay them and reward them at the mustering-out with a bonus and land. The general now had to have political power in order to get the necessary funds and lands to distribute. Inevitably popular commanders drifted toward the populist political program.

Marius also democratized the army. The old *maniples* were now organized into larger unites called cohorts, of 100 men each. These were organized into legions of 6,000 men, in which all the troops were equipped with the same armor and weapons, the short javelin *(pilum)* and the broad, short sword, equally good for slashing or thrusting. Each cohort was under a centurion invariably chosen from the lower middle class. The legions now developed a classless cohesion which produced the high morale and single-mindedness that proved such an effective weapon in the hands of resolute leaders.

Marius quickly brought Jugurtha to bay, then he rushed northward to meet a German invasion of the Po Valley. Hysterically, the Romans overlooked legal and moral precedents and heaped honor after honor upon him. He held in all six consulships. The atmosphere became even more tense as troops were dispatched to control pirates in the eastern Mediterranean, and to put down a bloody slave revolt in Sicily, in which over 40,000 slaves were slaughtered. When the immediate crises were over, Marius returned to Rome, where he proved to be a very inept politician indeed. In his rise to power, Marius had depended on a group of unscrupulous politicians, who hoped to use the dull peasant for their own ends. Once in power, they wrested control away from him and by using gangs of cutthroats and mobsters they intimidated the electorate, rigged elections, assassinated opponents, and finally fell out among themselves over the spoils. Rome was turned into a battlefield and government became a mockery. The middle class joined with the Senate to restore order. When it was obvious that Marius no longer could maintain control over his party, the Senate called on an impoverished patrician of great courage and ability, L. Cornelius Sulla, to march on the city, retain his prerogatives as consul, and restore the Republic to order.

Sulla took the city in a lightning move and began to kill off the leaders of the Populist party. Marius and others fled to the north, while Sulla turned the city over to the Senate. He left immediately for the East to meet the attack of Mithrodates the Great, King of Pontus on the Black Sea, who was expanding his territories into the Roman sphere of influence. The war was bitter and bloody. Sulla was merciless and when Mithrodates sued for peace in 84 B.C. the price was high. An enormous booty was gathered from the whole region and an almost perpetual tribute was ordered. Sulla extracted a new oath of loyalty from his troops and marched back to Italy to seize power from the Populists, who had taken advantage of his absence to fight their way back into Rome and to restore their rule by force. For a year Sulla fought their armies, defeated them, and then entered Rome by assault in 81 B.C. He declared proscriptions of everyone, regardless of class, who was sympathetic to the Populist program. Hundreds of families were wiped out, and thousands of opportunists seized the houses and country estates of the murdered. Sulla freed thousands of the slaves of his enemies, and they took the name of their benefactor, Cornelius, and became his fanatical supporters.

Once order was restored, Sulla introduced reforms that in effect put the Senate back in power and turned back the clock to the pre-Grachian constitution. The tribunes and their assembly were put back under the control of the Senate, whose number was swelled with 300 of Sulla's noble supporters. The number of *quaestors* was raised to twenty, and all were members of the Senate for life; the *praetors* were raised to eight, and the number of provinces to ten so that the two consuls and the eight *praetors* would each have a province to administer as governor for a year upon leaving office. The minimum age for *quaestor* was set at thirty, for *praetor* at forty, and for consul at forty-three. No consul could run for re-election for at least ten years after he had served his term in office. Sulla also reformed the judicial system, welcomed the Italians into Roman citizenship and, having restored the Senate to power, retired to his country villa where he lived the life of a gentleman farmer until his peaceful death in 78 B.C.

To restore the Senate to power by means of a new constitution was one thing, to revivify it was another. Gaius Pompeius (or Pompey) had joined Sulla's forces in 81 B.C. at the age of twenty-four. Raising three legions of his own, he fought the forces of Marius in Sicily and Africa. In 77 B.C. the Senate was faced with a revolt in Spain led by Sertorius, a just and capable leader of the Populist party. Senatorial armies had been ineffective, so the Senate turned in desperation to Pompey and gave him an extraordinary command, even though he was under age and did not have the experience needed under the law. This was government by exception. While Pompey was defeating Sertorius by attrition, Spartacus led a full-scale revolt of the slaves of southern Italy. The Senate sent M. Licinius Crassus, the wealthiest financier of his day, as consul to put down the revolt, which he did with horrible severity. Remnants of the slaves were cut off in northern Italy by Pompey, who had just returned from Spain.

Crassus and Pompey now controlled the Roman world. Crassus' millions and his support among the middle classes, and Pompey's well-disciplined armies, were the important factors in their power. Pompey could not by law hold the consulship, but in the face of his military threat, an exception was again made in his favor. The two consuls proceeded to take control over the state, and the Sullan constitution fell to pieces. Control over the government was put back into the hands of the Equestrian order, especially in the courts. The young Cicero emerged for the first time as an important Roman statesman by working out the necessary legal details and by influencing the Senate to accept the reforms. The tribunes were restored to power over the Senate, but since they were kept strictly under the influence of the two consuls, it was the latter who really controlled the Senate as well as the tribunate assembly. Pompey was voted an extraordinary *imperium* to fight the troublesome Mediterranean pirates, a command that was not confined to any set territory. While his campaign was a great success, nonetheless the exception made in his favor pointed in new directions for ambitious commanders. Then the tribunes proposed that the command over the eastern provinces be taken away from the honest senatorial general Lucullus and given to Pompey. This represented another break with constitutional law, and though it was vigorously supported by the *equites* and Cicero, it was eventually the expediency that spelled disaster for Pompey and his supporters in the war with Julius Caesar. Pompey acted with characteristic swiftness. He defeated Mithrodates once more, turned all of Asia west of the Euphrates from the Black Sea to the Red into a Roman province, and came home with unbelievable amounts of booty.

The First Triumvirate

In the year 63 B.C. there were special tensions in Rome. The lower classes were angry at their still unsatisfied demands for economic reforms. The government was now obviously in the hands of a ruthless minority, since over ninety percent of Rome's citizens lived outside the city and did not bother to vote in elections. Finally rivalries between the great political leaders of the day led to dangerous intrigue.

Julius Caesar (102–44 B.C.) turned in this year to serious politics. He had lived a scandalous life up to this time, dissolute and debt-ridden, but he had kept some contact with political events. Though patrician, his sympathies were with the Populist party, as were his connections—his aunt had married Marius and he, himself, was the son-in-law of the Marian leader Cinna. By garnering Populist votes and borrowing very heavily from Crassus, Caesar won election to the praetorship and the office of *Pontifex Maximus*, signalling to all his moral regeneration. He chose rich Spain as his province, for he needed cash very badly to pay off his debts to Crassus. In the same year Cicero was elected to the consulship and openly declared himself a conservative supporter of Pompey against Crassus and Caesar, who were sponsoring the old Graccan land-distribution, this time from the lands that Pompey had added to the state in his wars. At the same time, Cicero uncovered and defeated with rather hysterical measures a conspiracy of a disgruntled aristocrat, Catiline, aimed at taking over the state to wipe out the debts of impoverished Romans, particularly noblemen.

In the following year (62 B.C.) Pompey returned from the East, expecting the Senate to ratify his treaties in the East, reward his veterans, and allow him to celebrate a triumph. Once his disbanded his armies, however, he was powerless. While he writhed in frustration, Caesar returned from Spain and offered a solution to the problems of all the political leaders. Since he had control over the vote, Pompey had his legions, and Crassus his middle-class supporters, and since all three needed power to satisfy their supporters, why not join forces, take over the Roman world and divide it up like a pie? Caesar was elected consul in 59 B.C., Crassus got favorable tax settlements in Asia for his friends, and Pompey's veterans were given their lands. As consul, Caesar acted in an outrageously high-handed manner to put down senatorial opposition and to serve the interests of his partners. All gained, but Caesar most of all, for he was assigned a five year term as governor of Gaul, where he trained the most efficient army in the Roman world and gained invaluable experience in politics and statesmanship.

The triumvirs engineered the exile of Cicero and other senatorial stalwarts, and met in Luca (56 B.C.) to renew their agreements. Caesar opted to return to Gaul, Crassus undertook a campaign in the East against the newly-emerging Parthian kingdom, and Pompey decided to stay in Rome or Spain to mend his political fences. The coalition was strengthened by marriages, and it was agreed that each commander could raise private armies, but that all commands would end in 49 B.C. One special agreement had to be made for Caesar. He had many enemies who were eager to get back at him by charging him with malfea-

sance in office as soon as his command would be up, and his accounts subject to audit. He knew that with rigged juries he would be in some danger. In office, however, he could not be touched. He decided to get to Rome and run immediately for the consulship. He sought special legislation which would allow him to leave his province before the end of his term so he could appear in Rome in person with his immunity still operative to run for the consulship. His partners agreed to the plan.

After the meeting at Luca, the triumvirate disintegrated rapidly. Crassus was killed in the East. Pompey drifted openly toward the senatorial party and was given almost dictatorial power. Pompey's wife, Caesar's daughter Julia, died, and he married into a senatorial family. Caesar's enemies brought him under their influence and every attempt to patch up the estrangement failed. Finally in January, 49 B.C., the Senate issued an ultimatum to Caesar to give up his command and return to Rome. On January 10, Caesar decided on a bid for absolute power, crossed the borders of his province at the Rubicon with his legions (clearly an act of civil war), and marched on Rome.

Pompey and the Senate fled to Greece, leaving behind the public treasury and all of Italy, that rushed to join Caesar's campaign. Within two months, Caesar held all of Italy, and after a swift campaign against Pompey's supporters in Spain, he crossed over to Greece and at Pharsalus (48 B.C.) administered a crushing defeat to Pompey who, barely escaping with his life, took refuge in Egypt, where he was murdered by the King, Ptolemy XIII, probably to gain Caesar's favor.

Caesar swept on after Pompey, reaching Egypt right behind him. Here he found a turbulent situation in which the young, charming Cleopatra (she was twenty-two at the time) was struggling with her brother-consort Ptolemy XIII, then with another younger brother Ptolemy XIV, for power over the descendants of the Hellenistic aristocracy. Caesar apparently was intrigued with the young girl, had an affair with her that produced a son, Caesarion, and lingered in Egypt for months, training her for her position as Queen of Egypt, and bringing the affairs of the whole Near East into order. He finally returned to Rome, bringing Cleopatra and their young son with him.

When Caesar returned to Rome, he was determined to introduce at long last the reforms that had been needed since the time of the Gracchi. He knew full well that the senatorial clan had failed to govern. He took the consulship for himself and held it each year but one until he died. He also had himself named dictator three times in succession to forestall tribunician veto. In addition he took the tribunician power without actually holding the office. This gave him control over the popular vote and also sacrosanctity. He was also a sort of moral prefect of the city, which gave him the power of the censor. To make the Senate a stronger partner, he packed it with 900 new members chosen from the lower classes and provincials. Otherwise, he did not disturb its constitutional position.

With these unprecedented powers, Caesar transformed the government. He united all of Italy and restored order in the city by outlawing clubs and gangs. He founded new colonies to reduce the excessive population of Rome. He settled his thousands of veterans in the new provinces he had acquired, which not only reduced Rome's population, relieving the poverty there, but helped spread Roman civilization

to the barbarians on and across the frontiers. His new colonies were set up as self-contained corporate bodies, modeled after Rome, and under the rule of the local middle-class aristocracy *(curiales)*. These *civitates* remained the basic unit of the Empire throughout its history. Caesar also turned to practical matters. He reformed the calendar by settling on a 365 day year with a leap year ever fourth year (the Julian Calendar). He even began a systematic codification of the law. There are indications that he was planning to dig a canal across Corinth and to move the capitol to ancient Troy when a group of would-be patriots, unable to comprehend the inevitability of his reforms, and that the Republic was indeed dead, assassinated him in the name of Liberty in the theatre of Pompey (where the Senate was holding its meetings temporarily) on March 15, 44 B.C.

The Second Triumvirate

When the assassins cut down Julius Caesar, they thought that the act alone would restore the old Republic. They had no plan to reform the government or the social order. As the matter turned out, Caesar's world survived his death. His close friend, Mark Antony, was consul and took swift command in the city. He obtained a copy of Caesar's will, which bequeathed to every Roman citizen 1,000 denari, and turned his extensive properties into a public park. When he read this at Caesar's funeral and had fanned alive the flame of public vengeance for their dead hero, the assassins took refuge in flight to Greece. As surviving consul, Mark Anthony seemed a worthy successor to Caesar. He had been a faithful follower in all his campaigns and in his public career. Handsome, of apparent decisiveness, he seemed cast in the Caesarean model. But Mark Antony was no Caesar. Emotionally unstable, behind an outer mask of resoluteness he hid an inner child-like need for constant reinforcement. He bathed in the glow of Caesar's strength and vitality. After the loss of his hero, he turned increasingly to public applause to keep up his inner strength and he hoped that by aping Caesar's career he could keep building up an ever larger audience.

His first steps seemed secure enough. His first rival was Lepidus, who had taken Anthony's place as Caesar's Master of Horse, but the two soon came to terms when Lepidus recognized the other's superior position and accepted the role of *Pontifex Maximus*. The most serious rival for power, however, was an enigmatic eighteen year old boy, Octavian, the son of one of Caesar's nieces. Precocious, the boy had early caught his great-uncle's eye, and Caesar had sent him abroad for education and military training. His plans are revealed by the fact that in his will Caesar named Octavian his adopted son and heir. Octavian was a quiet, resourceful man, not only of great ambition, but with an astonishingly mature self-control and capacity for turning plans into accomplishments. Upon hearing of the assassination, he swiftly crossed over to Italy and, with the counsel of Cicero, firmly made himself the leading power in Rome. Aided by his close friends, the capable Agrippa and Maecenas, he came to a working understanding with the conservative leaders of the Senate. He made a highly significant marriage with the influential aristocratic matron, Livia. By using the magic of his name Caesar, he won over many of his uncle's legions, who deserted Antony to join

his cause. Soon Antony was floundering. He was exposed as an embezzler of public funds and as an unstable man of inordinate pretensions. Octavian took command. He formed a second triumvirate with Antony and Lepidus. He forced the tribunate assembly to give them greater power than other magistrates, and they ordered a proscription of all possible opposition. Over 2,500 senators and knights, including Cicero, were murdered. Then he carved up the Empire, offering to his partners their choice of the spoils. He, himself, stayed at Rome to control the situation, but Antony, true to his nature, chose to fly after glory and fame in an Eastern campaign. This period of civil war ended with the defeat of the assassins at Philippi in 42 B.C. and the blocking of Lepidus' attempt to become an independent tyrant in Sicily.

Mark Antony and Octavian remained as the two masters of the world and cemented their friendship with the marriage of Antony to Octavia, sister of Octavian. Antony then went to the East and became involved in an unsuccessful war with Parthia. He also came into contact with Cleopatra, who had returned to Egypt after Caesar's death. Apparently she had devised an ambitious scheme to conquer the East and in partnership with Rome reestablish the empire of Alexander. Deceived by appearances, she thought Antony was the dominant power in Rome and the man for her scheme. She invited him to Egypt. He, meanwhile, needed Egyptian money and men, and decided to accept. It was a fateful decision for both, for almost at once all their plans and schemes of conquest were engulfed in a passionate love affair which fed on his inner weaknesses as much as on her desire to dominate. Out of touch with reality, they shocked the world with their blatant disregard for his wife. They had a series of children for whom they planned to conquer the world. But day by day Antony's army dwindled as his legions shipped back to Rome. Octavian portrayed him as a weakling deceived by an Oriental temptress who had robbed him of reason and manhood. When Rome was sufficiently disgusted with Antony's conduct, Octavian set out to capture the adulterers to bring them back to Rome in disgrace. The battle was fought by navies at Actium off the coast of Greece in 31 B.C. Decisively defeated, Cleopatra, who had been at the battle in person, fled back to Egypt, followed by the almost frantic Antony. Lost in hopelessness, they waited for their conqueror to arrive, and when he did, they chose suicide rather than disgrace. Octavian killed the young Caesarion, farmed out Cleopatra's children to Near Eastern powers, confiscated her treasure, buried the lovers in a common tomb, and turned Egypt into a Roman province. As he set out for Rome, the world waited to see how he would use his absolute power to restore permanent peace.

The Principate

It was obvious to Octavian, or Augustus as his countrymen now called him, that the stability of Rome depended on his retaining power in his own hands. But he refused to be a dictator. Instead he envisioned a partnership between himself as *princeps*, or first man in the state, and the Senate. His rule was essentially a dyarchy. The important provinces, that contained most of the legions, were assigned to him as proconsul and to the Senate. The rest were administered as before by governors, but now these were better trained and paid adequate salaries to keep down exploitation. Gradually his proconsulship was given authority over all other offices and troops in all provinces, so eventually Augustus was in command of all government outside Rome. At home he at first held the consulship consecutively, but as this cut down the number of ex-consuls available for administrative duties, he gave up the consulship and took the powers of the tribune instead. As tribune, not only did he have sacro-sanctity, but he became the people's protector and he could introduce or veto at will legislation in the Senate and in the people's assemblies. He also had power over all other magistrates. The Emperor's proconsular authority and his tribunician power were the basis for imperial authority, for it brought control over the army, over the government, and over public opinion firmly into the Emperor's hands.

Honors were heaped on Augustus by the Senate. He was given the right to initiate, veto, and vote first on any legislation he wished in the Senate. He was acclaimed as *Imperator*, Father of his Country and Restorer of the Republic. The secret of his success lay more in the confidence he inspired in the Roman people and in the seeming conservative restoration of republican liberty that he proclaimed than in the reality of this freedom. His work constituted a profound change in the government. He created a new state, and it was only a question of time before this would become apparent.

In the meantime Augustus undertook a revival of the morality of ancient times. He stabilized the Roman society by restricting the manumission of slaves, which had become a favorite way of freeing a family of the responsibility of the maintaining the expensive upkeep of slaves. He made adultery a crime, and penalized men and women who did not marry. He proposed religion as the cement that should bind together the Roman people so profoundly disunited by a century of civil war. He built numerous temples and revived ancient cults. He brought back the practice of family prayers and forbade Eastern cults, though he, himself, was worshipped as divine in the provinces. He claimed divinity for his family. He deified the genius of the dead Julius and he encouraged the artists to portray himself in all the symbols of majesty and sanctity that words and statues could convey. Though he was not worshipped in his own day as a god at Rome, it was obvious that the *numen* or genius of Augustus was so worshipped, and that after his death this *numen* would continue to secure good fortune for the Roman people and be worshipped as divine.

There is a quality of unreality in this attempt to legislate into the Romans a return to the stern morality of their ancestors. Augustus could turn Rome into a city of marble. He could introduce an Italian consolidation and peaceful prosperity to the provinces, but he could not solve all the problems of Rome. The Senate inevitably lost its legislative function in the state as it tended to follow the lead of the *princeps*. Increasingly it became a sort of high court. Its main power remained as the role it played in electing with the army the successors to the imperial power. The place of senators in the social hierarchy and in the civil service was increasingly taken by members of the equestrian order, which Augustus strengthened, and in the provinces by the thousands of veterans that had served the state in the civil wars.

The army still provided a good living for the lower classes, but in foreign policy Augustus chose to pursue a conservative course. He stabilized the frontier along the Rhine and Danube in the West, and in the East he secured the frontier with a string of provinces and friendly regimes. After the battle of Teutoberg Forest (9 A.D.) in which Varus lost three legions to invading Germans, Augustus gave up all thought of expansion and instituted a defensive policy of protecting the empire behind strongly defended natural frontiers.

The most difficult problem for Augustus, and one he never solved effectively, was the question of succession. He, himself, had no son, and he outlived all the members of his immediate family that he had hoped would succeed to his power. He was eventually forced to accept as his successor Tiberius, who was Livia's son from her former marriage. He carefully groomed Tiberius over the years by having him serve in the armies and in the provinces. He forced him to divorce his beloved wife to marry Augustus' debauched daughter, Julia. Finally, he bestowed upon him the same proconsular and tribunician powers he held, thus making Tiberius his partner in government. He himself retained the legislative control over the Senate and his power as commander-in-chief over the legions. Upon his death these last two powers, bestowed by the consent of the army and the Senate, were all that were needed to make him emperor. The army, though, held the ultimate key to imperial power, as became more and more obvious in later years.

Roman Culture

Roman art and literature must be viewed in the context of the late Hellenistic period. The trends towards grandiose conceptions, naturalness, exaggerated emotionalism, sterile themes, these were the elements Roman artists used. Yet the Roman genius instilled new life and an impressive form into this decadent art. Roman buildings, for example, were Greek only in superficial decorative elements. They were tall buildings, basically Italian, even Etruscan, in mood, set in dramatic arrangements of flights of stairs, elaborate enclosures, and symmetrical plantings of shrubs and trees. The effect was monumental. The arch became the symbol of Roman architecture and the circular temple its most common building. With these elements, the Romans were able to construct gigantic, vaulted and domed complexes of buildings that satisfied their taste for the grandiose at the same time that it made it possible to conduct public affairs inside and not in the market-place as in the Greek city-state.

Roman literature follows the same pattern. Since public careers in Rome depended on running for election, oratory was early developed into a fine art in Rome. The Roman orator found the Greek style of the classic period too dry, whereas the exaggerations of Eastern Hellenistic mannerisms offended his taste. Typically Roman were the measured speeches of the elder Cato, who exerted a strong influence on the creator of the Latin prose style, Cicero. He worked out a balanced, resonant style that combined the best of the Greek style with a Roman sense of proportion and sparseness. His texts on oratory and the speeches he delivered in the Senate and in the courts have had a constant influence throughout the history of western literature.

The chief beneficiaries of the Ciceronian style, perhaps, were the historians of Rome. The early histories have been lost, but Livy (59 B.C.–17 A.D.) expressed in excellent form the high moral tone of the Augustan Age. His extremely long narrative of Roman history from its beginning to his own age, most of which is lost, is an exciting adventure story of a people destined for greatness. Tacitus (55–117 A.D.), the best writer of the Silver Age, wrote masterful annals of the early empire which are important not only for the factual account they relate, but even more for the insight they give us into the prejudices of an aristocrat, seeing evil in the empire and yearning for the "good old days." This same bias colors his essays on Britain, *Agricola*, and on the Germans, *Germania*. Suetonius (69–140 A.D.) in his *Lives of the Twelve Caesars* continued the tradition of writing in graphic matter-of-fact style. Much maligned by superficial criticism for his tendency to incorporate into his work material of very dubious trustworthiness, nonetheless, his histories are a mine of very important information. At least he himself was not taken in by the stories he related.

Rome produced few philosophers or scientists, though the *Natural History* of Pliny the Elder (23–79 A.D.) was a true encyclopedia of all the Greek science that was known to the Romans. It contained many errors and distortions, but it remained the high mark of ancient learning until well past the Middle Ages. His nephew, Pliny the Younger (61–113 A.D.) left a series of important letters that illustrate the education of a well-born Roman. In one of these he described how his uncle was killed while investigating the eruption of Vesuvius that destroyed Pompeii. In another letter, to the emperor Trajan, he gave an important picture of the attitudes of the government to the early Christians.

There has survived little fiction from Rome, though the *Satyricon* of Petronius and the *Golden Ass* of Apuleius indicated that there was some of high quality. Poetry, on the other hand, survives in large quantities. Apparently every educated Roman tried his hand at poetry, and the form covered a wide range of material. Catullus (84–54 B.C.) was one of the more brilliant poets of the late Republic. He used adaptations of Greek meters to pour out a burning picture of his innermost emotions. His poems dealt with all aspects of the ties that bind people to each other: love, friendship, dependency. He also painted a lively picture of the hopes and longings, the incidents of the everyday lives of the Romans on the eve of their deepest social and political revolution.

Perhaps the most influential of all the poets was Vergil (70–19 B.C.). Vergil was the son of a northern Italian farmer, who dedicated himself to his friend and patron, Augustus, yet who never lost his deep love and yearning for the beautiful countryside in which he grew up. His *Ecologues* and *Georgics* are the epitome of Rome's faith in sober industry, the permanence of the land and the values of people who lived on it, the moral ties that bound together a Roman family and the Roman people. In his fourth *Ecologue* he lyrically described the "Golden Age" of the past and predicted its return would be signalled by the birth of a wondrous child. Many have seen in this passage a prophecy of Christ, though he himself probably alluded to the hoped-for son of his patron at the time, Pollio. His great masterpiece, the *Aeneid,* is a tremendous pageant of the historic mission of Rome. Aeneas, who fled from Troy with his father and son, was guided by destiny to journey widely, suffer vicissitudes, spurn the temptations of Queen Dido of Carthage, and eventually reach the site of the future Rome where he established the Roman race. Obviously, the story was an allegory of the vision that Augustus wished to publicize, that Rome had reached in him its foreordained greatness. But the poem also revealed the deepest Roman beliefs in *pietas,* sobriety, the good will of the gods, and the mission of Rome to conquer the world.

Horace (65–8 B.C.) was also of the lower classes, the son of a freedman. In his *Odes* and *Satires* he portrayed on the one hand the serious view that an ordinary hard-working Roman held of life with its frugal virtues, and on the other contrasted the frivolous, debauched and vicious life of the corrupted aristocracy that was losing its control over the state. A good example of this very class was the brilliant Ovid (43 B.C.- 17 A.D.) who wrote a series of witty and scandalous satires (*Art of Love, Metamorphes, Fasti)* that reflected perfectly the tone of the aristocratic court that resisted so effectively all attempts by Augustus to introduce moral reform. All the foibles, the ridiculous weaknesses of men were irreverently pictured in language that offended Augustus, who exiled the poet to the Balkans, where he pined and eventually died, broken-hearted.

Little philosophy was produced. Epicureanism, however, so congenial to the Roman character, found its finest expression in the long philosophic poem *On the Nature of the Universe,* by Lucretius (94–55 B.C.). The poet claimed that man ought not to fear death, for it was really a wonderful way to escape the pain of everyday life. Man sought happiness in this world, but he could not obtain it from the gods, for they did not exist in a universe of impersonal atoms. Happiness could only come from man's intellect. When man used science to understand the mechanistic order of the universe, and came to terms with its laws, he could rise above pain and reach the most sought-after state of *anorexia*, to be without those appetites which could not, after all, be satisfied.

The Stoic philosophy also found a natural echo in the Roman character. Seneca (5 B.C.–65 A.D.) approached the philosophy almost as a religion. He believed that God existed and that He made Himself manifest in nature. To live, then, in harmony with nature was to live the good life. The part of man that pulled away from nature had to be chastised, disciplined, and brought back to its natural direction by the constant exertion of will. Marcus Aurelius (emperor 161–180 A.D.) tried to put into practice this ideal, as well as the ethics of Epictetus (55–135 A.D.), who had taught that happiness was an inner light, that man's life was one of suffering, that all men found kinship in their common pain. In his *Meditations*, Marcus Aurelius showed us how difficult it was for a pious late pagan, who had lost his belief in the gods or in a personalized universe, to remain a moral, self-controlled gentleman.

The Early Empire 14–96

Tiberius (14–37 A.D.) came to the throne after a long life of disappointment and pain. His mood was conservative and apparently he wanted to continue the policies of Augustus without further reforms. He possibly dreamed of restoring the now defunct Republic. In any case he chose to share his power with the Senate. He transferred to that body the power of electing magistrates, but he continued to nominate the candidates. Unfortunately, he had become very suspicious and almost paranoic in his sensitivity to criticism. He began to rely on spies

and instituted numerous trials for treason. There were many senators, moreover, who had still not understood that the imperial power had come to stay. They still thought they could defeat the emperor. Gradually, Tiberius became more and more estranged until he finally exiled himself on Capri from which he ruled by decree. Open hatred flared and he died universally hated and unfairly charged with tyranny. His successor Gaius (37–41 A.D.), or Caligula as he was popularly called, was a disaster. Morbidly fearful of assassination, openly mad, he let loose an insane rule of terror in which he alienated the Senate and the army, which finally formed a plot to murder him.

Claudius (41–54 A.D.) had been a pedantic scholar all his life. His physical infirmities and prudent self-effacement had amused Caligula, so that he survived. The murderers of Caligula raised Claudius to the throne almost as a joke, but he became the most competent emperor in the early empire. He tried to reform the Senate by opening its doors to provincials to make it representative of empire-wide opinion. But the Senate was declining too rapidly to be of much use to him. He turned instead to a cabinet composed of freedmen who were specially trained and educated to be the heads of complex bureaucratic departments. He took an active interest in the provinces, extending citizenship to all army and navy veterans regardless of origin. In foreign affairs he was basically conservative, but to protect the northern provinces he launched a very successful invasion of Britain, which not only added that country to the empire, but tied the army even more closely to the emperor.

The last of the Julio-Claudian emperors was Nero (54–68 A.D.). Attractive, not without talent, he had morbid weaknesses that apparently slipped into open madness. He went on a tour of Greece to take part in singing contests as an ordinary candidate. The tour was a resounding success for Nero, who won all the prizes, and the Greek cities, who were freed from their taxes, but it shocked the sensibilities of the people of Rome. He launched a series of outrageous murders, including his wife and mother, and after the disastrous fire of 64 A.D., which his supporters blamed on the Christians, he began to build a new Rome on a scale that approached megalomania. In disgust, conspiracies broke out at Rome and among the troops on the frontiers. Three armies hailed their generals as Caesar, and Nero committed suicide in terror even as soldiers were rushing through the streets to cut him down.

In spite of the poor quality of government in the capitol, the empire had entered upon a period of unparalleled peace and prosperity. Money was stabilized, vast public works gave employment to the lower classes, and trade flourished as the whole world was brought into peaceful order. Even the farmer developed effective techniques to maintain himself in relative prosperity, although the imperial system favored the growth of large senatorial estates that provided stiff competition for the small land-holder. There was some increase in manufacturing, though here the lack of real interest in technological improvements was a dangerous symptom. Slaves still provided most labor, though their treatment was improving, and Stoic principles and the high costs of buying and maintaining slaves led to increasing manumission. All in all, Roman society at large was fluid, optimistic, and interested in high-minded reform.

The Flavians (69–96 A.D.) came into power with Vespasian, who was the fourth Emperor to rule in 69, a year marked by a short but bloody civil war. He was of peasant stock, and had worked his way laboriously to a successful career in the army. He officially took over all the legislative and military powers of the state, and had himself deified. Though he was in theory supposed to rule within the constitution, he was openly a full Emperor. His son Titus (79–81 A.D.) worked hard to be a good man and emperor, as did his brother Domitian (81–91 A.D.) who marred his important reforms in the provinces by a suspicious and cruel personality. Domitian demanded that he be addressed as Lord and God, and his reign of terror brought about a palace revolt and his assassination.

The Pax Romana 96–180

After the Flavians there ruled a series of emperors: Nerva (96–98), Trajan (98–117), Hadrian (117–138), Antonius Pius (138–161), and Marcus Aurelius (161–180), who were all sober, high-minded, hard-working men who took their reigns as a call to duty and greatness. Frugal, these men preserved the public funds of the government, and each at his death bequeathed huge sums to the treasury out of their personal fortunes. The Senate lost all its power, but the senatorial class was replaced by the productive middle class, the equestrian order. The people of Rome were assured of a constant supply of food at controlled prices, but it was the provincials that benefitted most from the regime. Roman civilization spread widely all over the world. Roman-type cities, roads, and governments sprang up everywhere. Governors were well-trained and well-paid for their work. Rome encouraged the formation of local provincial assemblies, and the emperors extended citizenship widely. The city-state *(civitas)* had always been the basic unit of the Roman system, and in this period local government under the local middle-class aristocracy *(curiales)* was strengthened. Even the frontier was stabilized as the last Roman conquests across the Danube took place and Romanization of the barbarian tribes along the frontier extended civilized conditions for miles northward. Only in the East did there remain an unsettled border facing the Parthians and later the Persians. All in all, the Roman world was living in a Silver Age, if not a Golden one, and the benefits of universal peace were so profound that they were nostalgically recalled for centuries to come.

Collapse and Reorganization 180–285

Commodus (180–192), son of the philosopher-emperor Marcus Aurelius, lived, it seemed, a life calculated to contrast in every way with that of his father. A voluptuary mystic, he lived in the midst of an oriental court filled with debauchery and murder. The Praetorian Guard struck down the Emperor, sold the crown to Pertinax, and then killed the latter after 87 days because he wished to introduce economy to government. The crown was auctioned to the highest bidder, and five years of civil war brought Septimus Severus to the throne (193–211). This Emperor had been born in the deserts of north Africa, and his dynasty inaugurated a rule by foreigners, mainly from the East. He was disliked by the Italians, so he organized a well-disciplined provincial army on which he relied completely

for authority. The Severi always courted army support by giving out enormous payments to the troops. They also depended increasingly on provincials for political and administrative support. The Italians were severely repressed, the army favored, and finally Caracalla (212–217) extended Roman citizenship to all freedmen throughout the empire *(Constitutio Antoniniana 212)* to offset Italian influence in the government.

The effect of the great power of the army on the government was seen immediately after the assassination of Severus Alexander in 235. Within fifty years no less than nineteen emperors reigned by terror and all but one died by violence. The army alone determined the succession, and the crown was always for sale to the highest bidder. The empire might have survived the period in better health if the conditions of the 2nd Century had remained constant, but in fact disastrous developments had taken place that called for vigorous action by the government, which was paralyzed by the effects of the military anarchy.

The Decline of the Roman World

The decline of the Roman Empire is one of the great catastrophes of human history, but for this very reason it has been studied by countless historians who have revealed with their research how widespread its causes were. Under the soldier-emperors expensive foreign and domestic wars drained the treasury and placed an intolerable burden on the tax structure. Furthermore, the monies collected were thrown away on wars and a foreign policy of paying tribute to barbarians along the frontier to keep peace, both policies becoming a serious drain of money out of productive use and circulation. There developed an acute shortage of specie and capital for industrial or technological investment.

The government was forced to collect taxes in an increasingly ruthless manner. The main tax was on land, and it was based on the size and quality of the lot *(iugum)*. To collect the tax on a piece of land, there had to be dwellers on it, so there was added a head-tax *(capitum)*. Thus a piece of land was assigned so many *capita* for purposes of taxation. The rate was not usually excessive, but assessment was only made every fifteen years. Rates were changed only every five years. There was a tendency for many farmers to fall into arrears, especially if their crops were to fail, which happened all too often in the 3rd Century. They borrowed heavily and finally either lost their land or abandoned it. Also, public lands had largely gone into large estates that were tax-exempt to encourage their development. These proved too much competition for small farmers and not only added to their tax burden, but robbed them of a chance to prosper. Since there were no land banks, nor farm cooperatives at the time, farmers had to borrow from the owners of these very same large estates. Thus, the estates became ever larger, and farmers sought refuge on them as life in cities and on the roads became less attractive. It was easy for a farmer to become a share-cropper or semi-serf *(colonus)* on the estate. Once he entered this status, however, his contacts as a citizen with the government were severed. He became a dependent of the lord of the villa or manor. Even a more prosperous farmer might enter some arrangement with the owner of a villa to escape taxes by turning over his lands and then receiving them back as a *praecar-*

ium, a sort of lifetime lease, not protected by law, that could be terminated at any time by the owner.

Thus, as time went on, the villa or manor became a large piece of territory on which there lived a nobleman surrounded by a large private guard held to himself by personal oaths of loyalty (patron-client or commendation), that was often rewarded by land-grants *(praecaria)*. On the manor lived praecarists, *coloni*, and slaves. In each category there were often groups of barbarians useful as soldiers in war or as farmers in peace. The government found that all these people had escaped taxation, and it was difficult to tax the lord, who often was too powerful. The burden became heavier on those who were still free, tax revenues shrank, and the government had to seek other remedies.

The collection of taxes had been the duty of local governments *(curiales)* for centuries. The *curiales*, however, found that it was impossible to collect sufficient taxes to satisfy the demands of the imperial government. Increasingly, officials abandoned their jobs, merchants fled the cities, urban proletariates melted away. Even though the emperors interfered increasingly to control the election of competent men, there began a steady decline of municipal government, then finally of the cities themselves. Trade languished, customs duties fell off, industry declined. All this meant not only less revenue, but a stagnation of the whole economy, which now tended to become local in nature.

One catastrophic factor in the economic decline was the rapid disappearance of gold and silver coinage, particularly the latter. There always had been an unfavorable balance of trade, since Rome produced so little in exchange for the luxuries imported from the East. Many people tended to hoard their money as the wars made investment unattractive. More important, mines began to fail, and no new mines were opened. Thus, there was an absolute drop in the amount of precious metals within the empire, which now was living on capital and not income. To make up the deficits, the government resorted to a frantic debasement of the coins, mixing ever-larger quantities of tin with the silver, then finally simply washing copper coins with a coating of silver. All good money immediately fled into hiding. The only alternative was an economy of barter. The taxes were collected in goods or services (*annona*), usually at a local military headquarters, and trade became literally the exchange of goods and service, with greater economic stagnation as the result.

A little understood result of the decline seems to have been a steady drop in population. Either a loss of optimism kept the number of children down, or it was a decline in the amount of nourishing food available, or the lack of expansion and immigration to make up for those killed during the wars, or the disastrous effects of plagues that ravaged the whole empire during the 3rd Century. In any case, the society simply did not have sufficient manpower to maintain itself. The government naturally turned to a regimented use of what talent there was, and slowly the state became a vast impersonal machine in which classes were made rigid, status hereditary, and citizens units of productivity to be assigned as the government saw fit. The psychological results of this were as important as they are difficult to assess adequately. There was a general decay in public spirit as men saw no benefit, no hope in the imperial system. The mood of the times was apocalyptic or escapist, as is reflected in the sometimes hysteri-cal, sometimes melancholy literature. Men desperately turned to salvationist religions as an escape from the reality around them. Superstition and magic were rife. And men turned rapidly away from intellectual pursuits that offered no comfort and no means of advancement. The educational system went into decline, men of science and originality in technology or the arts became scarce, so that even if there were solutions to be found, there were too few men equipped to find them.

Attempts to Stem the Tide

The last attempt to salvage the empire was made by Diocletian (284–305) and his successor Constantine (306–337). These men did not innovate so much as they brought order to the conditions that had developed within the empire by natural growth. There emerged a naked absolutism that replaced freedom with regimented control in every level of the society. The empire was divided into a western and an eastern half, each having an augustus, who adopted a caesar as his assistant. Each of the four had his own army and government. The augustus, and to a lesser extent the caesar, was transformed into an eastern potentate. He became *Dominus et Deus* (Lord and God), wore royal robes with a crown on his head, and had to be approached on bended knee in elaborate rituals. This whole procedure obviously symbolized the absolutism of the operations of the government.

The army was the first to feel the new reforms. It had proved inadequate to protect the vast frontiers of the empire. It was now enlarged to over 600,000 men, but it was reorganized to make it more flexible. Half the troops were garrisoned along the frontier, while the rest were gathered at strategically-placed encampments from which reinforcements could be rushed to danger spots. As the needs for manpower became greater, it became customary to enlist barbarian units, who gradually Germanized the whole army as their officers made their way up the ranks to the top. Members of the *curiales* were forbidden to enlist in the army. This was to prevent the rise of rival claimants to the throne, but the effect eventually was just the opposite. German leaders with personal guards became powerful war-lords all along the distant frontiers. The augustus was protected by the crack regiments that were stationed in the capitol *(palatini)*.

To put an end to the military anarchy, the administrative system was placed exclusively in the hands of civilians. The cities *(civitates)* were placed in the control of the *curiales* who, with their heirs, were compelled into their jobs by law. The provinces were broken up into numerous small units (120 by the 5th Century), which were grouped into dioceses, each under a *vicarius*. These in turn were administered by four praetorian prefects who had enormous administrative and judicial powers. Thus the government was drawn tightly together into a vast bureaucratic machine that employed thousands of civil servants. The objective was a more efficient technique of government and a more profitable collection of revenues. The result was the opposite. Government became unwieldy and extremely expensive.

Economic reform followed the same pattern. The government assigned a widespread system of requisitions and compulsory service. A new currency was issued, and to control inflation and profiteering prices and wages were set by law for almost every imaginable product or service *(Edict on Prices)*. This plan apparently did not work, but the edict that proclaimed it has survived as a crucial source for the period. Taxes were now to be collected in goods *(annona)*, and were assigned to all productive land. Since manpower was crucial if taxes were to be collected, the *coloni* were fixed to the land and the cultivation of wasteland was encouraged. Vast numbers of farmers became serfs by law and many more followed voluntarily as praecarists to find security. The government ordered the annona to be paid into local granaries or to the nearest military encampment. The city dwellers fared no better than their country cousins. Membership in trade guilds *(collegia)* was made obligatory and hereditary. Thus the trades were artificially maintained. Taxes had to be paid both in kind and cash and since escape was impossible, people were frozen to their crafts, to their customary obligations and compulsory service, whether it was in the government or in the army.

The reforms had saved Rome from total collapse, but the price was high. The state could now plan its economy and control its budget. Productivity was preserved as far as human ability made this possible. But morale had collapsed. Men had lost their identities as they became cogs in a vast machine. Romans had lost their will to survive as free men, for their own government had already robbed them of their freedom.

IV
CHRISTIANITY AND THE PRIMITIVE CHURCH
▼ ▼ ▼ ▼ ▼

▶ **Arch of Titus in Forum in Rome.** The sculpture depicts the carrying away of the sacred candelabra from the Jewish Temple in Jerusalem, which fell to Titus in 70 A.D. The expulsion of Jews from Palestine, the *Diaspora,* scattered Jews all over the Empire. The early Christians went to Antioch, where "They were first called Christians."

Waiting for the Messiah

Christianity emerged from Judaism at a time when the Jews of Palestine were deeply troubled politically and spiritually. A century of Jewish independence had come to an end in 63 B.C. when Pompey and his Roman legions had marched into the holy city of Jerusalem. Yet Jewish nationalism still resisted every attempt of the Romans to impose their pagan culture upon the land, particularly when they placed upon the ancient throne of David a puppet-king, the barbarous Herod the Idumean. Desperate rebellions broke out only to be put down with savage reprisals and massive numbers of crucifixions. As always in the past, the Jews turned to their God for help, for it was firmly believed that He would help His Chosen People by sending a redeemer who would again lead them out of bondage.

There was no agreement, however, as to who this redeemer would be. Would he be a king of the line of David, a leader of hosts? Would he be a lowly figure, riding upon a white ass, who would expiate his people's sins by his own sacrifice? Or would he be a Son of Man, descending from the heavens to redeem his people? All had been described in the ancient books. Nor was there any agreement among the people as to how they might hasten his coming or help him in his work. The first step was to overthrow the Romans, but that would mean a general upheaval in the East and great danger for all.

One group, the Sadducees, a wealthy and aristocratic minority, decided that collaboration with the Romans and deep involvement in public and civil affairs was the wisest course to follow. This stand mirrored their belief that immortality consisted of a happy and successful life on this earth with many descendants. The Zealots, on the other hand, were small bands of fanatics who felt that God would hasten to intervene once His people had launched a violent insurrection. They would not pay tribute to Rome, nor would they obey her laws. The Pharisees, who probably numbered less than 6,000, shunned contact with the Romans, but they would not join an open revolt. Instead, they took refuge in the Law. By obeying the strict letter of the Law and by mechanically performing every ritual exactly as the Law enjoined, they believed that they could hasten by their righteousness the coming of the redeemer. They were so steadfast in their resolution that they preferred to suffer even brutal execution rather than break the Law as they interpreted it.

Finally, there were those who withdrew from society altogether, either to solitary life in the wilderness, or into monastic communities such as those of the Essenes in the area around the Dead Sea. In these the members renounced private property, practiced celibacy, partook of solemn communal meals preceded by ritual bathing, and led quiet contemplative lives of study as they waited for the redeemer to descend from the clouds as an avenging Son of Man.

These groups did not represent the attitudes of the common people, who simply yearned for the anointed one, the Messiah, who had been promised by the prophets of the past and who would not long delay his coming. The time was short. The Romans were preparing new exactions. In the very year in which Jesus was born, Augustus Caesar ordered a general census of the empire so that he might have a precise idea of the number of potential soldiers and tax-payers. The Chosen People had already lost thousands of its young men; every family had felt the loss and new trials were to come. It is no wonder that there was excitement at the news that a prophet, the first in centuries, had appeared in the valley of the Jordan.

John the Baptist and the Appearance of Jesus

John the Baptist was an authentic figure from the past. Gaunt, fiery-eyed, clad in skins, he denounced the sins of the people and called upon them to repent, to fast and to pray. His practiced baptism, which for him was not a prelude to prayer, but a rite that was an outward sign of an inner desire to throw off a past sinful life and to enter a new life of righteousness. When asked if he was the messiah, John denied it. "One is yet to come who is mightier than I, so that I am not worthy to untie the straps of his shoes . . ." It was this one that he claimed to recognize among those who came to him for baptism in "the fifteenth year of the Emperor Tiberius' reign" (29 A.D.).

The Gospels

The portrait of Jesus of Nazareth, the story of his life, and the record of the acts of his early followers were at first kept alive in a collection of stories passed down by an oral tradition. In an age when books were scarce and not much used as texts, especially among the lower classes, this had been sufficient. But as the Christian community turned more and more to the task of organizing itself into an institution of this world while it awaited the millennium, it became necessary to reduce these writings to a canon, which was finally adopted in its present form in 185 A.D. The New Testament consists of four Gospels which provide the essential facts of the life of Jesus.

The earliest of these is probably that of Mark, which seems to have been written in Greek around 70 A.D. and presents Jesus as the miraculous and powerful Son of God. Those of Matthew and Luke are based partly on Mark and partly on a lost source called "Q" (from the German word for source, *quell*), and date from around 85–90 A.D. These present Jesus as a teacher in the ancient tradition and present Christianity as an outgrowth of Judaism. The last Gospel, that of John, was written between 95–100 A.D., and is a philosophical discussion of Jesus as the *Logos* of God, and links him to Platonic philosophy.

Attached to these there is a narrative of early Christian history, the Acts of the Apostles, and twenty-one letters, nine or ten of which were written by Paul of Tarsus. The Testament ends with a strange prophetic vision, the Book of the Apocalypse or Revelation, which exhorts Christians to display courage during a persecution in Asia Minor in the 90's A.D.

All of the New Testament as we know it today was written after the death of Jesus, the earliest book being Paul's First Epistle to the Thessalonians of 50 A.D.—and the last, Peter's Second Epistle of about 150 A.D. It also appears, though there is some controversy over this point, that none of it was written by anyone who actually saw Jesus.

The Life of Jesus

The life of Jesus emerges from the new Testament in sketchy and distorted fragments—his birth, an incident or two of his childhood, his appearance before John the Baptist in his thirtieth year, isolated incidents of the next two years, with a more detailed narrative of the last few weeks of his life. Such is the meager story. Yet a personality of astonishing force, consistency, and authenticity emerges. It is this personality itself that is the best evidence of the historical fact of the life of Jesus. No writer of fiction has ever conceived one so true.

Jesus was born in 6–4 B.C. He was the son of Joseph and Mary, and was of the line of David. He probably spent an uneventful childhood in the town of Nazareth and perhaps he became a carpenter like his father. He emerged from this obscurity when he came to the Jordan to be baptized by John. Then he disappeared again into the wilderness, undoubtedly to plan the way he would accomplish what he considered to be his mission, the moral rebirth of his people. His public life began in Galilee, where he healed the sick and exorcised demons. He preached to the people and attracted to himself a sizable following, particularly a group of twelve who became intimately attached to him. He broke off this phase of his career abruptly and went to the north with his disciples. There he made his final decision to go to Jerusalem as the Messiah and to await in his temple the coming of the Kingdom of God.

It is clear that the writers of the New Testament believed that he was the redeemer—"'And you,' he asked, 'who do you say I am?' Simon Peter answered, 'You are the Messiah, the Son of the living God.'" There is no real reason to doubt that Jesus considered himself one of the traditional prophets and that he felt he was to help in the coming of the Kingdom.

In any case he reappeared in Galilee and moved steadily toward Jerusalem. He entered the city in the Passover season, on the back of a donkey, as Zachariah had once said the Messiah would do, and went directly to the Temple, where he further strengthened his messianic role by throwing out the money-lenders. Each day thereafter he argued religion in the Temple with the scribes and Pharisees, whom he at first seemed to resemble since he was opposed to violent revolt against and for collaboration with the Romans. Almost immediately he aroused hatred. The Zealots were disgusted with a Messiah who preached meekness. The Sadducees and priests resented his challenge of their conduct in the Temple. The Pharisees considered him a blasphemer and an apostate. A plot was formed against his life.

He spent Thursday with his disciples, eating with them a last Passover meal, whose traditional bread and wine he interpreted as being his own body and blood through which a new covenant could be made between God and mankind. After the supper they retired to the garden of Gethsemane for a night of meditation. There he was arrested and tried that same night in the house of Caiaphas, the High Priest. Found guilty of blasphemy by the Jews, he was presented to the Roman governor, Pontius Pilate, to have the death sentence confirmed on the grounds that he had stirred up sedition against the state. This was done, and Jesus was taken to Golgotha where he was crucified.

The Teachings of Jesus

Jesus presented himself as a Jewish prophet and teacher. First he emphasized the traditional, uncompromising monotheism of Judaism. His was a God who loved His people and would send to them His Kingdom. The meaning of this term is not clear, though Jesus apparently had in mind a state of affairs in which God's will would prevail. He spoke of it as a form of society, sometimes as a political system, and most often as an eternal state of grace. He indicated that it had begun with his own appearance and that it would be further made manifest at a later moment during his lifetime and on the Day of Judgment. It surely represented a universal brotherhood of men, bound together by love of God.

Naturally the Kingdom obliged men to follow a strict ethical system. The Law was to be obeyed, as the Pharisees had said, but not just the empty letter of the Law, rather its inner spirit. He condemned the pious hypocrites of this earth and called for a spiritual rebirth. The Law cannot be changed, but men can. In this he represented a revolutionary attitude toward established priesthood. Man, he taught, needs to seek an inner communion with God. From this he will be inspired to turn outwards and to love his fellow man even if this love supercedes the ceremonial laws or even the material amenities of life.

This basic message was delivered in an unlettered, unadorned style, cloaked in homely parables drawn from the everyday life of Palestine. He did not represent any philosophical system, nor did he urge the ascetic life. He was not interested in science, certainly was unfamiliar with Greco-Roman culture, and did not advocate any political or economic revolution. His was a simple call for the birth of a better society in which men might live peacefully in harmony and love with each other.

The Birth of Christianity

The general reaction to the life and death of Jesus was a combination of boredom, bewilderment and disappointment. He surely did not fit any of the commonly held pictures of the Messiah. He had died shamefully, a criminal on the gallows. But his followers were drawn to him by the very poignancy of his lonely death on the cross, and for them his death was the very climax of his ministry. In their grief, they were held together by the belief that he had indeed been the Messiah. Jesus had not founded a church, nor did his followers feel that one existed at the time of his death. It was the resurrection that accomplished this and it is interesting to note in this connection that the earliest stories did not mention the empty tomb. They indicated merely that Jesus was seen after the crucifixion by Peter in Jerusalem, again by some in Galilee, and on another occasion by a group of five hundred of the brethren. He apparently also appeared, not in sight and sound, but as a vision, like he did to Paul.

The actual beginning of the Christian church, though, does not date from these appearances, but from the time of the first Pentecost after the death of Jesus. This holiday was the Festival of the First Fruits in honor of the descent of the Law to Moses on Sinai. On that day the Spirit descended like tongues of fire, filled the assembled brethren, and inspired them to proclaim Jesus as the *Christos* (the Messiah) and the Resurrection. It was their zeal to proclaim the Risen Christ that spurred the apostles to their dynamic mission to found a Christian church, and since Jesus was seen no more, in the absence of the Risen Christ it was the Spirit that was the source of all gifts and inspiration.

And so a church had been founded, and it was not long before this new Nazarene church was in trouble with the Jewish authorities. The followers of Jesus accepted him as the Messiah, therefore they no longer awaited the coming of the redeemer but rather the second coming of Christ. This put them outside the Jewish community as did the new practices they followed. They gathered weekly in private homes to celebrate the *agape,* or love-feast, and to consecrate the Last Supper, which was regarded as a re-enactment of Christ's death on the cross. The brethren sold their personal property and contributed the proceeds to a common treasury to which they added their earnings and out of which their common needs were met. Led by the apostle Peter, the group was intensely missionary in spirit, and began to carry its message to the Jewish lower classes of Palestine. Soon, however, converts were made among the Jews of the Diaspora and even among the gentiles. These new Hellenized members of the group were much less attached to Jewish practices and rituals, and even the Palestinian Christians were rather lax in observing all the dietary laws. The orthodox Jewish circles began to view the Nazarenes as a heretical group and open attacks began. The first victim was Stephen, the leader of the Hellenists, who was stoned to death because he had incited people to break the Law.

St. Paul

This outburst of hatred forced many of the Christian community to take refuge in the Greco-Roman world surrounding Palestine.

There the Christians came into contact with Platonic idealism and metaphysics and the principles of Stoicism. Such contact had already caused a deep split between the orthodox Judaism of Palestine and Jewish reformers like Philo of Alexandria. For Christians, the decisive step in this development was the conversion of Paul who, a "Jew of Jews," had been an avid persecutor of Christians and who had witnessed the martyrdom of Stephen.

Paul was from Tarsus in Cilicia, a Greek center of Stoicism. He went to Jerusalem to study under the great scholar Gamaliel in preparation for a rabbinical career. He was a devout and a strict observer of the Law, which led him to join the anti-Christian groups in the city. He was on his way to Damascus to help exterminate the members of the new sect there when he went through a profound mystical experience. He was blinded by a flash of light which he believed was the resurrected Christ, and he heard the words: "Paul, Paul, why do you persecute me?" He was led into Damascus blind, converted to the new faith and, when his sight was restored, became the most dynamic leader of the group. In fact, he is universally accorded an importance in the history of Christianity second only to that of Jesus and has been often referred to as the second founder of the faith.

Paul worked for many years at Antioch and Tarsus winning converts, organizing the Christian communities, and developing his theological outlook. He was drifting away from the attitudes of the Jerusalem Christians toward strict observance of the Law and Jewish exclusiveness. He decided to go on a long journey to bring the "Christ crucified" to the gentiles. Before he left, he went to Jerusalem, and attended a meeting of all the Christian leaders, the so-called First Council in 49 or 50 A.D. There he tried to compromise his differences with them. He did not succeed too well, and he soon set out for Greece. He visited Cyprus, Ephesus and the Anatolian cities, Thrace, Thessalonica, Athens and Corinth. He spent some six or seven years among the gentiles and in this time split completely from Judaism. Yet when he was called on for help, he returned to Jerusalem where he was attacked by furious Jewish mobs, rescued by Roman soldiers and put into prison in protective custody. He demanded as a Roman citizen the right to a hearing in Rome, and the last of him that we know definitely is that he arrived there and spent the next two years teaching. A persistent tradition relates that he was martyred there.

Paul's Contribution to Christian Doctrine

With Paul, Christianity passed from Palestine to the Greco-Roman world at large, and his ideas revolutionized Christian thought. First of all, he realized that the gentiles would have no real interest in a Messiah who was tied to the establishment of an historical Jewish state. Nor would they be attracted to a leader who had died on the scaffold. But many people were interested in the monotheism and ethical systems of both Jews and Christians. Furthermore, for centuries there had been circulating in the Hellenistic world ideas of saviors who had died and had been reborn and through whom men could achieve salvation. Paul's aim was to eliminate from Christianity all its exclusively Jewish elements so that its essential doctrines could merge with these Hellenistic ideas. Thus he preached a doctrine called the "salvation by faith."

The Christ was divine and had existed eternally with God. He was sent to become incarnate as a man and to sacrifice himself so that God would then save mankind. This linked Jesus with the Messianic tradition, but Paul paid little attention to the teachings and actions of the historical Jesus. He concentrated on the Christ crucified and taught that man must seek a mystical union with him as the focus of life rather than obedience to the Law. This could be achieved by ethical living, brotherly love, charity and the observance of certain rites like baptism and communion. A Christian might die in the flesh, but he would find eternal life in communion with Christ. Observance of the Law of the Torah was no longer necessary, since belief in Christ had replaced it, therefore Jewish practices were not obligatory. In addition, for Paul the good life was no longer a pre-condition to faith in God, but rather the good life was a dynamic course of action in response to the great gift God had chosen to give to man. Men lived good lives because God had sent them Christ.

Beyond this, however, Paul was not particularly ascetic nor was he a social or political reformer. A man was best off to stay where he was, for seeking one's salvation was the true end of life, not bettering one's position. He frowned on incontinence and marriage both, but he did not forbid them. He did believe that all men were brothers and that all were part of a cosmic historical process that had begun in the Garden of Eden, had climaxed on the cross on Golgotha, and would eventually be fulfilled on the Day of Judgment.

Paul's ideas were further developed by the author of the Fourth Gospel, attributed to John the Evangelist. Here the Jewish concept of the Wisdom of God was merged with the Stoic concept of *Logos* or Word, as it is often translated. This *Logos* was the creative principle of God in the world or His imminent or active intelligence implicit in the order of the universe. This *Logos* was identified with Christ, perhaps to make a link with Stoic philosophy. But there was one difference. Where the Stoics would have thought the body or flesh a kind of prison for the *Logos,* one to be abandoned as soon as possible, the Evangelist emphasized the fact that the *Logos* became flesh. Hence the concept of the incarnation was strengthened. Paul's concept of the rites of baptism and communion were also strengthened in the Fourth Gospel for there is a strong emphasis on the partaking of the flesh and blood of Christ. Yet for neither are these rites truly sacramental in nature, conveying grace by their very operation and divorced from the person administering them. On the whole, the Fourth Gospel emphasizes Paul's insistence on rebirth in Christ and eternal life in him.

The Spread of Christianity

Christianity spread rapidly after the work of Paul, and in each major city of the empire Christian communities were established. In the beginning these groups were fairly isolated from each other, each organizing itself around its pastor or bishop. Fervid in their sense of contact with Christ, these early Christians awaited eagerly the second coming which they expected sooner rather than later. They tended to concentrate on spiritual qualities and the good life rather than on contact with the material world around them. They lived communally, pooling their resources, practicing as best they could the injunction to love one another. The bishop,

naturally, handled the treasury of the group, re-enacted the Holy Supper, presided over the *agape,* and performed baptisms, marriages, etc. He became a busy man and had to choose assistants from the flock to help him. The deacon helped with financial affairs and helped prepare the altar for the liturgy. Soon a priest was needed to help in performing some of the bishop's religious duties. Acolytes, lectors, exorcisers, guardians also came into being. In effect, each bishop developed around himself a family of assistants who were attached to him and for whom he had to provide a living. He entrusted to them the traditions as he knew them. In ordaining his priests he passed on to them the powers as he had received them. Upon his death these assistants came together to bury him and while there they selected from among themselves a successor whom they then presented to the congregation for approval. The new bishop thereupon received the recognition of the other bishops. A hierarchy, then, emerged around the bishops, each one of whom extended his authority throughout a diocese, which was a political division of the empire. Each priest was assigned to a sub-division, the parish.

As the Christians lost their expectation of an imminent second coming, they tended to turn back to a more active life in this world. Disputes arose, inevitably, and increasingly complex problems were brought to the bishop for solution. He needed a more sophisticated set of rules to follow and so he began to adapt the Roman law of the community around him to the special needs of his flock. He developed, in short, a law court in which there arose a procedure and legal code which were derived from both Roman and Christian concepts.

The authority of the bishop was based on the faith of his people in his Christian faith. The older and more reliable this interpretation was, the more enforced by occasional letters from the apostles or revered leaders of the Christian world, the more authority and prestige a particular bishop and his successors had. Certain bishops, particularly those who presided over congregations in the larger cities, capitals of provinces, for instance, had more prestige and authority than others. These metropolitan bishops (*metropolis* was the name for a provincial capital) or archbishops, were called on to settle disputes between other bishops, to determine points of doctrine, and often to pass on an appeal from another bishop's court. Thus, the bishops within the provinces were slowly organized under the archbishops.

Among them, in turn, certain ones were called patriarchs, for they presided in communities which had been established by the apostles themselves (such as Jerusalem), or as in the case of Rome because it was a particularly important capital. These patriarchs emerged as the men of most consequence and influence in the Christian world.

Christianity and the Roman Empire

The Roman government followed a policy of pragmatic and discriminating toleration toward the many religions that existed within its boundaries. It was believed that the welfare of the state depended on the good will of heaven, and it was only prudent to keep peace with all the gods. Every people in the empire was urged, therefore, to follow its own religion so long as rites offensive to Roman laws and sensibilities were not performed. Such established religions were considered licit and were tolerated, whereas new religions might be considered illicit and subject to police action.

Furthermore, the cult of the emperor had been developed to bring some uniformity into the religious patterns of the empire. If no one religion was popular to bind together the many different ethnic groups, all could join in the worship of the emperor, who was associated with divinity during his lifetime and became divine upon his death. The cult provided the symbols and emotional response on which empire-wide political unity could be based, and it was accepted throughout the empire by all groups except the Jews.

The Roman government was willing to close its eyes to the uncompromising attitude of the Jews in return for peace in Palestine. They were annoyed at Jewish truculence and prosecuted them as seditionists, but they did consider the religion as licit. If Christians were Jews, they would enjoy the same leniency. If they were not, they would run the risk of being charged with subversion.

At first, the Romans protected Christians from the fury of Jewish mobs, but soon they themselves began a long policy of persecution. The change arose from a basic difference between Christians and Jews. Judaism was content to be left alone to worship its God and to follow His laws. It did not seek converts, and even after the destruction of the Temple in 70 A.D. and the dispersal of the Jews into the modern world, it did not influence public opinion very much. Christianity, on the other hand, was extremely active in seeking converts and in changing public opinion. Christians openly broke with Judaism and worshipped not only the one God in heaven, but also the *Christos* as Lord *(Dominus)* on earth. Their refusal to worship the emperor had overtones that clearly set Christianity apart from Judaism. This group belonged to a new religion, and Rome began to recognize the fact as early as the reign of Nero during the 60's A.D.

But even then the government's policy was hesitant and confused. There was no consistent persecution of the religion as such. When specific charges were brought against individual Christians, they were tried and, if found guilty, they were punished. For almost two centuries action was taken mainly against the leaders of the congregations, and the state tried to limit the spread of the new creed rather than to stamp it out. It continued to have hopes of absorbing Christianity as it had so many before.

The citizens of the empire were not so slow in focusing their reaction to the new sect. Coming from the lowest classes, Christians seemed to preach the overthrow of all social and moral values. Their pacifism threatened the safety of everyone. Furthermore, they met in private to practice their secret rites. Added to these charges was the fact that Christians were glad of the differences that separated them from others. Ugly rumors began to spread. Christians were accused of infanticide, incest, arson and sorcery. The public despised Christians and then began to hate them. Popular prejudice chose this easily identified group as a scapegoat for all general catastrophes. Mobs fell furiously upon the congregations from time to time, and the government was forced by public pressures to resort to brutal, if sporadic, persecutions.

The religion was not destroyed. Each attack left the Christians stronger in spirit and greater in influence, for their steadfast courage was an inspiration to an increasingly wide audience. Also the world-wide Christian community had emerged with its obedience to the Lord and His bishops, its laws and its loyalties. It was a state within the state, and the government of Rome had no control over it. This was particularly obnoxious to the emperors at this time, for the empire was disintegrating. Cohesion was sought in the strengthening of the central government by proclaiming the divinity of the emperor and declaring him the *dominus* of the world.

Christians already worshipped the *Christos* as *Dominus*, and the essential conflict between the state and the religion became clear. Either the Christians had to give up their belief, or the emperor's position would have to be secularized, or the state would have to become Christian. The state decided that Christians could not be loyal citizens and it set out to exterminate them. From 303 to 311 the persecutions were fierce, but the Emperor Galerius admitted defeat by issuing an edit of toleration in 311. This was reissued in 313 by Constantine in Milan, and the persecutions ceased.

Constantine favored Christianity and recognized the power of the Christian bishops because he found in the new creed the solution to his most pressing problem. The empire had been weakened by civil war and militarization. Christianity stood for harmony and peace. The imperial administration was becoming decentralized and ineffective. The bishops had a close working contact throughout the empire, and they had an efficient administrative apparatus. Above all, the empire had lost its hold on the loyalty of its subjects, and the emperor had no real position in it. The Christians believed that just as there was universal harmony in Heaven under one God and one Law, so too on earth there was one universal harmonious community with one set of institutions and one head, the emperor, God's vicar. On such a basis as this Constantine dreamed of forging a new state. The conflict between the new creed and the state was almost resolved.

The Christian Apologists

This dream was frustrated for a while by developments within the Church. During the period of the persecutions, the Roman intellectuals had launched a learned attack on the new doctrine to destroy it by logic. The most typical of these was Celsus, a Platonic philosopher of the late 2nd Century. He accused the Christians of immorality, since they associated with criminals and slaves; of superstition and sorcery, since they accepted miracles; of intellectual dishonesty or deficiency, since there were so many inconsistencies in the Scriptures. Above all, he accused them of subversion and disloyalty, since their ideas undermined the security of the state.

Christians felt obliged to answer such attacks and the threat from the rival Eastern salvationist cults in like kind. The first step was to determine the authentic Christian doctrine. All the writings of the apostolic ages that could be verified were gathered together into a canon text of the New Testament. This task was brought to completion in the late 4th Century. Inconsistencies in these writings were discussed by the bishops of the Church in synods and they often defined doctrine on the authority of a concept of a continuing revelation. Occasionally, an individual bishop intervened in a dispute using his traditional keeping of orthodoxy within his diocese as his authority.

Once the Christians were sure of their own doctrine, they turned to the outside world to convince it of the justness of their cause. In the East the apologists, as these were called, steeped themselves in the pagan philosophical works and used particularly Platonic arguments to demonstrate that their philosophy was superior to pagan beliefs. In Alexandria, for instance, there developed a center of Christian studies that incorporated Neo-Platonic concepts into Christian dogma. They emphasized the God-like aspect of Christ's personality. In Antioch, on the other hand, study concentrated on the Man-like aspects. In the West, emphasis was placed more on the legal and moral considerations of Christianity, putting forward the good life as superior to the life of empty philosophizing.

Heresy and Disunity

While the primitive congregations had been isolated and in obscurity, each had developed its own customs and its own concepts of Christian doctrine. As they came into closer contact with each other, these differences became more obvious and disputes arose. Should the Old Testament be rejected? Was revelation a continuing process? What was the date of Easter? Should lapsed Christians be readmitted to the Church? Such questions were limited in scope and were rather easily resolved.

But as the theorists began to refine doctrine, arguments arose over much more subtle questions, and much larger portions of the Church were involved. Soon after Constantine gave his support to the Church, for instance, a bitter quarrel broke out in North Africa. Christianity was very strong there, for it had given a focus to an ancient anti-Roman attitude among the Punic elements in the population. The Donatists expressed the opinion that a lapsed or, for that matter, any evil or ill-living priest could not administer a valid sacrament. The bishops of the Western part of the Church, led by the Pope, denied this and affirmed the principle that a sacrament was valid in its own right and was not dependent on the virtue of the person who administered it. In a fury, the Donatists rejected this new example of Roman interference, and resentment remained there for centuries.

Some ten years later a dispute broke out in Egypt that finally involved the whole Christian world. Arius, an archpriest in Alexandria, under the influence of the apologists, brought up the question of the relationship between the Father and the Son. He declared that both were divine, but that the Son had been created in a moment in time by the Father. This would mean that the one was less powerful than the other, that he was not eternal since there was a time before which he was not, yet since he was divine, there would appear to be two separate divinities. Bewildered by the intensity of the reaction to these arguments, which did not seem very important to him, Constantine called into session the First Ecumenical council, which met in Nicaea in 325 A.D. A group of 318 bishops argued the points at length and finally rejected the position of Arius. They drew up a creed of the fundamental beliefs of a Christian, the Nicene Creed, which answered Arius with the concept of the Trinity. The Son, and later the Spirit, was declared of one being, one essence, one substance with the Father, and there was never a time when he was not.

The Emperor found himself confronted with a religious problem that threatened the security of his whole government. Attracted by the Arian suggestion of a hierarchy of divinities that might include eventually the emperor himself, he and his successors tried for over fifty years to effect some compromise among the bishops. The Trinitarian bishops were adamant. They hounded the Arians out of the empire and they castigated the emperors. Theodosius finally brought the struggle to an end in the Second Ecumenical Council in 381, and the Nicene Creed became the basic statement of the faith thereafter.

It was the same Theodosius who declared the Christian faith the only licit one in the empire and launched the persecution of the pagan cults. The triumph of Christianity was complete. It had succeeded where so many other sects had failed because its god had been a man who had lived on this earth. The intimacy of knowing Jesus directly had been the privilege of the Apostles, it was a possibility for all later generations of Christians. It was the foundation of Christian introspection. Also, this was the first religion in the Greco-Roman orbit to place its emphasis not on the absorption of the initiate into the activities of a transcendent god, but on a spiritual rebirth within man himself. It provided an opportunity for change. Finally, the Christians created in a world of disintegrating institutions a visible Church, whose administrative system laid the foundation for the Christian commonwealth of the Middle Ages.

V

THE WORLD OF THE GERMANS
▼ ▼ ▼ ▼ ▼

▶ **Volubilis, Morocco.** Originally a Roman army camp used against the Berbers and then against the Vandals. The camp became a prosperous provincial town with temples, baths, markets. Note the odd design of the Corinthian columns.

► **Volubilis, Morocco.** All Roman army camps were built on the same pattern. Two streets crossed at right angles and emerged through four gates. The whole was surrounded by a wall. In Caesar's *Gallic War,* he points out the discipline needed to pitch camp this way every night when on campaign.

► **Arch of Constantine, Rome.** Constantine was of Germanic blood. The arch commemorates the victory over Maxentius, and was erected in 315 A.D. To build the arch, pieces had been taken from earlier structures. It demonstrates the cultural deterioration prevalent in the Western Empire.

The Early Germans

The best description of the early Germans before their penetration into the Roman Empire is in Julius Caesar's *Gallic War* and in the *Germania* of Tacitus. Both works are biased and give a distorted picture, one because of the military nature of the contacts that Caesar made with them, and the other because of the attempt by Tacitus to paint an attractive portrait of barbarians against which he could contrast the corruption and decay of his own world. Within these limitations, however, certain general statements can be made.

The Germans were a tall people, red-haired and blue-eyed. Though they eventually moved widely within the empire, mixed freely within Roman society, intermarried and learned Latin, they were never absorbed into the Roman culture pattern to the extent that the north African and Near Eastern upper classes were. Their lands were gloomy, swampy forests, in which only rudimentary agriculture had been developed. The Germans were primarily hunters, and their economy was based on large herds of cattle and swine. Iron was used among them to forge weapons, and they were skilled in the making of gold ornaments and jewelry. The social and political life of the Germans expressed their nomadic nature. They had no cities, living instead in poorly-constructed huts in temporary villages. There were clear distinctions among them between a nobility, a priesthood, freemen, freedmen, and slaves. Honors and obligations were assigned by class, the warrior-nobles doing the fighting, for instance, the slaves growing food in small garden plots.

The whole tribe constituted the folk, which is the largest political organization they knew. It was ruled by a king, who was really only a war chief. Sometimes several chiefs shared the kingly power. The folk acted as a whole in time of war to elect a king, or to settle some extraordinary dispute within the tribe. The king had little authority as a leader, except when he was personally a powerful warrior. The chieftains of the tribe were always involved in attempts to increase their power and authority. Each gathered to himself a band of younger, less powerful fighters who took an oath of loyalty to the leader that lasted as long as he treated them fairly and led them well. This *comitatus* (*comes*, or companion), as the Romans called it, was the most important institution among the early Germans, and each band was held together by deep and lasting ties of allegiance and mutual obligation.

The family, however, was the basic social unit. It contained not only the immediate members of a family, but also distant relatives, retainers, slaves, etc. The head of the family was responsible for maintaining order among his kinfolk, and he was held responsible for their behavior. Each family preferred to handle its own affairs, resorting seldom to outside legal remedies, and the blood-feud was the universal technique for settling disputes between families. Arising within the *comitatus* or the family, political ties were deeply personal, and the Germans never had much feeling for abstract institutions. It was always difficult to delegate authority among them, for they respected and obeyed the person of authority himself, rather than his office or title.

If a family preferred to avoid the blood-feud, there were available certain courts, which were called *moots* or *things*. These were assemblies in which all the males of the tribe gathered to settle disputes, determine policy or give justice. If a complaint was brought before them in a case that was not too serious, the accused could prove his innocence by taking a solemn oath. Primitive peoples considered the oath an extension of the personality itself that could become a weapon to be used to destroy the perjurer. To strengthen the oath, a man could have his friends take oaths to attest to his dependable character (compurgation). Oaths were weighted according to a man's status in the tribe. Penalties were assigned for every crime, even murder, and the money payment or other redress was set according to the ranks of both the injured party and the offender. Often in serious crimes, guilt was determined by ordeal, a test in which the accused (or accuser, for it could work either way) was put into a precarious situation—walking on hot coals, plunging a hand into boiling water, being thrown into a well—and his survival or safety was put into the hands of God. If he was innocent, God would protect and deliver him, thereby demonstrating his innocence.

The religion of the Germans was a primitive worship of the forces of nature and the spirits of the dead ancestors of the tribe. Certain holy spots, particularly gloomy forest groves, were visited to offer sacrifices to ensure the good-will and protection of the gods. The sacrificial offering was then eaten by the worshippers. Apparently humans were often eaten in this way, though a horse was the preferred sacrifice. To this day, as a result, there is an almost universal aversion to eating horse-meat. There was no ethical or moral system tied to their religion, though the Germans prized bravery above all things, loyalty to one's leader, and hospitality to the stranger.

The Wandering of the Tribes

By the 4th Century the German tribes had been in close contact with Rome for many generations. In the face of the Roman legions, the Germans had to draw together into more solid political organizations. Furthermore, many of them had been to Rome as hostages or had served in Roman armies. They introduced to their tribes the techniques they had picked up. Traders had circulated Roman goods among them, and had broadcast the benefits of a higher culture. More solid, though still primitive, kingdoms began to emerge among the tribes. Drawn by the better climate of the Mediterranean, these kingdoms began slowly to migrate southward and to the southeast where they encountered Roman opposition. The Ostrogoths (East Goths) finally reached the steppes of southern Russia. Behind them their cousins the Visigoths (West Goths) settled in the Balkans. The Vandals were along the upper Danube, the Burgundians along the upper Rhine. The Franks settled in two groups, the Ripuarians along the banks of the Rhine, the Salians in the marshy lowlands west of the Rhine estuary. Angles, Saxons, Jutes lived precariously along the shores of the North Sea. Behind this ring there were many more nomadic tribes, the Lombards and the Slavs, for instance, that were still at a very primitive level.

The Visigoths

The relatively stable arrangement along the frontier was shattered when the Huns burst forth from Asia around 370 A.D. This savage tribe had been pushed out of its homelands in Outer Mongolia and had ridden westward, collecting restless nomadic allies as it sped along on its swift ponies. By the time they reached Russia, the nomads had become a vast, loosely-knit horde that fell upon the Ostrogoths in savage fury. Terror-stricken survivors fled to the Visigoths, who asked for asylum within the Empire. The Visigoths were allies of Rome by this time and they had been converted to Arian Christianity by Ulfias, the renowned missionary to the Goths, who had translated the Bible into a Gothic dialect. The Emperor Valens was fighting on the Persian frontier and, thinking perhaps to establish a buffer against the Huns, gave the Visigoths permission to settle in the Balkan provinces on condition that they lay down their arms. In 376 the Visigoths crossed the frontier, and as they did so they were mistreated by the Roman troops and exploited by the merchants and slave dealers. In retaliation they took up arms and began to ravage northern Greece. The Emperor met them in the decisive battle of Adrianople (378). For the first time in history, a Roman emperor with two-thirds of his army were cut down in battle by barbarians. These troops were never replaced, and the frontiers were never again adequately defended. The battle also signals the end of the tactical reliance on infantry and the beginning of a thousand year reliance on cavalry.

The Visigoths under their leader, Alaric, had no plan of conquest. Theodosius, the new Emperor, made a quick peace which lasted until his death. His sons succeeded him, Arcadius in the east and Honorius in the west. They were under age and were dominated by rival ministers, particularly the Vandal Stilicho, who ruled in Rome. Alaric was made a Commander of the Armies and sought to profit from the general breakdown of order. He plundered Greece and was bought off with titles. He became governor of Illyria and then to escape Stilicho's armies, that were seeking to destroy him, he invaded Italy. Honorius killed the powerful Stilicho and sought to use Alaric, but when they could not come to terms, even with Galla Placidia, the Emperor's sister, in Alaric's hands as hostage, the Visigoths marched on Rome in 410 and sacked it. This particular attack, though one of many during the period, left a deep impression on contemporaries. St. Augustine wrote his *City of God* to answer to the charges that the city fell because the gods were angry at the new Christian cult. It was Rome's time, he maintained, to pass away, as all earthly things must when their purpose has been fulfilled. It had been Rome's mission to unite the world in preparation for the Coming of the Heavenly City. Having done so, it came to an end. Only the Heavenly City lasts eternally.

Alaric died soon after the taking of Rome and his brother, Ataulf, who had married Galla Placidia, led his tribe northward into Gaul south of the Loire, and Spain, where they finally settled as conquerors of the region. They established a Germanic kingdom within a Roman territory. The social and economic arrangements in the villa-system went on as before. Cities, however, declined as political centers, for the Visigoths preferred to live in the countryside as the new landlords. They continued their own customs, but they did provide a code of law for their Ibero-Gallic subjects, the *Breviary of Alaric*, a justly famous collection of Roman statutes adapted to the conditions of an early medieval Germanic kingdom. They slowly were converted to Trinitarian Catholicism, and priests came to have an important influence in the government and in the society at large.

The Vandals

To meet the Visigothic threat the Roman government had had to pull troops back from the frontier. Tribes began to pour across. The Vandals, for instance, with the Burgundians, Alans, and Suevi crossed over into Gaul. Sweeping down into Spain, the Vandals settled in southern Spain until 419, when the Visigoths defeated them in battle. Their King, Gaiseric (or Genseric), led them over to north Africa, which they quickly overran. Carthage fell to them in 439 and they established a kingdom which took to the sea. As pirates, they controlled the central Mediterranean, raiding the Italian coast at will and disrupting with fatal results dependable communications between the eastern and western halves of the Roman Empire. On one of their raids they sacked Rome (455), giving to the language a new word for wanton destruction. The Vandals were always a small group, and failed to establish any institutions of lasting value. Some historians point to their activities, rather than those of the Muslims, as the fatal interruption in shipping across the Mediterranean.

The Collapse of the Western Empire

The migrations of the Visigoths and Vandals illustrate much about conditions in the late Empire. Moving through every western province, nowhere did they meet any organized resistance. Everywhere they were accepted as rulers. They did not have to conquer by violence, nor did they have to destroy the systems they found where they settled. What is more, their numbers were not great. When Gaiseric led his Vandals across north Africa, he took a census and found his tribe numbered 80,000 males, only half of whom, at a most generous estimate, represented warriors. There was no effective Roman military or administrative machinery left that was capable of stopping the invasions.

The Burgundians established themselves across the upper Rhine, in what is still called Burgundy. They claimed to be representatives of the emperor, and set up a mixed German-Roman type of government. The Suevi moved into Spain, to be absorbed by the Visigoths. The Angles, Saxons, and Jutes began to invade Britain, which lay totally without defences after it was abandoned by Rome around 400. As a result, the destruction of Roman institutions was probably more complete there than anywhere on the continent.

As the northern provinces fell off, Italy remained nominally under the control of Galla Placidia, as regent (425–45), and her son Valentinian III (423–455), as emperor. The real power, however, lay with another German general, Aetius, who maintained an elaborate balance of power among the German tribes. He was able to gather together a large army of the German and Roman elements to meet the Huns who, united by their king Attila (434–453), were making an attempt to take over Gaul. In 451 Attila was defeated between Châlons and Troyes. He led exhausted, disease-ridden elements of his army into Italy. Persuaded by Leo, the bishop of Rome, to accept tribute and spare the city, Attila wandered on and died soon after. The Huns, a loose confederation at best, broke up into small groups and disappeared, either returning eastward or being absorbed into surrounding tribes. Aetius was assassinated soon after by order of Valentinian, who in 455 was himself cut down. The emperors after this time were powerless pawns of the generals of the army, the most powerful of whom, Odoacer, put an end to the farce in 476 when he deposed Romulus Augustus, the last of the western emperors, on the theory that one emperor, the eastern one, was enough for the Empire, and Odoacer was his representative in Italy. Thus came to an end the Roman Empire.

How did it come about? We have already seen the steady decline in the 3rd Century. In the 4th and 5th Centuries it continued. Germans roamed across the provinces at will. The Roman peoples accepted without a murmur the establishment of the kingdoms. For them, all that happened was the coming of a new class of landlords. The manors went on as before. Trade became essentially local, and was not interrupted, though the luxury trade was diminished by the Vandal raids. The cities had died, however, and people took no interest in politics. The empire had ceased to play any real role in their lives. It lived on only as a dream, an ideal of a perfect age in the past, as distant as Heaven was in the future. There was no will to save it, for it represented nothing worth saving. Of course, underlying the whole decline was a serious economic collapse. Isolated on their manors, men increasingly lost contact with each other, content to be ignored by the passing armies. They stopped paying taxes, gave up all service to the state, and preserved the Roman culture and way of life in units that became too small to support institutions of any great sophistication.

The Ostrogothic Kingdom

The kingdom that represents these developments best, and the one that worked hardest to preserve whatever possible from the collapsing Roman world, was the one established in Italy by Theodoric, King of the Ostrogoths (489–526). As soon as Odoacer took over the western Empire Zeno, Emperor in the East, raised Theodoric to the rank of Commander of the Armies, made him a patrician, and sent him into Italy as his representative to destroy Odoacer. The two Germans, each claiming to be acting in the name of the Emperor, fought it out until 493 when Theodoric murdered Odoacer and established himself as a King, technically under the suzerainty of the Emperor Zeno, whose administrative system was preserved in Italy, but actually as an independent German ruler who dominated the other German powers because of skillful diplomacy and the lingering memory of Roman prestige.

The Ostrogoths were in complete control of the army, and they established their own courts for their own affairs. The Roman inhabitants retained their own courts and their own administrative system. Many Roman noble families served the king, and there was at least some sense of continuity. The Germans were always few in number, so that clashes between them and the Romans were rare, and easily settled in courts of mixed German and Roman custom. The land was divided up, with about one-third going to the new lords of the land. The rest remained in Roman hands, and since much of Italy was underdeveloped land at this time, there was plenty for all, and no serious tensions arose.

Theodoric had been educated in Constantinople and he had a strong desire to maintain as much as possible of Roman culture. He encouraged the maintenance of schools, though by this time learning had largely retreated to the monasteries, and he made an attempt to attract scholars to his court. The call was answered by Cassiodorus, one of the last writers trained in the classical education, and Boethius, the last of the ancient philosophers, and one who attempted to translate Plato and Aristotle into Latin, and to reconcile their differences and merge them with the New Testament into a great synthesis of human knowledge. Theodoric labored to keep up the roads, the bridges and the cities. As an Arian he stood aloof from the Catholic church, intervening only to keep order, but as the emperors stepped up their attacks on heresy, Theodoric drifted increasingly into an anti-Catholic policy toward the end of his reign.

Theodoric's kingdom went into rapid decline after his death. Justinian, in his plan to reconstruct the ancient empire, decided to destroy the kingdom. His armies invaded in 536 and ravaged Italy until 554 when the last Ostrogothic king was killed. Without sufficient means to establish a strong government in Italy, Justinian had created a vacuum by destroying the one power strong enough to stabilize the west. New barbarians began to move in, such as the Lombards. These were a people of Germanic stock who had been living deep in the northern forests. Untempered by civilizing contacts with Roman culture, their invasion was violently destructive. Under some thirty-five chieftains they swept down the length of the peninsula. They were strongest in the north where their institutions had profound influence. In the south they were weak, dividing the lands with the eastern

emperor, who concentrated on the few lands left to him in the far south, where Byzantine institutions remained almost intact. The cities of Genoa, Rome, Naples and Ravenna remained nominally under the eastern emperor, but in fact the Church, led by the bishop of Rome, was left as the only effective government in the cities and most of the cultivated lands of central Italy. Thus began the persistent division of Italy into separate cultural and political entities. Venice began to emerge at this time, its population swelled by refugees who fled to the little settlements established as a haven in the time of the invasions of the Huns. Italy fell into chaos as Lombard princes fought each other. Byzantine forces only rarely were able to marshall enough strength to establish order, while the Pope could provide government sporadically in urban centers.

The Church in the German World

Documents relating to the early history of the Church in the West are very scarce. Tradition is clear, however, that St. Peter, who had been given special powers by Christ to act with His authority and to establish His Church, was martyred in Rome, probably in the reign of Nero. Tradition has also always maintained, moreover, that St. Paul was martyred in the capital city. Thus the Patriarch of Rome could and did claim that he had powers passed down to him from Christ Himself, and that his authority was based on a tradition that went back to the teachings of the two most important saints of the early Church. In all the West the Pope alone could make a claim for such apostolic

▶ **Tomb of Theodoric, Ravenna.** The Ostrogothic king had the tomb built in 520 A.D. for him and his descendants. The cupola is a single block of stone 36 feet in diameter, weighing 600 tons. The overall effect is somber and Gothic in mood.

tradition, which together with his prestige as Bishop in the capital of the Empire, gave him an authority over the other bishops which he never hesitated to use.

In 90 A.D., for instance, Pope Clement I intervened in the affairs of the Church of Corinth, claiming that his authority stemmed directly from God. In 107 St. Ignatius, Bishop of Antioch, acknowledged Rome's leadership in the letters he wrote on the eve of his martyrdom. In the treatise of St. Irenaeus, Bishop of Lyons (d.c. 202), directed against the Gnostic heretics, he pointed to the doctrines of the Roman churches as the true tradition of Christian belief. Toward the end of the 2nd Century Pope Victor I (189–198) intervened in the dispute among the Eastern churches over the proper date of Easter and excommunicated those who rejected his position. Cyprian, the outspoken Bishop of Carthage, disputed violently with Pope Stephen I in the 250's over the question of the re-baptism of lapsed Christians, but he accepted the role of Rome as final judge in matters of doctrine. This role was further confirmed by the condemnation by Pope Dionysius in 262 of the theology of the bishop of Alexandria.

There can be no question that during the early centuries of Christian history the bishop of Rome was accorded great respect by the other bishops of the Church. He was considered at least as first among equals and his authority in matters of theology was very great. But the claims of the primacy of Rome rest on stronger ground than this.

The earliest Christian communities in the West had been rather isolated with little direct contact with each other beyond an occasional letter from an apostle or some important bishop. As the outer structure of the Church emerged, however, these communities were brought into closer contact with one another. This contact made clear the fact that in each one there had grown up a specific Christian tradition of ritual and dogma. It was obviously of supreme importance to determine in every case of conflict which tradition was the correct one, the only one that led to ultimate salvation. Christian teaching had been oral during these early years, and there was no dependable canon to turn to. The only guarantee of a tradition's reliability was the trustworthiness of the person who transmitted it. Thus, each tradition was judged in terms of the character of the bishop who taught it and the reliability of the source of authority. All bishops at their consecrations became heirs to the tradition of their sees. Each link in the chain of authority, each bishop's name, that is, that reached back to the infallible source of Christian doctrine, Christ, was carefully recorded. Every see could list many bishops, but only Rome could claim an unbroken line of bishops that reached back to Sts. Peter and Paul and through them to Christ.

Thus the primacy of Rome rested first on the claim to apostolic succession. The Roman tradition was most trustworthy because it had kept alive in an unbroken line of succession the traditions of the two apostles. No other church could claim double apostolic succession. Indeed, in the West no other church could claim apostolic foundation at all. Apostolicity was always the basis for her primacy over the Western bishops. But in the East many sees could claim apostolic foundation—Ephesus, Jerusalem, Antioch, etc. There apostolicity was not a particularly effective claim to primacy, especially over Antioch, which had also been founded by St. Peter. The Roman bishop, therefore, added to his claims the prestige of being bishop in the capitol of the Empire. An important figure, experienced in law and administration, he could claim in his own religious jurisdiction the same appellate authority that the Roman jurists claimed in secular affairs. Many bishops of the various churches turned instinctively to the capitol for guidance in matters of a disciplinary nature. But, of course, this particular claim to prestige did not give the Roman pontiff any authority in doctrinal matters. Nor did Rome remain for too long the capitol. In the 3rd Century, the capitol moved eastward, and after 330 it was in Constantinople. In fact, this unique claim to primacy was used thereafter by the Patriarch of Constantinople to claim equal, if not superior, powers with Rome.

Ultimately, the strongest claim to primacy that Rome could make was the claim to orthodoxy. In all the disputes of the early Church and in the stormy debates over the great heresies of the 4th, 5th, and 6th Centuries, Rome always supported the side of orthodoxy. Oftentimes the orthodox opinion was known at the time, often it only became known later, but in any case the Roman Bishop could assert that his tradition had never included even briefly any heresy or wrong thinking. This claim in the long run, proved most effective, and it was on this basis that the Roman popes began to build an institution that would eventually bring all of the Western churches under their sway.

The triumph of Christianity under Constantine had brought about great changes in the position of the bishops within the Church. At first there had been no agreement as to the size a bishop's territory ought to be. Eventually it was decided in the Western provinces that the bishop's diocese ought to correspond to a *civitas*, the Roman equivalent of the Greek city-state and the basic political unit of the Empire.

Furthermore, the bishops and their clergy were exempt from the jurisdiction of the secular courts. The clergy and all lay disputants in ecclesiastical cases were tried in the courts of the bishops. Their decisions were recognized by the civil courts. The state also enforced a bishop's sentence of excommunication. Thus, all bishops had a strong claim to leadership in matters of doctrine and by the 5th Century their decisions in questions of faith were accepted without question throughout the Western Church, and even at tines in the East as well. But their influence in administrative affairs was much more limited. Each diocese elected its own bishop, and managed its own government. The next task for the pope was to overcome all controls from secular government, and at the same time extend his administrative control over the other bishops of the Church.

The Emperor Constantine supported the Christian Church because of a sincere conviction of the worth of the new religion. But he was an acute politician who had before him the task of rebuilding his Empire. In the new creed he saw a means of establishing his authority on a new basis. He viewed himself as the head of the Christian community and, in the traditional wisdom of the Roman emperors, he took as his responsibility the religious welfare of his subjects. Giddy with the flood of material benefits showered on them after years of privation, and grateful for their new legal authority, the leaders of the Church were anxious to please the Emperor. They viewed him as "equal to the Apostles," and accepted his leadership even in matters of dogma. It was the Emperor, for instance, who called the Council of Nicaea into session, and it was he who presided over its sessions.

Between the reigns of Constantine (d. 337) and that of Theodosius (379–95), the whole Empire was Christianized. This made the problem of defining the relationship between the Church and the emperor even more acute. The emperors summoned councils, they made ecclesiastical laws, they appointed and removed bishops at will. In short, they exercised a complete control over the Church in its visible aspect. Even in matters of conscience their will was usually obeyed. But opposition was growing.

The Arian controversy of the 4th Century threw the Church into chaos. The Eastern emperors were Arian, while those of the West were Trinitarian. Each supported his bishops, the Arian bishops becoming ascendent in the East, but the bishops of the West led by the Roman pope supporting the Nicean position. Finally, Theodosius came to this position and firmly established Nicean Trinitarianism as the official orthodoxy at the Council he called in Constantinople in 381. The Emperor was still master over the Church, but the influence of courageous bishops over him can be seen in the dramatic way St. Ambrose refused Theodosius entrance into his church until the Emperor recognized that he was in the Church and not above it.

The next opportunity to demonstrate his authority was afforded the Pope by the debates over the Nestorian heresy, that taught that there were two persons in Christ, the divine and the human natures. This teaching, supported by the Patriarch of Constantinople, Nestorius, denied the role of Mary as mother of God. The archbishop of Alexandria led the attack on the heresy and he sought the help of the pope of Rome. At the councils that were held to settle the dispute, the doctrinal issue was determined by the pope, though the emperor settled this controversy by banishing Nestorius and affirming the authority of the bishops of Rome and Alexandria.

The followers of the archbishop of Alexandria now slipped into an equally dangerous heresy, teaching that Christ in effect had only one nature (*monophysis*, in Greek), the divine, which had absorbed the human element into itself. These doctrines may seem somewhat esoteric to us today, but at the time it was felt that salvation depended on the proper definition of Christ's nature. To promise Redemption, He had to be Divine. To achieve it by His death, He had to be human. Flavian, Patriarch of Constantinople, denounced the Monophysite position, and he was supported by Pope Leo I, who wrote his famous *Tome* to defend the anti-Monophysite stance. This *Tome* was used at the Council of Chalcedon in 451 as the basis for the orthodox position that Christ was one person, with two natures. The controversy dragged on after this, causing the emperors to resort to any means to restore peace in the Eastern church. Rome rejected every attempt at negotiation, even the *Henoticon*, a desperate compromise between the heretical and the orthodox positions. The issue was finally settled in 519 when Justin I officially denounced Nestorianism and Monophysitism, and declared that the Roman bishop, speaking with the authority of St. Peter, was infallible in matters of doctrinal orthodoxy. The Bishop of Rome had established his primacy. Already the emperor of the West had ceased to rule, and far from the imperial court at Constantinople, the Pope was able to translate this primacy into real power.

In the meantime the decline of the Eastern Roman Empire had led the pope to exert his influence increasingly in the temporal affairs of the West. As the secular government disappeared the pope remained as the head of the only effective administrative machinery that could keep society going. When the Huns invaded Italy, it was Pope Leo I who organized the defense of Italy and who negotiated with Attila in 452. In 455 Leo again had to negotiate with an invader, this time the Vandals. He could not prevent the sack of the city, but he did prevail upon the Vandals not to burn it nor to massacre its citizens. In this same period Pope Gelasius I (492–96), protesting against the interference of the Emperor Anastasius in ecclesiastical affairs, enunciated his theory of the dual nature of society. There are two powers on earth, that of the secular government and that of the pope. Both are divine, both are absolute, both are necessary to achieve peace.

In the 5th Century imperial control was again restored over Italy. The Germanic invasion had taken place. The Western provinces had been plucked from the Empire and a series of German kingdoms had been established. The Germans, however, had been converted by Arian missionaries. They were not only invaders in the eyes of the peoples of the West, they were heretics as well. This tended to maintain a cleavage between the ruling aristocracies and the masses of the peoples, who turned to the pope as a symbol of orthodoxy. The pope, moreover, was the only remaining symbol of a universal state, It was the Church that was the heir of Rome, not the ephemeral German kingdoms.

As a result, when Justinian invaded the West and restored the Empire, he naturally focused it on the pope. Justinian strengthened the role of all the bishops in their dioceses, but he gave the Roman bishop pre-eminence. The pope was declared "the chief of all the holy priests of God" and "the source of all the priesthood." However, the pope, who unlike other bishops was elected freely within his diocese, nonetheless had to submit his election to the emperor for approval. The wars of Justinian exhausted Italy. And when he died, the people turned to the pope as the only element of imperial administration now left. The Lombard invasions of the time cut Rome off from the East and it was the pope who signed the various treaties as head of state in Italy.

Gregory the Great

The 6th Century saw Rome pass from the rule of the Caesars to the rule of the popes. The first papal monarch was Gregory I, the Great (590–604), whose career shows clearly the way in which Christian beliefs and Roman customs combined to produce the medieval Catholic Church. Gregory was born into a wealthy senatorial family of Rome. He was educated in the law and rose rapidly in the administration of the city to become prefect of the city while still a young man. Suddenly he withdrew into a monastery. For three years he lived a happy life of asceticism, but he was too valuable a man to be allowed such a life of withdrawal. He was selected as one of the deacons of Rome, and then was appointed papal representative to the imperial court in Constantinople. There he gained much knowledge of the details of the imperial administrative system, though he apparently disliked the Greeks, a prejudice which affected his later career.

Gregory returned from Constantinople to become abbot of his old monastery, and there in 590 he was unanimously elected Pope. His first task was to defend his city from the Lombards. Ignoring his secular overlord, Gregory negotiated directly with the enemy and signed a treaty that brought peace to Italy after thirty years of war. This made him the undisputed temporal ruler of the Patrimony of St. Peter. But he was also anxious to consolidate his control over the churches of the West. He asserted his authority successfully over north Africa. He brought Spain back into the Catholic orthodoxy. He sent representatives to the Franks and began to spread Trinitarianism among the Arian Lombards. Above all, he sent missionaries throughout the areas still pagan in the West, especially to England, and began to bring them under the control of the Church. By the time of his death in 604, Gregory had established once and for all the temporal and spiritual powers of his office. He had thrown off imperial control and he had affirmed his position of supremacy against the claims of the Patriarch of Constantinople, who took the title Oecumenical Patriarch. Gregory called himself *Servus servorum Dei*, "the servant of the servants of God"—equally superlative, though humbler in tone.

Monasticism

The success of the papacy in establishing its primacy was symptomatic of the changes that had occurred in Catholicism as it had emerged as a successful Church. This emergence had been resisted by many early Christians who saw in the material success a snare of the Devil to delude the righteous. These early ascetics felt that the Church no longer protected them from the dangers of the world, so they withdrew into lonely places to live lives that would prepare them for the day of Judgment. The first reports we have of these hermits give a repelling picture of excessive fasting, self-flagellation, mortifications of the flesh, and out and out filth. By the 4th Century there were thousands of these monks in the East, particularly in Egypt. They began by leading solitary lives. Then they gathered together in communities called *lavras*, each one of which had its common rule and superior. St. Anthony wrote regulations for these *lavras* in Egypt, and a disciple of his introduced them into Palestine. The movement spread to Anatolia, where St. Basil (329–79) became its leader. He laid down the rules of monastic life that set the pattern for Western monasticism, and which remain to this day popular throughout Eastern monasteries. He insisted that the monastic community be kept small, and that the monks occupy themselves with hard work. He frowned on extreme asceticism and insisted on a novitiate, during which time an initiate could test his reactions to the discipline of monastic life.

Monasticism was introduced into the West by Athanasius and St. Martin of Tours in the 4th Century, and it spread rapidly through Gaul and to Ireland, where it was carried by St. Patrick in the 5th Century. This early Western monasticism took some strange forms, especially in Ireland where it merged with the clan structure of the society to produce hereditary abbots, but it did provide the zealous missionaries that Christianized Gaul and western Germany.

Monasticism was converted into a strong weapon, to be used by Gregory the Great and his successors in their fight for Church unity, by the efforts of St. Benedict of Nursia (480–543). Benedict was born of a noble Italian family, but he withdrew in disgust from the corruption of society when he was fourteen. He spent three years in a lonely cave at Subiaco in the Apennines, tried cenobitic life at the invitation of a group of rebellious monks who resented him, but then he moved southward to Monte Cassino, where he established a quiet, well-ordered community of monks. He based his rule on the three essentials of monasticism: poverty, chastity, and obedience. He added a fourth vow, stability, in reaction against the vagabond monks he'd observed. Every monk had to swear to observe these. All private property was forbidden, and each monk was issued what he needed from a common stockpile. The monks were organized under an abbot, who assigned each one his tasks for every hour of the day. Their lives were filled with hard work, study and prayer. Idleness and extreme asceticism were alike forbidden. Each monk was to eat enough to keep up his strength, and he was allowed a pint of wine a day.

The rule was strict, but not fanatical. It offered men of good will an opportunity to live peaceful lives, filled with constructive work and charity. In the unsettled conditions of the 6th and 7th Centuries, the order spread rapidly. As civilization declined, the Benedictine monasteries became centers of learning. There were no class distinctions recognized in them, so that men of the lower classes could rise to positions of authority. Thus the Church had a steady source of trained men of talent. Gregory I was the first Pope to use these men and, as we have seen, he was most successful in establishing his control over the Western church.

The Church Fathers

Another reaction against the growing secularism of the Church can be found in the writings of the great theologians of the early Church. These men tried to protect the Church against both heresy and worldliness by stating its principles in clear terms. Often these Church Fathers resorted to pagan Greek philosophy to buttress their arguments, but according to St. Jerome any idea from the pagans that could be converted into a support of Christian dogma was permissible.

St. Ambrose was an active man of affairs as Bishop of Milan, but his main contribution to the Church was his allegorical approach to the Bible. He believed that every statement in Holy Writ was to be understood in two sense, the literal and the allegorical. His method was immensely popular through the Middle Ages and accounts to a large degree for the universal use of allegory in medieval literature.

St. Jerome, on the other hand, was an intellectual in his approach to the Bible. He studied the Greek and Hebrew texts and compiled a standard version which he issued in Latin as the Vulgate, the basic Catholic text to this day. He also studied the pagan classical writers to develop his style so that he could produce a Christian literature that would be cultured and literary.

The greatest theologian of the period was undoubtedly St. Augustine of Hippo (354–430). In his *Confessions* he describes how he moved from Manichaeanism to the salvation of his soul in Christianity. The burning passion of this book has always endeared it to believers, but any serious student of the later Roman Empire can find in it a deep insight into its spiritual climate.

His *City of God* is the first and still one of the greatest works of Christian philosophy. In it he tries to reconcile the presence of both good and evil in God's world. He pictures the universe as a duality of good and evil that are locked in a struggle, the outcome of which is foreknown to God, but which is the means by which God chooses to make Himself manifest to man. A Christian must accept the ephemeral ills of this world, for he knows that within them a Divine Will is at work and that in the end he will have salvation. St. Augustine wrote voluminously on almost every phase of Christian theology, and his works were studied for centuries after his death.

We have already seen the close cooperation that existed between the Church and the Franks. The results for the Church were that it came to hold a monopoly over the schools and the training of skilled administrators for the high offices in the state. More and more, laymen entered the Church and religious life just to obtain these offices. This led the Church into a deep involvement in politics, which eventually brought the Church itself under the control of the lay aristocracy, who came to look on Church offices as their private property. Corruption spread, and if it were to continue as an effective instrument of Charlemagne's government, the Church would have to be reformed. It is for this reason that Charlemagne practically Christianized his state. He called councils, appointed bishops, controlled church schools. In every way he could, he made it clear that he would always use his secular power to strengthen his religious leadership. It is curious that Charlemagne did not realize that he was laying the foundation of the papal monarchy of the High Middle Ages. Society was unified under a theological control. The prime function of the secular arm was to strengthen this control. Under kings of lesser ability than Charlemagne, this control would pass to the Church.

However, the Carolingian empire disintegrated during the 9th Century, when the ferocious attacks of the Vikings, Magyars, and Muslims plunged Western Europe into chaos. Feudalism offered local centers of control as the only defense. The universalism of the Church was broken up into local churches, each under the control of a feudal lord who looked on church property as his own, and on ecclesiastical offices as an opportunity to reward men who served him well. The effect was to bring the Church to the lowest point in its history. The papacy was usurped by the feuding families of Rome who fought over it as if it were a political football. With no control exercised from Rome, bishops all over the Western Church treated their dioceses as their personal possessions. The lower clergy fell into gross ignorance and immorality. Clerical marriage was a common practice, an evil in a feudal age, for it led to the conversion of the office of priest into a fief to be handed down to a son, however unqualified. Few priests were appointed because they possessed the ability to serve the spiritual needs of the community. Reform was obviously needed. But who had the authority and the power to reform the Church? The Holy Roman Emperors, who were the heirs of the Frankish kingdom in Germany, needed competent administrators and felt that only a reformed Church could provide them. They undertook the task by marching into Italy and placing qualified men on the papal throne. But the cure was worse than the disease. Secular control was itself one of the causes of Church corruption. The reform had to come from within the Church itself.

VI

THE EARLY MIDDLE AGES: THE EAST

▼ ▼ ▼ ▼ ▼

▶ **Mosaic icon, Christ Blessing, Santa Sophia, Constantinople.** The fineness of the features demonstrates the skill of the artist. The small bits of stone give the appearance of being pigment. These mosaics were covered by the Turks with about a foot of cement, For many years, bit by bit, they have been being uncovered.

► **The Gate of Belisarius, Rome.** Belisarius fought the Ostrogoths for almost twenty years. He strengthened the walls of Rome and erected this gate. The crenellations show it was defended by men who shot arrows at the attackers, while sheltered by the crenellations. Few people at that time could maintain a siege for long.

► **Santa Sophia, Constantinople.** The dome and the pendentives are clearly visible. Earthquakes have damaged the building and the heavy walled buttresses were put up to prevent further damage. The Ottomans used the church as a mosque and erected the minarets.

The Founding of Byzantium

When Diocletian divided the Empire into two parts he was tacitly recognizing that the Empire was too large for one effective administrative center. Moreover, he saw that the demographic and economic focus of the Roman world had shifted to the east. There trade was heavier, cities more vital, the land more productive. He usually maintained the capitol in the Balkans, at Split, but Constantine decided to move it permanently to the east. He chose to build on the site of ancient Byzantium, a brilliant move. Poised between two continents, the focus of the important trade routes from the east and south, New Rome (or Constantinople as it came to be called) remained for over a thousand years after its dedication on May 11, 330 the strategic center of the western world. It was the first city Christian from its very beginning and in it Hellenistic culture, Christianity, and Roman political institutions fused to produce a civilization eventually known as Byzantine. Its peoples, to be sure, always called themselves Romans, and their history was the continuation and adaptation of the Late Empire, though eventually the changes became very pronounced.

The eastern part of the Roman world had been deeply affected by the crisis of the 3rd Century, but there was a vitality there that made possible not only a rapid restoration of stability, but the development of a highly successful state. Diocletian and Constantine had created an absolute monarchy, which was strengthened by Constantine's conversion to Christianity. He was now considered as God's special agent on earth, entrusted with the task of protecting God's church. His person became sacramental and he was revered as though he were a living icon. The Church believed it was in partnership with the emperor to rule the Christian world, to attain common objectives, and to defeat common dangers. Occasionally, a clash developed between them, but church-state rivalry was rare in Byzantium. As we have seen, to protect their absolutism, the new emperors had broken up the Empire into numerous small provinces, which were gathered into prefectures. Civil and military power was carefully separated, the one put into the hands of the Praetorian Prefect, the other in those of the *dux*. As time went on, the prefects tended to become very powerful and to absorb military authority, but under their guidance there developed a vast bureaucracy, the most efficient administrative machinery of the Middle Ages. Though offices tended to disintegrate into mere titles, Byzantium was well-served throughout its history by a class of professional civil servants that transcended all political upheavals in the court.

The Emperors and Religion

Constantine's main problem as Emperor had been religious. He had acted vigorously when the Arian controversy threatened his plans for the new Christian Church. At Nicaea he, in spite of his limited knowledge of Greek, had led the discussions and had been very active in formulating the creed that emerged from the debates. The Emperor was generous in his support of the Church and hoped he had healed its wounds. But he had miscalculated the strength of the Arians, and toward the end of his life tried to conciliate them and to force the Church to readmit Arius. He was bitterly opposed by

Athanasius, Bishop of Alexandria, who maintained a fight for orthodoxy until his death in 373. The dispute was a foreboding of the religious tensions that were to keep the eastern world in turmoil for centuries. Christianity's claim to exclusive truth was not universally accepted for many years. Furthermore, Greek philosophical speculation always led to a challenging analysis of Christian concepts that caused acrimonious debate. In many parts of the Eastern Empire, particularly in Syria and Egypt, national pride often demanded particularist churches. The emperors, striving to maintain unity, were beset by pressures of all sorts, but their first consideration had to be the strength of the state. All too often heresies developed in the very areas that were most vital for their economic or military needs. To put down the heresy might lead to rebellion, but to compromise was sure to lead to furious attacks from the orthodox bishops, which might lead to civil war. No satisfactory solution was found before the Arab conquest of the affected areas made the debate academic.

Constantine died in 337 A.D. after receiving baptism from an Arian bishop. His son Constantius (337–361), sole ruler after 351, supported Arianism and during his reign Ulfias, an Arian bishop, translated the Bible into Gothic and spread Arian Christianity to the German tribes. Julian "the Apostate" (361–63), who followed Constantius, attempted to revise paganism as an answer to Christian dissension. He failed completely, for paganism was not only dead as a religion, but it no longer served the needs of the state.

The religious controversies and the earlier civil wars threatened to weaken Roman policy on the frontiers. In the east, Persia was a threat, even though the emperor, like Jovian (363–64), tried a policy of conciliation, while in the north, the Germans were pushing against the whole frontier. Valens (364–78) had to fight a war on both fronts and lost his life in the effort. Theodosius the Great (379–95) salvaged the Empire by abandoning any attempt to defeat the Visigoths by force of arms. He enlisted them as allies (*foederati*) and gave their leaders titles. This became standard Byzantine policy for dealing with barbarians, even though the effect was to barbarize the army and to place important commands in the hands of non-Romans. The policy was also expensive. High taxes led to the descent of the free peasant into the ranks of the *colonus*. Theodosius had come to the throne from the Orthodox West. An ardent foe of Arianism, he called together the Second Ecumenical Council in Constantinople (381) to establish orthodoxy; the Nicean Creed was drawn up in its final form, and the controversy came to an end.

The Empire was still in great danger, however. Theodosius divided the Empire between his two sons, Honorius in the West, and the elder, Arcadius (395–418), in the East. The split in the administration now became permanent, though in theory the Empire remained a unity. The new emperors ruled under the control of regents and German military commanders. The German element became predominant in both capitols, though eventually it was overthrown in the East. The immediate danger from the Visigoths was eased when Alaric led them to Italy, beginning the process that ended in a German take-over of the Western provinces. The respite was not of great value in the East, for the next Emperor, Theodosius II (408–50), was ineffective. He did found the University of Constantinople (425) where the Greek, Latin, and Christian classics were taught in a harmonious curriculum. In 438, the Emperor promulgated the Theodosian Code, which gathered together all the imperial edicts from the time of Constantine.

The Code was published in both the East and the West, but the Empire was really splitting apart. The Western government collapsed after the invasions of the Huns, and the Roman pope became the only effective leader within the Western part of the Empire. The East was becoming increasingly Greek in its tone, and New Rome had supplanted the ancient Rome of the Caesars. The growing pretensions of both the pope and the eastern capitol clashed repeatedly during the religious controversies that resulted from the theology that developed at Antioch. The Orthodox had answered the Arian attack with the doctrine of the consubstantiality of the Father and the Son. Now the question arose as to the relation between the human and the divine in Christ. At Antioch, scholars concluded that there were two distinct natures in Christ, the human vessel and the divine godhead that was absorbed into it. Mary was not the mother of God (Theotokos), but only the mother of the man Christ, who at some time was infused with the Holy Spirit (Logos). At Alexandria, theologians insisted that the divine and human natures were actually only one (monophysis). In 428, Nestorius, Patriarch of Constantinople, preached the Antiochene theology, and Cyril, Patriarch of Alexandria, launched a skillful attack against him. Nestorius was condemned at the Third Ecumenical Council at Ephesus (431), and was driven from the Empire.

But the anti-Nestorians, in their zeal to deny the separate natures of Christ, now over-emphasized his single nature. Monophysitism was condemned by the patriarch of Constantinople, and Leo I of Rome wrote his *Tome* to condemn it. The Pope's statement that Christ was a single Person with two perfect natures became the orthodox position. The Emperor Marcian (450–57) called the Fourth Council at Chalcedon (451), which was guided by the *Tome*. Christ was at the same time Perfect God and perfect man. Constantinople had gained leadership over the Church by its vigorous action, and the 28th Canon of the Council stated the equality of the See of Old Rome and New Rome. The pope was accorded primacy of honor alone, which did not satisfy him. Even more serious, the Monophysite heresy became the symbol of Syrian and Egyptian nationalism. The more the emperor tried to put down heresy, the more he was viewed as a tyrant. The Syrian and Coptic (i.e., Egyptian) churches became the instruments of a national separatism that would eventually welcome Arabic conquest as a liberation.

The religious problems were intensified by internal tension in the capitol. The Germans had become very strong, and a growing national feeling that swept through the capitol forced the emperor to take measures against them. Leo I (457–74) was elected by the German army, but he took his crown from the patriarch, which introduced a religious element into the coronation that eventually offset the military. He also used Zeno, an Isaurian, to hold down German pretensions. When Zeno became Emperor (474–91), riots and civil war broke out against him. The Eastern emperor was in no position to take any measures in 476 to prevent the final collapse of his Western colleague. Zeno tried to settle the religious dispute with his *Henoticon*, a compromise between Chacedon and the Monophysites, but he failed to achieve anything but a schism between Rome and Constantinople that lasted thirty years. When he died, the populace of the capitol insisted on a Roman emperor, and an aged court official was crowned as Anastasius I (491–518). He had already reorganized the tax structure to the great satisfaction of the merchant class and he had been able to reintroduce the wide use of gold coinage. He was, however, an avowed Monophysite. His religious policies caused bitter civil wars and rioting in the capitol. Constantinople was divided into *demes*, which were organized into two factions, or parties, the Blues and the Greens, each of which had a leader appointed by the government. The Blues were Greek, aristocratic, Orthodox; the Greens were middle-class, Monophysite, and Oriental. The political and religious attitudes of the factions were reflected at the Hippodrome, the center of the city's life. Riots often broke out during the horse races that swept mobs to the very palace. The popularity of the reforms and frugality of Anastasius could not redeem his religious bias. A Monophysite policy might win over Egypt and Syria for a time, but the resulting chaos at the heart of the Empire was too high a price to pay.

Justinian, the Last Roman Emperor, and His Reconstruction of the Roman World

The fall of the Western Empire to the Germans had not gone unnoticed by the Eastern emperors, but they had been powerless to prevent it. By the 6th Century, however, the East had survived its most pressing attacks, and its recovery had been so marked that a serious attempt to reestablish imperial authority in the West was feasible. Justin

I (518–27), a Macedonian, who had had a distinguished career in the army, had been chosen to follow Anastasius on the throne. His nephew Justinian, however, was really in charge of the government until he became Emperor in his own right (527–65). Justinian was one of the best educated, most sophisticated men of his age, a remarkable achievement for the son of an ignorant peasant. His spirit vitalized the work of the brilliant men he chose to surround him, and his greatness of vision must be judged more by its objective and eventual impact on the civilization of the West than by its achievements in the immediate sense. He was ably assisted by one of the most remarkable women of all time, his wife Theodora. The daughter of a bear-keeper in the Hippodrome, Theodora grew to be a seductive, beautiful courtesan and actress, who gained a wide range of knowledge on her travels through the Orient. Justinian was captivated by her charm and intelligence, and fell in love at their first meeting. They married, and he had her elevated to the highest aristocratic rank. Thereafter, she lived a highly moral, productive life, interesting herself in religion and social reform. In addition to his wife, Justinian leaned heavily on the generals Belisarius and Narses, the jurist Tribonian, and the sinister but effective administrator John of Cappadocia.

Justinian dreamed first of restoring the ancient Empire, the realization of a dream that had haunted men for generations, as it was to remain an ideal for centuries to come after the transitory success that he achieved. In 533, Belisarius destroyed the Vandal kingdom in north Africa, though ominously local Berber tribes were not pacified until 548. In 535, he began the invasion of Italy to destroy the Ostrogothic kingdom. The campaign was a harsh one, lasting for twenty years and taxing to the utmost the ingenuity of both Belisarius and Narses. Meanwhile, an army landed in southeastern Spain (554) and began to push back the Visigoths. The Empire appeared to have been restored, but the cost was staggering. Justinian had freed his troops for the western campaigns by paying heavy tribute to Chesroes I, the King of Persia. In the Balkans, hordes of Slavs swept past the frontier forts and began to lay waste the whole territory as far south as the Aegean shores. Soon they would settle permanently in Greece.

Justinian, in the tradition of the past, considered himself a true autocrat. He was determined to rule without any restraints from the city *demes* and their factions. He sought to restrict both the Greens and the Blues, who in response joined forces to oppose the Emperor. The Hippodrome became the scene of wild disorder in 532 when a small riot, fed by widespread discontent with the tactics used by John of Cappadocia to squeeze revenues from the people, flared into a general revolt. Crying "Victory! Victory!" *(Nike)*, mobs rushed through the city setting fire to public buildings, churches, and even the royal palaces. An emperor was acclaimed, and Justinian was on the point of fleeing the city when Theodora, who had kept her head in the crisis, strengthened his courage and rallied their forces. Narses and Belisarius intrigued to split the factions, then attacked the Hippodrome where thousands were massacred. Autocracy had triumphed over the last vestiges of popular government.

Justinian eagerly turned to the task of rebuilding the state. He erected a new Senate House, public baths, the Chalke gate and above all, the daring new church of the Holy Wisdom *(Hagia Sophia)*. By constructing a great dome on pendentives over a square building, his architects were able to enclose an immense space under a breathtaking sweep of mosaics, shimmering in the light streaming in through innumerable windows. His success led him to build the churches of San Vitale and Sant' Apollinaire at Ravenna in Italy; St. Demetrius at Salonica; St. Irene, Sts. Sergius and Bacchus, and the Holy Apostles at Constantinople.

John of Cappadocia was assigned the task of reorganizing the administration of the state. He attempted, with little success, to check the growth of the large estates of the landed aristocracy by destroying the clear distinction between the civil and military authorities in the provinces. The roll of offices was abolished, and the collecting of taxes was made more systematic and successful. Byzantine trade and industry were given strong support. The goods of her factories were exchanged with the peoples north of the Black Sea and with distant China for a wonderful variety of luxuries: amber, silk, porcelain. All too often, however, gold shipments had to supplement her insufficient exports, and Persia was always a stumbling block. The importation of silkworms and the production of domestic silk eased the problem somewhat.

Justinian's greatest achievement was his codification of Roman law. In 529, Tribonian published the *Justinian Code*, a carefully-edited collection of the valid edicts since the time of Hadrian. The *Digest*, the opinions of leading Roman jurists, followed in 533. The *Institutes*, a textbook for law students, came next, and the work was rounded out by the *Novellas*, the laws passed by Justinian since the Code. The first three were in Latin, but the *Novellas* were in Greek, and Greek translations of the whole work soon began to circulate. The *Cornus Iuris Civilis*, as the completed collection was

◀ **Santa Sophia, Constantinople.** The church was the wonder of its day because of the light that streamed through the many windows. This was made possible because of the dome and the pendentives that carried the weight without closing space for windows.

▶ **Byzantine Senator, Byzantine Museum, Constantinople.** In the early years sculpture was common, but icons were always more popular. The senator is wearing the traditional toga. The statue has the classic Roman look.

called, gave a structure to the centralized state that had been developing in the East. The total life of the community and its citizens, both private and public, was presented in a homogeneous unity that reconciled Roman principles with Christian morals and Hellenistic practice. Above all, the *Cornus* institutionalized the absolute authority of the emperor. It preserved the idea of monarchy and had a profound influence on the West as it was introduced later in the Middle Ages.

Justinian was a Roman Emperor, probably the last, but he was also profoundly Christian. He saw his state as a Christian Roman Empire, and he involved himself in religious matters with a will. In 529 he closed the pagan Academy in Athens, its scholars taking refuge at the Persian court. He had complete control over the Church, both in the West and in the East, and he not only called councils, and supervised the details of Church administration, but he wrote theological treatises, composed hymns, and in general determined the dogmas of the Church. He was willing to reinforce the position of the papacy for support in his Italian campaign, but when Syria and Egypt fell away in disgust, he realized the dilemma and, at the Fifth Council of Constantinople (553), he attempted to compromise with all sides. The policy was a failure, as was so much of his work. By destroying the German kingdoms without the means of replacing them effectively, he had created power vacuums that were filled by the destructive invasions of the Lombards into Italy, the expansion of the Visigoths in Spain, and the interminable raids of the Berber tribes in north Africa. His successors were forced to give up his Western dream and to concentrate on the East.

Under Justinian's successor, Justin II (565–78), a war broke out with Persia that lasted through the reigns of Tiberius I (578–82) and Maurice (582–602). Maurice achieved peace with Persia and was able to salvage Byzantine rule in the West by establishing two exarchates, one in north Africa and the other at Ravenna. The exarchs had complete civil and military authority to organize their provinces. He had little success in the Balkans, where the Slavs now began to settle down in groups that would in the end give rise to permanent Slav kingdoms within the territories of the Empire. Maurice fell victim to a reaction against the heavy hand of the governmental machinery Justinian had constructed. The *demes* began to re-emerge as voices of popular discontent, which spread to the army. An officer, Phocas, was proclaimed Emperor in 602 and marched on the capitol. Riots broke out, Maurice was deposed, and Phocas was accepted as Emperor (602–10). He executed Maurice and his three sons, and unleashed a reign of terror against the old aristocracy which had been, after all, the mainstay of the autocracy. They retaliated with plots, which caused more terror, until the government dissolved into anarchy. The Persians took advantage of the chaos, invaded from the east, and overran all Asia Minor. Slavs and Avars took all the Balkan peninsula. The Empire was falling to pieces. The exarch of Carthage, Heraclius, rose to the occasion. He sent his son, also named Heraclius, with a fleet to save the Empire. He arrived at the capitol on October 3, 610 and was crowned two days later. Phocas was overturned and with him the Roman Empire came to an end. With Heraclius, Byzantine history, properly so called, begins.

Heraclius and His Successors

The reign of Heraclius (610–41) began with a series of disasters. The Balkans were taken over completely by the Slavs, who pushed all the way down into the Peloponnesus and to the vicinity of Constantinople. The Greek population was forced to flee into isolated valleys, remote southern peninsulas, or to the islands. The population became heavily Slavic in the conquered areas, but eventually Hellenic culture reasserted itself. In the south, the Persians were everywhere victorious. They took over Armenia, Syria with its rich cities, and finally Jerusalem, where they destroyed the principal churches and captured the Holy Cross, the most venerated relic in Byzantium.

Heraclius set to work to retrieve the situation. He organized the areas in Anatolia still his into large military zones called *themes.* Each *theme* was under a commander, called a *strategos,* who had complete military and civil jurisdiction. The *theme* was peopled with soldier-farmers (*stratiotai*), who were given inalienable grants of land in return for military services under the *stragegoi.* Thus, a fair means of recruiting an army had been found, and expensive mercenaries were no longer needed. Also the state had found a way of pacifying troublesome elements on the frontiers. By giving them lands as *stratiotai* not only was their pressure relieved, but they could be used against others as well. The *theme* administration of the provinces was matched by the emergence of *logothetes* in the central administration. These were well-trained professional heads of the financial and bureaucratic departments of the government.

With a reinvigorated state behind him, supported by the funds of a church

anxious to defeat the enemy of the faith, Heraclius trained a new army, in which light cavalry played an important role, and launched a series of spectacular attacks on the Persians (April 5, 622). By 628 he had isolated the Persians diplomatically and had defeated them in battle. In 630 he made a triumphant visit to Jerusalem to return the Holy Cross. In 626 he had defeated a strong attack by the Avars on the capitol. Their defeat led to new invasions by the Bulgars, the Serbs, and the Croats, who now moved in to fill the vacuums. The *theme* system held, however, and was extended to become the backbone of the Byzantine administration.

It is with Heraclius that the Eastern Empire became definitely Byzantine. Greek replaced Latin, not only as the language of the people, but as the official language of the government and the Church. The Emperor abandoned his Latin titles and became known as the *Basileus,* a Greek title that originated with the Persian emperor in ancient times. The *Basileus* also sought to solve the religious disunity which had contributed a great deal to the initial Persian successes. He supported a compromise with the Monophysites based on the idea that Christ had a single energy that activated His two natures. The heretics seemed to accept the theory, and Pope Honorius agreed to go along with it. The Patriarch of Jerusalem, however, rejected it vehemently, and the Pope expressed certain reservations. The *Basileus* accepted a new suggestion from Sergius, Patriarch of Constantinople, that it was a single will *(thelema)* in Christ that gave unity to His dual nature, and he promulgated this teaching in the *Ecthesis,* which he posted in the narthex of the church of Hagia Sophia in 638. Both sides rejected the compromise, and the way was open to the Arabs who began to move into the Near

East at this time. The battle of Yarmuk on August 30, 636 broke all Byzantine resistance. Antioch surrendered without a fight. Jerusalem fell quickly. By 639–40 the Arabs had taken all Mesopotamia and Persia, and in 640 the invasion of Armenia and Egypt began. Heraclius was crushed. His conquests had only served the Arab cause. He died on February 11, 641, a suffering, embittered old man.

Heraclius had a son, Constantine, by his first wife, and another, Heraclonas, by his second wife, his niece Martina. To prevent a feud, he left his throne to both sons as co-emperors. A civil war broke out which eventually placed a son of Constantine, Constans II, on the throne (641–668) by an act of the Senate, which could still exert influence on the course of affairs in the absence of imperial authority. During the reign of Constans, the Arabs continued their advance. By 646, the Copts of Egypt had surrendered willingly to the Muslims. The Arabs built fleets which took Cyprus in 649, Rhodes in 654, and Cos soon after. Civil war between Muâwijah, the leading general of Islam, and Alî, the son-in-law of Muhammed, gave Byzantium a respite. In 658, Constans led an expedition against the Slavs in the Balkans with some success, and then he turned to the West, where the Arabs had attacked the exarchate of Carthage in 647. The *Basileus* had tried a last attempt at conciliation with the Monophysites of Africa by promulgating in 648 the *Type* which forbade the discussion of the divine will and the divine energy. The *Type* failed to stave off the Arab advance. Furthermore, it was condemned by Pope Martin I, who had become Pope without the customary approval of the Emperor. Constans ordered the Pope's arrest and transfer to Constantinople, where he was tried for treason, found guilty, and sent to southern Russia where he died in exile.

Constans had become unpopular in the capital as a result of his cruel treatment of Martina and the murder of his brother to remove him as co-emperor. He decided to go to the West, where he landed in 663. He made a token attempt to free Italy from the Lombards, visited Rome, then sailed to Sicily to defend it against Muslim attacks. Apparently, he had some thought of returning the capital to Rome, which may explain the palace revolt which broke out on September 15, 668. Constans was murdered in his bath, some said by being smothered with his soap. His young son, Constantine IV, became *Basileus* (668–85).

The reign of Constantine IV was occupied mainly by Muslim and Bulgar attacks. Having won the civil war, Muâwijah took up the war against Byzantium. For fifteen years after 663, Anatolia was laid waste. By 674 Arab fleets had encircled Byzantium and began a siege of the city. For four years they made repeated attacks, all of which were beaten by the strong walls and by Greek fire, a technique of hurling lighted explosives through a siphon. The Arab failure was the first real stop in their advance and it raised Byzantine prestige through the Near East. Constantine was able to turn his attention to an invasion of Bulgar tribes into the Balkans across the Danube. He led an expedition by sea to the area north of the Danube. He failed to stop the Bulgars, who settled in the area south of the Danube, mixed with the Slavic peoples living there, and established a Slav-Bulgar state which the *Basileus* was forced to recognize.

He had better success in solving the religious problems of the Empire. Since the areas controlled by the heretics had fallen to the Arabs, there was no longer any need to reconcile them. At the Sixth Council which met at Constantinople in 680–81, all compromises with Monophysitism were condemned, and the doctrine of two energies and two wills was declared Orthodox. The popularity which he gained by leading the discussions at the Council toward so happy an issue led Constantine to eliminate his two brothers, who had shared his rule as co-emperors. The principle was established that only one autocrat could hold supreme power in the state.

Constantine died at the age of thirty-three, and his son Justinian II (685–95; 705–11) became *Basileus* at the age of sixteen. His father's victory over the Arabs kept peace in the devastated Anatolian provinces. He was able to make a highly successful expedition against the Slavs in the Balkans. He moved some 30,000 of them into Anatolia, where he colonized them as *stratiotai*. This worked quite well, and Justinian set up new *themes* in Greece. At the same time that the *themes* strengthened the military defenses of the Empire, they helped stimulate the economic life of the whole area as well. Since the oldest son always had to inherit the military obligation of the *stratiotai*, the younger sons were encouraged to go off to open farms of their own. Thus, the system encouraged the growth of a class of vigorous free peasants, whose rights to their property were confirmed by the famous *Farmer's Code* that undoubtedly dates from this period. The farmers were listed in village communities by the government, each village being assessed a communal tax that had to be paid by all jointly.

Justinian was a very devout Christian, and he held a Council in 691–92, the *Quinisextum* (Fifth-Sixth), which confirmed the Canons of the two preceding councils. It also condemned vestiges of paganism which had survived, and it laid down rules for Church administration. Practices which were becoming common in the Western Church were condemned, which led the Pope to condemn the Council. Justinian's unpopularity in Rome was matched by a growing resentment among the aristocrats, who felt that their great estates were threatened by the spread of the *theme* system. The *Basileus* was an extravagant builder, which added to an already heavy tax burden. A revolt broke out in 695. Justinian's nose was cut off, and he was sent into exile. Ten years later, he led an army of Slavs and Bulgars on the capital, sneaked into the city through a sewer pipe, and recaptured his throne (705). He rewarded his Bulgar allies by naming their Khan a Caesar of the Empire, and he created a blood bath of revenge against his enemies. Finally, an Armenian general was proclaimed *Basileus* by his troops and he marched on the capital. Justinian and his son were murdered, and the dynasty of Heraclius came to an end.

The new Emperor, Bardanes-Philippicus (711–13), was an open Monophysite, who tried to establish the heresy as orthodoxy. The pope denounced him. More serious, the Bulgars attacked to avenge their late friend. The *Basileus* was deposed by his troops, and Anastasius II took the throne (713–15), only to withdraw to a monastery after an ineffective attempt to launch an offensive against the Arabs. The figure that emerged as the real power during this period of anarchy was the *strategos* of the Anatolian *theme*, Leo, an Isaurian from north Syria, who had laboriously worked his way up through the army ranks. On March 25, 717, Leo entered the capital as undisputed *Basileus*.

VII

THE EARLY MIDDLE AGES: THE WEST

▼ ▼ ▼ ▼ ▼

▶ **Segovia, Spain.** 14th Century castle renovated in the 15th Century. As the Moors retreated before the Christian advances, they left behind fortifications that were quickly strengthened by new castles.

▶ **Avila, Spain.** In the wars between Moors and Christians such walls were common. In this town lived and died St. Teresa, a mystic who practiced extreme acts of piety.

▶ **Church of St. Anthony, Padua, Italy.** The church was built by Byzantine architects and resembles St. Mark's in Venice as a result. Padua was a Venetian possession and had close contacts with the East. The church is an example of the opulent style that resulted from trade with Byzantium.

The Franks

With the destruction of the Ostrogoths, the only strong kingdom left in the west was that of the Franks. Originally, the Franks were a rather weak tribe living in two groups along the Rhine. Their movement westward differed in one vital respect from all other German migrations. They moved out in an orderly expansion, never losing contact with their homeland. They were always able to call in reinforcements, and their state always had a tone of permanence and stability never fully attained by other German nomadic peoples.

Gregory of Tours in his *History of the Franks* (late 6th Century) has described the origins of his people in quasi-mythical terms, though his description of their institutions and their later history is fairly accurate. Apparently the Franks invaded Gaul in small bands under rival chieftains. Under Clovis (481–511) a Salian band defeated the last Roman forces in Gaul, absorbed the Allemani, expelled the Visigoths from all Gaul north of the Mediterranean coastal region, and forced a union with the Ripuarian Franks. Vicious, crafty, totally amoral, Clovis became the strongest man in the West. He married Clotilda, a Burgundian princess who was a Catholic Trinitarian. Under her influence Clovis and all his tribe received Baptism by representatives of the Pope. At that time, political loyalty was expressed only in religious terms. By his conversion, Clovis won immediately the loyal support of all his Roman subjects. He could also depend on the enthusiastic assistance of the Catholic bishops and their administrative apparatus. When he was named consul and patrician by the emperor his kingdom became the most cohesive and

substantial of all the German states. His wars took on the aspect of holy missions against the Arians, though the Franks remained for centuries a particularly immoral and blood-thirsty people with strong pagan survivals.

After the death of Clovis the kingdom was divided between his four sons. Seldom has a family been so torn apart by hatred and murder as the Merovingians (as the Frankish royal house was called). This situation arose from a Frankish custom of dividing an inheritance equally among the surviving heirs. The title could not be divided. Naturally, each wished for it all, and the rule became one of "despotism tempered with assassination." Four states emerged eventually within the Frankish lands: Austrasia, Neustria, Aquitaine, and Burgundy. The kingdom as a whole was too large to be governed in these Dark Ages by any one king, so that the attempts of the royal rivals to eliminate each other were doomed to failure as far as efficient government was concerned, for each part was better governed by local institutions. Power was delegated to counts who ruled large areas, often an old Roman city-state, and dukes, who ruled several counties combined into frontier provinces. These officials lived off the income of their own lands, provided local justices, and gathered together fighting forces to defend their districts. They were opposed to the central government and as a group were more powerful than the king. Around the person of the king there was a group of personal servants, the constable, for instance, who was in charge of the stables, the butler in charge of the pantry, and most importantly the *major domo* (mayor of the palace), a sort of ranch foreman who was in charge of the administration of a whole royal estate or the household around the person of the king himself. These servants were used for public as well as personal duties. They had prestige and political power, and the offices were eagerly sought after by the nobility.

The king provided practically no government beyond the defence of the realm, and some law courts. He was not interested in maintaining Roman civilization, which went into serious decay. The expenses of this system were very low, and the king was expected to live on his own personal income, without the support of taxes. Even the army was inexpensive, since all free men had to serve voluntarily and they had to bring with them their own arms and equipment. Towns declined as they fell into the hands of local noblemen, who also controlled the villa system. The Gallo-Romans were still governed by Roman law, now usually combined with German customs. The Church also used Roman law and some of the old administrative skills. Its schools were the only ones to survive the period, and even in these education was reduced to learning the rudiments of reading, writing, grammar and rhetoric. Scientific and technological study disappeared. In general the Roman elements withdrew from active participation in politics. Their mood was to turn toward their own affairs, and to allow the more sophisticated elements of the culture to collapse. German law, customs, and finally creativeness began to provide a new direction for cultural development.

The Carolingians

During the 7th Century the power of the Merovingian kings continued to decline as the nobility grew in power. Open warfare among the mayors of the palace was put to an end by Pippin of Heristal, who first took control of Austrasia, then Neustria, and finally the whole realm. From 687 to 714 he secured more peaceful conditions by encouraging the missionary activities among the Germans of monks brought in from Ireland. He was succeeded by his illegitimate son, Charles Martel (714–741). Charles had to put down immediate opposition from the other Frankish noblemen. When he invaded Aquitaine to reconquer the province, he came into conflict with the Moors, Muslims who had crossed over to Spain in 711 and were now raiding in southern Gaul. To stop them, Charles had to raise a new army based mainly on cavalry units, which were expensive to train and equip. The only inducement he had to offer his followers to undertake the heavy expenditures was land which he confiscated from the Church. The Church retained technical title to the land and received a nominal rent, but the main income and the immediate control over the estates went to noblemen who committed themselves by oath to serve in Charles' new army. The result was victory over the Moors at Tours-Poitiers in 732, but a long step toward the establishment of the medieval fief had been taken.

In spite of his high-handed confiscations of Church property, Charles was well aware that the Church would be very useful in civilizing the restless Frankish nobility and in pacifying the rebellious lands across the frontier in Germany. His greatest assistant in this mission was the English monk, Boniface, who as bishop took upon himself the task of reorganizing the Frankish Church under the authority of the Pope, establishing the Benedictine Order throughout Frankish lands, and converting the heathen across the eastern frontiers of the realm. Charles and his sons gave him encouragement and real help in numerous councils, called and presided over by the mayors, not the king, in which the secular as well as religious affairs of the kingdom were settled. The important business of government passed into the hands of the bishops of the Church.

Charles had to ally himself with the Lombards during his war with the Moors, so he refused to enter Italian affairs to assist the Pope. His son and successor Pippin (747–768), however, reversed this policy. He vigorously pushed the Moors beyond the Pyrenees, but he entered a much closer and warmer friendship with the Pope. He gave back to the Church title of much of its confiscated property, though the military service owed by these estates still had to be given to the state, and he continued to assist St. Boniface in his work. Most important, he entered into an alliance with Pope Zacharias (741–752), who was menaced by a Lombard expansion that had captured the Exarchate of Ravenna in 751. Pippin felt the time had come to take over the royal power from Childebert III, the last of the Merovingian puppet kings. In a famous exchange of letters the Pope sanctioned the usurpation, and Pippin in 751 deposed the king and was, himself, elected and crowned by the noblemen of the realm. Later Pope Stephen II (752–757), temporarily expelled from Rome, took refuge in Gaul (754), where he anointed Pippin and his sons, declared the family "kingworthy," and forbade the Franks ever to select a king from any other family. Pippin fulfilled his bargain by fighting two successful campaigns against the Lombards in Italy. In 756 he was able to turn over to the Pope, as Bishop of Rome, a deed to a strip of territory that stretched across central Italy and included Rome, Ravenna,

and Spoleto. This was the *Donation of Pippin*, which was renewed by the later Carolingians and eventually led to the formation of the Papal States.

Upon Pippin's death, rivalry for the throne broke out between his two sons, Carloman and Charles, who had married daughters of Desiderius of Pavia, King of the Lombards. Carloman died in 771, and his sons fled to their grandfather in Italy. Charles (later called Charlemagne) was left as sole King. His long and important reign (768–814) began with a full-scale invasion of Italy. Pope Adrian I (772–795), harassed by Desiderius, called on the Franks to come to his assistance. Charlemagne was only too happy to eliminate the support his nephews were receiving, and he crossed the Alps in 773. He defeated Desiderius and sent him off to a monastery, renewed and perhaps enlarged the Donation of his father, conquered all Lombardy, and finally took its Iron Crown for himself. Lombardy became a possession, but it was ruled separately and was not absorbed into the Frankish kingdom.

Charlemagne then turned to a lifetime of war. For over thirty years (772–804) he carried on a bitter war against the Saxon nation. By its end thousands of Saxons had been slaughtered, Saxon national institutions were destroyed, and the survivors were converted to Christianity. Frankish lands stretched to the Elbe and beyond. Bavaria was also taken (787–788), and the power of the Avars was shattered in Bohemia (788–805). He was less successful in his wars against the Moors in Spain. Taking advantage of local rivalries, he hoped to take over the land down to the Ebro. But his politics failed and he had to retreat in haste. On his way through the Pyrenees, his rear guard commanded by Count Roland (the only fact known about him) was attacked by Christian Gascons in the valley of Ronces-valles. In the 11th and 12th Centuries when Crusades became popular, his campaign against the Moors was glamorized and the lowly Count was immortalized in the *Chanson de Roland*. Charlemagne's campaigns were in the main successful, though he failed in his attack against Venice, and he stabilized his frontiers with a ring of provinces called *marches* (or *marks*), under military leaders who had complete authority to defend the districts by any means necessary.

Imperial Administration

Einhard, an official at the King's court and one of his personal friends, has left an intimate biography of Charlemagne, who is pictured as the ideal king. He was moderately tall, robust, his bulging belly hidden by his manly gait. He loved the hunt, took frequent baths, was moderate in his habits and friendly with his men. He was interested in learning (though he was illiterate), and he was dedicated to the interests of his government and the Church. Einhard fails to mention that he was also lusty, often stubborn, and almost always arrogant.

In 799 Pope Leo III (795–816) was driven from Rome by his enemies. He fled to Charlemagne who reinstated him in Rome and planned to leave some soldiers to guard him. Leo felt he needed to strengthen Charlemagne's position in the city so as to be himself more secure. With this plan in mind, on Christmas Day, 800 (or possibly 799, for the New Year was reckoned from Christmas at that time), while the King knelt in prayer in St. Peter's, the Pope suddenly placed on his head a crown and made him

Emperor and patrician of Rome, a dignity that only the emperor could bestow. According to a later account, the people in the Basilica immediately hailed him three times as Augustus. In an oft-quoted passage Einhard, who is our source for the coronation, claims that Charles would not have entered the church that day if he had known what the Pope was planning. It is true, perhaps, that he did not want the crown from the hands of the Pope, though even this may be a later distortion, but there can be no question that he wanted to become Emperor. He had conquered many lands, and his realm had become an empire in fact. In the East, where the theoretical unity of Christendom was still represented by the one universal emperor, a woman, Irene, had schemed her way to the throne. By tradition only a man could hold imperial dignity, so it could be argued that there did not, in fact, exist an emperor. Charles was already negotiating with Irene. If the Pope's action disturbed him at all, it was surely only because of its timing. He was determined on the crown. Immediately after the event, he sought recognition for his new dignity. Certain western kings became his lieges and the great Abbâsid Caliph, Harun al-Rashid, entered an alliance with him. Finally the Byzantine Emperor Michael I in 812 accepted the accomplished fact and recognized Charles as the Emperor of the West.

Though Charles was proud of his title and apparently used it all his life, his real achievements lay in his administration of the affairs of his kingdom. He was not a true originator, but his vigorous attention and desire to be in charge revitalized the existing system. He recognized the powers of the counts, the dukes, and the rulers of the *marches* (*mark-graf* or margrave), but he kept them under control by the use of his *missi dominici.* These were officials, half laymen, half bishops, that he sent into all the districts of the realm to inspect local affairs and to hold courts to hear and settle complaints. They and the King exchanged *capitularies,* which were reports, instructions, legislative decisions, and which regulated all the affairs of the kingdom.

Charles formalized even farther the officers of the Merovingian court. The constable became the head of the army, the seneschal became the chief administrative head of the government, and the chancellor (originally a literate priest acting as the king's secretary) became the head of the state secretariat.

The basic weakness in the administration could be seen in certain developments in the control of the army. All free men were still required to serve, but since fighting techniques had become so expensive and required such skill, only the nobility could really afford to serve. So poorer farmers were allowed to pool their obligation to send a representative to fight for them. Thus, military service in person was restricted to an aristocratic elite. At the same time the lesser nobility were commending themselves to strong leaders for protection, while the magnates were building private bodyguards. Charles had to recognize the trend by allowing men to come to the army in bands under their own leader.

Another weakness in the system which would eventually become fatal was the lack of any means to recompense the servants of the crown or the army except with land. Charles Martel had used Church lands for this purpose, but Charlemagne began to use *benefices* carved out of the royal domain, which had been swelled by the spoils of his wars. As the nobility became stronger on the land in administration and defence, as they took over more and more responsibility in the king's entourage, their lands were destined to become more extensive while the crown lands shrank. Eventually, most of the power would lie with the armed retainers of the nobility.

Charles' greatest efforts lay in the field of education, for his whole system depended, as all sophisticated government does, on the keeping of records and administration by correspondence. He gathered together at his palace at Aachen (Aix-la-Chapelle) under Alcuin of York a group of scholars from all over the civilized Western world.

Theodolphus, a poet from Spain; Peter, a Pisan grammarian; the historian Paul the Deacon, and others began to gather the remnants of classical learning. Charles bade them recopy all the manuscripts available in a legible new script (the beautifully clear Carolingian miniscule from which all our own lower-case letters are derived), and to teach the young sons of the nobility the skills necessary to make them effective administrators in his system. The plan did not work, nor did it stop the relentless decay in culture, for there were too few learned men in a world that depended more on action than on reason, but the effects of this so-called "Carolingian Renaissance" were felt for many years. Germans for the first time entered with full equality with Romans into the world of scholarship. Gaul became the center for early medieval studies and in the next few generations would produce a John Scotus Erigena, a Hincmar of Rheims. Also, in every cathedral schools with teachers of theology and grammar were established. Though these languished for long generations, from them eventually came the great intellectual revival of the 12th Century.

The Collapse of the Carolingian System

Charlemagne was succeeded by his son, Louis the Pious (814–84). He was an austerely religious man who imposed a severe discipline upon the Gallican Church while he allowed the Papacy to grow in independent strength. His reign was of special note because of his frustrated schemes to ensure a peaceful succession to his throne. By his first marriage Louis had three sons, among whom he divided his lands equally in 817: Lothaire, Pepin, and Louis. By a second marriage, however, he had a fourth son, Charles, for whom he had to provide by taking lands away from the older children. A general war broke out in which Louis was attacked and deposed by his sons, then restored when they fell out and attacked each other.

By the time of the embittered Louis' death, the kingdom was in total turmoil. Pippin died, but Charles took over his inheritance and allied himself with Louis to defeat Lothaire at Fontenoy (841). In the following year the two allies met at Strasbourg to cement their friendship with solemn oaths of mutual loyalty. These Strasbourg Oaths sworn by the brothers and their men had to be repeated in the two languages in use in the western and eastern portions of the empire. They are justly famous as the first written appearance of the languages that would become medieval French and German. The alliance held, and after some bitter fighting the three brothers agreed to arbitrate their differences and signed the Treaty of Verdun (843). The division was as significant in its own day as it has proved fascinating for later historians. No regard was made for geographic or ethnic considerations. The decision was made strictly along the lines of an equitable division into three parts of all the properties and feudal holdings. Charles took his portion in the west, Neustria and Aquitaine. Louis received the east, Saxony, Bavaria, and the lands west of the Rhine including the capitol, Aachen. In general, in the west the French-speaking peoples were gathered into what would become France; in the east, the German-speaking into Germany; but in the middle there was hopeless confusion. Here both languages were spoken and there was no geographic basis on which a natural structure could be built.

When Lothaire died his three sons divided up his kingdom, and in 870 it was further divided by the Treaty of Meersen into two parts (the future Alsace and Lorraine). The empire had fallen into its independent constituent parts, each pursuing its own affairs, while the imperial title became an empty prize over which the later Carolingians fought bitterly until it went into disuse upon the deposition of Charles the Fat of Germany by his nobles in 887. He and his western French cousins had dissipated their power in the Middle Kingdom as well as in their respective territories by distributing ever increasing parcels of their domains to the nobles to secure their allegiance in the civil wars. The result was that the Carolingian domain lands became too weak to produce sufficient power to control the nobility who now established themselves as the real government, each in his locality, dominant over the kings whom they elected or deposed at will.

New Invasions

The dangers inherent in the failure of central government were not obvious to the nobility, who were intent on breaking up territorial units into smaller and smaller pieces. The Church alone had a vision of the total European situation, and it sought desperately but in vain to organize some sort of defense against new invaders that began to swarm all around the continent.

From Africa Muslim pirates began a series of devastating raids on Sicily, the whole Italian coastline, and the French Riviera. They then occupied Sicily and the other major islands, established themselves in Italy midway between Rome and Naples, and on the north Italian Riviera. From these outposts they terrorized Provence, the Alpine regions, and all of Italy. Cities disappeared as trade withered. Monasteries lived precariously in lonely terror.

Even more damaging were the attacks of the Norsemen, who first made contact with civilized Europe as rude traders, then as rapacious pirates. Finally, forced out of Scandinavia by overpopulation and the attempts of strong chieftains to establish orderly kingdoms, boatloads of adventurers, the Vikings, set out to make their fortunes by rapine, pillage and murder. Everywhere they could reach with their shallow-draft long-ships, along the coasts of Europe and far up its rivers, they spread destruction. Hardly a single settlement of any size survived, whether it was a monastery, a town, or a manor. The whole movement covered a period of about two hundred years, though the last phase of it saw organized invasions of Britain and northern France in the West, and along the Russian river system in the East. Ireland and the outer is-

lands, even Iceland and Greenland, were sporadically settled, but in England, which had been ruled by seven rival Anglo-Saxon kingdoms, the Danes were able to establish a permanent kingdom. Alfred the Great in 878 signed a treaty with them whereby they were given, after they had converted to Christianity, the Danelaw, all of northeastern England and southern Scotland.

In France the raids were even more devastating. Taking advantage of the civil wars, the Vikings attacked savagely the whole coastline of France and followed the rivers to Paris, Orleans, Ghent, and Rheims. The counts did what they could, and often they organized effective defenses, but the kings were powerless. Eventually Charles the Simple, to the disgust of all the nobility, brought a halt to the raids by ceding to them in 911 the area around the mouth of the Seine as tribute. Under their chieftain, Rollo, now a count, the Vikings settled as Normans and gradually the attacks came to an end.

In the East, out of reach of the Muslim and Norse assaults, the invasion came from across the steppes of Russia. Around 890 the Magyars suddenly appeared on the German frontier and for about sixty years they harassed Italy, southern Germany, and eastern France. Though they did extensive damage, they were intrinsically a weak threat. They did not assimilate civilized techniques with the amazing rapidity of the Northmen, nor did they organize subject peoples to fight for them. As a result, they were always short of manpower, and the German King Henry the Fowler (918–36) restricted their incursions with a line of forts on his frontier, which his son and successor Otto I destroyed their army at Lechfeld (955). After this the Magyars settled in Hungary and directed their attacks against the Slavic

▶ **Cathedral, Bayeux.** This church is closely associated with William the Conqueror and his wife Matilda. Across from the church is the historic Bayeux Tapestry, which is a principal source for the invasion.

▶ **Castle complex, Blois, France.** One of the best-preserved castles in France. The moat was always filled and the only entrance was across the narrow drawbridge. This was a favorite castle of the kings of France, who also had a palace nearby.

peoples who were now divided into the Poles and Czechs in the north, and the Serbs and Croats in the south.

The Feudal-Manorial System

As the Carolingian Empire failed as an effective administrative system, men had to turn to other means of organizing and regulating their affairs. Already men were tied to each other by commendation. Manors existed as isolated economic units that provided sustenance for a fighting aristocracy. Counts and dukes treated as private possessions their obligations to give justice in courts of their own devising and to offer administration to large territories. Of course, men still lived in kingdoms and felt some loyalty to the king, but as communications broke down they had fewer and fewer contacts with him. They turned instead to their immediate superior or the local strong man for leadership, and these men, in turn, developed the technique of governing at the local level. Overlapping territories and jurisdictions brought about endless feuding, but the tendency toward smaller holdings and the decentralization of power prevented the emergence of any really strong men. The unit of government became the county, whose head, the count, kept a fairly firm control over the courts and military defense, while he allowed his vassals to take over the running of their own estates.

The origins of the system were present in the institutions of the late Empire that had been taken over by the Germans. The *precarium* was a personal agreement between an owner of a piece of land and a tenant in residence who was given the use of the land for life, or until the owner wished to oust him. Often a landowner wishing to extend his holdings would offer better contracts and larger holdings to his precarists. In addition to the precarists, there lived on the land *coloni,* tied to the soil and to their status by law. When the Germans took over the Empire they actually took over a collection of large villas peopled by workers who did not own the land but who were tied to it.

The Romans also had the patron-client relationship whereby a man sought security by placing himself under the protection of a wealthy or powerful patron in return for services rendered. These services became primarily military in the late Empire, and every Roman nobleman had a large bodyguard. The Germans had a similar arrangement in the *commitatus,* though they formalized it by an oath of allegiance and much closer commitment between the chief and the warrior. As the two merged, a class of noblemen, German or Roman at first, then increasingly German, was established that employed large bands of devoted followers.

Feudalism begins when the two systems of land and personal dependence merge. It is obvious that in an age of declining economic activity, the use of the produce of land will become the only sign of value. Noblemen began to pay their men by giving them an income from pieces of land, or from some monopoly or service. This was also done to strengthen the personal tie, just as it was often done to gain fighters or servants. At first the land was not only owned by the lord, but it came directly under the laws of the land, or as these declined, under the jurisdiction of the owner. But in Merovingian times the custom of immunity arose. At first, it was granted to lands given by the Church to protect them from powerful local lords. No tax collector or judge could enter the lands from outside. The holder of an immunity, on the other hand, had the right to collect public funds, whether in money, kind, or service, and soon he began to administer justice to fill the vacuum left as public justice was barred. Immunities spread to laymen and by the end of the Carolingian period all land holdings were under the control of their immediate lord. The early name for a piece of land given out with immunity for the lifetime of either party to the transaction was *benefice*. As the *benefice* became more widely used in secular circles, it came to be called the fief.

We have already seen that in Merovingian times the king had come to rely on his nobility to fill the offices of his government. These noblemen tended to turn the office into a hereditary right. Counts and dukes by the Carolingian period regularly passed on their offices and titles to their sons. Furthermore, it was a Germanic trait to give more importance to an allegiance to a person near at hand, than to the idea of a distant state. In the unsettled conditions of the 8th and 9th Centuries men preferred to commend themselves to members of the nobility for safety. Often they turned their lands over to the lord as an inducement for protection, and then received them back as fiefs. The kings also recognized that commendation was the only method available to secure the necessary manpower to keep the society in operation. They encouraged commendation, or vassalage as it came to be called, as a technique of bringing all men under some form of order. They also tried to impose royal vassalage on the upper ranks of the nobility as a control. Vassalage did not work as well between the distant king and his counts as it did between the count and his nearby fief-holders. Thus vas-

salage increased the strength of localism. The Merovingians had found it expedient to transfer local government to the counts and dukes, content that order be established even if through a local agent, hoping that loyalty to the crown would secure the king's prerogatives. Charlemagne had tried to control the system with his *missi* and the extension of vassalage, but all power fell to the nobles, without restriction, when the Carolingian dynasty ended. The central government was finally willing to settle for the principle that every piece of land must have some local lord over it.

Feudalism emerged as a political system whereby government passed to strong local lords who gained supporters by giving out fiefs. These were types of tenure that varied widely, but they were always a source of income, and (though there were variations) were usually given in return for military service. On the whole, the system can be viewed in negative terms as the breakdown of central government. But it is more fruitful to see it as the establishment of a system of government designed to provide society with its essential services with the best means available at the moment.

The use of the word "system" is somewhat of a misnomer, for in the beginning there was no system. In fact, in many ways the feudal arrangements never became a consistent, planned system, but there did arise a fairly well-defined pattern that spread from France to all areas and was adopted to one degree or another, always subject to local custom, by medieval Europe as a whole.

Certain types of tenure, for instance, can be defined. *Frankalmoin* and ecclesiastical *benefice* were grants of land to the Church that owed in return no obligations at all, or merely spiritual ones. Much more common was the military tenure, or fief, which might be given to either ecclesiastical or secular holders. The fief had attached to it the obligation of the service of so many knights that had to come with the holder of the fief to perform military service for the lord either in the field, on garrison duty, or on home guard. Fiefs also were given in return for all non-military services to the lord. These were called sergeantries and could vary from a reward to a personal servant to an outright gift. Eventually, the fiefs would be given in cash, or the services rendered by a money payment, a development that in the end destroyed the basis of feudalism.

All tenures were based on the feudal contract. A vassal knelt before his lord, placed his hands within the lord's, and swore fealty and to become his man *(homage)*. The lord accepted his oath and invested him with the possession *(seisin)* of the fief. It was understood that the lord had obligations to his vassal. He had to protect him in his holding, provide a court of justice for him, and provide for his children if he were to die. The vassal, on the other hand, undertook the military or other obligations of the fief. He had to sit in the lord's court to give counsel and help provide justice. He also had to pay a relief whenever the fief was inherited either by a new heir or from a new lord. Aids had to be paid. These were contributions toward extraordinarily expensive activities of the lord—the knighting of his son, the marriage of his daughter, a crusade, the payment of ransom, etc. If either party failed in his obligations, the contract was broken and the fief either stayed with the vassal or escheated to the lord.

Infeudation was complicated by the granting of secondary fiefs, a practice called subinfeudation. A vassal might divide his fief into domain land which he kept and parcels which he gave out as fiefs to vassals of his own. Each of these might do the same until a whole hierarchy of vassals were holding parts of the original fief. The basis of subinfeudation was obviously the belief that many people might enjoy and control the same piece of land, ownership being in a sense multiple rather than private. In the vertical structure that emerged each man was tied to the man above, and all those tied to him, and he was tied to the men below him that were tied, in turn, to him. He could seek redress in his lord's court only for cases involving men obliged to answer there. In any instance where no court was provided for him, he resorted to violence to settle his affairs. The lack of horizontal controls explains the anarchy of the Middle Ages. It is also important to notice that it was quite possible for any vassal to acquire many more fighting men from his fief than he owed to his lord for it. Thus private armies grew relentlessly and added materially to the general chaos of early feudalism.

Feudal courts were places where the customs of the fief were studied and the appropriate precedents applied to the particular case before the court. The customs were written down in books, though written codes of law as such were rare in the Middle Ages. The assembled vassals demanded justice, though the whole court had to be ready to help the lord enforce decisions. The ordeal and compurgation were regularly used, and in Frankish lands the ordeal by combat became the most popular. Under the direction of the court, the parties to a dispute fought a juridical battle, the judgment going to the victor. There was no effective appeal from the decision of the court. The lord's lord might be called on for relief, or the loser might challenge the individual members of the court, but both were rarely used expediencies; therefore, the most frequently used appeal from the decision was to escape to one's fief, take refuge in a well-defended castle with one's retainers, and to sit it out until the court was ready to compromise the decision.

The Church was deeply involved in the feudal system. Much of the land given over to the Church was held by some form of feudal tenure, for which the Church had to fulfill its obligations. Also the high offices of the realm were often (in some cases, like the chancellorship, always), given to bishops, which made them feudal officers of the realm as well as lords of the Church. A layman often built a monastery or a church on his fief. These were his property, and he retained control over them and felt he had the right to appoint the abbots or priests to them. Out of this involvement would grow a conflict of interest for the bishops and a secular control over many members and institutions of the Church.

The Village

The basic economic unit of the Middle Ages was the village. In it, the dwellers of a manor huddled together in primitive huts attempting to raise enough food to keep alive. The lord of the manor was usually too involved in war to pay much attention to conditions in the fields. As a result, there was little direction, little inventiveness, little incentive on the farms. The fields were usually divided into farm land, fallow land, and pasturage, and a primitive system of rotation was practiced. The village in the early period had to grow all its own food, usually on soil and in climates not well suited. Yields were low. Furthermore, there was insufficient power to cultivate enough land to grow food in large enough quantities to feed animals, which would have produced the power and fertilizer necessary for better crops. It was a vicious circle, and the medieval villages barely kept alive.

The village, forced as it was to use its resources to the fullest extent possible, did develop a sense of communal effort and balance. The fields were divided up among all the peasants and the lord, each person getting some good, some bad land. Work was done collectively, the results being apportioned according to custom. Village affairs were regulated in the manor court, where the lord settled all disputes. By custom the villagers had certain rights. They were protected in their holdings, for they could not be forced off the land, nor could it be passed on to a new holder without them. There were both free men and serfs, or villeins, in the village. Both owed many obligations to the lord. The villager had to share with the lord the produce of the land, doing all the work himself. He also had to perform certain prescribed duties (corvées). The lord enjoyed monopolies (banalités). All wheat had to be ground in his mill, all bread baked in his ovens, wine made in his press—all of this at a price, of course. The lord could move at will over the peasant's lands and he could collect set taxes and fees, as well as extraordinary ones when he saw fit.

All in all, the manors were of low productivity, worked by peasants that were more animal than human. Population was of necessity sparse. Such talent as there was was lost in the absolute necessity of every man to submerge his individual effort in the common struggle to subsist.

The German Empire Survives

During the reigns of the last Carolingian kings in Germany, there took place the same march towards aristocratic anarchy so fateful in the West. The "stem duchies," large feudal states in the hands of powerful ducal families, emerged in Saxony, Franconia, Bavaria, Swabia and Lorraine. These duchies became virtually independent kingdoms and the king was helpless against them. Upon the death of Conrad I (911–918) the dukes elected Henry the Fowler, Duke of Saxony (919–936). The office remained an elective one through the Middle Ages, but the legitimate emperors were always chosen from the royal family. Henry took vigorous action against the other dukes, forced them to recognize him as King, and added new conquests to the royal domain. For armies, he could rely on the old custom that brought all free men to serve in the army, and by controlling the elections of bishops in his lands, he was able to secure dependable men of talent to assist him in his government.

Otto I (936–973) succeeded to his father's throne without serious opposition, but as soon as his power began to be felt, the dukes rose up against him. He made large grants of property to the Church to strengthen the bishops whom he used to create an effective administrative apparatus. He attempted to control the dukes by strategic marriages and family alliances, but the dukes, even when relatives, were in constant revolt against him. His prestige soared, however, after his crushing defeat of the Magyars at Lechfeld. He began to dream of reviving the old Carolingian Empire, and in 951 he invaded Italy to ally himself with the Carolingian house by marriage and to be crowned in Rome. He was also probably interested in reforming the Papacy, again to strengthen the Church which had become so important a part of his government. In 962 he was crowned Emperor, and in 963 he gained control over the Papacy by exacting from the Romans an oath never to elect a pope without the permission and approval of the emperor. He immediately called a council which deposed the Pope, the corrupt John XII, and elected a candidate put forward by the Emperor. No doubt, Otto dreamed of restoring Charlemagne's church-state, but he was also sure that the Church would be an obedient junior partner in the arrangement.

His activities in Italy brought him into a conflict with Byzantine policies there, which was resolved by the marriage of his grandson, the future Otto III, to Theophano, daughter of the late Emperor Romanus II (959–963).

Otto II (973–983) came to the throne with the usual rebellion of the nobles. This time, however, the Emperor found a permanent method of weakening the great duchies. He created new duchies in Carinthia and Austria, and within the old ones he greatly reinforced the holdings of the bishops. In this way he raised so many rival powers that a coalition became very difficult and no single power could arise strong enough to pose a serious threat. Unfortunately, Otto went south to fight the Muslims in Italy and, after a humiliating defeat, died prematurely of disease and chagrin, leaving a three-year-old son to succeed him.

A general insurrection swept across Germany and among the Dane and Slavs to the north and east upon the accession of Otto III (983–1002). Under the skillful regency of Theophano the crown was secured, though eastern Germany was lost to the Poles. Otto was trained by his mother in Latin and Greek, and apparently he was indoctrinated by her into a dream of re-establishing the ancient Roman Empire. He found an occasion to invade Italy in 996 to settle disturbances in Rome. He had his cousin Bruno elected Pope, and as Gregory V (996–999) his cousin crowned Otto Emperor. Otto returned to Aachen, where he tried to revive Charlemagne's court. There he met and became deeply involved with Gerbert, the most learned man of his day, who was teaching at Rheims. The two men fancied themselves a second Constantine and Sylvester I, the Pope who by tradition had been of great assistance to the Emperor. They dreamed of establishing a universal theocratic empire in which the Gelasian theory of the two swords would become a reality. As Pope and Emperor, the two would unite in harmony the whole world and the restoration of the Roman Empire would usher in a Golden Age. They went to Rome when Gerbert became Pope Sylvester II (999–1003), and Otto issued a new Donation of Constantine, built a great palace on the Aventine, and showered favors on the people and nobility of Rome. He never won their favor, however, and they rose up and besieged him in the Castel Sant'Angelo, where he died of fever at the age of twenty-one. The dream was over, but it was an omen for the future. The pursuit of empire in Italy had lost eastern Germany to the Slavs. In Italy, the result was hostility toward the empire and bitter rivalry among petty princes for control over Rome and the Papacy.

Otto left no direct heirs, so the nobles elected his cousin Henry II (1002–24), who spent his whole reign zealously reforming the Church in Germany, desperately and unsuccessfully trying to push back the Poles, and making three expeditions to Italy to bring some order out of the chaos that was spreading down the peninsula. His death again left no direct heirs, and the nobles elected his nearest relative through the female line, Conrad II (1024–39), who started the Salian line. He began to introduce feudal practices to reinforce the lower nobility so that he could offset the power of the bishops, whom he seems to have mistrusted. His policy was to balance a feudal nobility tied to the service of the crown by hereditary titles and fiefs against the more powerful dukes and bishops, who were further weakened by freeing monastic lands from their control. The whole system depended on the canniness of the emperor and was doomed by the lack of any firm royal institutions of central authority. He achieved no success in Italy, but he did add the great kingdom of Burgundy to the empire when Rudolph III willed his title to Conrad. On Rudolph's death in 1033, the emperor moved in and took over his inheritance.

Henry III (1039–56) succeeded his father and began a mad juggling game to keep his empire in order, To control the great nobles, he had to create new ducal families, who in the end became just as troublesome as their rivals. He carried on a long series of wars in the East and by their conclusion Bohemia, Poland, and Hungary were nominally his vassals, though only Bohemia remained loyal. He tried to dominate the Church by encouraging reform, but the strengthened Church turned against him. In 1046 a half century of corruption in Roman politics had ended in a fight between three rival claimants to the papal power; Sylvester III had been elected after the ouster of the criminal Benedict IX, who reclaimed the papal tiara only to sell it to the reformer Gregory VI. Such a scandal could only end with the intervention of the Emperor. Henry was delighted to go to Rome to support the cause of reform so that he could depend on a renewed Church. In 1046 he called a council at Sutri that deposed all three Popes. Henry searched for a worthy candidate. His first choice, Clement II, died in a few months; his second choice, Damasus II, lived only twenty-three days as Pope. He finally settled on Bruno, Bishop of Toul, who took the name Leo IX upon his election (1049–54). Bruno was a sincere reformer and refused to accept the office from the Emperor. He went to Rome and insisted upon being elected in the proper manner. Leo immediately began a reform which was eventually to free the Papacy from all secular control. He called a council at Rheims, without bothering to ask permission of the French king, who forbade his bishops to attend. Most did not and they were excommunicated by Leo. The Pope began to investigate cases of simony and other serious ecclesiastical crimes, which he insisted had to be moved for trial to his own court in Rome. By the time of his death, Leo had freed the Papacy from dependency on imperial support, and had re-established control over his northern bishops. Henry, who had been so helpful in this development, did not live to see the consequences of his sincere support of the reformers. The emergence of an independent Papacy in control of the bishops of the Church obviously was to pose serious problems for the empire.

The empire itself had survived as an obsolete fossil from the past. It had based itself on the bishops of a strong Church, who made it possible for the emperor to pit force against force in the complex game of internecine German ducal rivalries. In the long run the lack of solid imperial institutions made it impossible to rule so vast an area as Germany. The empire prevented feudal anarchy, but it also prevented the growth of feudal institutions better suited to the needs of medieval Germany than itself.

VIII

THE WORLD OF ISLAM
▼ ▼ ▼ ▼ ▼

▶ **Rabat, Morocco.** A typical Islamic interior. Water is always an important feature. Decoration is elaborate, but never contains human representation of any kind.

▶ **Group of Bedouin at Giza, Egypt.** These are modern Bedouin who live in the same manner they lived in when the Prophet was born. In the background are the Pyramids.

▶ **The Blue Mosque, Constantinople (Istanbul).** The Muslims were awed by Santa Sophia and they turned it into a mosque. But soon the Blue Mosque was built to rival the Christian church. The name refers to the blue glass windows that fill the interior with a blue tint.

The Arabs before the time of Muhammed were a loosely-organized people who filled the vast expanse called Arabia, that stretched from the Mediterranean Sea and Egypt in the west to Persia in the east. At heart they were and remained a collection of nomadic tribes, but a collection of town centers sprang up along the routes of trade that carried goods from the Far East to the Mediterranean. These southern Arabs spoke their own form of Arabic and developed a culture of their own. Gradually this culture moved northward and mixed with an Arab culture of the cities of the Fertile Crescent. The Romans encountered them in the rich cities of Petra and Palmyra in the period up to 200 A.D.

Thus, Arabs lived in two basic cultural systems. There were, on the one hand, the nomadic Bedouins. Those fierce desert-dwellers wandered across the wastelands of Arabia, tending their camels and sheep. They had no political organization, but were gathered in clans under tribal sheiks. The only concept of law that they had was a primitive right to self-help, revenge, and the blood-feud. Their religion was nature-worship (animism) of the *mana* or power that lay in rocks, wells, stars, the moon, etc. The personality of these people, however, was quite striking. Brave, self-reliant, and austere, they conducted themselves with a simple dignity in the formal aspects of daily life. Their hospitality was lavish, since to them the guest was sacred. Yet the Bedouin was capable of explosive, almost maniacal, violence at times. Perhaps the utterly merciless character of the environment in which he had to live, with its burning sun, its uncertain water supply, its terrible sandstorms, kept him always in a tense state verging on hysteria. He found release for the tension in endless tribal wars with his fellow nomads and periodic raids on wealthy cities. For the most part, his attitude toward the universe was that it was immense and filled with powers over which he could exercise absolutely no control. Fate (*qisma* or kismet) was the only recognizable principle that motivated it. All that came to man was his destiny, that was to be accepted with stoic resignation.

The Bedouin were an important element among the Arabs, but they by no means characterized them all. Along the southern and western coasts of the peninsula there existed a string of very powerful trading centers that controlled the flow of goods from India to the Mediterranean world. Sophisticated cultures combining Semitic, Hamitic, Persian and Roman elements flourished in these cities. Occasionally, strong kingdoms were established, such as the one that became so powerful at Palmyra in the 3rd Century A.D. under its Queen Zenobia, or the Jacobite Christian kingdoms, the Ghazanids and the Lakhmids, of northern Arabia that clung to a precarious existence during the 6th Century wars between Byzantium and Persia.

There was a constant movement among the Arabic tribes, generally of a circulatory sort. Southern tribes made their way northward, as those of the north wandered to the south. Many of these tribes were Jewish or Christian, but they were usually unorthodox or heretical in their theology. As they moved through the peninsula, they spread rather bizarre versions of the Judeo-Christian religious tradition. These mixed with the native gods and produced a somewhat uniform religious pattern. All the tribes worshipped gods and goddesses that were the embodiment of powers that were seen in the physical world. These many gods were, in turn, understood to be manifestations of a vaguely defined universal deity called Allah. This monotheism was not very strong, though the Prophet always gave importance to it. It certainly did not give rise to an ethical system or to a public morality. Infanticide was widespread, especially of female children. Women had no social status whatsoever. Extreme violence and brutality were taken for granted.

The religion, however, did provide a basis for the one sign of unity among the tribes. In the city of Mecca there was a black rock, the Ka'ba, which tradition associated with the prophet Abraham. It was an object of worship for all the Arab tribes. A structure was built to house it and also the idols of all the gods worshipped in Arabia. Once a year, a month's truce was declared in the tribal wars so that people might journey to Mecca to worship and to trade. For that one month the Arabs were a united people, and the city of Mecca was their focus.

It is not clear when the Jews first entered Arabia. Of course, Muhammed associated the building of the Ka'ba with Abraham, and it is possible that Abraham began his journey toward the land of Canaan, the promised land, in southern Arabia, but later Jews fled into Arabia whenever persecution became unbearable in their homeland. Under the Romans this was especially true, for they found the Jews troublemakers. Their religion demanded a certain lifestyle which Romans resented as nonconformist. Jews tended to take refuge in Arabia. There has been, for example, a community of Jews in Yemen from the 7th Century B.C. until today, when the modern state of Israel has called them back to their ancestral home.

Jewish settlers spread across the Arabic world and became very prosperous. Soon they dominated the commercial and agrarian worlds, settling in Mecca and in Yathrib (Medina). Not only did the Jews bring a higher level of culture which attracted many Arabs, but their monotheistic religion brought many converts. Monotheism became the main cultural push for change.

Christianity entered Arabia almost from the beginning. Individual Christians, then whole tribes, were known long before Islam. Like the Jews, Christians tended to flee into the deserts of Arabia to escape persecution, in the beginning from Romans, and then later from fellow Christians. As we have seen, controversies about the Mother of Christ led to bitter disputes. Many Arabs who converted to Christianity became Nestorians or Monophysites. All Arab Christian communities were led by bishops and deacons. The orthodox sought aid from the Byzantine church against the heretics, while those communities in Persian hands, though free from the charge of heresy, met persecution as Christians. All in all, Christians in the Arab world hated the Greek Byzantine church and the Persian emperor. When the new Islamic state began to expand, they became a major force in that expansion.

The Arabs, then, before the coming of Muhammed, were a people by no means without culture. Their personality was that of the nomadic Bedouin, to be sure, but in the cities they had achieved a fairly high degree of civilization. There were serious social evils, however. Deep cleavages separated the rich from the poor. There was no social justice. Cruelty and brutality were common. Serious men of good will were deeply disturbed. They thought of reform, but this could only be achieved by a unified people working for a common social goal.

Muhammed

Muhammed was born in 570 A.D. in Mecca. His father, who belonged to the Hashimite clan, an impoverished branch of the ruling house of Mecca, the Quraysh, died before his birth, and his mother died five or six years later. The young orphan was raised by his grandfather, and then an uncle, Abû Talib. He entered the service of a wealthy widow, Khadijah, who sent caravans of goods along the trade route to Palestine and Syria. It is probable that Muhammed came into contact with Jewish and Christian ideas in his travels, but he never had a very clear picture of either religion.

In 596, at the age of twenty-five, he married Khadijah and became a man of wealth. This made it possible for him to withdraw into the kind of life he found most congenial. Muhammed was of a meditative nature. It is said that he suffered occasionally from epilepsy, which no doubt accentuated this tendency, and he spent long hours alone, in contemplation, wandering through the hills around Mecca. He was sensitive to the injustices of his day, apparently, and had early begun to think in terms of reforming the cruel polytheism of his tribe. One day as he rested in a cave on Mount Hira, close to Mecca, he went through the typical mystical experience that marks the careers of all such reformers. He later reported that he heard in his sleep a voice, which he later identified as that of the angel Gabriel, crying to him, "Read: In the name of the Lord Who createth, createth man from a clot of blood. Read: And thy Lord is the Most Bounteous, Who teacheth by the pen, teacheth man that which he knew not." This was his call to the mission that was to occupy the rest of his life.

He confided in his wife, his cousin Alî, and his friend and future father-in-law Abû Bakr, a wealthy merchant of the city. These accepted him immediately as a prophet of the Lord. A series of revelations followed, and the new prophet began to preach a message of hope for the downtrodden. He warned the wealthy that a day of reckoning was at hand and that only the merciful could expect mercy from the one, merciful God. His influence began to spread slowly among the lower classes. The rulers of the city, however, were frightened at his attack on idolatry, for this would interfere with the revenues that derived from the annual pilgrimage to Mecca of all the Arab tribes, and they resisted all his attempts to win them over to his new ideas. He did not in the beginning set out to create a new religion, nor did he hope to effect a social revolution. This can be seen in his willingness to compromise with the old religion. He made Mecca a holy city and recognized the Ka'ba as a sign of the covenant between God and Abraham. He thought himself just a prophet come to make man mindful of the wrath of God against the sinful. But others saw more accurately that as an apostle his ideas would lead to economic and political consequences that would bring into being a new order. The Qurayah nobility began to attack him. His wife died at this time, as did his uncle Abû Talib, and Muhammed left Mecca for a time to recuperate. He married a widow, and also Aysha, daughter of his friend Abû Bakr. At this time he met with some citizens of Yathrib who were converted to Islam. They promised to preach the new religion in Yathrib.

The crisis came in 622. The Umayyads, the aristocratic branch of the Qurayah, had begun to persecute the Prophet's followers, some of whom fled to Abyssinia. On the night of September 24, word came to Muhammed that the Umayyads had decided to have him assassinated. He had been planning a trip to Yathrib, whose leaders had invited him to come to their city to put an end to a factionalism that was destroying their trade. He already had relatives there, for it was the home of his grandmother. When he heard of his danger, he decided to make the journey. The flight from Mecca is known as the *Hijra,* and is considered by Muslims so important an event in the history of man that they date their calendar from it.

The Prophet remained in Yathrib (which was known thereafter as Al-Madinat Al-Nabi, the city of the Prophet, or Medina) for ten years, and established a theocratic state dedicated, as he said, to the glory of God and the spreading of the Word. The rulers of Mecca declared war, but within six years their armies were defeated, their cities had been raided, and they had to sign a treaty with Muhammed. After that, all the tribes of Arabia accepted the leadership of the new Prophet. For ten years Muhammed had been the ruler of a rapidly expanding state. He believed his leadership was inspired by God, and he announced the receipt of hundreds of revelations that covered the administration of the state and the establishment of a new law. In 632 the Prophet made his last journey to Mecca, the "farewell pilgrimage," during which he delivered his most beautiful sermon. He died a short time later on June 8.

The Quran and Islam

The religion that Muhammed founded was revealed to him in a series of messages called *suras.* Together these constituted the Quran or the "Reading." It was Muhammed's contention that God had chosen him as an instrument through whom He would make known His will to all mankind. He had already chosen other prophets in the past, Noah, Abraham, Moses, Jesus, all of whom were shown to be prophets by a miracle. Noah built the Ark as a covenant with God, Abraham and Ismael rebuilt the temple of the Ka'ba after it was destroyed in the Flood, Moses looked on God's face and received from Him the Law, Jesus was born of a virgin. To each of these God had revealed His Divine Plan, but each time mankind had rejected His Prophets. Now, one last time, God had chosen the Seal of the Prophets and to him He had revealed His final message. The Quran is that revelation, and it was delivered by God through the medium of Muhammed while he was in an ecstatic trance. To Muslims the Quran is the living Word of God.

The *suras* that were given to the Prophet in Mecca dealt mainly with the establishment of the new religion, and the creation of a new vocabulary. They were delivered in a rhythmic, prophetic style of great poetic beauty. As he became immersed in the complicated affairs of organizing a state in Medina, the *suras* began to deal with intricate legal and ethical problems. They became longer and are marked by a looser, more flowing style. Most of the *suras* were preserved in memory by his companions until they were written down during the time of Uthman, the third Caliph. The Quran was the first book written in Arabic script, which was invented for the purpose, and it surpasses any other book ever written in Arabic in its poetic and flexible use of the language. To Muslims, the style itself makes evident the Quran's miraculous nature. The *suras* were arranged arbitrarily by length beginning with the longest and ending with the shortest, with no regard for chronological order.

The attitude of Muslims to the Quran raises for them a serious problem. If the Quran is God's word and contains all that is needed for the good life that will lead to salvation, the ultimate goal for all Muslims, then it follows that every word, every accent in it is sacred and cannot be changed. Islam prohibits the translation of the Quran. All Muslims must learn Arabic. It also follows that the Quran is open to elaborate interpretation, since it must be made to fit any human contingency. On the other hand, if all that is needed is in the Quran, then whatever is not there is not needed for the good life. As the centuries passed, this led to a conservatism and a resistance to change which has had serious consequences in Islam. Foreign ideas and foreign technology spread very slowly into the Muslim world.

The core of the religion of the Quran is a strict, uncompromising monotheism. "There is no God but God and Mohammed is the Apostle of God." Man must surrender himself to His sovereign will. Islam, in fact, in Arabic means "to surrender," i.e., to God's will. The Arabs already worshipped *al-ilah, t*he God. A shortened form of the word, Allah, now became the word for the one God, and Muhammed outdid himself in creating poetic terms to describe Him. There are ninety-nine "most beautiful names" of God in the Quran.

God is the eternal Creator of the universe, the terrible Punisher of all sinners, and the compassionate and merciful Forgiver of all those who repent. Muhammed rejected the Christian concept of the Trinity, which to him compromised God's unity. He forbade the use of images to portray God and even to portray men, since they were created in His image. He even objected to the Jewish use of the word rabbi (my lord or master), since it seemed to be a misuse of the word for God. This rigid monotheism had its roots in the Judeo-Christian tradition, but it is not at all certain that the connection was made consciously by the Prophet. It would appear that his monotheism stems from ancient Judeo-Christian influences that had centered on the figure of Abraham. Muhammed adopted many Christian and Jewish practices and he always considered them "the people of the Book," the people God had chosen to receive this message, but in the end he rejected both groups. He quarreled with the Jews of Medina because they refused to accept his prophecy. He rejected the Christian priesthood and monasticism, for he insisted that his religion was one of action in this world.

This is reflected in the second principle of Islam, the insistence on prayer as an act of devotion. The Quran does not specify the pattern to be followed by the devout in their prayers, but over the years it was established that there ought to be five prayers a day: daybreak, noon, midafternoon, sunset, early night. The prayer is a combination of recitations and prostrations in the direction of Mecca, and can take place anywhere, provided the worshipper is in a state of cleanliness and kneels on a clean rug. The hours of the prayers are announced in a haunting chant by a Muezzin, usually from the top of a minaret. The noon prayer on Friday every week is marked by the Quran as a special one, and all work is prohibited during it. It is customary for devout Muslims to recite this prayer in a mosque, which is merely a meeting house and not a church.

The third principle of Islam is the giving of alms. The Quran enjoins that every

Muslim must give free-will offerings to widows, orphans, and the like for the welfare of his soul. This offering was elaborated fairly early into an obligatory contribution to the brotherhood of Islam. Rates were set for this contribution later on, usually at one-fortieth of a man's income, though it was never considered an income tax. It was, rather, a loan to God which would be returned with great interest as He rewarded the protectors of the unfortunate.

The fourth principle of Islam is fasting. Every year throughout the ninth lunar month (Ramadan), all those who are not sick or on a journey must abstain from all food and drink from the moment in the morning when a black thread can be distinguished from a white thread by the naked eye until they can no longer be distinguished in the evening. The fast is considered an expiation for sinfulness.

The fifth major obligation is the pilgrimage, or *Hajj,* to Mecca. Once in his lifetime, if he is at all able, every Muslim ought to go to Mecca to visit the places associated with the life of the Prophet. The ceremonies include walking around the Ka'ba and kissing the black stone, running back and forth between two sacred hills, and gathering with other pilgrims at Mt. Arafat, twelve miles east of Mecca, to sacrifice sheep and camels. Once a pilgrim has performed all of these acts, he is in a special state of cleanliness. Ever after he is known as *al-Hajj,* the pilgrim, and he receives special honor from all Muslims.

These five obligatory acts of devotion are known as the "five pillars of Islam." In addition, Muhammed provided a theology which is quite as elaborate as that of the Judeo-Christian tradition. God is served with a host of angels, who worship Him, as men do, and hold up His Throne in Heaven.

They carry His messages to man, and in return record the acts of man, and will serve as witnesses at the Last Judgment. They often appear to Muslims in moments of crisis to assist them against non-believers. The Muslims especially venerate Gabriel, who communicated the Quran to Muhammed and announced the conception of Jesus to the Virgin Mary.

The heavens are peopled with devils as well as angels. These are called *jinn* and were created by God, not of dust as man was, but of fire. They are rebellious creatures who oppose Muhammed and try to lead man to evil. They teach him sorcery, which they learned, according to legend, from Solomon, to whom they were made subject. Their leader is the Devil, Shaytan, who fell from the ranks of the angels because he refused to worship Adam at God's command.

Helped by the angels, hindered by the *jinn,* man must still strive in the Way of God. The Quran commands: "Fight in the way of Allah against those who fight against you, but begin not hostilities. Lo! Allah loveth not aggressors" (*Sura* II, v. 190). This fight (*jihad*) is a way of life for the good Muslim, but it is also the Holy War that is so often discussed in the West. The Muslim must protect the Muslim community against Christians and Jews. The war need be carried only to the point where they accept Muslim control and pay a special tax. Against idolaters, however, the war must end in either death or conversion to Islam, a simple choice that did much to spread the religion. All those who die during the *jihad* are assured of a wonderful life in Paradise.

The Paradise of the Muslims has always seemed attractive to Westerners. It is described in sensuous terms as a place of cool, green pastures, well-watered by

▶ **Mosque, Cairo.** Part of the ritual of prayer is a series of prostrations while passages from the Quran are recited. Everyone has taken off his shoes, which must be done as one enters the mosque.

▶ **Topkapi Museum, Constantinople (Istanbul).** These are examples of Muslim artistry. They are mainly ornamental, but are of the finest Damascus steel. The bows, arrows, and quiver complete the classic weapons of a Muslim knight.

sparkling fountains and brooks. There, lying on silken cushions, the blessed and charitable men, who have feared God, will be served by the lovely *houris*, ever-young and lovely maidens, with all the delights that are denied them on earth. Eternal bliss is the reward for the righteous. But on that terrible day when the Trumpet will suddenly announce the Last Judgment and the heavens will burst and the mountains crumble to dust, when each man's soul is weighed in the Balance, those who do not merit Paradise will be plunged into a pit of eternal fire.

In addition to these major doctrines, the Quran lays down many rules for everyday living. Wine is forbidden, as is the flesh of swine. A good Muslim must not gamble nor deal in usury. The Quran allows four marriages, provided that all four wives are loved and served equally. Also each wife must be given a dowry. Divorce is allowed to the husband, who need do nothing more than repeat three times before a judge that he divorces his wife, and he is divorced. However, she takes her dowry with her. Rules for the care of orphans, the management of inheritances, the punishments for crime, and the regulation of social behavior are scattered all through the Quran, and form the basis later of the *Sharia*, Islamic law.

These then, in brief, are the major tenets of Islam. They are not particularly original, since they reflect the basic insights of many faiths, especially Christianity and Judaism, yet taken together their tone is original. Islam combines the strict monotheism with the universality of Christianity. Islam does not identify itself with Arab nationalism. It offers itself to men of all nations, of all races. Yet Islam is not a salvationist religion. Man faces God directly. There is no re-deeming intermediary between them. Each man is responsible directly for his acts to God, and to Him alone is he responsible for his faith. It is a stark and lonely religion in some aspects, but by placing such great responsibility on man, it has aroused him to great efforts and creativeness to prove his worth.

The Hadith

The Quran was the revelation of God's Will spoken by Muhammed while in trance, but the Prophet was an active leader who had much to say when he was not seized by religious fervor. All of these sayings were preserved reverently by his companions. The average Muslim saw and still sees in the life and actions of the Prophet an ideal model for each man to follow as best he can in his daily life. The customs that were laid down by the Prophet, in his acts and his words, the *sunna* as they were called, became very important for Muslims. The *sunni*, strictly taken, refer only to the customs laid down by the Prophet himself. This view is upheld by the Shîa groups. Sunnis, on the other hand, maintain that the Islamic community continued to create its traditions after the Prophet's death, by an elaboration of his specific injunctions.

The traditions of Muhammed were handed down in short narratives, each of which is called a *hadith*. Everyone connected with the Prophet obviously had many such tales to tell. In a short time hundreds, then thousands of them appeared. Obviously all could not be true. The true traditions were being contaminated by an extensive apocryphal literature. To guard against this, scholars began to gather the *hadith* into collections in which each story was prefaced by sources that established its connection with the Prophet himself or one of his companions. From this practice, there arose a science of *hadith criticism. This includes not only an emphasis on textual criticism, but also on biography, for the reliability of the transmitters of the hadith* had to be established.

Hadith criticism is not an idle pastime in Islam, for Islamic law and often religious canons depend on it. As a result, down through the centuries enormous collections of the traditions have been compiled following strict scientific techniques for arranging them as of sound, good, or weak authority. Unfortunately, many matters arise in society which are not dealt with either in the Quran or in the official collections of *hadith*. Yet the Muslim community will accept as law only what has a basis in the Quran or *hadith*, which together have become sacred scripture. The result is that new *hadiths* have been found as needed. They now number in the hundreds of thousands and the collection keeps growing. Of necessity, these later traditions are very weak or in some cases even false. This has led many legal experts, especially those trained in the West, to call for a rejection of the whole system. The Muslim community cannot do this, however, and must strive instead to regulate the rise and growth of the *hadith*. Each generation has applied its own criteria, and historians can trace the religious history of Islam in the pattern of these changing regulations.

The History of the Moslem State

When the Prophet died, no provision had been made for choosing a successor. It was already obvious that Muhammed had founded a theocratic state, not just a religion. His successor would have to be the head of an integrated society, Islam. The important members of the community entrusted it to Abû Bakr, one of the Prophet's earliest converts. It was he who had comforted the Prophet in his last illness, and who had been chosen to lead the prayers. Abû Bakr took the title *Khalife al-Nabi*, Representative of the Prophet, or Caliph. For two years he struggled to win back the allegiance of several Arab tribes who felt tied personally only to the Prophet, and who withdrew from the community on his death. On his deathbed, Abû Bakr appointed 'Umar ibn al-Khattab, another companion of the Prophet, as his successor. 'Umar ruled for ten years, and it was during his caliphate that the great Arab expansion began. 'Umar offered foreign expansion to the feuding Arab tribes as a means of uniting their energies, but the phenomenal success the Muslim armies achieved was due to circumstances outside their own efforts. The whole Middle East was exhausted by the wars between Byzantium and Persia. No effective fighting forces were left to withstand the Muslim attack. Also, the inhabitants of the area were for the most part Christian schismatics and heretics who suffered under the rule of the Orthodox emperor of Byzantium. They welcomed the Muslims as liberators, for Islam recognized no distinctions between Christian sects and allowed the majority within each Christian community to rule the whole upon payment of a tax. Thus the Christians opened the gates of Damascus to the Muslims in 636 and of Alexandria in 642. The Arabs took Chaldea and Assyria in 637, Iran in 641–42, and by 643 they were near India.

'Umar became the prototype of all subsequent caliphs. He was a strong warrior, devoted to the expansion of Islam. He was a devout follower of the Prophet, who applied the law of the Quran in the political and social life of the community. He was the Imam, who presides at prayer and who "walks at the head of the people."

One of his important acts from the viewpoint of later history was to appoint to the governorship of Syria Muâwiyah, son of Abû Sufyan, the scion of the Umayyad family that had come to capture the Prophet on the night of the *Hijra*. The old Arab aristocracy had been growing restive under the leadership of the Prophet and his close companions. They were ready to make a bid to capture control of the Arab empire that had emerged. But they bided their time. 'Umar had set up an electoral college to ensure a peaceful transition of power after his death, so that when in 644 Umar was stabbed by a Persian slave, six electors were appointed to choose his successor. After a hotly-contested election, they chose Uthmân, a very old man who had married one of the Prophet's daughters. His only claim to fame was his authorization of an official text of the Quran. After a reign of nepotism, corruption, and religious laxity, he was assassinated in 656 by a group of Muslims who gave the leadership to Alî, cousin and son-in-law of the Prophet, his favorite and most steadfast convert.

At this moment the Arab aristocracy chose to make their bid for power. Muâwiyah refused to acknowledge Alî. Raising the blood-drenched cloak of his cousin Uthmân in the mosque in Damascus, he declared himself Caliph. The two contenders met at the battle of Siffin in 655. Alî would have won, but Muâwiyah attached pages of the Quran to the heads of his soldiers' spears.

Ali had to refrain from attacking, and in the ensuing negotiations he was tricked into abdicating. In disgust, a group of his most loyal and pious followers withdrew and went to the distant provinces of Iraq and Persia. They were known as the Kharijites and became the first schismatic sect in Islam. They were fundamentalist in their approach to Islam, and fanatically insisted that a man's religious worth is only known by his works, and not by his faith. A Kharijite assassinated Alî in 661 as a punishment for his having negotiated for the holy caliphate. Muâwiyah remained as Caliph. He moved the capitol of the empire to Damascus, where his dynasty ruled until 750 as the Umayyads.

Alî had had two sons, Hasan and Husayn. Hasan was accepted as Caliph in Kufah, but he gave up all his claims in return for a generous pension. He retired to Medina, where he spent his time with his wives. He is said to have collected over a hundred of them. Later the younger son took up Alî's claims, and it was then that an Alid party developed to support his claims to his father's caliphate.

In the meantime the Arabs began a great expansion. At first the Caliphs found the Bedouin restive, and drew them into Islam by offering them raids on their neighbors. Ironically, both the Byzantine and the Persian empires were so exhausted by the many wars they had fought against each other that they could put up only token resistance. The battle of Yarmuk on August 20, 636 was decisive, and Byzantine troops pulled back into Anatolia. Damascus was lost in 636, and the coastal cities of Palestine fell one by one—Tyre, Beirut, Antioch, and finally Jerusalem in 638. Soon after Persia was taken in a series of brilliant battles, and Alexandria as we have noted opened its gates in 641. It is true that the Arab armies were well led and fought valiantly, but the decisive factor was the dissatisfaction of the subject peoples with both Persian and Byzantine rule. Many heretical Christian groups, particularly the Monophysites, had taken refuge in Persia, where they were badly treated. All Christian groups came to hate the Byzantine emperors, who tried to maintain an orthodox religious policy. The Muslims were welcomed as deliverers, because Islam recognized Christians and Jews as "people of the Book," and since all Christian communities were treated equally, wherever local Christians were in the majority they were allowed their own form of Christianity and encouraged to join with the Islamic community. The stereotypical idea that Islam spread because people were offered the choice of conversion or death is only true in certain cases. The fire-worshippers of Persia and the believers in the polytheistic gods of Hinduism were offered this choice, and the tension created in India still separates the two halves of India. But in fact the new community of Islam had too much to learn to take such a narrow attitude.

The Umayyads made early and profitable contacts with Byzantine culture and technology. In fact, they did everything they could to discourage Jews and Christians from converting to Islam. Their communities not only did not have to convert, but they were taxed less than Muslims as an inducement. Naturally, with their higher levels of culture, they were feared by the Umayyads as potential rivals should they convert.

The Umayyads had to face a serious consequence of their very success. As Islam spread more and more widely among non-Arab peoples, the Arabs themselves became a smaller and smaller minority within their own empire. The revolt of Alî's second son

Husayn was to a large extent fueled by this development. It is also important to point out that Islam is marked by an inability to distinguish between political and religious opposition to the caliph. Since the caliph is both the head of the new religion and the state that resulted, it is almost impossible to distinguish between the two roles. Any political opposition to the caliph as political leader can be and is always expressed in opposition to him as religious leader, and the reverse is true. So Islam came to be racked with interminable civil wars.

This tendency still goes on today. It began with Husayn, who was supported in his revolt by the Alid party, which attracted non-Arabic Muslims, lacking a means of expressing their opposition to the Arab leadership. They developed two positions in Islam, the *sunni*, who accept the Umayyads and the *hadith* as a continuing source of authority, and the *shîat-alî* (or Shîa) who accept only Alî as the true successor of Muhammed. They also reject the *hadith* as authoritative. The split became permanent after Husayn was killed at the battle of Kerbala in October, 680. The Shîa took the attitude that Husayn had been the last true Caliph, and that his young son who escaped the massacre that followed was a mystic imam as were all his descendants. The imam is the true head of the Islamic community. It is often said that the split is similar to the one between the medieval Roman Church and the Protestant churches that resulted from the decline. In a superficial sense the comparison is valid. In both cases the basic beliefs of the two religions are two religions are preserved and in both cases the two opposition groups have split into many sub-groups. There are hundreds of minor Protestant churches today, just as there are many Shiite groups.

The Shiite groups are very political in nature, but they have extended the role of the imam to a point where the basic position of the Prophet is in question. The Shiite say that the imam was the basic source of orthodoxy in Islam. Some came to believe that he appeared in every generation, sometimes known and at other times unknown. Others believed the first imam was before Muhammed. Still others felt he was more important than Muhammed, who may have been a false prophet. Another group believes the imam is preparing the way for the *Mahdî* (the "guided one") who at the time of the second coming and the day of judgment will restore truth and righteousness to the world.

An important offshoot of the Shîa is the Isma'iliya. To them there is a mystic who has power second only to God. In fact, the Aga Khan who headed the group in recent times was considered a god by his followers. The group has always been very secret. In the time of the Crusades they were called the Assassins, because they took hashish to be able to carry out their mission, which was to kill anyone the imam wanted killed. In Lebanon they were called the Druzes. They believe that an imam who died in 1021, Darazi, is still alive and is the ultimate connection between God and man.

So the Shîa groups have developed many variations within the framework of Islam. Originally they were led by their opposition to the Umayyads. Truth to tell, they had developed close ties with Byzantine technology. They learned to build ships and eventually attacked Constantinople on many occasions. They also began to carry goods across the Mediterranean. They began to absorb Greco-Roman philosophy and literature; though not particularly creative, they did establish universities in their lands to teach the new culture in Arabic translations. Certainly they became good administrators. Their adoption of foreign ways led many new converts to think of them as not orthodox Muslims, and that fueled the Shîa group. But it also led to expansion. They reached and penetrated India, establishing governorships in the Punjab (713). Goods from all these areas began to enrich the Umayyads and a whole class of merchants and manufacturers.

The move westward was even more momentous. Carthage fell in 698. The Berbers fell, and in 711 a Berber convert, Tarik, crossed at Gibraltar (*Gib al Tarik*, or Rock of Tarik), and began the conquest of Spain. As so often happened, the attacks in Spain were not planned, but the results were momentous. The Visigothic kingdom collapsed and in a short time all Christians retreated to the northwest corner of the peninsula, while tentative thrusts across the Pyrenees were met eventually by Charles Martel at the Battle of Tours-Poitiers (732). Several Muslim states evolved in Spain, and several Christian states as well. The ensuing history of Spain is most complicated as Muslim states allied with Christians against fellow Muslims, while Christians allied with Muslims against fellow Christians. The wars went on while a Hispano-Muslim culture developed that transferred when needed Greco-Roman culture absorbed by the Umayyads. In the meantime, the Spaniards were excused from the Crusading movement since they were already involved in the perpetual Crusades against the Muslim.

The Umayyads brought a new sophistication to the Arab tribes, it is true. They brought a new architecture, new sciences, new concepts of government, but as we have seen this was done at a high cost. In opposition to the Umayyads in 747 the black banner of the Prophet was raised the name of al-Abbâs, great-great-great grandson of Abbâs, uncle of Muhammed. He attracted all those who opposed the ruling family, especially the Shîa groups and non-Arab Muslims who had come to resent Arab rule. The revolt was settled in one battle (Zab, January, 750). Abbâs entered Damascus and proceeded to kill every member of the Umayyad family. One escaped, Abd ar Rahmân, who crossed the north African deserts and was eventually recognized by the troops in Spain. He established the emirate of Cordova and his descendants became the Caliphs of the West.

The expansion of the Muslim world westward led the Belgian medievalist Henri Pirenne to state a theory that has been very influential, though now it has become controversial. He theorized that the Mediterranean world was culturally a basic unity, held together by trade and a common culture. He put forward the thesis that the Muslim expansion put an end to this unity. When Muslim shipping broke this unity and the Muslims introduced an eastern culture into the midst of the Mediterranean, the Western world fell back on basically Germanic elements within the Roman world, and Byzantium developed Greek elements of the Roman world. The result was the Germanic empire of Charlemagne, cut off from the Roman empire of the East, while in the East there emerged a Greek-speaking Byzantine empire along different lines. The thesis has stylistic symmetry that has made it attractive to this day, but many others have found that modifying adjustments must be made.

In any case, with the building of a new capital in the new city of Baghdad, where the Abbâsids ruled from 750 to 1258 A.D., Islam began to move away from the Medi-

terranean world. Under the Abbâsids the Muslim Empire reached its greatest heights. The democratic rule of the Companions of Muhammed and the Arab despotic rule of the Umayyads were now replaced by a theocratic despotism. The caliph ruled as Commander of the Faithful over all Muslims. Regardless of their race, all Muslims could enter his service and according to merit could rise in his administration to become chief ministers. The Empire shifted its focus from the Hellenic Syrian provinces to the oriental Iraqi and Persian ones. Muslim culture was now infused with Indian and Persian elements. Luxury such as it had never known became a commonplace as the riches of the East poured into the new capitol. The result was the rapid corruption of the reigning house. After a century of vigorous rule, the Abbâsid caliphs became puppets of their palace guards and chief ministers.

With a vacuum of power at its center, the Empire began to fall apart. Spain, the provinces of north Africa, Egypt, all set themselves up as independent states. Then nomadic peoples swept out of Asia and posed a new problem to the Muslim world. Islam had begun within an urban setting. This had been consolidated in the Umayyad dynasty, which had thereby lost its influence with the nomadic elements of the Muslim world. Now it had to adjust to a world in which tribalism predominated. The Berbers of Africa and the Turkish tribes of Asia took over the Abbâsid world.

In Spain Abd ar Rahmân had established an Umayyad state at Cordova. His descendants developed an empire in Spain that rivaled the Abbâsid capital at Baghdad in splendor, but like the Abbâsids themselves, luxury soon corrupted the Umayyads. They developed royal guards (the Islamic guard) which soon came to dominate the caliph. Usurpers took over Tangier and other parts of north Africa. The last Umayyad was deposed in 1031 and Spain broke up into several competing states.

In Egypt a new dynasty, the Fâtimids, bought its way to power. They defeated the various groups across north Africa, then they entered Egypt and from a new capital city, Cairo, they began in 973 to rival the Abbâsids in power. Their fleets controlled all shipping in the Mediterranean Sea. They invaded Arabia, took Mecca, Medina, and even Damascus. At the height of their power their empire stretched from Morocco to Mosel. The Fâtimids were of the Isma'iliya sect of the Shîa. As we have seen, they believed that after the Prophet there would appear a series of imams that would end with the coming of a *Mahdî*, who would be hidden until the Day of Judgment. A curious extension of the Isma'iliya was preached by Fâtimid Caliph al-Hakim (996–1021). He declared he was God and began a tyranny that was insane. He survived twenty years before he was assassinated, but as we saw above, the Druzes of Lebanon worship him to this day.

Islam has become a major force in history. Today it is still a most vital religion, and is returning to its old ways and traditions. Led by the Shîa a resurgence of Islam in the world can be seen everywhere. One can only wonder if the Muslims have learned how to solve the historic problems which led to its decline in the first place.

IX

THE WEST AWAKENS
▼ ▼ ▼ ▼ ▼

▶ **The House of the Snail, Venice.** The rich home of a Venetian aristocrat. Venice accumulated huge treasures from its trade with the East. The house has a double circular staircase, hence its name.

▶ **Church of St. Francis, Assisi.** There were some who were repelled by the resurgence of town life, and St. Francis was one. He rejected wealth, but in time the movement he began became very successful. The saint is buried in this church in his hometown.

▶ **The Campo Santo, Pisa.** Pisa was an early trader with the East. The complex includes the Baptistry, the Cathedral, and the Bell Tower. The dome is elliptical in shape and probably was built by Syrian workers. The Bell Tower began to sink while it was being constructed.

Civilization in the West had barely survived the collapse of the Roman world. Men expended all their energies in social and economic groupings that made subsistence possible, but which left no room for growth. Political institutions kept alive the ideal of government rather than its reality. Men seemed to have lost the skill of organizing themselves in ways of sufficient sophistication to provide the ingredients for a life of opportunity and security. Suddenly around the year 1000 all began to change. Political, religious and economic revivals took place that transformed the whole life of medieval Europe and laid the groundwork for one of the most productive and inventive eras in human history.

Political Stirrings in France

During the 10th Century France had fallen into a state of anarchy. Late Carolingians tried desperately to dominate the affairs of the whole kingdom in the face of a rising feudalism that had already made government on such a scale impossible. Finally the magnates of the realm gathered at Senlis to discuss the succession to the last Carolingian, Louis V, who had died without heirs. They decided that the monarchy was elective and chose one of themselves, Hugh Capet, as a gesture of feudal independence. Thus Hugh, a strong noble, became a weak king. During his reign (987–996) he was barely able to keep the throne, let alone maintain any authority over his subjects. His successors Robert II (996–1031) and Henry I (1031–60) demonstrated clearly the inherent weakness in the position of the king. Both wasted their energies in attempting to control all of the kingdom instead of

concentrating on building up power in a restricted area close at home, as the other magnates of the realm were doing. Robert at one time actually conquered Burgundy, only to have to give it up again. They had to enter the turmoil of French affairs on a par with their leading vassals, almost all of whom were more powerful than they. They did keep alive, however, the concept of a French monarchy and by the good fortune of having sons as heirs in every generation, the Capetian kings kept alive their dynasty until they become a custom of the French people. Philip I (1060–1108) was a particularly weak king, which in a way was his good fortune, for he was forced to restrict his activities to his own domains. He consolidated the lands between Paris and Orleans and began to build some real authority there.

Power in France lay with the great vassals of the king. Some of these, like the Dukes of Aquitaine, Brittany, or Burgundy, were faced with lands that were too large and filled with vassals too powerful to be controlled by one man. On the other hand, in Flanders and Normandy techniques were developed by the dukes that made it possible for them to extend their control over the whole duchy. They both dotted their lands with fortified castles in which they placed the Flemish castellan or the Norman viscount. These servants of the duke were able to dominate the surroundings lands, establish courts, enforce feudal obligations, and restrict private warfare. These dukes raised large amounts of cash from tolls and taxes on merchants which allowed them to hire mercenaries. Military service was carefully assigned according to the actual strength of a fief and all the vassals owed liege loyalty to the duke. The Duke of Normandy, furthermore, had complete control over the bishops and abbots of the duchy, and he could always count on their help in an emergency. All in all, these dukes had discovered the method of marshalling their resources by delegating carefully-controlled authority. This type of government began to spread all across France and from there to distant places as well.

The Normans in Sicily

In 1000 southern Italy was a battleground for Muslim, Byzantine, and Lombard princes who were strong enough to keep each other in check, but too weak to win through to some settlement. In 1016 a band of Normans stopped off at Salerno on their way to a pilgrimage. Hired as mercenaries by local lords, they saw the opportunities for profit in the petty wars. Word spread among the Normans in the north, and soon a steady stream of adventurers started to come into southern Italy. In 1036 or so the two sons of Tancred of Hauteville, William of the Iron Arm and Drogo, appeared. They quickly established themselves as leaders of the Normans and carved out a state in Apulia. Two more brothers arrived to join the family, Robert Guiscard and Roger. Robert was nothing more than a robber baron, but he quickly took over his brothers' state in Apulia. In 1053 Pope Leo IX attempted to subdue the Norman chieftains, only to be taken captive in battle. Robert came to terms with Pope Nicholas II, who recognized his authority by investing him with the Duchies of Calabria, Apulia, and Sicily. Roger invaded Sicily in 1060 to force out the Muslims, while Robert laid siege to the Byzantine cities on the mainland, Riggio, Taranto, Brindisi, and finally Bari,

which fell in 1071. He then crossed over to the Greek mainland, where he captured Adriatic cities and threatened to march across the peninsula to the capital itself. Greek diplomacy and Venetian control of the Straits of Otranto forced Robert to return to Italy, where he became involved in the fight Pope Gregory VII was conducting with Henry IV. The reduction of Sicily was stepped up, and victory was in sight when Robert died in 1085. The last Muslim outposts on the island fell in 1091.

Roger I (1061–1101) was succeeded by his son, Roger II, who was able to unite the possessions of Guiscard in Italy to his own in 1127. In 1130 he was recognized by Pope Innocent II as King of the united Kingdom of the Two Sicilies. The main power of the new King rested on his naval force which made it possible for him to dominate the coast of north Africa as well as the mouth of the Adriatic Sea. His administration was the most advanced of any court in Europe in its day, making Roger one of the most powerful monarchs in the world. The Normans inherited a highly centralized bureaucracy from their Muslim and Byzantine forerunners in Sicily. To this they added their own institutions, particularly the use of itinerant justices that carried the king's justice to all parts of the realm. Soon the king's justices were handling all criminal cases in courts where professional lawyers and justices used the Roman law. The king was papal legate, which meant that all ecclesiastical cases came into his court as well. The king made use of officials of all nationalities and religions, and his records were kept in Latin, Greek and Arabic. The efficiency of his government made possible a great economic revival of all the seaports of southern Italy and Sicily, and fabulous wealth began to accumulate in the Norman capital, Palermo.

England

The Normans brought with them a canny knack for good government and a genius for frugal economic management to every place they settled. The invasion of England and the rapid establishment of a strong central government there is as much a tribute to Norman genius as to the effectiveness of feudal institution.

Anglo-Saxon Britain in the 9th Century was divided into seven small kingdoms that carried on fitful war with each other. In 866 the Danes invaded York and piecemeal they began to take over the country. The petty kingdoms were united by Alfred the Great, King of Wessex (871–899), who stopped the Danish advance. England was divided into two parts, the Danelaw and the rest of England, including Kent, Wessex, Sussex and Mercia, which went to Alfred. The young King built many castles and maintained a navy to protect his kingdom. He introduced a series of courts throughout his lands, and he encouraged the opening of schools.

The successors of Alfred (899–975) continued his work. The kings used their officials, the ealdormen, to control local affairs. Royal courts were strengthened. Commerce flourished. The Danes and the Saxons were merged into one people, and peace was generally maintained. However, the promise of this period was not fulfilled. Between 975 and 1016, the year in which Ethelred the Unready died, royal power passed to the great noblemen. The Danes renewed their invasions, this time as the carefully-planned expansion of a strong kingdom, Ethelred collected a general tax, the Danegeld, sought allies on the Continent, but the King's own noblemen failed to support him

and he was defeated by Sweyn, who was elected King by the English council in 1013. His son Canute (1017–35) fought his way to the throne, and eventually united England, Denmark, Norway and Sweden into a vast North Sea empire. His reign was a time of great prosperity for England. Trade with the northern regions flourished. The kingdom was divided into four great earldoms, under which English law and customs were respected and strengthened.

After his death his sons began a disastrous civil war which undid most of Canute's work. Finally the English council, led by Earl Godwin, invited a descendent of Alfred the Great who had been raised in Normandy to return to England as King. Edward the Confessor (1042–66) brought with him a whole staff of Norman officials and advisors to whom he gave important posts in the kingdom. The strongest man in the realm was Godwin. A quarrel broke out between him and the King in 1051. Godwin was expelled, and Edward sought an alliance with William, Duke of Normandy. It probably was at this time that he promised William succession to the English throne. Godwin took over the kingdom, dominating King and country until his death in 1053. His son, Harold Godwinson, kept the power until the death of Edward in January, 1066. William claimed the throne on the grounds that he was distantly related to Edward, that the childless Edward had promised him the throne, and that Harold had confirmed the promise in 1064. The council, however, rejected the claims and crowned Harold, which was their legal right. William, however, was determined to invade to secure his rights.

Harold had angered his brother Tostig, who called on Harold Hardraga of Norway to invade England as his ally. The two landed in the north, but Harold met them at Stamford Bridge, defeated and killed them. At this juncture William landed an army, on September 28, 1066, at Pevensey in the south, and started marching north. Harold rushed down to meet them. On October 14 the two armies met near Hastings. Harold's men were tired, Harold too eager. Tricked by a feigned retreat, they rushed from their defensive positions and were decisively defeated. Harold was killed in the battle, and William was conqueror of England.

Pre-Conquest English Government

When William arrived in England, he found a set of institutions that were almost purely Angle-Saxon, Roman culture having largely disappeared after the first Germanic invasions. The society was structured on the clan. Every man belonged to and was under the discipline of a clan, and the clan was held accountable for his conduct. Slowly the clans broke down as they spread more widely over England, and men early sought more personal ties. The land, which was originally all folk land, that is held directly from the king under the customary laws of the folk, now came to be held as "bookland" from some lord, to whom the holder had commended himself. The lord was held accountable for his dependent's behavior. Men without lords were organized into tithing groups that were responsible for their members.

The vil was the basic political unit. A simple farm complex, it provided a market court in which farm problems were settled. More important was the hundred, apparently in origin a grouping of a hundred families and their land. Its court met monthly and was composed of four local representatives, a reeve, and a priest from each vil. Above this court was the shire court. This, too, was composed of four local representatives, a reeve, and a priest from each vil. An alderman (earl), a bishop, and the shire-reeve (sheriff) presided. The earl was originally an elected official, but he rapidly became an important magnate, extending his authority over several shires. He was the chief military leader, and his office became a hereditary one. The king's representative in the shire was the sheriff, who was a royal appointee. As the earl extended his power, the sheriff came into charge of the judicial and military administration of the shire. Charges could be brought in the shire-court, though it also acted as an appellate court from the hundreds court.

These local institutions were overlaid by a centralized authority that focused on the king, who was chosen by the councilors sitting in the *Witan*. He was selected from the royal family and the anointment of his coronation made him almost a priest-king, responsible for the welfare of the church as well as of his people. He appointed bishops at will and used his courts to enforce Church regulations. He was also the leader of the military forces of the realm. These consisted of the *fyrd*, the army of all the free farmers of the folk, who owed service to the crown; a private guard of house-earls, paid mercenaries of the king; and the troops sent up by *thegns*, the members of the king's *comitatus*. Of course, the king appointed the sheriffs, but this was his only control over local government, though the concept of the king's peace, which protected the king's highways and the area around his person, introduced some measure of safety throughout the kingdom, while at the same time it provided a sizable income in fines to the crown.

The king's council was the *Witangemot,* the council of the chief nobles and bishops of the kingdom. They elected and on occasion deposed the king. They advised the king and approved all his laws and treaties. They levied such taxes as existed, though the king lived on the income from his own estates, fines, customs duties from royal ports, tolls on the king's highways, inheritance taxes on the nobles, and the fees collected in his mints.

Superficially, the government seemed to have some degree of centralization, but the king had no really effective control over the earls. When Edward the Confessor came to the throne, he brought with him from the Continent a host of Norman officials and friends. His English subjects, offended, tended to transfer their loyalty from the king to the earls, who steadily increased their power over the shires. Free villages tended to disappear, and private armies and courts became characteristic of the whole country. This tendency explains the rise to power of Godwin and his sons, but it also explains why Harold was faced by strong opposition from rival earls.

The Invasion

William claimed the throne of England as his rightful inheritance and invaded with papal blessings. He had gathered together an army of some seven thousand men who had joined his cause not only from among his own vassals, but from all over France, eager for profit and advancement. The Battle of Hastings did not win the whole realm, but after his coronation in London on Christmas Day, 1066, he was able to put down isolated revolts all over the land. To accomplish this, on Salisbury Plain he exacted an oath of liege loyalty from every vassal in the realm, theoretically eliminating private armies and warfare. He joined to his feudal army the Anglo-Saxon *fyrd,* which he retained to give him a loyal militia. William preserved the Anglo-Saxon government he found, especially the prerogatives of the king and the use of the sheriffs in local courts. He added to this the customary feudal controls of the Norman dukes. Not only did he have strong personal authority over his vassals, but when he distributed the conquered land, he gave it out in scattered small parcels, carefully designated and tied to specific obligations. His right to take back the fief kept the nobles in line, while at the same time no noble could assemble extensive enough a holding to support any serious revolt.

The local courts were preserved, but the sheriff became identical with the Norman viscount. Side by side with the shire courts, there arose feudal courts given out as fiefs to noblemen. In general, there was a rapid extension of feudal relationships as the king and all his nobility settled their armed retainers on the land as vassals. The *Witan* was also feudalized and was converted into the *curia regis* in which nobles and bishops sat because they held fiefs from the king. By demanding attendance in his court, the king was now able to keep close watch over his stronger vassals. At the same time, from among members of the *curia* he selected certain experts who formed a smaller *curia* in constant attendance around him. Thus he had an effective instrument that was most effective in dealing with feudal nobles, who tended to shy away from the tedious details of government.

William was very aware of the need of a steady income. He had confiscated huge estates from the Saxon nobles that had fought with Harold, and he exacted large reliefs from those that had submitted. He received a substantial income from his own manors as well as all the customary levies and fines of the English king. For instance, he collected Danegeld three times. More important, he ordered the famous Domesday Inquest of 1086. Commissioners were sent to every shire in the kingdom to find out what every manor in England had owed to Edward, and what it was now worth. The survey gave the king an exact picture of his rights, how much revenue he could expect, and how much more each manor could give if necessary. The survey is on unique importance to modern historians for the picture it gives of 11th Century England.

William was careful to reform and strengthen the English Church, which had tended to lose its distinct personality as its bishops sat in the local civil courts to hear ecclesiastical as well as secular cases. Also, bishops were indistinguishable from secular lords in education and loyalties. William replaced the native clergy with Normans, starting with Lanfranc, whom he appointed as Archbishop of Canterbury. William owed much to the Pope, and he was willing to show his gratitude. Ecclesiastical courts were established to handle all clerical affairs. Bishops were given rich residencies in principal towns, and the ancient English custom of clerical celibacy was enforced. On the other hand, William retained firm control over the English Church. He oversaw the election of all bishops and invested them himself. He insisted that all church lands were liable to military service. He also reserved the right to approve and enforce the promulgations of the councils and episcopal courts. He was willing, in other words, to reform the Church so that it could become an effective arms of his royal power.

The Norman Kings

When William died in 1087, he left Normandy to his oldest son, Robert, and England to his second son, William II Rufus (1087–1100). It was immediately apparent that much of the Conqueror's power had rested on his personality. Revolts broke out against the King all over England, in favor of his brother, the weak Duke of Normandy. Even after Robert went off on the First Crusade, leaving his duchy in his brother's hands, the nobles still resisted William's attempts to exact heavy reliefs from them. He also fell out with his Archbishop of Canterbury, Anselm, a member of the reform party so widespread throughout the Church at that time. When in mysterious circumstances he was shot by an arrow in the back in August, 1100, no one was particularly grieved. His younger brother Henry I (1100–35) seized the royal treasury at Winchester, and within three days was crowned King by the curia. He immediately fell into a dispute with Anselm, who maintained strenuously the right of the Church and its bishops to be free of secular control. Henry insisted on the right to select and invest his bishops. A compromise was worked out in 1105, whereby Henry selected the bishops and invested them with their temporal powers, their spiritual powers then to be granted by the Archbishop of Canterbury, subject to papal approval.

Henry was distracted by attempts by his brother and nephew to lead rebellions against him, but he was able to concentrate on strengthening the royal power. He married Matilde, a Saxon princess of Scotland, and he worked hard to merge the Normans and Saxons into one English people. The *curia* began to break up into specialized groups and agencies. The exchequer was the room to which royal revenues were brought to be counted and recorded by members of the *curia*, who also began to hear cases involving the financial rights of the crown. The exchequer became a special court in which specialists in finance from within the *curia* heard all disputes with the crown in financial matters. Henry also began to use more effectively the itinerant justices, imported to England by the Conqueror. These justices travelled into the shires to set up courts to relieve the pressure in the crowded shire courts, but they soon became royal administrative officials.

Henry's only son, William, was drowned in the sinking of the *White Ship* in 1120, so that his only heir was his daughter Mathilda, who had first married Henry V, Emperor of Germany, and then Geoffrey, Count of Anjou. In 1135 when Henry died she claimed the throne, but it was seized by her cousin, Stephen of Blois (1135–54), who was popular in England and preferred to his cousin. Civil war broke out and for the rest of the reign the great nobles of the realm built up private armies and castles, taking advantage of the weakness of the King. By 1150 Mathilda was tired of the war and turned over her claim to Norman lands in France and to the crown of England to her son, Henry Plantagenet. Henry took possession of Normandy in 1150. His father died in 1151, leaving him Anjou and Touraine, and in 1152 he married Eleanor of Aquitaine and took over southwestern France. When Stephen died, Henry was universally acclaimed King and was crowned on December 19, 1154.

The Angevin Kings

Henry II (1154–89) came to the throne at the age of twenty-one to become perhaps the greatest king in English history. His responsibilities were mainly on the Continent, and he spent only about a third of his reign in England, but his work there was to be of decisive significance. Short, fat, barrel-chested, red-haired, Henry was a thorough Frenchman. He always considered England peripheral to his empire; but like his canny Norman ancestors, he had a sharp eye for finances. He had great need for the revenues from his English lands and he concentrated on creating there an efficient administrative system that would maintain order and the flow of money to France.

During the civil wars of Stephen's reign, the country had become tired of anarchy, and the people enthusiastically supported Henry in his first task, the restoration of order. Private castles were captured, mercenary bands expelled, and the central government re-established. The exchequer, the sheriffs, and the itinerant justices began to function again. A crucial development in English common law was the extended use of the inquest and jury. Henry ruled that any man involved in a civil suit over a piece of property or the title to a feudal holding could upon the payment of a small sum call an inquest in a royal court. Large numbers of people were eager to use an alternative to trial by combat, as was the practice in feudal courts. The inquest was conducted by judges, who took testimony from a jury, usually of twelve men, who answered questions about the piece of property. The extension of the use of the inquest weakened not only baronial courts in general, but also the control of nobles over their lesser vassals, who could find favor in the king's court. By the Assize of Clarendon (1166) the jury was extended to criminal procedures. The itinerant justices were given specific circuits and they and the sheriffs were ordered to call twelve men from every hundred and four from every vil to give testimony under oath about any crimes of robbery or murder that had been committed. The accused were put to the ordeal of water ("ducking"), and mutilated or hanged if they failed the ordeal. At a stroke all criminal cases were transferred to the royal courts, and the nobles were further weakened. It is interesting to note that Henry used this grand jury to seek out infringements on his prerogatives, or any misconduct in the administration of his affairs, a function the grand jury has retained to this day.

Henry devised many new courts to handle the great increase in cases the crown had to hear. Any shire court, for one thing, could be turned into a king's court whenever three king's justices presided. The Court of Common Pleas was established in 1178 to hear all civil cases in which the crown was not involved. All cases involving the crown went into the special section of the *curia* that eventually grew into the King's Bench. To transfer cases from feudal courts to the royal courts, the king provided a series of writs. The king's secretary, the chancellor, was empowered to issue orders on behalf of the *curia* that transferred the case.

Henry's reforms inevitably brought him into conflict with the Church. During Stephen's reign bishops had risen to great power. They insisted that all cases involving sacraments had to come into their courts. Now they claimed the exclusive right to try all cases in which clerics or Church property were involved. Finally they made the demand that all cases involving the giving of an oath, in other words all questions of contract, had to come before them. Since the Church did, in fact, give a better brand of justice than the King, and since the King's claim to jurisdiction over all his subjects would collapse if all categories of defendants included in the term "cleric" were to escape his justice, the King understandably was disturbed. He demanded that clerical privilege be withdrawn, and this brought him up against his stubborn Archbishop of Canterbury, Thomas á Becket.

Thomas was the son of a wealthy Norman merchant of London, educated at Canterbury and at Bologna in canon law. When Henry became King, Thomas had already proven himself an able administrator and loyal to the crown. Henry called him into his service and appointed him his Chancellor. The two became inseparable friends and Thomas, richly rewarded for his faithful service, became the leading lord of the realm. At his first opportunity, Henry appointed his friend Archbishop of Canterbury, with the firm expectation that in the continued understanding of their relationship, Thomas would make the Church the firm right arm of the state and would use all of his resources to help build Henry's government. But Thomas, apparently awed by his call to so high and holy an office, had converted to a sincere asceticism and vigorously undertook to carry forward the general reform movement that was sweeping through the Church.

The quarrel broke out in 1164 when the King demanded that "criminous clerics," that is, clerics charged with grave crimes, be judged by their bishops, but then turned over to the secular authorities for punishment. Thomas refused to agree. The King, in a rage, bullied other bishops to his support and Thomas was persuaded to swear to uphold the "customs of the realm." Then a council called at Clarendon (1164) drew up these customs as the Constitutions of Clarendon, which cut the Church of England off from Rome, stripped it of its independent powers, and placed it directly under the authority of the King. Thomas refused to accept them, and finally had to flee to the Continent to escape the King's wrath. Unable to raise effective support, he returned to England, bitter and angry, though nominally still the King's friend. Once back in Canterbury, he excommunicated all the bishops who had supported the King against him and he seized all the lands that had been taken from his See during his absence. Henry heard of the defiance while campaigning in France. He exploded in another of his rages and unthinkingly called out to be rid of this "false priest." His four closest companions set out for England and murdered Thomas at the altar of his own cathedral. England, all Europe, the King himself, were horrified at the sacrilegious murder. Henry did public penance and gave up his attempt to dominate the Church in England. The experience had so profoundly shaken the conscience of the realm that no further attempt was made to bring the Church under the power of the state until the Reformation.

The immediate result of the murder was a great rebellion. The nobles had been growing increasingly resentful of the growth of central government, particularly when Henry began to convert feudal obligations into money payments (scutage). With the moneys that his vassals paid him, he hired mercenaries who gave him a dependable military force at all times. This was so threatening to the privileges of the nobility that they took advantage of the general indignation at the murder of Becket to launch a general rebellion. The King put it down swiftly and effectively, but 1173 proved to be the year his policies began to go wrong.

Henry's reign was marked by wars from the very beginning. His first act abroad as King was to absorb Brittany, which he assigned to his son Geoffrey. Aquitaine and the south of France were given to his son Richard. Henry, the oldest, was given the title of King of England, while John, the youngest of Henry's four sons, was given nothing, for he was too young at the time of the partitioning of the empire in 1170. Henry loved his sons, but he did not trust them, and he did not allow them to take over the administration of their lands on their own. In 1173 Henry tried to establish a portion for John. The young Henry fled to Paris and was joined by Geoffrey and Richard. To wrest power from their father, a war was launched that was to keep the whole empire in turmoil for a decade. Truces were made and broken. The sons struck furiously at their father and at each other, until young Henry and Geoffrey died, leaving the King and John, his favorite, to face Richard. Harrowed by the coalition of his wife Eleanor, Richard, and Philip, King of France, Henry did everything he could to keep the loyalty of John, but in vain. When Philip and Richard finally defeated him, and he was shown the list of his barons who had deserted to the enemy, the first name on the list was that of John. Henry never recovered from the shock, and died two days later on July 6, 1189.

Henry had created a solid government. It would be soon put to the test by the neglect of his son Richard, the bad character of his son John, and the poor judgment of his grandson Henry.

Richard *Coeur de Lion* (1189–99) was the great hero of the medieval world. His exploits on the Third Crusade had won him lasting fame, which he surely merited as a great warrior and general, but as King of England he was a near disaster. He saw England only as a source of revenue for his activities in southern France and his great Crusade, and he went there only to raise moneys at the time of his coronation, and after his return from the Crusade to raise more moneys for his ransom. The kingdom was left in the hands of William Longchamps, Bishop of Ely, whose heavy-handed regency soon caused the nobles to raise a revolt that focused on John, who was named regent in 1191.

The only important measures taken while Richard was away were in the area of raising revenues, which never seemed enough to satisfy the adventuring King. The Saladin Tithe, a general tax on all movable goods, had been introduced by Henry II in 1188. This idea of a uniform tax collected throughout the country was extended to raise money for the Third Crusade, Richard's ransom, and his French wars. Perhaps nothing shows more clearly the results of the work of Henry II than the fact that the realm was consolidated enough to accept this advanced concept of a sovereign state. Apart from the introduction of coroners to protect pleas of the crown from the jurisdiction of the shire courts, tax reform was the only advance made by the regency, and there was little time left. When Richard returned from his Crusade, he found that mismanagement and neglect had prevented any effective defensive against inroads into his lands in Normandy by the King of France. He hastily raised a new army, and spent his last days in a dreary war in north-central France. He was killed in a private war with the Viscount of Limoges over some treasure the Viscount had found and which Richard claimed. His death seems as pointless as most of his exploits. Immediately on receiving news of his death, John seized the throne. By the end of his reign the work of his father had been strongly undermined. England had been cut off from its Continental interests, and the English Constitution had taken definite shape.

The Capetians Establish a Monarchy

Philip I had barely been able to maintain himself in the midst of his great vassals, but when he wearily turned the government over to his son Louis in 1100, he did point out the one direction in which a French monarchy could grow. Louis VI, who became King in his own right in 1108 and ruled until 1137. He gave up any attempt to rule all France in order to concentrate on his own domain lands and the immediate problem of strengthening and extending them. Throughout his reign he fought tenaciously to pacify and consolidate the *Ile de France*. Within his domains it was clear that any appeal to the King for help against any unlawful seizure, whether of monastic or secular estates, would be met with swift action by the King. He brought the level of law and justice in his lands to the level that had become customary in the other duchies of France. Grateful for this, the Church offered him important assistance in his task. Suger, Abbot of St. Denis (1081–1151), was his chief adviser. The most capable administrator of his day, Suger reformed the royal Abbey of St. Denis, rebuilt its church in the new

A town house, Blois. The towns of France accumulated great wealth, as can be seen here. Close by was the great castle that offered protection, but also involvement in feudal wars.

Clock tower on guild hall, Munich. Towns were self-governed. Each guild was represented in the town council, which made its own laws. There was a saying, "Cities make free men" (*"Stadluft macht frei"*).

Gothic style of architecture, wrote an account of his work as Abbot, and created the policies of both Louis and his son after him.

Louis used clerics as his administrators. He helped spread the ideals of the Cluniac reform movement, and he was a firm opponent of lay investiture. However, he never gave up the traditional power of the French king to appoint his own bishops. He was not particularly clever in foreign affairs, but he held his own against the Norman kings of England, as well as powerful neighbors like the Count of Flanders. His greatest victory was the marriage he arranged for his son, Louis, with Eleanor, wealthy heiress of William X of Aquitaine. By the time of his death, Louis had established an effective government, composed of officials drawn from the ranks of the lower vassals and the clergy.

Unfortunately for the reputation of Louis VII (1137–80), historians have concentrated on his failure to exploit the powerful alliance with Aquitaine. This is not quite fair, for the young King (he was only sixteen at the time of his accession) began his reign with enthusiasm. He was extravagantly in love with his bride, the vivacious Eleanor, who had been raised in the sophisticated courts of southern France, and exerted a strong influence over her husband's early policies. When St. Bernard of Clairvaux launched the very popular Second Crusade, Louis placed himself at the head of the host and set out for the Holy Land, his wife at his side. The kingdom was left to the regent, Suger. When they arrived in Antioch, Eleanor became so intimately involved with her uncle, the prince of that city, that Louis put her aside and determined on divorce. After their return this "monk in king's clothing" lost himself in jealous brooding. The government remained in the hands of Suger, who was determined to block the divorce, which would mean the loss of Eleanor's dowry, Aquitaine. As soon as Suger was dead, however, maddened by a flirtation between his wife and young Henry of Anjou, Louis called together a council in 1152 and had his marriage dissolved on grounds of consanguinity. Within two months Eleanor and Henry were married, and Aquitaine passed to the English crown.

Louis spent twenty-five years of bitter fighting to hold back Henry's attempts to extend his French territories, and though he was unable to exploit effectively Henry's struggles with Becket and his rebellious sons, he did manage to hold his own. In fact, his reign strengthened the emerging French monarchy. He was able to extend his protection to bishops harassed by secular lords throughout the kingdom. His dependable government attracted many lesser vassals, who transferred their allegiance from exacting nobles to the King. Many towns sought charters from the King for the same reason. Most important, as conditions slowly became more settled in France, and people from all classes sought better government and more efficient legal institutions, they inevitably turned to the King's court, which was the only one available to settle disputes between great lords, or between laymen and clerics, or the affairs of the bourgeoisie. Thus, the power of the crown had grown, less as a result of vigorous action on the part of the kings than as a natural emergence of an instrument of order.

The opportunities inherent in this growing prestige of the monarchy were consolidated by Philip II Augustus (1180–1223), who came to the throne at the age of fourteen. Unlike his father, Philip was a wily politician who found every means to manipulate the weaknesses of his enemies to his own advantage. He began his reign with an alliance with Henry II of England that allowed him to absorb Artois and Vermandois, which had been part of his wife's dowry. As soon as his lands in the north were secure from threats by the Count of Flanders, Philip turned against his ally and supported Henry's sons in their rebellion against him. During the Third Crusade Philip and Richard had nursed a growing animosity between them into open hatred. Philip rushed back to France to launch an open attack on the Angevin territories. Checked for a time by Richard's return, Philip was able within five years after Richard's death in 1199 to wrest most of his French lands from the harassed and incompetent John.

Philip's campaigns were interrupted by the complicated affair of his divorces. After the death of his first wife, Philip had married Ingeborg of Denmark as a diplomatic maneuver to obtain the use of Danish fleets against Richard. Philip suffered from some neurasthenic disorder and was unable to consummate the marriage. He took a bitter aversion to the poor Queen and forced his bishops to annul the marriage. Ingeborg and her brother King Canute appealed to Pope Celestine III, but Philip ignored the protests of the feeble Pope and married his mistress, Agnes of Merau. When Innocent III became Pope, he ordered Philip to put Agnes aside and to take back Ingeborg, who had been immured in a nunnery. When Philip again defied the Pope, Innocent laid France under interdict in 1200. After a year the King yielded outwardly. He took back his Queen, but threw her into a dungeon. He continued to live with Agnes and legitimized her children. Innocent thundered, but Philip held out until 1213, by which

time Agnes had died. Furthermore, John of England was by now in serious trouble with the Pope, and Philip was anxious to take advantage of his plight. He could afford to restore Ingeborg to her queenly dignities, which she enjoyed for the rest of her life.

John had meanwhile in 1200 given Philip an excellent excuse to attack him. On a visit to Angoulême, John had carried off as his bride the Count's daughter, who had been betrothed to Hugh de Lusignan. Hugh threw off his loyalty to John, his lord, and appealed for justice to the court of King Philip, his lord's lord. Philip summoned John to his court, and when he failed to appear Philip laid claim to all the English lands in France, and launched an invasion. The war seesawed back and forth for a dozen years during which Philip quadrupled the royal domain of France. In 1213 John in desperation made his peace with Innocent, and formed a coalition with the Count of Flanders and Otto of Brunswick, Emperor of Germany. While English armies attacked from the south, Flemish and German armies met the French at Bouvines in Flanders on July 27, 1214. The French victory ended the effectiveness of Otto's rule in Germany and brought Frederick II to power. It sealed the fate of John's pretensions in France, and it brought him directly to Runnymede and the signing of *Magna Carta*. As for Philip, his conquests were now secure, and he could turn in the last nine years of his reign to the task of establishing his administration of his new lands.

The French kings had already begun to use *prévots* to collect the revenue due them from their scattered territories. A *prévot*, originally a non-noble, paid the king a lump sum in return for the right to collect royal revenues in a particular district. The *prévots* cheated the king, squeezed every ounce of profit from their districts, and tended to become members of the local nobility. To check their power, Philip began to use *baillis,* called *seneshals* in southern France. The *bailli* was an official chosen from the lesser nobility for his talent, and was sent to take under his supervision the affairs of a group of *prévôtés.* He had full financial, judicial and military powers to protect the interests of the crown. The *baillis* were paid large salaries and given generous staffs of trained assistants, who were given ample opportunities to rise through ranks of service to the position of *bailli* itself. The *baillis* had to give accountings of their activities three times a year to the king in Paris. Frequently changed from district to district, rewarded for good service, dropped from office if inefficient, the *baillis* and their staffs became a royal civil service. Because he had his own loyal servants supervising local affairs and protecting his interests, the king could allow the *prévot* to continue to collect the royal revenues and be responsible for the maintenance of public works. He also respected local customs and legal institutions, since he knew that nothing injurious to his interests would be allowed.

Philip reorganized his *curia regis,* turning it into a high court of appeal under the Twelve Peers of France, but it did not break down into specialized bureaus as the English *curia* did. In fact, Philip preferred to depend on the bourgeoisie for his administrative personnel. He was too eager to support the newly-formed towns of France and gave more and more responsibilities to the bourgeois classes, especially the lawyers, who were busily introducing the principles and techniques of the revived Roman law. Philip derived a substantial income from the towns. He extended the use of scutage, and maintained careful financial accounts. He amassed the wealth necessary to extend and maintain his control over all authority in France. By the time of his death, the kingdom had become a centralized bureaucratic state.

The Gregorian Reform

The first attempt at reform within the Church was a monastic movement that began at Cluny in 910. The Cluniac abbots insisted that they be free from secular control and placed themselves under the papacy. Within the monasteries, the Benedictine rule was reestablished, and soon a network of well-run, productive houses began to spread over western Germany and southeastern France. Shamed by the example of the Cluniacs, bishops in these areas began to take a stronger control over their dioceses. Secular lords, seeing the productiveness of the Cluniac houses and appreciating the element of law and order they introduced into a world of feudal anarchy, encouraged other monastic establishments to reform themselves. A general groundswell of reform swept across Europe in the 10th Century. But the administrative problems of the Church needed more than good will to solve them. A strong reform from the top was needed and this was provided by a series of popes of the 11th and 12th centuries who were influenced by Cluniac ideals, and more deeply by the work of Gregory VII. The whole movement bears his name, though Leo IX (1049–54), who emphasized the right of the Roman clergy to elect the pope; Nicholas II (1058–61), who proclaimed that after 1059 the pope would be elected by the College of Cardinals, the higher clergy of Rome; and other ardent reform-minded popes contributed much.

The first objective of the reformers was to stop simony, the sale of Church offices. The evil was an ancient one, but under the feudal system it had become an open scandal. Every secular lord who built a church or monastery believed that he had the right to appoint the clergymen who would rule them. These offices he offered to men of his choice, usually the ones who bid the highest for the sinecure. Many of the most important administrative offices were thus filled by men of no particular talent beyond the ability to pay a large bribe. The reform of this malpractice was achieved by convoking councils, stating the dogmatic position, and then enforcing it with the threat of excommunication.

The second objective was to enforce celibacy among the lower clergy. The secular clergy, those not in monastic orders, had regularly married throughout the history of the Church, as indeed they still do in the Eastern Churches. However, feudalism, as we have seen, added a new danger. The Church as an institution had to keep her doors open to men of talent. This was the only way capable administrators could be secured. If the Church were to become an institution of vested interest, in which offices passed by inheritance from father to son, it would soon fail. Gregory was uncompromising in his attitude to this matter, though the reform was resisted violently for many years.

Bringing the whole Christian Church under the primacy of the pope was the third objective. The Greek Church of the East had already been at odds for centuries with the Roman bishops. At various times the Churches had been out of communion or in schism. Strong statements from the reform popes on such matters as Communion in two kinds, the use of leavened bread in the Eucharist, the wearing of beards by the clergy, the form of the Nicean Creed, all of which distinguished the Greek Church from the Latin, had aroused the suspicions of the Patriarch of Constantinople that the Roman pope might attempt to exert his authority over him. The break came in 1054 when a delegation from the Pope, in Constantinople to negotiate the differences that kept the Churches apart, excommunicated the Patriarch. He, in turn, excommunicated the Pope and all his clergy. The two Churches were in schism and have remained so ever since.

The Investiture Controversy

The most important objective of the reform was to free the Church from secular control. This applied to local churches, but the main focus was on the election of the pope and the other bishops of the Church. The problem was not an easy one to solve. Everyone agreed that both state and Church were divinely instituted as the "two swords of God." The disagreement arose over the relation between the two. The kings felt that since bishops were among the leading vassals of the realm and filled important administrative positions, they had a right to appoint men of their own choice to the bishoprics. The popes, on the other hand, building a centralized Church which would have to be served by these same bishops, insisted that they had the right of appointment and that the bishops owed first allegiance to them. The issues were clearly drawn, and the Investiture Controversy, as it is known, kept Europe in turmoil from 1075 to 1122.

The Controversy was begun by two worthy antagonists, Henry IV of Germany (1056–1106) and Pope Gregory VII (1073–

85). Henry was only six years old when he succeeded to his father's throne. Immediately the nobles of Germany rose up to usurp the royal power. Henry was passed from faction to faction as the work of the earlier emperors crumbled. By the time he was of age, it was obvious that the weakness in the government was its reliance on the cooperation of the nobility and the absence of effective imperial institutions. When Henry became King he began to build these. He concentrated on absorbing Saxony with its silver mines. He began to rely on his *ministerales*, non-free subjects that he trained to be his administrators and his fighters. Both these measures were aimed at freeing the Emperor from his nobles and becoming a basis for independent royal power. His actions infuriated his vassals, who rose up in rebellion against him. Henry appealed for help to Pope Gregory.

Gregory had risen steadily in papal circles during the pontificates of Leo IX, Gregory VI, Nicholas II, and Alexander II. He had become one of the most vociferous spokesmen for the new reform movement. Ironically, he himself was elected not by the new College of Cardinals that he had been instrumental in forming, but by public acclamation, in the absence of any other worthy candidate. Once Pope, he struck a series of heavy blows for an independent Church. He declared all marriages that members of the clergy had contracted dissolved, and he ordered the priests to leave their wives and children. A storm of protest swept through the clergy of northern Italy and Germany. In Milan the Church split into the established clergy and a reform party, the *Paterini*, and rival bishops were installed.

Gregory VII began the attack in 1075 by issuing his First Decree against Lay Investiture. A bishop was elected in three steps: 1) he was elected by the clergy of the diocese; 2) he was consecrated with his spiritual authority; 3) he was invested with the temporal or non-ecclesiastical power. The kings had confused, in the opinion of the Pope, the second and third steps, conferring both powers at one time. Gregory demanded that the practice be stopped on the grounds that he alone could invest a bishop with his spiritual power. He found himself immediately in conflict with the Holy Roman Emperor, Henry IV. Henry, who had refrained from entering the struggle in Milan because of his Saxon wars, was outraged. The Saxons were subdued, he invaded Milan, and placed his own bishop in charge. In January, 1076 he summoned a council of his bishops in Worms that helped him compose a letter to Gregory that accused him of criminal acts and of usurping the papal throne. The Pope excommunicated Henry, and deposed all the bishops who had signed the letter. Saxons broke out in rebellion, and the great dukes met to invite the Pope to Germany to depose the King.

Henry, in a brilliant move, slipped over the Alps with a handful of followers, and came to the Pope, who had gotten as far as the castle of Canossa, that belonged to his powerful friend, the Countess Mattilda. For three snowy days in February, 1077, the King waited in penitential garb for the Pope to receive his submission. Gregory, as a priest, was obviously forced to receive him, accept his plea for forgiveness, and lift the excommunication. The King sped back to Germany and renewed the struggle, this time with the help of his dukes, who felt the Pope had betrayed their cause. When Gregory again deposed the King in 1180, Henry retained his hold over his vassals and was able to invade Italy. He formed a coalition with Alexius Comnenus and north Italian barons, while Gregory enlisted the aid of the Normans under Robert Guiscard. Henry entered Rome in 1083. But Gregory was reinstalled there in 1084 by the Normans, who sacked and burned the city to the ground. They then retreated, taking with them the heart-broken Gregory, who died in exile on May 25, 1085.

The war went on. Urban II (1088–99) stirred up rebellion in Germany, and he organized a league of the towns of Lombardy against the King. Finally, Henry's sons Conrad and the future Henry V were persuaded to turn against their father. Henry fought back bitterly, but he was finally captured in 1105 by the young Henry, humiliated and forced to abdicate. He died a few months later, in August, 1106, a bitter, lonely excommunicant, deserted by almost everyone.

Henry V (1106–25), once he became King with papal support, turned ungratefully on his ally. Paschal II (1099–1118), a weak man, tried fitfully to keep up the war, but Henry forced him to give up his attacks on lay investiture and finally chased him out of Rome and replaced him with an antipope. The next pope reigned only a year, to be followed by Calixtus II (1119–27), who began a vigorous attack on the Emperor. The nobles by this time were thoroughly sick of the whole affair, and they forced the Emperor to call a Diet to make peace. The Concordat of Worms stipulated that the Church was to elect the bishops and the Pope to consecrate them with spiritual authority, while the secular government was to invest them with their temporal power. In Germany the bishops were to be elected in the presence of the emperor, invested by him with their temporal authority, then with the ring and staff as emblems of their spiritualities by the Church. In Italy

the investment of the spiritualities was to precede the investment of the temporalities. The compromise was ratified by the Church and the struggle over appearances came to an end. The realities of the contest, however, remained, and were to break out in later reigns with savage warfare.

The Hohenstaufen

Henry V died without heirs, and the nobles elected Lothair of Saxony to the throne. In Swabia, two nephews of Henry, angry at being passed over, rose up in rebellion. They took the name Hohenstaufen from a favorite family castle, while they were popularly known as Ghibellines, the Italian pronunciation of the name of another of their castles. The followers of Lothair were known as Guelphs, the Italian form of Welf, the name of the Bavarian duke who had married Lothair's daughter and who led the war against the Hohenstaufen. The two names Guelph and Ghibelline came to stand for parties and programs. The Guelphs generally supported the papacy; the Ghibellines, the empire, and all over Italy local political parties lined up either in the one camp or the other.

When Lothair died in 1137, the younger Hohenstaufen, Conrad III, was elected Emperor (1138–52). Conrad was a weak ruler, who had as much trouble with his vassals as Lothair had had. He chose to go off on the Second Crusade, from which he returned in defeat and disgrace. His nobles, meanwhile, had begun the great German march to the east. Individually, the dukes carved out new duchies for themselves beyond the eastern frontier, then in 1147 they united in a crusade against the

Slavs. A vast new territory was opened to exploitation. The farms of western Europe were thinned out by a general migration to the east. The new nobles had a much firmer hold over their lands, since there were no old prerogatives that had to be respected. On the new farms, however, they offered better arrangements than were customary in the old manors of the West, and many new towns with liberal charters were founded to tap the wealth of the Baltic coast. The balance of power began to shift to the eastern magnates, while the Emperor concentrated his power in southwestern Germany and Italy. Conrad recognized the danger around him and passed over his own sons to name his powerful nephew, Frederick, as his successor.

Frederick I Barbarossa (1152–90) has often been called the greatest Emperor in the history of medieval Germany. Even if this reputation is exaggerated, he is certainly the Emperor who understood best the basic problem of the German crown, the growth of the power of the independent dukes and the inability of the crown to control them. The solution he offered was to encourage the growth of the dukes, particularly in the east, but at the same time to develop even more the strength of his own estates in Germany. Thus, he hoped to develop the dukes into strong instruments of the even stronger royal power, that had some means of keeping the dukes, the bishops, and the prosperous towns under control. The plan was not wrong in itself, but it did require a government that would be constantly alert and of high caliber, a condition that proved impossible to be met.

Frederick began by making peace with the Guelphs, his relatives through his mother. Then he slowly began to concentrate his holdings in the Rhineland. He also began to raise new families to the nobility to offset the power of the older families. He encouraged the foundation and growth of powerful towns, that would not only be sources of taxes, but would also be centers of administrative authority over their surrounding districts. In these centers he stationed his *ministerales* to safeguard his interests. The steady progress toward the establishment of a solid kingdom within the empire was interrupted by Frederick's decision to enter Italian affairs. Undoubtedly he was anxious to consolidate northern Italy into a dependable source of men, money, and talent. Also he was ambitious and the lack of order in Italy was an irresistible challenge to an organizer. His need of support from a healthy Church may also have been a factor, for in 1154, when he made his first march southward, the Church was having serious difficulties with Arnold of Brescia.

By this time the cities of northern Italy had become largely independent of their feudal lords and had established themselves as free communes. The movement had spread to Rome, where a revolt broke out against Pope Lucius (1144–45). He was killed in the rioting, as a commune was set up and it fell into the hands of the heretic Arnold of Brescia, a student of Abelard, who had been expelled from Italy and France for seditious activity. Arnold came to Rome from exile in Zurich, and attempted to interest Conrad III and Frederick I in a romantic scheme to revive the ancient Roman Empire in a dyarchy of emperor and Roman Senate. Frederick decided to put his faith in the Pope and the northern communes instead, and invaded.

He crushed all opposition as he marched, though some towns, especially

Milan, showed ominous signs of intransigence. He was crowned King of Italy at Pavia, and marched into Italy, where he was crowned by the new Pope, Adrian IV (1154–59), the only English Pope in the history of the Church. Arnold was expelled, fled to Tuscany, where he was captured, and finally was burned to death for heresy.

The Pope and Emperor had cooperated to bring order to Italy, but at Sutri, where the Pope had gone to meet Frederick on his march southward, there had occurred a highly significant breach between them. At their first encounter, Frederick had haughtily refused to hold the stirrup of the Pope's saddle as he dismounted, the customary sign of respect due to the Pope. He would not become the Pope's squire. After much argument, he acquiesced, but he had made it clear that he would not take the position of the Pope's vassal to any degree. Later in 1157, at a meeting of the imperial Diet in Besancon, in Burgundy, legates from the Pope read out a letter from him protesting the seizure of a certain German bishop. Reference was made to benefits (beneficia) that the Pope would like to confer on the Emperor. Frederick was enraged at the word used, for it could also refer to benefices, i.e. feudal tenures, which would have inferred that the Emperor was the Pope's vassal. He prevented his men from attacking the legates bodily, but he sent off a scathing letter to Adrian maintaining that his authority came through his election from God alone. The Pope immediately backed away, explaining that his use of the word beneficia referred only to "good deeds." Again the Emperor had made his point.

In 1158 Frederick led a second expedition into Italy. He held a great Diet at Roncaglia, where his prerogatives (regalia) in Italy and over Italian communes were put forward and accepted. He assigned imperial governors (podestàs) to take over in all the towns, and all rights not specifically named in charters were invalidated. The towns had to be governed by bishops, generally ones favorable to the Emperor, or consuls elected to office by town councils and always answerable to them in the application of their military and political power. The consuls usually fell under the control of some particular class or party. In fact, all the communes were split into factions, that usually fell into the Guelph or Ghibelline party. Government crumbled in the face of savage civil wars or the internecine rivalries that were to plague Italy for centuries. Thus control by an outsider, whose only interest was the maintenance of order and the protection of imperial interests was actually a real improvement. The towns did not always see it this way, and many refused to admit their podestás. Milan was particularly defiant, and Frederick decided to make of it an example to all Italy. After a siege of two years (1160–62), he ordered Milan's enemies to destroy the city and disperse its armies. The lesson was not lost, but it was not exactly the lesson Frederick planned.

The communes and the Pope made an alliance against the Emperor. The new Pope, Alexander III (1159–81), had already shown himself an enemy to the imperial pretentions when he had appeared at Besancon as one of Adrian's legates. Frederick named an antipope, Alexander fled to France, and Frederick made a third expedition to Italy (1166–68). He quickly took Rome, but an epidemic forced him to make a hasty retreat to Germany. In 1167 the communes formed the Lombard League. Milan was restored, and all the important towns of the north (36 altogether) joined the League. Alexander, back in Rome, allied the Byzantine Emperor

Manuel, William of Sicily, and the papacy to the new League, which built the city of Alexandria in his honor. Frederick was forced to invade yet another time (1174–77). On May 28, 1176, at Legnano near Como, the imperial army was attacked by the town militias of the League and suffered a crushing defeat. The victory is still celebrated to this day in Italy. Frederick quickly made peace with Alexander III, who confirmed the Emperor's control over the Church in Germany, and with the League. He gave up all the prerogatives he had claimed at Roncaglia, and the towns became completely free. They immediately went to war with each other, and Frederick still retained a great deal of influence in Italian affairs.

When Frederick returned from his setback in Italy, he realized that Italy would not provide the resources he had expected. It was now even more important than before that his power in Germany be secured and enlarged. He decided to crush the independent powers that the dukes had built up while he had been preoccupied in italy. He summoned his vassal, the powerful Duke of Saxony, Henry the Lion, to answer charges made in the Emperor's court by his vassals. Henry refused to come, and Frederick led his loyal dukes against him in a victorious campaign that destroyed Henry's power and brought Saxony into the royal domain. The war was a good example of the manner in which feudal institutions could be used to strengthen the Emperor. However, it was too late to build up feudalism under the control of the central government. It had made too much progress at the local level.

Frederick never outgrew his ambitions to establish himself in the south. It is quite possible that he had some dream of a Hohenstaufen Mediterranean empire. In any case, he arranged a marriage between his son Henry and Constance, the Norman heiress in Sicily. He made one last journey to Italy in 1186 to attend the marriage of his son. Then in 1189 he turned his government over to Henry and went off on the Third Crusade. He drowned in June, 1190, while bathing in a little river in Anatolia. His efforts had been unceasing, his work exhausting, and he carried the medieval empire to its greatest heights.

The reign of Henry VI (1190–97) was a short one, that left behind many unanswered questions. Crowned before his father's death, he did not have to face a rival claimant to the throne. But his powers were too great, too threatening to go unchallenged. His father's work had secured for him in Germany a solid base of operations in the north, while the highly centralized and prosperous government of Sicily gave him huge revenues and a jumping-off place for any Mediterranean venture he may have devised. The papacy was uneasy, surrounded as it was by Hohenstaufen power. The Norman barons of Sicily hated Henry as a foreigner, and set up a king of their own, Tancred. Henry the Lion rebelled again in the north to support them. The Pope had crowned Henry Emperor, but he now recognized Tancred as King. King Richard of England, in Sicily on his way east to the Third Crusade, also supported Tancred and made a bitter foe in Henry. When Richard decided to rush back over land from the east, he was recognized in Austria in spite of his disguise, and was turned over to Henry, who threw him into prison. He finally released Richard for the enormous ransom of over 100,000 pounds. These funds gave Henry the edge over his rebellious dukes, and they submitted to his authority. Tancred died, and the Norman rebellion fell apart. Henry was now the most powerful monarch in German history. The north was secure, the Tuscan cities had been organized into an imperial league. The Norman kingdom in the south was completely his. As he turned his cold, unscrupulous eyes eastward, even the once mighty Byzantine Empire trembled, for it is quite probable that Henry had the ambition to extend his power throughout the Mediterranean world. It is certain that had he lived, he would have been in a position to consolidate his father's work in the north, and there was no power in the south to oppose his pretentions there. It is intriguing to speculate on what chances of success he really had. In point of fact, he died unexpectedly at the age of thirty-two, and Germany was left without an effective ruler for eighteen years. The enemies of the Hohenstaufen had a chance for a second breath.

X
THE HIGH MIDDLE AGES
IN THE BYZANTINE WORLD
▼ ▼ ▼ ▼ ▼

▶ **Monastery on rock, Meteora, Greece.** Byzantine monks sought out of the way places to build their monasteries. There is a large group of monasteries built on these rocks that is still in use. In many cases the only access is by basket, rope and pulley.

▶ **The Church of the Virgin Pammakristos (14th Century),** Constantinople. This church became a mosque, but is now abandoned. Other such churches are now museums.

▶ **Mosaic Icon, Christ Blessing, Santa Sophia, Constantinople.** Christ is often shown in Byzantine iconography as stern and frightening. Icons are highly stylized, which makes it difficult to date them. Notice the realism of the features in stone.

Leo III (717–41) came to the Byzantine throne at a time of great danger for the Empire. The Arabs were massing for another assault on the city, and within six months after he began his rule they had invested its walls. Through the winter of 717–18 and into the summer the city fought back with Greek Fire. Finally, exhausted, stricken with plague, harassed by the Bulgar allies of the Empire, the Arabs withdrew, never again to threaten the very existence of the Empire as they had just done.

Leo hastened to strengthen his position. He began to break up the larger themes into smaller units, so as to prevent the development of rivals to the throne. In 726 he published the *Ecloga,* a compact legal manual that made readily available the important legislation of Justinian's *Corpus.* The *Ecloga* made many modifications in the older laws by introducing Christian ethics. At the same time, mutilations, brandings, and other horrible punishments reveal the moral tone of the 8th Century.

The main work of the reign, however, was the assault that Leo mounted against the use of icons in the Church. The use of holy pictures, or icons, by the Church as a means of instruction and of encouraging devotion went back to at least the 5th Century. Down through the years, portraits of Christ, the Virgin and the saints, and painted scenes from the Old and New Testaments had multiplied by the thousands. A veneration of these representations had developed that often bordered on the superstitious, especially in the case of certain wonder-working icons. In reaction, there had always been an iconoclastic ("image-breaking") movement that viewed icons and statues not only as superstitious, but as blasphemous and sacrilegious. This reaction was strongest in the Near East where Christians had to counter

the influence of strict Jewish and later Muslim prohibitions of any portraiture of divinity. After the Muslim conquest, missionary activity along the borders of Byzantium began to win many converts from among the Christians. To blunt the appeal of Islam, Christians of Anatolia turned to an austere, puritanical Christianity, that stripped away any suggestion of idolatry or paganism. They especially condemned the veneration of icons and statues.

In 726 Leo, who was an Isaurian from that very region, began his attack. Like all Byzantine emperors, he was convinced of his responsibility to guard and cleanse the Church, and in this instance to dominate it. He began by delivering a series of sermons to point out to his people the uselessness of venerating the icons. Then he ordered a famous icon over the Chalke gate be removed. A fierce riot followed, and Leo moved cautiously. He consulted with Germanus, the Patriarch of Constantinople, and Pope Gregory II; but both men repudiated iconoclasm. The most outspoken opposition came from the theologian John of Damascus. John explained icons in neoplatonic terms, the physical image being but a representation of and an avenue to the essence behind it. Icons were not worshipped, as God was. They were merely venerated, worship being reserved for the essence they represented. Furthermore, he insisted that when God took flesh in Christ, in effect He became the first icon. This brought back overtones of the Monophysite controversy, for if Christ had been man, than He could be represented, but if He had been merely essence, without real body, then obviously He could not be pictured. All later discussion of icons was colored by this reversion to the old dispute, so much so that it has been suggested that the whole attack on images was nothing but a renewal of the Monophysite heresy.

In 730 Leo began to take more positive steps. He issued an order that all icons were to be destroyed. He deposed the Patriarch, and the conflict broke into the open. Troops began to strip public buildings and churches, and to persecute the iconodules (venerators of icons). The Pope condemned Leo's action, and the estrangement between the Eastern and Western Church was increased. Leo brought many of the rich sees of southern Italy and Sicily under his own patriarch. When the Eastern Church emerged from the struggle, these sees remained in its hands.

Constantine V (741–75) followed his father to the throne, and after putting down an early revolt he pursued iconoclastic policies with savage brutality. The civil wars that preoccupied the Islamic world as the caliphate was moved from Damascus to Baghdad gave him an opportunity to stabilize the eastern frontier. In the north the new *Basileus* took the field against the Bulgars, who were by now a most serious menace to the Empire, and after a long series of campaigns he won a decisive victory in 763. The Bulgarian state was crippled by the wars, but it was not destroyed. It continued to exist and to nurse a fierce hatred of Byzantium. Constantine's preoccupation with Eastern affairs led him to abandon the West. It was at this time that the pope turned westward and made his alliance with the Franks.

The *Basileus* carried on a mortal war against icons. He deposed bishops, ransacked monasteries, confiscated ecclesiastical lands. He bitterly denounced the veneration of icons on the grounds that the God-like nature of Christ could not be represented and that it had totally absorbed the man in Christ. From here, the *Basileus* went on to attack the veneration of saints, relics, and even the Virgin. His attack became an attempt at a general reformation of the whole Church. But the violence of public reaction matched his own. The monks and the lower classes resisted him with a hatred that lived on for centuries after his death.

The reign of Leo IV (775–80) was an interlude in the struggle. He eased the attack on images, and had some success against the Muslims. His most important move was to marry a beautiful Athenian, Irene, who combined deep religious feelings with a passion for power at any cost. Leo died prematurely, and his son Constantine VI (780–97) came to the throne at the age of ten. Irene took over the regency and immediately moved to restore the icons. Step by step, she removed iconoclast bishops and officials, and finally she was able to assemble the Seventh Ecumenical Council at Nicaea in 787. Images were restored, but the Council split over the treatment of iconoclasts. Moderates won the day, and former iconoclasts were admitted back into the Church, but zealots, principally monks, wished to take violent measures against them and the government that had inspired them. The moderate opinion prevailed because it reflected the basic attitude of the Byzantine Church toward the state. So long as the state was orthodox in belief, the Church was willing to adapt to political circumstances and to cooperate with the *basileus*.

Irene was delighted with the popularity that followed her restoration of the icons. When her son reached his majority, she refused to give up the regency. The army would not support her, however, and she had to retire. But the *Basileus* was a weak, unstable man. He had been deliberately debauched by his mother to keep him out of public affairs, and she had been quite successful. He took cruel measures against members of his family whom he feared, and he put aside his wife to marry his mistress in an outrageously lavish ceremony. The Church attacked the divorce and refused to sanction the new marriage. The *Basileus* furiously cut down all opposition, but he had alienated the army, who now supported Irene. In 797, by order of his own mother, the young *Basileus* was blinded, and Irene became *Basileus,* the first woman to rule the Empire in her own right, though she wore men's clothing to keep up the pretense that the *Basileus* was a male. Her government was a failure. Intrigue filled the court. To gain popularity, she remitted all the major taxes, which soon brought the state almost to collapse.

The most far-reaching development of the period was the emergence of the Western empire. The Franks had succeeded where Byzantium had failed. They had restored order in Italy, and the Pope entered into a close alliance with the new Frankish Kings, the Carolingians. Charlemagne was never too clear about the Monophysite overtones in the controversy over icons, but he wanted to assert his own authority in religious matters, not only as a Frankish king, but possibly because he felt that with a woman on it, the Byzantine imperial throne was legally vacant. In any case, in his *Libri Carolini*, Charles rejected both the veneration of icons and, at the same time, the destruction of icons, an attitude that can only be understood in terms of his attempt to assert his independent authority. His alliance with the Pope led by inevitable logic to his coronation as Emperor in the West by the Pope in St. Peter's at Christmas, 800. Thus, the pretentions of the Pope to speak for the whole Church in religious matters had been largely ignored in the East, and he had lost control over the southern Italian sees, but the Byzantine *basileus* had lost as well. His claim to universal imperial authority had been successfully challenged, and though for a while Byzantium refused to recognize the existence of a Western empire, in the end they were forced to accept the accomplished fact. East and West were steadily pulling apart.

The Macedonians and the Apogee of Byzantine Greatness

A palace revolt finally deposed Irene on October 31, 802. In the next few years the government took measures to put itself on a more secure financial footing. Church lands and the peasants living on them were added to the tax rolls. The state forbade private money-lending, and offered state loans at 16% interest. The themes had deteriorated, and the government forced small groups of peasants to pool their resources to send one *stratiotes* to represent them. This made it possible to extend the themes to Greece, to assert Byzantine power over the Slavs who had settled there.

This was a timely and crucial policy, for the destruction of the Avar kingdom in central Europe by Charlemagne had freed the Bulgars in the southeast, and had permitted them to reorganize themselves under a new King, Krum, who launched a series of attacks against Byzantine frontier fortresses. The Emperor Nicephorus marched north to meet him, and on July 26, 811 the Byzantine army was trapped and annihilated. The Emperor was killed, and

Krum made a drinking cup from his skull. Krum advanced on Constantinople, destroyed the lands lying outside the city, but suffered a stroke on April 13, 814, and died.

The capital was spared as the Bulgars withdrew to the north, but Muslim forces were more difficult to handle. The Empire lost Crete to them in 826, and they began their invasion of Sicily in 827. In desperation, an alliance was formed with the Khazars in the north and with the Ummayyads in Spain. The crisis forced the state to find a final solution to the struggle over icons. In 843 the Empress Theodora was able to arrange a compromise with the zealots, and the icons were restored. Iconoclasm was dead as a political and a religious issue, but the tension between the moderates, led now by prelates of broad secular education, and the zealots, narrow-minded monks fearful of the effects of worldly learning on spiritual values, went on unabated. The one group followed the policy of *oeconomia*, accommodation to necessities of state, the other upheld the superiority of the Invisible Church over the Church Visible. Both groups, to be sure, condemned the Paulician heresy, an extreme form of iconoclasm that borrowed heavily from Persian Zoroastrian dualism. The Paulicians, or Manicheans as they were called, were driven out of Anatolia and moved to the Balkans, where they came to be known as Bogomils. They finally made their way to Bohemia, north Italy, and southern France, where they became the nucleus of the Albigensian movement of the 12th Century.

The period of iconoclasm had been crucial in the history of Byzantium. The iconoclast objectives of the emperors, drawn mainly from the eastern frontiers, had constituted an attack of easternism on the basic Hellenism of Byzantium. The victory of the iconodule position was actually a victory of the Greek religious spirit, which now was released to inspire a great cultural renaissance. The loss of the western provinces allowed the Empire to concentrate on its immediate problems with the Bulgars and Muslims. The Church, once it had defeated the iconoclasts, was free to assert its autonomy, and it pursued a vigorous drive into the Balkans. Once converted and organized into Byzantine-type churches, the Slavs ceased to be so mortal a danger to Byzantium. The 11th Century, then, promised to be a time of great cultural and political advances. Byzantium under the inspired leadership of the Macedonians became the cultural center of the medieval world. Its influence was decisive in the emergence of culture in the East, but as cultural awakenings took place in the West, Byzantine civilization was adopted and was incorporated into the heritage of the West as well.

In 856 the young Michael III (842–67) became Emperor. His uncle, Bardas, became Caesar and took control of the state. Michael has become notorious in history as the "Drunkard." He was a rather weak, self-indulgent man, though he did at times attempt to fulfill his obligations with courage. However, the important developments of his reign took place in spite of his presence, rather than because of it. Bardas set to work vigorously to give focus to the first signs of the political greatness that Byzantium was about to achieve. He founded a new university at the Magnaura Palace, where a stream of brilliant scholars began to lecture under the leadership of Leo the Mathematician. The most famous student and professor at the university was the brilliant and dynamic scholar Photius. On Christmas Day, 858, Photius was elevated to the Patriarchal see. Immediately, zealots formed a party and denounced the election of Photius as uncanonical, which it probably was, though their real objection was to his secular education and his policy of close cooperation with state policies. The party appealed to the pope at Rome to help them. Photius took a conciliating attitude, hoping to avoid a conflict with the Western Church that could only widen the gap already opening between it and his own Eastern Church. But on the papal throne sat Nicholas I (858–67), a harsh, uncompromising politician dedicated to the establishment of Roman supremacy throughout the universal Church. He refused to recognize Photius as Patriarch, and declared him deposed. The Patriarchate, however, had emerged triumphant from a period of bitter warfare with the other patriarchs of the East, the Muslims, and lately the iconoclast emperors. It had survived and was ready to use its unique position to bring all the Eastern world under its sway. Photius was in no mood to bow before a Roman Bishop.

The opportunity for greatness was waiting. Michael had lead a campaign against the Muslims that turned the tide in those wars, for now Byzantium went on the offensive. In the north, the Russians had established themselves around Kiev, and had even laid siege to Constantinople in 860. Photius saw an opportunity to serve the interests of the Church and the state by using conversion to Christianity as a means of pacifying and Byzantinizing the Russians and their neighbors the Khazars, and countering Jewish and Muslim influences in southern Russia. The Moravians, moreover, had settled in central Europe, and to offset Frankish missionaries introducing pressure from his powerful Western neighbors, their King, Ratishiv, sent to Constantinople for missionaries to bring the benefits of the Christian Byzantine culture. Accordingly, Photius sent two brothers, Constantine and Methodius of Salonika, to him. They had worked out an alphabet based on the Slavic dialect in use around Salonika, and they translated the Bible and liturgy into Slavonic. Thus they introduced not only Christianity to the Slavs, but their first written language. The brothers eventually came under the sway of the Roman pope, so much closer at hand than their own Patriarch, but their work ensured the permanent influence of Byzantium throughout southeastern Europe. While Constantine went to Rome, to die there as the monk Cyril, the Moravian church began to send missionaries to other Slavs. The Bulgars could not resist conversion, now that their enemies had done so, so their King Boris, after some negotiations with Rome, received baptism from Constantinople and took the name Michael. A Bulgarian church was organized under the Patriarch, and a cultural fusion of the Bulgars and the other Slavs began. The King used his new church to overthrow his *boyar* aristocracy, and to establish himself as an autocrat. Christian political theory always favored an imperial structure of society, and time after time it was used by kings to wrest power from the *boyars*, aristocrats who clung to old pagan ways.

Photius was now in a position to take action against Rome. He denounced certain practices of the Western Church, especially the use of the *filioque* in the Creed, as heresies, and excommunicated the Pope. He hoped to launch a spirited ecclesiastical invasion of the West when he was suddenly toppled by a palace revolution.

Michael III had made a friend of a shrewd Armenian peasant from Macedonia, Basil, who used his great strength as a wrestler to move from extreme poverty in the provinces to a position of some fame in Michael's pleasure-loving court. The Emperor, captivated by the fellow's charm, made him his groom and his constant companion. He gave Basil his mistress to marry, and shared his power with him. Basil had Bardas murdered on April 21, 865. Basil became co-emperor, and finally Emperor when he had Michael killed in his bedroom, while in a drunken stupor. Basil I (867–86) immediately took steps to win friends. He deposed Photius and opened negotiations with Rome, accepting the excommunication of Photius, now confined in a monastery. He also granted to the Bulgarian church a certain amount of autonomy. He was able to send effective help to the Serbian kingdom that was first being organized at this time by protecting the Dalmatian cities with his fleets. Byzantine missionaries spread Christianity rapidly throughout the Balkan peninsula. He was even able to send armies under Nicephoras Phocas to southern Italy, and Byzantine rule was again firmly established there, although there was little success against the Arabs in Sicily. In the East Basil was able to win some victories, weaken Muslim control, and encourage the growth of an independent Armenia.

Basil soon found that his policies toward the impass between the two Churches had to coincide with those that were traditional with strong emperors. Accordingly he brought Photius back to court as tutor for his sons, and reinstalled him as Patriarch. The Emperor was also very much involved in the cultural activities that were spreading from the new university. He was especially interested in the new studies in the Roman law. He began a vast revision of the Justinian *Corpus*, though he only actually published a textbook, the *Procheiron*, and an introduction to his proposed revision, the

Epanagoge. In this book there is spelled out a theory of government based on the close cooperation of Church and state that must have been written by Photius.

Leo IV (886–912) continued the energetic advances of his father. First, he deposed his former teacher, Photius, as Patriarch, and replaced him with his own brother Stephen. The chief monument of his reign, and the one that earned him the nickname "the Wise" or "the Philosopher," was the revision of the laws that his father had begun and which he now completed and published as the *Basilica*. The whole body of imperial law was systematized and brought up to date. Also, Leo promulgated a whole series of new laws that expressed the final emergence of imperial absolutism over all other elements in the government. The Senate and *curia* disappeared, and the only check on the Emperor was now the Church, for he was bound by canon law and the decisions of Church councils. The administrative apparatus of the state was reformed, centralized and put under the control of the *strategoi* in the themes and the Emperor in the capital. The *Book of the Eparch*, published in the next century, described the economic life of the Empire. Everywhere the heavy hand of the government was felt as every trade and craft was organized into guilds, based on the old Roman *collegia*. However, though everyone was forced into a guild, membership was no longer hereditary, but was now based on proficiency, judged by a state examination. The guilds were controlled by the city *eparch*, the government's official, to ensure the prosperity of the state and the solvency of the government.

Leo concentrated so much on reforming his government that he allowed foreign policy to collapse. In the provinces, especially within the themes, powerful magnates began to amass large holdings and to assert a great deal of autonomy. Boris-Michael of the Bulgars had been followed on the throne by his powerful son Symeon (893–927). He invaded Byzantine territory and won a decisive victory with Patzinak help, while the Empire had allied itself with the Magyars. Arab marauders began to lay waste the eastern frontiers, capturing and sacking Salonika in 904.

The last years of Leo's reign were obscured by his marital difficulties. To obtain a son and heir, Leo had had to marry four times, clearly against canon law, and the Patriarch, Nicholas Mysticus, had denounced him. Leo received a dispensation from the pope, but the tensions between the *basileus* and Patriarch had flared up again. When Leo died, his son Constantine was only six years old. The troubles of the regency were intensified by a new invasion by Symeon, who now hoped to topple the Byzantine government and seize the imperial crown for himself. He devastated the Balkans, destroyed imperial armies, and was checked only when a palace revolution brought Romanus I Lecapenus to the throne (920–924). The new *Basileus*, like Basil I, had laboriously worked his way up from humble origins. Finally, as admiral of the fleet, he was able to get strong influence over young Constantine, married him to his daughter Helena, and became *basileopater*. In 920 he became co-emperor. Against Symeon he pursued a policy of patient waiting. So long as he was secure within the walls of Constantinople, he knew he could hold out until Symeon's allies fell away from him. The Croats and Serbs were encouraged to throw off Bulgar domination, and Symeon died during a war with them. His son Peter was a weakling who married Maria Lecapena and fell completely under the domination of

her father. The Bulgarian frontier was finally at peace again. The Balkans fell into anarchy as the Serbian and Croatian kings expanded under Byzantine cultural influences, and the *boyars* began to reclaim their independent authority from their king.

Romanus conciliated all parties. He made peace with the Church and with aristocratic rivals to his power. His most important measure was his attempt to protect the small land-holding soldier-peasants from the growing provincial magnates. He knew full well that the tax structure and the army depended on them, but it was very difficult to stop the growth of proto-feudal developments in areas so often under foreign attack and so far from effective help from the state. The same tendencies were emerging within the Islamic world, where small emirs were establishing independent states within the framework of the Abbâsid empire. Romanus held his own against them, and he fought back a Russian invasion in 941. His end came ironically at the hands of his own sons, who deposed him in a desperate attempt to seize power, only to die violent deaths when they failed. Romanus died a lonely death on June 15, 948.

When Constantine VII Porphryrogenitus (913–959) finally took over his throne, he was already forty years old. He occupied himself with the literary activities for which he has become famous. His treatises on court ceremonies, the themes, and the imperial administration were encyclopedic in the picture they gave of the workings of Byzantine government. Probably the most important event of the reign was the reception of Olga, princess and regent of the Kievan state, who came to celebrate her recent baptism into the Christian faith.

Romanus II (959–63) came to the throne possibly after poisoning his father at the instigation of his wife Theophano, the daughter of a tavern-keeper, who rose from courtesan to Empress. She had complete domination over her dissolute husband, whose reign is important only because it introduced two great generals to Byzantine history, Leo and Nicephoras Phocas. Nicephoras carried on a brilliantly successful campaign in Crete in 960. He also was able to defeat the Muslims in Syria, and captured their capital, Aleppo. When Romanus died unexpectedly on March 15, 963, Theophano, left with two small sons, Basil and Constantine, shrewdly offered the aging general Nicephoras the crown as co-emperor with Basil and Constantine. After he had won his way to the capital, and had been crowned in Hagia Sophia, the two were married.

The Soldier-Emperors

Nicephoras Phocas (963–69) filled the reign with spectacular military successes. He invaded northern Syria and captured the great city of Antioch. He invaded Mesopotamia and extended his conquest of Crete to Cyprus. He allied himself with Olga's son, the Russian Prince Sviatoslav, to defeat the Bulgars in the north. He even planned a campaign in Italy in alliance with Otto I of Germany. His internal policies were somewhat less brilliant. He allied himself with the landed aristocracy, and under his protection their large estates began to spread across Anatolia, while military holdings fell into the hands of rich farmers. Even the commercial aristocracy began to invest heavily in large estates.

Nicephorus was an extremely pious man. He was a close friend and supporter of St. Athanasius, who founded the monastery of the Lavra on Mt. Athos in Greece. He spent a great deal of his time at prayer, wore a hair shirt under his clothing, and lived a monastic life. Repelled by his austerities, Theophano turned to a brilliant aide of the Emperor, John Tsimisces, husband of Theodora, sister of Romanus II, and plotted with him to kill the aged general. Nicephorus was struck down in his bedchamber by John in December, 969, and John was crowned co-emperor.

John Tsimisces (969–76) continued the brilliant victories of his predecessor. He repudiated the scandalous liaison with Theophano to keep peace with the Church, then turned to the Bulgarian war. He conquered eastern Bulgaria, and shattered the old Bulgarian empire. The czar was taken captive to Constantinople, while Sviatoslav, now allied to the Bulgars, had to withdraw when Tsimisces paid the Patzinaks to attack Kiev. He opened negotiations with the West, and gave Theophano, a daughter of Romanus II, to Otto II in marriage. While pursuing a successful campaign in Syria, he died of typhus on January 10, 976.

Basil II (976–1028) by this time was a young man of eighteen and had been co-emperor with his brother Constantine since 963. For a decade he struggled to hold off the pretentions of aristocratic armies that had been encouraged by the policies of the two late co-regents. By 985 he was able to assume the power of the *Basileus* which he still shared with his brother, who willingly left affairs of state to his energetic brother.

During this period, Samuel, a son of a governor of Macedonia, had founded a state of his own at Ochrida. Slowly, he united all the lands of the old Bulgarian empire, reestablished the Bulgarian Patriarchate, and launched an attack on Thessaly. Basil was handicapped by another revolt of the Anatolian magnates that laid siege to the capital. Basil called on the Russians for help, and their Prince Vladimir led his *druzina* of 6,000 men to the capital and saved the day. The Varangian Guard became a permanent part of the Byzantine army. Vladimir married Basil's sister Anne, was baptized, and forced his people to convert. A Russian church was organized under Byzantine bishops. Civil disturbances lasted for thirteen years, but Basil was able to continue the anti-aristocratic policies of Romanus II, and held back the incipient feudalism. This had become by now a main concern for all Byzantine emperors.

In 991 he was able to renew the war against Samuel. He made alliances with the Serbs and the Croats, fought back a Fâtimid attack on Syria, and then concentrated on a final five-year campaign in Macedonia. The wars had been fought since 986, and in 1014 Basil won a final victory. Fourteen thousand prisoners were blinded and sent back to the czar in batches of one hundred, each under a one-eyed guide. Samuel suffered a stroke at the sight and died on October 6, 1014. By 1018 the capital of Ochrida fell, and the whole Balkan peninsula was Byzantine once more. The entire area was organized into new themes. The triumphant Bulgar-Slayer, as Basil has been called ever since, intervened successfully in Armenia, the land of the Khazars, and was preparing to take an active role in Italian affairs when he died. Basil had been a morose, introspective man with no interest in cultural diversions. He never married, and spent his whole life in active campaigning. He may have had unattractive personal characteristics, but he was probably the greatest emperor after Heraclius.

The Decline of the Macedonians

Constantine VIII had been theoretical co-emperor during his brother's reign, but he ruled for three more years by himself (1025–28), during which time he tried at this late date to provide husbands for his three daughters, all past their forties. The eldest retired to a nunnery, but Zoe and her sister Theodora turned out to be silly and pathetic old ladies, trying desperately to regain youth with creams and lotions, and falling under the spell of those who flattered their vanity in order to use their weaknesses to get ahead.

Intrigue absorbed the last years of the Macedonian dynasty. The bureaucracy exploited the provinces without mercy. The government was left in the hands of a court party led by the brilliant Michael Psellus. They founded a new university in Constantinople, which taught the Greek and Roman classics in the *trivium* and *quadrivivium*. But the aristocracy continued to gain power, and the state armies continued to shrink. Increasing use had to be made of mercenaries from England or Norman Italy.

The main event of the next reign was the final break with Rome. The forces that were drawing apart the two Churches, the one so deeply involved in the affairs of feudal Europe, the other in the emerging Slavic national churches, were too strong to be reconciled. In 1043 Michael Cerularius had become Patriarch. Haughty, strong-willed, he was determined to maintain the gains Photius had made for the Church. Pope Leo IX was just as determined to maintain Roman supremacy throughout the Church. Both agreed to a meeting to negotiate their grievances. Humbert, the Cardinal Leo sent to the East to negotiate, was extremely hostile to the Greek Church. Inevitably, the Cardinal and Patriarch clashed. Reconciliation between Eastern and Western church practices became impossible. Humbert excommunicated Cerularius and his supporters, while the Patriarch retaliated in kind. The schism that resulted was never expected to be permanent, but as time went on it became more and more difficult to find a formula of compromise, so it lasts until today, and still it is difficult to compromise.

Zoe and Theodora finally died, and civil war erupted. Surrounded by enemies on all sides, Normans, Patzinaks, and Seljuk Turks, the Empire seemed about to collapse, especially after the disastrous defeat of Manzikert at the hands of the Seljuks on August 19, 1071. Yet as so often happened in Byzantine history, there emerged a savior, a young, vigorous military commander, Alexius Comnenus, who was crowned Emperor on April 4, 1081.

The period of disintegration had been a disaster. Everywhere the great magnates were on the rise. Not only did the government stop trying to keep them under control, but it became their tool. The taxes on peasant holdings that had been paid by the aristocracy were abolished. The magnates began to swallow up all the small peasant and soldier holdings. In fact, the free peasant himself disappeared. The army declined rapidly to be replaced with mercenaries or private feudal-type bands. A crucial development in the process was the appearance of the *pronoia*, originally a way of rewarding prominent men, who were given a holding and its income to administer for a definite period. The land could not be alienated, nor could it become a hereditary holding. Now the government was forced to resort to this technique increasingly to administer its

holdings. At the same time, ecclesiastics were given the right to collect taxes in certain areas *(solemnia)*. The tax collectors and the pronoiars began to build their own administrative systems, and Byzantium was well on its way to feudalism.

The period was also marked by the appearance of many new enemies. From the West came the Normans, who carved out of Byzantine territories in Italy a kingdom that whetted their appetite for further expansion in the East, an idea they passed on to the Hohenstaufen. In the north the people of the steppes had become a menace. We have already seen how the Bulgars settled on the Balkan frontier and became the first foreign power to establish itself within the Empire to be recognized as permanent by the Byzantines. It was also the only state that could claim an imperial crown and patriarchate of its own.

The Russians were the people destined to achieve permanent greatness in the steppe region. Led by adventuresome Vikings, Swedish bands began to move up the river systems of Russia in the 9th Century. Legends claimed that a certain Rurik and his brothers established the *Rus* at Kiev. Their first known appearance, however, was the raid of 860 on Byzantium. Oleg (880–912), who united Kiev and Novgorod, attacked again in 911, and by that time the Russians had spread to many trading centers on the Don and Dnieper rivers. By 945 these centers were flourishing, and a trading agreement was signed with Byzantium. Sviatoslav (964–72) brought his state into the orbit of the Bulgar-Byzantine struggle, as we have seen, though he failed in his attempt to conquer territory outside Russia. Vladimir (978–1015) Christianized his country and extended his lands to the Black Sea. Yaroslav the Wise (1019–54) was the most powerful of the Kievan princes. The wealth from their commercial enterprises with Asia and Byzantium, and the high degree of culture they developed after the country's conversion, made the Russians an important power in the 11th Century, and Yaroslav was able to make marriage alliances for his many children with many important rulers in western Europe. He established an odd system of ensuring succession to the throne, however, whereby each prince was given an *appanage.* As each prince died, all moved up a notch until each in turn reached the throne. The system failed to achieve unity, and the Kievan state fell apart into small competing principalities soon after Yaroslav's death.

The Fall of the Abbâsids

The Islamic world was also disintegrating as Byzantine power declined. For a while this made it possible for the emperors to hold their own, but soon Muslim peoples began to move into the collapsing Abbâsid empire to become a serious menace to Byzantium. The Abbâsids had had a short period of real power from 754–861, the most important Caliphs being Harun al-Rashid (786–809) and Al Mamun (813–33). The dynasty was fabulously wealthy because of the enormous trade that traveled through its lands, and because of the age-old crafts that produced marvelous goods in its ancient cities. The caliphs had great armies of mercenaries, but the government was in the hands of viziers, who came from certain powerful aristocratic families. After Al Mamun, the caliphate became a prize over which many families fought. In 836 an army of Turkish mercenaries rose up and cap-

tured the caliph. The caliphate moved to Samarra, where the caliph lived as a puppet ruler until 892. Persian schismatics then kept the caliphs captive from 945–1055. The government became a mad scramble for power all through this period. Slaves, eunuchs, robber-chieftains all fought to win control over the captive caliphs.

Understandably, the empire broke up into large independent states. Spain, seceded under Abd-ar Rahman in 755, and an Umayyad state was established there, only to break up into emirates that carried on the perennial wars with each other and the Christians. The whole Abbâsid empire from Morocco across to Afghanistan was taken over by dynasties that came and went, always with violence. The most important of these were the Fâtimids of Egypt. In the early 10th Century a supposed descendent of Fatimah captured central north Africa and Egypt. A new capital was built at Cairo in 973. With fanatical zeal they swept across Arabia and conquered Syria. They were Shiite Muslims and bitterly denounced the orthodox caliph at Baghdad. The Fâtimids declined rapidly. They depended on mercenary captains, who tended to be untrustworthy. They also retreated into debauchery, and left the state to be run by ambitious governors. The most interesting group of these people were the Assassins of Lebanon, who kept the whole Muslim world in a state of terror because of their fanatical hatred of all earthly government, and their use of assassination to destroy it.

In the midst of the chaos there appeared the Seljuks. The Seljuks were a Turkish tribe whose leader, Noghril Beg, captured the caliph in 1055, supposedly to protect him. Alp Arslan, his successor (1063–72), invaded Anatolia, which he won at the battle of Manzikert. A sultanate was established there at Rum. His cousin Qutlu-mish carried on the war against the Greeks, capturing Nicaea which he held until the First Crusade. Under Malik Shah (1072–92), the Seljuks took over all the Near East. But they ruled the territory through governors called *atabegs,* each one of whom tried to seize power and to establish a dynasty. The Seljuk sultanates play a significant role during the period of the Crusades.

It is clear that the two worlds, the Byzantine and the Muslim, were going through profound changes that would lead to their disintegration, and the Crusades were the first sign of the world that would emerge.

THE HIGH MIDDLE AGES IN THE WEST
▼ ▼ ▼ ▼ ▼

▶ **Westminster Abbey, London.** Edward the Confessor restored the Abbey shortly before the Conquest in 1066. Down through the ages the Abbey has been repeatedly enlarged, but remains pure in style. Almost all the monarchs of England have been anointed here.

▶ **Cathedral of Notre Dame de Chartres.** This church is the most perfect example of 13th Century Gothic style in the world. The sculpture is serene, as confident as the soaring upward thrust of the building. How the colors of the stained glass windows were obtained is still a mystery.

▶ **Cathedral of Notre Dame de Chartres.** The town of Chartres nestled around its great cathedral. The amount of stone that was cut, the perfection of the artistry raises the question of how this small village could achieve such a great cathedral?

Economic Revival

Medieval society was based on an agrarian economy, based in turn on the types of soil and climatic conditions that prevailed in Europe. In the Mediterranean basin the soils are thin, the sun is hot, and there is a general lack of water. Here, farmers from ancient times to the present have had to limit themselves to crops that grow on the cooler slopes of the many mountain ranges that are so characteristic of the area. Olives, grapes, etc., which are suitable, take a great deal of time and labor to cultivate. The plains require a special type of plowing that will disturb the deeper soils as little as possible, but which will in frequent passes over the surface create a layer of fine dust to keep in the water. Again it is a technique that requires many man-hours. Little land was suitable for grazing on a large scale. There was a shortage of meat, but also of fertilizer, which kept down productivity in the grain fields. The agrarian community found itself badly fed and occupied almost all of its time in eking out a subsistence. To change this situation, large irrigation works would be needed, and these required efficient and wealthy governments.

In the north the soils are heavier, but here the problem is one of too much water, rather than too little. To cultivate the land, a special heavy plow is needed to slice deeply into the earth and turn over the furrow so that the soil will dry out in time for sowing. Elaborate drainage systems are needed to carry off the spring rains. At the same time, the growing season is short, and the work in the fields must be done quickly. In the ancient and early medieval periods, local government was able to help the farmer in his needs, and when this broke down, owners of large villages took over the task for a while. But Roman technology was such that even with the better soils and rain supply, farmers could barely produce minimum crops.

Oxen were the only animals in general use. Though sentimentality recommended use of the ox for ages, it is not an efficient animal. It eats hay, which contains a relatively small amount of protein for energy per acre. The ox moves so slowly that plowing had to be restricted to very small plots to get it done in time. The Romans had devised only one type of harness, the central feature of which was a strap that was thrown around the neck of the animal. The weight, whether of a plow or a cart, pulled by the animal was kept to a minimum so as not to choke it. Apparently there was also no way of hitching one animal in front of the other, so the greatest animal power available came from two oxen yoked side by side. It is obvious that without continuous technological advancement agrarian conditions would continue to deteriorate. Population would be kept low, and general economic and social stagnation would result.

These are precisely the conditions that prevailed in the early Middle Ages. The size of social and economic groupings dropped so low that it became impossible to maintain more than the concept of large-scale, sophisticated government. During the Carolingian period some changes began to occur. The heavy plow began to come into general use in northwestern Europe. On heavy wheels, with a mold-board attached, this plow could be used by the pooled labor of the manor to open the fields. Its use spread very slowly, until more efficient harnessing techniques were introduced. The horse-collar was introduced from the East at this time, a simple change which moved the strain from the neck to the shoulder of the animal. This made it possible to get more work out of the oxen, but even more important, it made the use of horses possible. The horse eats oats, a more efficient source of power than hay, and is a quicker, more alert animal than the ox. It was always a very expensive animal in the medieval period, and could not be used in large numbers. With the horse-collar, metal horse-shoes (to save wear on the ungulate hoof), and a harness to hitch horses one before the other, much more efficient teams were available to do the spring plowing more quickly.

At the same time, the saddle and stirrup came into general use, increasing the speed and maneuverability of horsemen, which led to the use of cavalry and helped establish the mounted feudal class. This military development made it possible for Europe to defend itself better against the Asiatic, Muslim, and Norse invaders of the 9th and 10th centuries. The new security meant that more people survived to provide manpower to work the farms with far better chances of actually reaping a crop.

The windmill spread from Byzantium after 900, making better drainage systems possible and providing more efficient power for grinding grains. Finally, the three-field system spread widely after 1000, providing a method of increasing the amount of land under cultivation from one-half to two-thirds, without sacrificing time to let land lie fallow or be used for grazing.

The result of more settled conditions, the introduction of new technological inventions, the growth of a cooperating and enterprising spirit on the farms led to the steady growth of population after 1000. Villages became overcrowded and peasants emigrated to clear new lands and establish new villages. Those who stayed at home found they had more time for draining marshes, building dykes and canals, and in general improving and reclaiming lands. This, in turn, led to more production and more population. A general eastward migration began to move across Germany, pushing back the Slavs and opening whole new areas that had to be organized under the protection of powerful lords. The work was difficult, and to induce men to hazard the dangerous trek to the East, lords had to offer attractive terms on the farms and charters in the villages and towns. Feudal manorial conditions improved. Food production rose dramatically, and for centuries Europe had a steady supply of manpower and leisure that made it possible for much of this manpower to be put to other uses than simply maintaining subsistence level living.

The most dramatic evidence of the changes that were taking place in the medieval system was the emergence of towns, trade, and large-scale manufacturing. The developments within feudalism itself provide one of the explanations of the revival of towns as economic centers. As feudal holdings tended to break down into smaller and smaller units, manors and fields no longer could support a group of skilled artisans to provide the manufactured necessities of life. Groups of these artisans began to emerge to serve whole districts instead. These people provided a market for farm goods, and trade developed as these were exchanged for the goods of the town. Furthermore, the increase of the population itself produced a need for supplies that had to be brought from widening distances.

Italy was the first area suited to satisfy this need. There, towns had never wholly disappeared after the deterioration of the Roman Empire. On the coasts men had practiced piracy and illicit trade with the

Arabs so that ships and sailing skills were available to take advantage of the collapse of Byzantine and Muslim power in the central Mediterranean. By the 11th Century Genoese and Pisan fleets were advancing into the area. The Norman state in Sicily made it possible for these fleets to make contact with the East, and by the time of the First Crusade regular shipping routes to the Orient were possible. Spices, citrus fruits, rice, indigo, sugar began to flow into Italy and from there northward over the Alps. Merchants carried the precious goods largely in pack trains along primitive roads. They made frequent stops along the way at monasteries or castles. People from the surrounding area would come to buy and soon regular stopping-off places were formed into permanent settlements clustering around a castle as nucleus. A protective wall would be built and a town had come into being. As people came to the town to settle, it had to be enlarged. The lord of the castle was put under pressure to remove himself to other fiefs and to provide some means whereby the burghers could handle their problems. Soon some form of self-government had emerged, the lord had left, and the town had become an island in the feudal area.

Not only did towns spring up along the routes from the south, but they rose in the north to produce the goods needed to exchange for the luxury items from the east. In Flanders, for instance, improved conditions and more effective manpower had developed a large steady supply of wool. Too bulky to ship, the Flemish found it expedient to turn the wool into cloth. They soon perfected their techniques and Flemish wool became famous. To produce the cloth, many skilled artisans had to come together to cooperate in the manufacturing process.

Towns were founded and they flourished. This same growth took place all over the north as specialized crafts began to emerge. Each town attracted immigrants and became a large market not only for luxury items, but for everyday foodstuffs as well. Thus the towns specialized in their trades, while the farmers could now concentrate on the raising of crops, finding they themselves no longer had to produce every item they needed, a condition that had been so characteristic of the earlier period. Foods were sold in the towns for cash, which, in turn, supported a host of small merchants and shopkeepers that offered bread, dried fish, clothing, everyday tools and necessities.

The effect of the towns was profound. Feudal lords found in them a steady source of income if they could squeeze it out of the burghers, but they also found they could buy the means of living aristocratic lives. They needed cash, however, so they began to force the serfs to convert their work and service obligations into money payments. At first the serfs resisted, but soon they learned to use their time and labor to supply the needs of the towns. The custom spread and serfs were able to become, first, tenant farmers, then they bought their way to complete freedom. Areas of agrarian specialization also began to emerge, once the farmer was not tied down by economic and feudal necessity. Some areas produced wine, others wool, still others special food. Trade was even more stimulated.

To handle these new and complicated activities new techniques were needed. The use of money, for instance, brought a need for a system of finance. Banks emerged in Italy to issue insurance for voyages to the East. Money had always circulated to some extent, but by the 12th Century, the West had begun to issue its own silver coins, and by the 13th, its own gold coins, particularly the Florentine *florin*, first issued in 1252. Money led to the need for credit, and though the Church always frowned on usury, there were many ways of making loans that would in fact bring a profitable return. The Templars, for instance, originally founded to help Crusaders in the Holy Land, began to make loans to lords going to the East. They also set up banks in the West and the East and facilitated the flow of money with letters of credit, and many of the methods of modern finance. By the 12th Century the papacy and secular governments had begun to borrow, first from bankers, like the Templars or rich Italian families, then by issuing state bonds in the form of forced loans. These loans were not usurious, for the interest they paid was not only in compensation for the bondholder's sacrifice in the interest of the state, but it was paid in the form of a "life-rent," an income payable until the death of the bondholder.

Manufacturers were organized into guilds or corporations *(collegia)*. A guild was a protective association composed of masters, journeymen, and apprentices. Starting at the bottom a young man could work his way up the ranks until he had perfected his talent so well that a sample of his work, his masterwork, assured a committee of the guild that he ought to be enrolled as a worthy master. The guild was governed by the masters, who set prices, standards, and regulations. All the guilds sent representatives to a council that handled the affairs of the town. Government of this sort was outside the feudal experience. Townsmen wanted to be free of feudal dependency, and it became customary for anyone who came to a town and stayed there for a year and a day to become a free man, whatever his former status. Also, the town as a whole regulated its affairs with its lord by establishing a yearly money payment in place of arbitrary feudal exactions.

Finally, the town developed its own government. Special courts were needed to handle the affairs of merchants. Towns had to be policed in new ways. Taxes and town maintenance called for special officials. Even the relations between the town and other towns called for new procedures. All of these needs were outside the competence of a feudal lord, who was disposed to allow the town to handle its own affairs, but was afraid of losing all control, lest he lose his income as well. The townspeople united themselves into communes, corporate entities composed of free men. They struggled bitterly with the nobility and the upper clergy to establish their independence, often turning to the king for assistance. Some towns always remained unprivileged groups of serfs, others had charters of limited freedom, but the free commune had its own government, consisting of some sort of head official (consul in Genoa, *podestá* in other Italian cities, mayor in England), and council. Citizenship was often restricted to guild members, though in "sworn communes" all the inhabitants were citizens.

Towns were very unpopular with the upper classes, who saw in their independent spirit a desire to overturn all legitimate order, but the towns prospered. Sometimes they banded together in leagues (the Baltic Hansa, Lombard League, etc.), but more often they kept up a steady rivalry that stimulated the growth of Europe, but also proved destructive and wasteful in the later Middle Ages.

The Crusades

The most dramatic sign of Europe's reawakening was the First Crusade. The loosening of older ties, the general rise in energy and activity, the breakdown of earlier localism, all led to a general feeling of restlessness. People felt they were on the move, whether it was to change economic or social status or simply their physical position. Better government had led to a widespread recognition of its benefits and a desire for more law and order. The vigilante committees, as well as the Church's Truce of God and Peace of God, were putting pressure on the fighters of Europe to curb their lawlessness or to remove themselves. The opportunities to rise, that had recently opened to people at all social levels, held out a lure to those who dreamed of getting rich quickly. A general wave of piety had followed in the wake of the reform movements within the Church in the 10th and 11th centuries, and was leading men to go on frequent and distant pilgrimages. The Italian towns were already on their way eastward and saw opportunities for great profit in Levantine trade. The Pope, locked in the Investiture Controversy, was looking for a dramatic means of advertising his real leadership of the European community. These and many other factors help explain the enthusiasm with which the First Crusade was met. Whether for selfish motive or personal gain, or pious sympathy with the Eastern Christians, whether to re-establish contact with the Eastern Empire and Church, or to sweep the West clean of its unwanted, the people of Europe responded with unbelievable fervor to the call.

The occasion for the First Crusade came from the East. The *Basileus* Alexius I Comnenus was beset by many problems.

Harassed by civil war, foreign invasions and financial decay, his government was deeply in need of mercenaries. As was the custom, the Emperor hoped to acquire them in the West. He sent letters to friends there and finally sent envoys to discuss the matter with the Pope, who could act as a spokesman for the West as a whole. Urban II, meanwhile, was anxious to further the cause of Church reform. He was involved in his turn in the fight with Henry IV and he felt that by subduing the activities of the nobles, he would find himself in a better position to control Henry. He was particularly eager to find some means of putting into practice his theoretical claims to primacy in Christendom. In 1095 he had travelled to Piacenza on his way to a council to be held at Clermont in France. The Byzantine request for aid touched off an involved series of discussions, out of which the Pope and his advisors constructed the idea of a crusade. The crusade had already become well-known in Europe. The wars against the Moors and the Slavs had been, in a sense, holy wars. The Seljuk Turks had begun to harass pilgrims in the Holy Land. The Byzantine Empire was Europe's chief line of defense and were it to fall, Asiatic hordes would be on the Adriatic in no time. The schism of 1054 with the Greek Church was still fresh and could perhaps be healed if the Greeks were in a particularly grateful mood. The creation of a great host of armies under papal leadership would settle once and for all the balance of power in Europe.

By the time Urban arrived in Clermont he had prepared one of the most successful speeches in the history of propaganda. Playing on every mood of his listeners, he aroused a wild enthusiasm in the throng of clerics and laymen who had gathers from all over France. Preachers, led by the opportunistic Peter the Hermit, wandered all over the West preaching the holy mission to almost hysterical crowds. Soon hordes of the unattached lower classes started moving toward the East in undisciplined, unorganized mobs. Looting and robbing as they went, they fell on infidel Jew and unprotected Christian alike. The Pope turned to the nobles of Europe to organize the military expedition that he was planning. Raymond of Toulouse, Robert of Normandy, Hugh of Vermandois, Robert of Flanders, Godfrey of Lorraine and others joined the movement and began to lead their troops either to Mediterranean ports to sail to the East or overland using the routes that passed through Hungary. The plan was to meet in Constantinople to discuss the campaign with Alexius and to get his assistance.

The first the dumbfounded Alexius heard of the expedition was a flood of reports and complaints that rushed ahead of Peter the Hermit's mobs, moving relentlessly through the Balkans. When they arrived in Constantinople, the *Basileus* offered them help, but he was soon disgusted with their turbulence. He shipped them over to fight Turks in Anatolia, where they were quickly annihilated. Before he could assess the situation, the better organized military units began to arrive. As each came into the city, Alexius exacted from its leader an oath of fealty and another that all former Byzantine territories would be turned back to him. He obviously was mindful of the activities of Robert Guiscard in the Balkans, and was afraid of the Crusaders. At the same time, he wanted to use them. The Norman contingents led by Bohemond and Tancred were particularly dangerous, for their leaders refused to take the oaths.

Settling their jealous rivalries for the moment, the armies attacked Nicaea in

1099. The city surrendered to Alexius, and the Crusaders were annoyed and began to suspect Greek treachery. While Alexius began to recapture his cities along the coast, the Crusaders cut straight across the desertlike Anatolian plateau and won a great victory at Dorylaeum on July 4. Encouraged, they moved on toward Antioch. Some lesser nobles left the expedition to establish fiefs for themselves. The only important one was the County of Edessa, created by Baldwin, brother of Geoffrey of Bouillon. The host arrived at Antioch late in 1098. The Crusaders laid an ineffective siege and began to quarrel. Bohemond craftily came to terms with a defending officer on the walls, led his troop into the city, and claimed it as his principality. A Turkish army led by Kerbogha, a local prince, now besieged the Crusaders inside the walls of the city. Food supplies ran low, morale was bad. Many escaped over the walls. One of these, Stephen of Blois, rushed northward to meet Alexius' army that was coming to the rescue. He advised the *Basileus* to turn back, since he was sure the city had fallen. Alexius did so and later was accused of treachery.

Meanwhile, in desperation, the Crusaders launched a surprise attack on the Turks, crushed them and found the way open to Jerusalem. Bohemond stayed in Antioch while the rest of the army went on. They arrived in Jerusalem on June 7, 1099. The siege was short, and on July 15 they stormed the walls and captured the city with one of the most horrible massacres in the history of warfare. In the Holy Sepulchre itself, riders rode up to the knees of their horses in the blood of the women and children who had sought asylum there.

The Crusade had been an astonishing success. The explanation lies in the fact that the Muslim world was disintegrating. A lack of union inhibited any effective defense. Furthermore, the Western knights were man for man far superior warriors to the Muslims. No Eastern army was ever able to withstand a well-handled charge of the Western heavy cavalry. But now the weakness of the expedition made itself clear. The Church would have liked to establish a theocratic state in the East, but the host elected Godfrey of Bouillon as Defender of the Holy Sepulchre. He died in 1100 and his heir, his brother Baldwin of Edessa, insisted on the title and power of King, which he was given by the barons with the reluctant approval of the patriarch Daimbert, the head of the clergy. Baldwin I (1100–18) established the kingdom. A Fâtimid army from Egypt had been defeated at Ascalon in 1099, but many cities had remained unoccupied along the Syrian coast. Baldwin allied himself with the Italian city states, and while their fleets attacked from the sea, his armies entered the towns from the land side. The Italians received generous trading privileges and quarters in each town. By the time of his death, Baldwin had extended the lands to their farthest point.

During his reign the government of the kingdom was constructed. Four feudal states were set up: the principality of Antioch, the county of Edessa, the county of Tripoli, and the kingdom of Jerusalem. Each was led by a lord who distributed fiefs to his vassals. Each set up a feudal court and operated completely within the institutions of 11th Century France. The king of Jerusalem had no real power over the other states unless he could employ his own vassals in Jerusalem to force the others to obey him. He did have a vague superiority over all the crusader states, and he established a system of courts, with the High Court for his nobles, bourgeois courts under viscounts in the towns, and special courts for the Syrians. The other states began to expand in the north on their own. There were hostilities with local Turkish lords and with the Byzantine *basileus*, but there was some success due to the Italian fleets and reinforcements that flocked to the East upon hearing of the fall of Jerusalem. The Templars and the Hospitallers were also of great help. These orders began as groups of lay brothers organized to assist pilgrims in the Holy Land. They were given extensive lands throughout the kingdom, turned into elite fighting groups, and became immensely powerful, extending their influence all through Europe.

The Crusaders slowly became colonists. They never conquered all the lands of Syria, so they lived side by side with the Muslims, whom they came to respect. Soon agreements were reached that led to alliances. The Franks, as the Crusaders came to be called throughout the East, were always an upper-class minority. They had to depend on native labor and services. They began to live in the Eastern manner, adopting Eastern dress, foods, and medicine. The society and the kingdom were fairly well-established by the death of Baldwin II (1118–31). The crusading spirit had waned, the Italians had established themselves in the towns and wanted peace to pursue their trade. The king's armies were strong enough when reinforced with fresh Crusaders from the West to maintain themselves in the disunited Muslim world, but never strong enough to extend the frontier.

The turning point came with the rise of Zangi, Prince of Mosul, who was interested in creating a strong, independent state in northern Syria. In 1144 he captured the county of Edessa. St. Bernard of Clairvaux

Church of St. Sirnan, Toulouse. This has remained the largest Romanesque building in France after the destruction of Cluny during the Revolution. It is built of brick in a style that is reminiscent of Spanish cathedrals. It marks the difference between northern and southern French styles.

▶ **Cathedral, Siena.** Begun in the 13th Century, it was completed in the 14th Century, but the plan was to enlarge it so that the present nave would become the transept of the new cathedral. The plans were dropped after the work began. St. Catherine was born in this most typical of late medieval towns in Italy.

preached a new Crusade to bolster the divided kingdom of Jerusalem. The Second Crusade (1147–49) was led by Louis VII of France and Otto III of Germany. Badly led, mismanaged, the Crusade ended in total failure, and the kingdom was worse off than ever. Baldwin II had left the throne to his daughter, Melissande. Her husband, Foulque of Anjou (1131–43), and she took over the regency for her young son until 1152. Baldwin III (1143–62), once he reached his majority, proved to be a vigorous ruler, but he died prematurely at thirty-three, and his brother Amaury I (1162–74) made the serious mistake of embarking on an expedition against the decadent Fâtimid rulers of Egypt. Here he became embroiled in Muslim politics dominated by the attempt of Nureddin, son and heir of Zangi, to take over the south. Amaury fought four wars in Egypt against Nureddin's general Shirkuh that eventually exhausted him and the kingdom. Shirkuh's nephew, Salah ad-Din, took over the crown of Egypt and when Nureddin died in 1174, Salah ad-Din was the undisputed leader of the Muslim world. He began a determined effort to take over the Frankish states and to drive the infidel into the sea. The kingdom was hopelessly divided. The King, Baldwin IV (1174–85), was an incurable leper. His cousin, Raymond of Tripoli, was his regent, but he was not trusted by the other lords of the realm. The court split into two factions that spent the little time left to them in intrigue and machination to dominate the throne. Raymond had kept Salah ad-Din's friendship with an alliance, but when Guy de Lusignan became King in 1186, Salah ad-Din became suspicious and decided to invade. The crucial battle was fought at Hattin. It was a disaster for the Frankish kingdom. The leaders were unable to trust each other, nor were they able

to lead the 20,000 men that had been called to the host from all the ports and towns of the kingdom. After his victory at Hattin on July 4, 1187, Salah ad-Din marched leisurely through the kingdom to Jerusalem, which capitulated on October 2, 1187. The civilized and compassionate treatment accorded the city by the Turk contrasts starkly with the horror of its capture by the Christians on the First Crusade.

News of the fall of Jerusalem and the collapse of the kingdom sped westward. Pope Innocent III immediately called for a new Crusade. The Third Crusade (1189–92) was the best-planned and best-financed of all the crusades. It was led by the most powerful rulers of the day, Frederick Barbarossa, Philip II of France, and Richard of England, yet it ended in dismal failure. Frederick died before he ever reached the Holy Land. Richard and Philip were already at war in France and only considered the Crusade an interlude, a temporary truce in their hostilities. Philip hated the idea of the Crusade, went only to satisfy public opinion, and wanted to get it over as quickly as possible. Richard enjoyed himself hugely. He was a born warrior and hero, and he was sincerely interested in victory in the East. The two kings set out by sea and met in Sicily. There they quarrelled bitterly, and Philip left for Syria. Richard stayed behind. He became engaged to Berengaria of Navarre for her dowry. He antagonized Tancred of Sicily and then the Emperor Henry VI, who were involved in a war for the crown of Sicily. Finally, he set sail for the East. A storm scattered his fleet off Rhodes and Berengaria's ship was blown to Cyprus where she was captured by Isaac, the ruler of the island. Richard in vengeance took possession of the island, which he turned over to the Templars. He arrived in Syria with Guy de Lusignan, who had left the kingdom after he lost the throne with the death of his wife, and had gone to Richard in Cyprus to seek his help in taking back his throne. The Crusaders settled down to besiege Acre, the most important town in Syria. Hatred flared openly between Richard and Philip and between their armies as well. The siege lasted twenty-one months, the city finally surrendering on July 12, 1191. Philip had been ill through most of the siege, and he left in disgust to get back to France and his attacks on the Angevin lands. Richard remained another year in the East, accomplishing nothing more than a treaty whereby Christians were to be allowed to visit the holy places, though the kingdom was reduced to a coastal strip. Finally Richard slipped off in disguise to get back to the defense of his lands. His capture and subsequent ransoming and pointless death in Limoges were in keeping with the tenor of the whole Crusade. Obviously, the papacy had lost control of the movement, if in fact it had ever been in real control. Religious idealism fired the Crusaders. The call of the Pope was answered each time, but his influence was never able to enforce peace on the rival factions in the Crusade; nor was he able to enforce his will on the crusader states themselves. The Crusades had emerged clearly as expansionist moves of an awakened Europe. The real control of the Crusades lay in the hands of the Italian states, and soon the East became the arena in which the great powers of the 13th Century would act out their drive to power.

The 12th Century Renaissance

The new horizons of the 12th Century led men to find the intellectual and artistic means of expressing the new world that had emerged. First, a more effective language was needed. Ciceronian Latin even in ancient times was an aristocratic language, emphasizing style, and used primarily for orating and polished writing. The language of everyday life employed far more flexible forms, a vocabulary and style suited to ordinary living situations. As the language passed into the medieval period, the more formal language was lost, and the vulgar vocabulary and style became accepted usage. Latin remained a living language, but it had to be adapted to the changing situations of the medieval scene. People needed simpler, more direct forms of expression as the more sophisticated aspects of culture were lost. New words were needed to express Christian and feudal situations. In short, a new language, medieval or vulgar Latin, replaced the balanced Ciceronian prose and it was a language suited to the needs of the age. In the 12th Century educated men began to perfect and expand this language so as to have a more perfect instrument to express their new social and political institutions and the new spirit that swept across Europe in the wake of the "great awakening." They studied the classics closely, seeking more accurate grammatical forms and a more precise vocabulary. Almost all the Latin authors that are known today were studied in the 12th Century. The Latin prose that emerged was far more precise than the classical language, though it was not so artistic in form.

The Latin poetry of the age, however, is of real stylistic merit. The complicated metres and calculated style of classical poetry held no interest for the medieval period. Strong, emphatic rhythms based on simple metres that coincided with the natural pronunciation of words and patterned rhymes, unknown to the ancients, were more pleasing to the medieval ear. The love and drinking songs of the *Goliardi*, university students who were determined to live life without care, are vivid, often irreverent pictures of life as it ought to be. Even the religious poetry of the day, some of the most moving ever written, was written in rhymed verse. The *Dies Irae* and the *Stabat Mater*, among many others, illustrated the fact that the medieval poets were more interested than the ancients in expressing as intensely as possible the deepest and most personal emotions that a man can feel.

Perhaps the most striking and original literature of the period was that written in the vernacular. French had already emerged as a literary language by the 12th Century, and Italian, Spanish and German rapidly followed suit. The earliest vernacular literature emerged at the courts of the feudal aristocracy or in the homes of the wealthy burghers as a form of entertainment to help pass long evenings in an age made dull by a lack of diversion. Troubadours wandered across France as welcome guests, singing or chanting their polished *romans*, imaginative tales of love, supernatural powers and tragic death, largely addressed to courtly ladies and usually of Celtic origin; and the rougher *chansons de geste*, strong tales of feudal adventures, battles and moving quests to fulfill vows to God or one's lord. The cycle of poems connected with King Arthur and the knights of the Round Table, the Parsifal and Tristan stories are examples of the *romans* that grew out of popular legends and folk takes. Sometimes classical themes were their inspiration, as in the *Roman d'Alexandre*. The *chansons* were often composed to glorify a particular noble family *(Raoul de Cambrai)*, a great adventure *(Chanson d'Antioche)*, but the most popular of all were those connected with Charlemagne, the oldest and most famous being the *Chanson de Roland.*

In both types of poem assonance (the succession of the same vowel sound in line endings) and rhyme were used together with pronounced rhythms to keep the attention of the listener through long recitations. Often the poems relied on clichés of style and stock phrases, but on the whole they portrayed vividly the ideals of the medieval age, the chivalric code, love of adventure, and dedication to one's lord or lady. Organized religion was largely ignored and kings were not pictured well. The poems obviously reflected the prejudices and culture of the wealthy classes. One of the most famous of all medieval works of poetry, the *Roman de la Rose,* begun by William de Loris in 1230 and finished by Jean de Meun in 1265, went so far as to satirize this life in almost 13,000 elegant satirical lines. The life of the bourgeois classes was portrayed in amusing satires like the cycle of *Renard the Fox*, the clever animal, the burgher, who outwits the lion, bear, and wolf. *Aucassin and Nicolette* Illuminated perhaps the romantic vision of the lower classes as it told the story in verse and prose of the son of the noble who loves and finally wins the lowly peasant girl.

A special category of 12th Century verse was the lyric poetry of southern France. In Provence a sophisticated culture had developed in the flourishing cities which borrowed heavily from Muslim Spain. An elaborate artificial court life emerged and it was one of its conceits to hold Courts of Love, in which problems of courtly love were debated in witty and elegant verse. Precious letters in verse sped back and forth, and every lover had to be able to win his lady in song. No person or institution was immune from their clever pointed lampoons. The most popular forms were the *salut d'amour,* a letter to one's beloved; the *aube,* to be sung at dawn as lovers part; the *serenade,* to be sung under a balcony in the evening. The *rondeaux* were dances, the *tencons* debates over points of love, and the *sirventers* satiric attacks on a rival or a frustrating convention. The life portrayed in this poetry was sort of silly. The beloved ought to be a married lady; her love-smitten wooer, someone who looks from afar, languishes in agonies of love and is afraid to come too close. The court life that inspired and sustained the poems died out rapidly, but the poetic forms themselves spread very widely and have had a permanent effect on European literature. Dante's *Divine Comedy,* that created a literary language for Italy, was largely inspired by Provencal lyrics. The German *Minnesinger* (troubadours), especially Walther von der Vogelweide, were obviously inspired by the same poems.

Scholarship

Men of the 12th Century in a sense were busy developing the world around them. For the first time since the ancient Greeks, scholars were asking profound questions about its origins and its nature. Men wanted to acquire skills to control it and subject it to their will. The search for knowledge became a passion of the age. Scholars journeyed to distant Byzantium, to the polyglot Norman court in Sicily, and most in particular to Muslim Spain to find the texts of the ancient Greeks, in which questions similar to their own had been asked and answered. A vast amount of material was found in Greek or more commonly in expanded analytical Arabic translations of the Greek. Without dictionaries or grammars, with no exact contemporary equivalents for the ancient expressions, they nonetheless made available an immense collection of texts. Often the translators were indiscriminate in what they thought was important. Often they repeated each other's work without knowing it. But their work was so important that it constitutes the greatest intellectual awakening in European history.

Above all, the 12th Century discovered Aristotle, whose works outside of a few works in logic had been largely ignored down through the late Roman and early medieval centuries. Aristotle unfortunately for these eager scholars came to them in a difficult form. He was a true scientist, who raised profound questions and put forward stimulating, provocative answers. However, he did make errors, and his surviving works, voluminous as they were, consisted only of lecture notes, that were often vague, inconsistent and abbreviated. Commentaries were necessary, but these were often difficult to absorb in themselves. Furthermore, Aristotle was the only Greek scientist to survive. Others, often more accurate than him, often more provocative, were lost so that there was a lack of balance in assessing his value. It was inevitable that Aristotle would become the foundation of all scientific investigation at the time, but even then many men saw his errors, his inconsistencies, and tried to find better answers.

The scientific awakening could be seen in many areas. Mathematics developed as the works of the late Greeks, Euclid, Archimedes and Ptolemy, were absorbed. Arabic numerals, particularly the concept of the zero, algebra and trigonometry were introduced. Astronomy emerged as a science again as the astrolabe and quadrant came into use. Sailors benefited immediately, though astrology was popularized and held an important hold over learned men until the Renaissance. Even in medicine, men made progress. Hypocrates and Galen were studied, though the practical arts of pharmacology, hospital care, diet, etc., were advanced by contacts with the Muslim doctors in Spain and in the Levant during the Crusades.

The "queen of the sciences" was philosophy. Scholars had a persistent desire to fit all the knowledge they were accumulating into some sort of universal system. At the same time, they felt they needed a tool to find new knowledge, to solve the mysteries of the universe, as it were. The new logic of Aristotle gave them just such an instrument. By its rules it seemed possible to take any problem, no matter how abstract, no matter how far removed, and reduce it to simple statements that could be organized into logical patterns of deduction. What was already known could be stated in these formulae, they believed, and by the patient operation of the rules of logic, they could be forced to give forth an infinite series of new truths that would eventually explain the whole universe. The Church was suspicious of the new method at first, as were traditionalists, but the New Logic swept across Europe.

The problem that occupied the attention of most philosophers of the day was one that had intrigued the ancients as well, How does one relate to the world? Is a perceived phenomenon real? If it is, how does one communicate the perception? Do all men perceive the same phenomenon in the same manner? Can the sense perceptions of two men be identical? Do phenomena, rather, only exist in universal prototypes, that men perceive through immediate intel-

lectual apprehension? In other words, it is possible to conceive of the universe as existing in an absolute sense, perhaps in the mind of God, apprehensible by man through his mind, while an earthly representation of it is perceptible through the senses. This position was maintained by the Realists, led by Anselm (1033–1109), who believed the universal came before the thing (*universalia ante rem*). Nominalists, on the other hand, led by Roscellinus (d. 1121), maintained that only the physical world had real existence and was worthy of study, and that the universal was merely a concept suggested by an examination of the thing (*universalia post rem*). The implications of the two positions are obvious. On the other hand, knowledge is revealed through transcendent eternal institutions, such as the Church or empire, and must be applied by men in their daily lives. Society is orderly and authoritarian. On the other hand, society is composed of individual parts, individuals or congregations that gather together to form larger units. Knowledge comes from the investigations of men who set up general hypotheses to serve their needs and to find more knowledge.

Peter Abelard (1079–1142) is the philosopher who carried the debate to its most exciting heights. The son of a minor Breton noble, Abelard studied logic and philosophy in many schools before he settled at Paris. There he rapidly became famous as an impudent, arrogant student, who outraged his teachers with his taunting questions and his audacity to start lecturing on a subject almost before he had completed his studies in it. He wrote an outrageous book, *Sic et Non (Yes and No)*, in which he quoted passages from Scripture and the Church Fathers to prove both sides of many articles of faith. In another work on the Trinity, he emphasized the elements of the Mystery so well that the whole seemed to be denied. These daring writing, the attacks they aroused from the authorities, particularly from churchmen and traditionalists, his flair for provocative, even brilliant lectures, made him the darling of the younger generation. Students flocked to his classes, and when he was barred from the schools, he set up his own school at St. Genevieve, from which the furute University of Paris was to spring.

In the debate over universals, Abelard suggested a compromise, Conceptualism. He denied the reality of the universal in God's mind, just as he denied the reality of individual things. What was real was the concept of the universal that existed in the mind of man as a result of his observation of individual things (*universalia in re*). This form of realism became later on the generally accepted philosophy of the Church and has persisted in philosophical circles to this day. At the time, however, it was rejected, largely because of the conduct of Abelard himself. Carried away with his own importance, he felt he was above ordinary restraints. He seduced Heloise, a lovely girl put in his charge by her uncle to be tutored, Outraged, the uncle had Abelard castrated. He took refuge in monastic life. He soon quarreled with the monks and went back to teaching. St. Bernard led a general attack on his works, however, and he was condemned and forced to flee for protection to Cluny, where he died in angry despair.

An important extension of philosophy as it applied to the practical needs of everyday life was the law, and men earlu sought to find rational principles to understand and improve the legal institutions current in the ecclesiastical and secular courts of the day. In italy Roman law was still in general use, though it had to operate within the framework of customary law. As society became more complex, and more involved problems came into the courts, legalists began to study the ancient legal texts, particularly the *Corpus Juris Civilis* of Justinian. In Bologna, particularly, Irnerius began to give lectures on Justinian's *Digest*, which helped establish the university there. The 12th Century was a time of change, and men found it difficult to change time-honored customs. Instituted law, however, since it is the work of men, applying universal principles of natural laws of equity, to be sure, can be changed by men. The logic and completeness of Roman law were far superior to Germanic custom and soon replaced it. This was particularly important in the Church, where canon law had been accumulating in thousands of canons and precedents that were often obsolete, inconsistent and inadequate. Using the principles of Roman law, Gratian in his *Decretum* brought systematic order to the canon law. His text was popular at Bologna, and it brought the Roman law into every part of Europe.

The Universities

The rapid accumulation of new knowledge raised a srious problem of communication. The old cathedral and monastic school could not handle the thousands of students who were wandering all over Europe seeking teachers. Also, the Church was suspicious of the new knowledge, the new teachers and the new students. If it could not stop the studies, as St. Bernard would have liked to do, at least it could control them in specific centers where students and teachers could gather. The new universities answered both needs, and they spread rapidly with the hearty backing of the Church.

The first universities were, as the name indicates, associations or guilds to protect and regulate the interests of both teachers and students. Faculties wished to protect themselves from unscrupulous competition, to secure a livelihood and to regulate the quality of teaching. Students wished to secure the best teaching possible for their money and to protect themselves from the hostile townspeople among whom they had to live. At Bologna, for instance, the students of law organized themselves into a guild and set up regulations that governed the quality and frequency of the lectures given by the many teachers that had gathered in the town. The teachers, in defense, set up their own guild and stipulated that no one could call himself a professor of the law until he had passed qualifying examinations and had been accepted into the guild. The master's examination became the test of having mastered the subject. Formal lectures were given in regular courses. Examinations were given and, if passed, a formal degree, or license to teach, was received. Several faculties organized themselves into guilds, though the university as a whole remained largely under the domination of the students.

The University of Paris, which became the model for all major northern universities, was less under the control of laymen and students. A cathedral school had existed in Paris from early times. In the 12th Century so many students and teachers flocked to Paris that teachers began to lecture in many parts of the city, especially across the Seine on the Left Bank. The chancellor of the cathedral still granted the teachers their liecenses to teach in the city, and he kept control over them. The teachers began

to form their guilds, in which students entered as apprentices, as it were, perfected their knowledge, submitted themselves for examination, and were admitted into the ranks of the masters and given a liecense to go out to seek students of their own. The Church kept its control over the teachers through the chancellor, and Paris remained a center for the study of orthodox philosophy and theology.

Life in the universities was not easy. There were no school buildings as such. Books were very expensive. Lectures were long and involved. It took many years to prepare for examinations, which were extremely difficult. Students were usually very poor and lived from hand to mouth. Students grouped themselves for protection into nations according to their point of origin. Later public-spirited benefactors began to donate dormitories, called colleges, to house groups of students. In the college a tutor helped the students and soon regulated their affairs. A library accumulated, lectures were given, and the college eventually emerged in many universities as their basic unit. Of all the institutions passed on from the Middle Ages, the univesity remains closest to its original conception.

The Cathedrals

The most creative expression of the 12th Century renaissance was its cathedrals. The original Christian church was modeled after the *basilica,* or law court, a rectangular building divided into three aisles by two rows of pillars. Often the building was used as a lecture hall, and at one end on a raised platform stood the chair of the teacher set into a rounded apse to throw his voice out into the room. The church combined the two forms of the building, placing the altar in the apse, and raising the roof over the central aisle (the clerestory) to provide walls to support windows for illumination. Often a cross-aisle, a transcept, was placed across the other aisles, separating them from the altar and giving the building the form of a cross. As the *basilica* came into use in northern countries, it showed certain inadequacies. The flat roofs were a liability under heavy weights of snow, and the wooden construction was a firs hazard. The problem was solved by the introduction of barrel-vaulted roofs, so called because they look like the inside of a low barrel cut lengthwise in two. The weight of such a roof was too great for the thin walls of the clerestory. By crossing two vaults at right angles, a groin vault was formed that concentrated the weight of the roof at four points that could be reinforced and opened up a wider space for light and air. The building that resulted was rather heavy in feeling, since the walls that soupported the roof had to be thick, but its rows of solid columns leading down the nave to the altar, its soft light and rounded arches over the doors and windows were very beautiful. Usually the west facade was decorated with elaborate sculptures. The Romanesque style, as this type of cathedral was called, remained popular in the southern regions of Europe, where cool, dim, quiet buildings were prized.

But in the north the mood had changed. Men were more experimental, imaginative and daring. They wanted new buildings to express this feeling. Also the Romanesque church was too heavy, too earthbound. It did not express the new piety, the new mystical soaring upward in search of God. Above all, it was impossible to build one large enough to hold the great crowds that now sought entrance to the church. The Abbot Suger desired to build a large and impressive church at St. Denis. He wanted to flood the interior with light. To do this he emphasized the vertical lines of the building, raised the roof and opened up much more window space. These principles remained the elements of the new Gothic style. The points of contact in the groin vault were reinforced with specially cut stone. This rib vaulting concentrated the weight of the roof at specific points as before, but architects kept the columns and piers small by using outside supports to the wall. Piers were built along the wall as buttresses, or they were built away from the wall and flying buttresses were extended betwwn the piers and the wall to brace them. The walls could now be opened. Arches were heightened into points, and many glass windows could be set into the wall space. The church could now rise to unprecedented heights, the use of the pointed arch making it seem even higher. Broad wall space was a challenge to the makers of stained glass and the sculptures, and soon the cathedral became the perfect expression of the sensuous ardor of medieval man.

THE AGE OF THE WESTERN MONARCHIES

▼ ▼ ▼ ▼ ▼

XII

▶ **The Tower of London.** William the Conqueror was a most distrustful man. One of his first concerns after the Conquest was to begin to fortify the city of London. His son completed the Tower by 1101 A.D. It has been a home, a place of execution, a stronghold ever since.

▶ **Carcassone, France.** This medieval town was reconstructed with historical accuracy so that one has the sense of being there at the time it functioned as a castle complex. Successful war was defensive, for it was impossible to take by assault one such castle, except by starving its inhabitants into surrender.

▶ **Sforza Castle, Milan.** This castle is a sign of the emergence of the strong men of the new age that followed the Middle Ages. The emphasis is on brute force. Italian culture has always met that with a sense of elegance that has the last word.

England

John Lackland (1199–1216) has the worst reputation of any English king and largely deserves it. He was bright, inventive, and had a good eye for the future of his own interests and those of the realm, but he was crafty, sly and greedy. He trusted no one and lacked the courage and persistence to carry his schemes through to completion. By 1204, as has been described, he had lost almost all his French lands to Philip Augustus.

The English vassals who had lost their fiefs on the Continent were angry and began to turn away from the King and his plans to reclaim his power on the Continent. They were further disgusted by the outcome of his struggle with the Pope. In 1205 the Archbishop of Canterbury had died. A disputed election followed, one bishop being favored by the clergy, another by the King. When the dispute came before Innocent III, he appointed a third candidate, Stephen Langton. John refused to accept him, and seized the lands of Canterbury. Innocent answered by laying England under an interdict, which forbade the celebration of all sacraments. John was furious and confiscated all the Church holdings in England, his terrified bishops fleeing to the Continent. In 1209 he was excommunicated, yet he still refused to yield. Actually, though his subjects were repelled by his situation, the interdict had not been very effective. However, the Pope called on Philip to invade England, and John had to yield in May, 1213. He received Langton as Archbishop, gave up England to the Pope and received it back as a fief. He turned back to the Church all its confiscated lands. Again the barons were angered at his conduct. The final straw came with the disastrous campaign John launched in 1214 to win back his French lands in alliance with the Emperor Otto IV. His conduct was so ignominious, his defeat at the battle of Bouvines so complete, that the barons united and marched against the King, who met them in conference at Runnymede. The outcome was *Magna Carta*, which was finally signed and sealed on June 19, 1215.

Magna Carta was in due time declared to be the first Statute of the Realm, and later generations tried to read into it the origin of all English constitutional freedoms. The document itself was a compromise between two warring factions. It was strictly a feudal contract, in which the King was forced by his barons to swear to uphold their traditional rights. But in two respects at least it established new and important principles. On the one hand it stipulated that the king was bound to obey the laws of the land and was subject to punishment if he broke them. On the other hand it was the nobility of England that had the duty to force the king to obey the law. The most important application of this in practice had to do with the collection of taxes, and the idea was stated and preserved that the king could levy taxes only with the consent of the nobles. Once the position of the king in relation to his barons was clarified, all his powers resulting from the work of Henry II were sustained. The benefits of strong government had been recognized, and so long as it was not used against them, the barons were willing to support it.

No firm provisions had been made to enforce the charter. John quickly appealed to Innocent III, who released him from his vow. He was preparing a strong fight against his barons, who had raised a new revolt, when he died from eating too many green peaches. William Marshall, as the head of the King's party, had John's nine-year-old son, Henry, crowned, took over the regency and put down the baronial revolt.

Henry III (1216–72) was a well-educated, capable and charming man, whose one lack was the political acumen he badly needed to get on with his nobility. Ever since the loss of their lands on the Continent, the nobility had turned to their affairs in England. They were becoming aware of their Englishness. English was becoming the language of the realm, and the barons were uninterested in involving themselves in disputes in Europe, whether in the cause of the pope, or any secular faction. Henry was very religious, and was eager to support the papacy. Furthermore, his closest friends and relatives were Frenchmen, and he was equally eager to involve himself in their affairs on the Continent. His great fault was that he failed to see that the universal pretentions of monarchy had become obsolete. He was an English King and it would have been better for him had he limited his activities to his own realm. Any king would have had difficulty in adjusting to the nobility after *Magna Carta*, but his troubles were complicated by his ambitious foreign policy.

He made three unsuccessful attempts to win back his French lands. He favored the Church with many money grants and gave his support to the Church in its war against Frederick II. He also had to invade Wales on several occasions. His policies were expensive and he had to go often to the council, now called the Parliament, to get monies and military help. At first the barons gave him what he asked for, but later they began to refuse him aid. A bitter quarrel broke out in 1238, and the barons drew up the Provisions of Oxford, which set up a permanent council to take the place of the king in the government. The council came slowly under the control of Simon de Montfort, who

was determined that the barons give England better and more centralized government than the King had. Many barons distrusted him and threw their support to the King, who attempted to reassert his rule. Simon led an army against him, and at Lewes in 1264 defeated and captured the King.

Simon called a new council, but to enforce its power, he called together a meeting of the Parliament. To offset the weight of the barons, who were not very strongly behind him, he summoned two knights from each shire and two burgesses from each borough. This meeting of the Parliament in 1265 was important because it demonstrated that the nobles were not the only class in England concerned with and responsible for national affairs. Simon never won the support of the barons, and Henry's son, Edward, raised an army that defeated and killed Simon at Evesham later that year. Henry was firmly back in power, but his mood was one of conciliation. He gave up his foreign adventures, gave back all lands confiscated from rebellious nobles and found himself and the country at peace. He called a Parliament in 1268, modelled after Montfort's one of 1265. The barons in gratitude granted him a generous tax. The reforms of Henry II were expanded. The common law emerged quite clearly at this time. The king's courts took over all the criminal and civil suits, and the use of "petit jury" was introduced to make decisions about the guilt of persons indicted by the grand jury. At the same time the King's legalists were consolidating the customs of the realm into a consistent body of common law that was finally summed up in a treatise by Henry of Brackton.

Edward I (1272–1307)

Henry died while his handsome, chivalric son Edward was on his way home from a crusade in Syria. The country remained at peace in solid support of the new King. Edward's reign (1272–1307) was largely taken up with military problems. His first task was to pacify Wales and Scotland. Henry had tried unsuccessfully to come to terms with the rebellious Welsh led by their national hero, Llewelyn. Edward fought a series of difficult campaigns from 1277 to 1284. The country was a royal principality. Another campaign had to be fought, during which the long bow was perfected, and in 1301 Wales was finally pacified and assigned to the king's eldest son. The union has proved a lasting one.

The kings of Scotland had been forced to accept English sovereignty since the time of Henry II. In 1286 the Scottish crown fell by legitimate inheritance to Margaret, the "Maid of Norway," who set out for Scotland to claim her throne. A committee of Scottish barons was appointed to rule in her name. Edward decided to arrange a marriage for her with his eldest son, thus securing a peaceful solution to fighting between the two countries. But the Maid died on the voyage and the wars went on.

Edward assigned the throne to a claimant, John Balliol, who was rejected by the barons. Edward invaded Scotland and a war broke out that lasted into the reign of Edward's son. A whole series of claimants, William Wallace and Robert Bruce among them, fought every attempt of England to subdue them, while they fought each other just as bitterly. In the end, Edward II was defeated at Bannockburn in 1314 and Robert Bruce, grandson of the hero, became King of an independent Scotland. It is noteworthy that in these wars with Wales and Scotland new weapons, the longbow and the pike, broke the power of the English cavalry charge.

The King's dealings with the Continent were just as unsuccessful. A series of half-hearted campaigns against Philip IV of France left the English holdings much as they had remained at the time of John's death, though Edward and his son did contract marriages with French princesses, which later added some weight to the English claims that precipitated the Hundred Years' War.

Edward I's main work had to do with the growth of the English Parliament and Common Law. The King was determined to destroy feudal rights and privileges. It was not always clear to him or to the feudal barons that a system was being destroyed, however, for it was done piecemeal. Written legislation replaced customary law and as the old laws were defined and new ones promulgated, England emerged as a constitutional monarchy. *Quo Warranto* (1278) limited baronial courts. The Statute of Mortmain (1279) limited grants to the Church. *De donis conditionalibus* (1285) prevented the passing of baronial estates to anyone but direct heirs or to the crown. *Quia emptores* (1290) eliminated subinfeudation. These statutes, taken together, spelled the eventual destruction of feudalism in England.

The barons and bishops of England had been growing increasingly restless in the face of this legislation. Finally they rebelled in 1297 and, to pacify them, the King issued the Confirmation of the Charters, whereby he confirmed *Magna Carta* and agreed that he could only enact taxes with the consent of Parliament. Edward had been making extensive use of parliaments, though their composition varied from time to time. In 1295 he called the Model Parliament, which assembled the secular and ecclesiastical nobility, the knights and the burgesses, and the lesser clergy. They heard the King's request, separated into their constituent groups to debate, then reassembled to give their answer. The men who came to Parliament were always those that had business there. If the matter under discussion affected certain groups, only they would be summoned. If it affected all the realm, all would be summoned. At the meetings of Parliament it became customary to petition the crown for redress of grievances, since the king was more receptive when dealing with the body that had control over his purse-strings. Thus, the two were linked together, and it became a tradition to grant the king money only when he had given redress in the grievances of the kingdom. By the end of Edward's reign England had emerged as a strong monarchy. Its strength, however, lay largely in its influence on future events. At the moment, if feudalism was dead, the feudal nobility was still powerful and dangerous, since the restraints of the feudal order had been removed.

France

The death of Philip Augustus brought to the throne his son, Louis VIII (1223–26), whose short reign is noteworthy only for some gains he made for the crown in its crusade against the Albigensians in the south. He also established the custom of assigning to each prince of the royal family a large fief *(appenage)* which would divide up the royal domain without destroying the unity of the kingdom. As it turned out, the custom was fatal, since it set up rivals who all had good claims to the throne.

Louis IX (1226–70) came to the throne at the age of twelve. His mother, Blanche of Castile, as regent was faced with an immediate rebellion of the barons, who brought in English help to fight their haughty foreigner. The war did not get very far, as much because of the reluctance of the barons to destroy the central government, as because of Blanche's ability. When Louis began to rule in person, he had the efficient government of his grandfather in his hands. It is to his credit that he used it so judiciously. Jean of Joinville, one of the King's courtiers, has left a magnificent biography of the King. It draws a moving portrait of a saintly King, who loved justice, his subjects, and God. He was also a gentleman, a strong warrior and a firm upholder of the prerogative of the crown. He was the most popular ruler of his day, and his saintliness brought about his canonization within a generation of his death.

The reforms of Philip Augustus were further developed. The *bailis* continued to be used, but now *enqueteurs* were sent out to hear any complaints against them. The *curia regis* began to split up into specialized groups as had the English *curia* a century before. The judicial work of the court, for instance, was put into the hands of the *Parlement* of Paris. Another body took over finances. All through the administration a group of well-trained bourgeois bureaucrats increased the rights of the crown, especially since they could keep far better records than the feudal vassals of the king. Roman law was introduced into the king's courts, and they were open to all his subjects. The high degree of justice he offered in them attracted an increasing number into them. This in turn weakened the feudal courts. By the time of his death, Louis had raised the prestige of the French monarchy immeasurably within the country by his upright life, and throughout Europe by his restrained charitable conduct toward his enemies as well as his friends.

The reign of Philip IV the Fair (1285–1314) completed the building of the French monarchy. Philip fought to eliminate rivals to his power by war and by institutional inventiveness. He was successful in resisting all attempts of Edward I of England to reclaim his lands. In Flanders, he was eventually successful in controlling the government there, though during the wars with the Flemish he suffered a terrible defeat at Courtrai (1302). He also had some moderate success in German politics, but his biggest *coup* in foreign affairs was his capture of the papacy, which will be discussed below in connection with the misadventures of Boniface VIII. Philip's wars had been very expensive, and he had turned to the Templars for help. He fell so deeply into debt to them that he decided to take advantage of the general hatred for the Order, which had become the main banker of the time, to disband it and confiscate its vast holdings. He felt it was best to convict them of heresy, which would wipe out his debts, since oaths to heretics were not valid, and which would give him the backing of the Church. The Order was accused of heresy and other infamous crimes, and the King forced convictions by using the Inquisition, secret trials, torture, false testimony. The whole procedure was a violation of every canon of justice, but the King was relentless. In 1311 the Order was disbanded, and the King took over all its property in France. He had already gained considerable wealth by expelling the Jews in 1306 and confiscating what he could from them. He also juggled the

value of the currency and encouraged the payment of bribes in his courts.

These mean expediencies to solve his financial problems indicate a serious weakness in his government. He had, of course, his *curia regis* and he always consulted with them before he issued a tax. Unfortunately for him, however, and very unlike the English council that had become the Parliament, his *curia* had no influence in the country at large. He still had to negotiate with local councils to raise revenues. This took time, but of course in the long run, the determined opposition to taxes that was characteristic of the English Parliament could not develop in the weak local councils of France. The French equivalent of the Parliament, the *Estates General*, did begin to meet regularly during Philip's reign. Yet it was never representative of the whole country. The French always considered it an onerous duty to have to go to Paris to meet with the king. They much preferred to await his agents in their local assemblies. As a result, the French never saw in the *Estates General* an instrument for putting pressure on the king to redress their grievances. The assembly became simply a sounding-board for the King, where he publicized his propaganda attack against Boniface VIII in 1302, the first meeting of the *Estates*, or against the Templars in 1308. It is true that in 1314 he summoned an assembly to discuss taxes, but he had assumed that the delegates had come simply to hear his ideas. He was not wrong, for the tax was accepted in principle, the amounts worked out individually at the local level. Philip IV had worked ruthlessly to consolidate the reforms of Philip Augustus and Louis IX. He had succeeded, but by the time of his death, his reputation had been irretrievably lost. He had used trickery, murder, deceit. His expediencies loom in sharp contrast to the saintliness of his grandfather. The strength of the nobles had been held in check by force. At the first opportunity, they would strike back.

As soon as Philip was dead, they rose up against his son, Louis X (1314–16), and forced him to issue a series of charters guaranteeing the feudal liberties of the nobility. The charters were issued in local assemblies and never became a French *Magna Carta*. Instead, they introduced a resurgence of feudalism that would plague France until the end of the Hundred Years War.

The Papal Monarchy

The pontificate of Innocent III (1198–1216) is without question the high water mark of the medieval Church. The Investiture Controversy had been won, the launching of the Crusades had demonstrated the leadership of the Church, the Church-sponsored learning of the 12th Century had made available masses of classical learning, and Innocent was to bring all three developments to fulfillment in less than twenty years.

Innocent was a trained lawyer when he came to the papal throne at the age of thirty-seven. He viewed himself as the visible embodiment of God's power on earth. All kings, all men, all elements of the Christian community came directly under his control. He kept an intimate contact with every part of this community as is shown by the more than 6,000 letters that have been preserved from his correspondence.

It was the intention of Innocent III to consolidate the advances made and to establish himself as the arbiter of all Christian affairs. He believed that it was his right and his duty to be the conscience of Europe.

Secular authorities might govern, to be sure, but he felt that all disputes ought to be put before him for jurisdiction. He claimed the right, first of all, to nominate and control the Senator of Rome, who was elected by popular vote. He them took effective control over his lands in Italy. He then intervened to settle the disputed succession to Henry VI. The Guelph candidate was Otto of Brunswick, the Ghibelline was Philip of Swabia. Henry's brother, Otto, made elaborate concessions to the Pope, and Innocent backed him. Once he became Emperor, however, Otto broke his oaths, and Innocent, in desperation, put forward as a rival claimant Frederick, Henry's young son and heir, who had already been crowned in Sicily with the Pope's backing. The Pope formed an alliance with Philip Augustus, and the decision was made at the battle of Bouvines. By 1215 Frederick was the Emperor of Germany.

We have already seen the extent of Innocent's involvement in European affairs. He forced his will over Philip Augustus, John of England, and the rulers of many lesser European states. He launched the Fourth Crusade and entered into negotiations with the Frankish states of the East. This activity was moderately successful in its immediate objectives. The Pope was called in to judiciate in disputes, and his voice carried great weight. But there were ominous signs of weakness. Philip took back his wife only when he was ready. John capitulated in the face of a political and military threat, not a religious one. In other words, Innocent seems to have been more powerful as one of the great rulers of Europe than as a spiritual leader. Europe began to think of him more and more as a monarch than as a Pope. This was the result of the pope's political maneuverings during the Investiture Controversy. But Innocent continued the trend and stamped upon the Church a strong secular mark. The danger was that if Europe considered the pope to be a political ruler, then they might begin to treat him as such. The experiences with John and Richard were a good indication of what that might mean.

His only protection was to strengthen the Church and use it to improve and dominate the spiritual tone of the secular world. He was determined to construct a mighty Church that could resist all attacks made upon it. Thus, the pope's position would be secure as the sun, from whom all other bodies shine by reflected light. He called together the Fourth Lateran Council in 1215 to accomplish this task. This Council was the largest and most important held in the West up to that time. A widespread reform of the Church was instituted. Bishops were made responsible for establishing schools to train candidates for the priesthood, and they were to control the moral and spiritual lives of their priests, who were granted a decent income to live on. The Council forbade pluralism (the holding of more than one Church office at a time), and tried to make the bureaucratic administration of the Church more efficient. The sale of relics was forbidden, though the practice continued. A far-reaching decision of the Council was to forbid clerics to take part in trials by ordeal or combat. England immediately banned them, as did the rest of Europe more slowly. To replace such trials, governments had to devise new court procedures and to probe more deeply the nature of justice. In England, as we have seen, the jury trial was the outcome.

The Council gave the medieval Church its final form. The Pope, as heir to St. Peter, sat at its head. He was assisted in his enormous task by his *Curia* in Rome. The *Curia* was composed of the cardinals and officers of the papal administration. It was divided into four sections: the chancery, which handled the papal correspondence; the *dataria*, which handled dispensations, absolutions, and the like; the *camera*, which handled financial matters; and the *rota*, which handled legal matters and appeals from lower courts.

The elaborate administration carried on in this *Curia* was financed by revenues drawn from a relatively restricted source. There were the *servitia* and *annates* which prelates paid when appointed to an office. Monasteries paid annual fees, as did clerics whenever they visited Rome. Peter's Pence was a tax of one penny per household collected in England, Poland, and Scandinavia. There was a variety of other smaller fees that were augmented by the rents collected from papal lands. A large part of the revenues came from legal fees and indulgences. The monies were extensive, but they never actually covered the expenses of the Church. This was a basic weakness that in the end brought about the collapse of the medieval Church.

The pope administered his government through legates, who were special agents he sent out on his business. There were three types of legates: the *legatus natus*, who was a resident legate, often the king, in a given territory; the *legatus missus*, who was a special agent sent to settle disputes among the lower clergy, or to preside over local ceremonies and councils; and the *legatus a'latere*, who was always a cardinal, and who had the actual power of the pope in his hands for the duration of his mission.

The pope was also at the head of a system of appellate jurisdiction that began in the bishops' courts, moved to the archbishops' courts, and ended in the papal

Curia. In these courts the Church used canon law, which originated as a mixture of Roman law, papal decrees, opinions of the theologians, the Bible, decisions of councils, etc., and which Gratian had codified in his *Decretum.* The law was commonly divided into the laws that governed the actions of clerics and those that dealt with the Church organization. This latter part controlled any case connected in any way with a sacrament of the Church.

The Church was based on the sacramental system. In theory, the Church was considered a divinely-appointed institution which provided man with a path that led to salvation. Using that as a guide in his daily life, man could be sure that he was acting within the bounds of the true faith. By the time of Innocent III there were seven recognized sacraments. Baptism was the act by which all previous sins were washed away, and the new Christian was brought into God's Church. Confirmation, which could be performed by a bishop, was the strengthening of the new Christian by the reception of the Holy Spirit. The Eucharist was the partaking of Christ's flesh and blood so that the partaker was incorporated into Christ. The bread and wine of the ceremony were transformed during the Mass in their essential nature by the priest into flesh and blood, though their outer or accidental nature remained bread and wine (transubstantiation). Originally the communicant received both the bread and wine. In 1095 the practice was banned, and thereafter the communicant received only the wafer, while the priest drank the wine.

Penance was the fourth sacrament. It was the process whereby a sinner might expiate his sin and regain the grace that he had lost. Originally penance was a public affair, performed before the congregation, but un-der the influence of the Irish monasteries the practice of making private penance was introduced after the 6th Century. By the 13th Century it was the general rule, though it was not clear how often confession of sins had to be made.

Ordination was the sacrament whereby a priest was consecrated and given the power to administer the other sacraments except conformation. The priesthood was considered indelible which meant that, once ordained, a priest never lost his power to administer valid sacraments regardless of his own state of grace.

Marriage was a self-imposed sacrament, administered by the man and woman to each other, that was blessed by the priest. It was considered indissoluble, the only grounds for annulment being consanguinity or previous vows. The last sacrament was extreme unction, which was the anointing with holy oil and was administered to the dying.

The use of the sacraments provided man with grace which helped man on his journey to God. No one, however, could be assured of this entrance of his soul into heaven immediately after his death. His concupiscence, his innate tendency to sin, made it almost impossible for him to have atoned for the whole burden of his temporal punishment for sin on this earth. The Church taught that man was provided with an opportunity to complete this atonement in Purgatory. To die in a state of grace did not of itself eliminate the possible necessity of a stay in Purgatory, but man could stand the pain of Purgatory when he knew that eventually his fate would be in Heaven. The unrepentant sinner, however, must suffer for eternity the agonies of Hell.

The soul's stay in Purgatory could be shortened by the performance of good works done by a man in his life, or in his name by a man's friends or relations, such as praying or almsgiving. In effect, by these good works the merit earned by the extraordinarily meritorious lives of Christ and the saints could be transferred to the needy one's account. The name for such a transferral was an indulgence, of which there were two kinds: plenary, which was the remission of all temporal punishment for sin; and partial, which removed a certain part of temporal punishment. In all cases, the indulgence could only operate when the sinner was truly penitent and it could only involve the temporal punishment for sin and never external punishment, such as imprisonment.

The pope had a variety of means of enforcing obedience to the decrees of the Church. The first of these was excommunication, which cut the sinner off from the body of the faithful. No one could associate with him, and all obligations owed him, debts, loyalty, oaths, etc., were forfeited. Anathema, the most severe form, followed the sinner into the grave. On earth, the civil authorities made many claims on the excommunicant, though these varied from place to place. In France his property was forfeit. In Sweden he was executed if he remained excommunicated over a year. Nowhere could he appear in court, marry, carry on business, or fight under arms. He could not be buried in consecrated ground.

The interdict was a sort of collective excommunication. In any area placed under interdict all the churches had to be closed and the sacraments suspended. This was often attached to a person, especially a king, so that it operated wherever he happened to be. As he approached a town, for instance, the church bells would toll, the churches would close and all Christian life would come to a halt. As soon as he left, the bells would ring out, the people cheer and life would begin again.

The third method the Church used to enforce obedience was the Inquisition. This was merely a court that met to gather information concerning the accused's guilt or innocence. In origin it was a sworn inquest. However, as heresy grew to be a serious problem in the Church, witnesses, it was felt, had to be protected. Thus testimony was taken in secret from unnamed accusers. Furthermore, the accused was considered guilty until he had cleared himself of the charges, obviously an impossible thing to do under the circumstances. The ill repute of the Inquisition stems from this circumstance. However, the great majority of cases heard by the Inquisition ended in fines and penances. Only a small percentage ended with the *auto-da-fé*, death at the stake by burning, conducted by civil authorities.

In the 10th and 11th centuries the Cluniac movement reformed most of the monasteries of western Europe. However, there were many men who felt that the Cluniac houses were too worldly and involved with secular studies and pursuits. Those men were also repelled by the very success of the Church so well represented in the pontificate of Innocent III. To satisfy their need for a stricter asceticism, the order of Grammont was founded in 1076 and its austerities made it popular in the 12th Century. Even more popular was the eremitical Carthusian order founded in 1084. These monks lived in separate cells, worked alone, ate no meat, and were sworn to perpetual silence. The most popular of these orders was the Cistercian, founded in 1098. It became immensely celebrated in the 12th Century due to the reputation of its most illustrious member, St. Bernard of Clairvaux. The Cistercians stripped their churches of all decorations. They also specialized in spiritual work and manual labor, repudiating scholarship and materialism. Ironically, they moved into underpopulated regions, opening up new rich lands and developing them so well that the Order became immensely wealthy by the end of the Middle Ages.

A phenomenon of the 12th Century was the establishment of the two great Mendicant Orders, the Franciscans and the Dominicans. Many people resented the fact that cloistered monks withdrew from society to live the good life. They sought some way to live a religious life, but one that entered into the daily lives of common people. St. Francis of Assisi (1182–1226) is surely the man who has come closest to living the ideal Christian life. He was utterly simple and direct in his conviction that one must simply approach the world with faith and love. The world would provide in return, he felt, all the good man needed. He made a virtue of poverty and taught that God was everywhere. His creed was naive, pantheistic and completely inapplicable, and would certainly not have survived its inspired founder if more practical men had not modified his principles.

St. Dominic (1170–1221) was a completely different type than St. Francis. He was a well-educated Spaniard who believed that the Church's doctrines had to be brought to the people by a well-educated clergy in inspired sermons. The Dominicans became famous wandering preachers who brought religion into every aspect of the daily lives of the common people.

The two orders grew rapidly and borrowed each others' techniques. The Dominicans adopted the rule of poverty, owning no property or land, and the Franciscans stressed education and became able administrators. Both produced great preachers and both took over the universities of Europe. Both orders were directly under the supervision of the Pope. Each was headed by a Father General, answerable to the Pope, who ruled through a council of representatives of the local houses. The Mendicants were given special rights to hear confessions and administer sacraments, which aroused jealousy in the secular clergy. The common people always supported the Mendicants, and the Church recognized their value in satisfying the spiritual needs of the common people in an age when the Church had become an enormously successful, but an increasingly impersonal institution.

It is paradoxical that a main objective of the Mendicant Orders was the fight against heresy, when one considers that what gave rise to heresy also gave rise to the two Orders. Heresy is as old as the Church itself for every time the Church defined a point of dogma, disagreement with its definition was bound to lead to heresy. The more the Church defined its dogma, the more widespread disagreement became. The 12th Century saw the creation of a monolithic Church and everywhere in Europe men turned away to find their own paths to salvation. The two most important heretical groups of the many that existed at the time are the Waldensians and the *Cathari*.

The Waldensians claimed that the Bible ought to belong to everyone and that any inspired man or woman could preach the Word of God. They believed that a sinful priest could not administer valid sacraments. They denied the real presence of Christ in the Eucharist and rejected infant baptism. They held services in the open and in the vernacular language. In short they gathered together a wide assortment of beliefs that had been current for a long time. In turn, their ideas were passed on to the early Protestant reformers and have become familiar in modern Protestantism.

The *Cathari*, unlike the pacifist Waldensians, were extremely militant. They lived mainly in southern France around the city of Albi, hence they are often called the Albigensians. Their beliefs were a mixture of Zoroastrian and Manichean dualism that entered France by way of the Balkans, Bohemia and northern Italy. The Cathari taught that there were two gods, the good god and the evil god, Jehovah. Jehovah had created the earth and had killed Christ when He came to redeem mankind. Thus, the cross is the sign of Christ's defeat, not His victory, and should be spat upon. Jehovah, in the meantime, had taken over the earth and ruled in the false church that pretended to be Christian. The *Cathari* rejected almost every point of Catholic doctrine. They practiced extreme asceticism since all things of the flesh were evil, and upheld suicide as a final rejection of the flesh.

In spite of the grossness of many of their beliefs, the *Cathari* were learned preachers who wandered all over the rich provinces of Provence and Languedoc, where they were quite popular. St. Dominic began his preaching to counter them. Innocent III preached a crusade against them, which was undertaken by the northern French barons. By the time the crusade had come to an end in 1229, not only had the *Cathari* been eliminated, but the culture of southern France had been destroyed. Louis VIII formally annexed the provinces to the royal domain.

The Church and the German Empire

When Innocent III died, he had no idea that he had raised to the Imperial Throne the bitterest foe the Church was to encounter in its whole history. Frederick II (1215–50) has often been described as the first example of the "universal man" of the later Italian Renaissance. He was raised at the cosmopolitan court of Palermo and early in life developed a profound skepticism. For him all religions were the same, all cultures equally interesting. A brilliant amateur, he dabbled in every phase of science known in his day. Utterly cruel, he considered himself above the rules and laws that govern ordinary men. He was promiscuous in his private life, but it was his contempt for the religious conventions of the day that shocked his contemporaries. He welcomed Jews, Muslims, and schismatics at his court, though he burned heretics because they defied his authority. He was truly *Stupor Mundi*, the wonder of the world.

Frederick's policy was to establish himself firmly in his southern possessions and in northern Italy as well. Two things, however, stood in his way. To win the support of Innocent in his fight to the German throne, Frederick had taken a vow to give up Sicily once he was crowned in the north, and later he had given his oath to go on the Crusade. Obviously, the Pope was apprehensive about being encircled by Hohenstaufen power, but he died before any serious threat materialized. Honorius III (1216–27) was a mild man, who tried to get Frederick to fulfill his vows. As an inducement he arranged a marriage between Frederick and the heiress to the crown of Jerusalem in 1225. But to no avail. Frederick

Albi, France. This church was used by the Albigenesian heretics. It had to serve as a fortress at times. There are no windows or openings that were not guarded. Next door to the church was the family home of Toulouse-Lautrec, artist and descendent of the Counts of Toulouse.

▶ **Cathedral-mosque, Cordova.** By the time this structure was completed a merging of Christian and Moorish lifestyles had taken place. The main structure was a mosque, with minarets to the left, and on the right is a Christian cathedral.

was too busy consolidating his government in Italy to go off to the Orient. Gregory IX (1227–41) was of sterner stuff. Seriously alarmed at the growth of Frederick's power and animosity, he ordered him to leave Italy and set out on the Crusade. Frederick procrastinated, the Pope marshalled public opinion. Finally, the Emperor did set out in September, 1227, but sickness broke out among his men, and he turned back. The Pope was outraged and excommunicated him. Actually, there was irony in the situation. Frederick had been acknowledged King of Jerusalem by the barons of the kingdom. He had come to terms with the Sultan of Egypt to give him aid in his wars in Syria in return for the surrender of Jerusalem. He was anxious, therefore, to get to the East to fulfill his bargain when he was forced to turn back to Italy. The following June he set out again for Syria, and Gregory excommunicated him again for not getting the first excommunication lifted before he left. The Crusade was a complete success, but its gains were the result of negotiation, not fighting. Jerusalem, Bethlehem, and Nazareth were turned over to Frederick, who agreed to keep a ten years' truce, and to allow Muslims to pray in Jerusalem. He was then crowned King in Jerusalem. Gregory denounced the agreements and sent an army to invade the kingdom of Sicily. Frederick easily defeated the Pope and a truce was signed in 1230.

Frederick then turned to his serious task of reforming his government. In 1231 he issued at Amalfi the constitution for the kingdom of Sicily, which destroyed feudalism in his kingdom. Private war was abolished and all criminal cases were removed from feudal courts. Ecclesiastical courts were deprived of all jurisdiction over laymen, and clerics were barred from public office. The freedoms of towns were severely restricted and an imperial *podestà* was placed in each one as governor to control local assemblies. The Emperor established an elaborate system of courts and appellate jurisdiction in which Roman law was applied in the interests of a highly centralized state. The work of government was placed in the hands of well-trained professionals, usually Muslims or Greeks, who used Byzantine or Arabic procedures. The coinage was stabilized, and the economy of the kingdom was consolidated. Sicily became the most advanced and prosperous state of its day.

In 1232 Frederick also issued a constitution in favor of the princes of Germany that was a serious setback to his growing power. In Germany he and his son, Henry, had been building up their power in their domain lands. Germany, however, had fallen almost completely into the hands of the German princes. It now seemed obvious that no real chance remained for a strong centralized government. Germany had become in fact a collection of powerful states. Frederick hoped to temporize, but by the terms of the constitution he recognized the independence of the princes and the towns, putting an end, as it turned out, to the reality of the German Empire.

His son was angered by the concessions and in 1234 he allied himself with the Lombard League, revived in 1226 to defy the Emperor. Frederick marched north in 1235. He forgave the princes, who deposed the young Henry and sent him to prison. In 1237 the Emperor invaded Lombardy and won a total victory at Cortenuova on November 27. The League was broken up, but his terms were so harsh, resistance continued. In 1239 Gregory excommunicated him yet another time, and the war took a new tack. Both the Pope and Emperor appealed to popular opinion. Most people were willing to take Frederick's side. The Pope had obviously been motivated by personal rancor and selfish hopes for gain. But Frederick's free-thinking and his open attacks on the Pope disturbed the conscience of Europe. He made a fatal error in 1241. At that time, Gregory called a council in Rome to depose the Emperor. Frederick's fleet attacked the ships carrying the bishops to Rome and so many prelates were killed or carried off to prison that the council could not be held. Europe was shocked. Frederick's attack on the Pope had now become an attack on the whole Church. His supporters began to drop away from him.

Innocent IV (1243–54) carried on the bitter struggle. He turned the whole Church into a weapon to use against Frederick, whom he hated venomously. Europe was just as repelled by the secularism of the Pope as it was by the skepticism of the Emperor. The Pope slipped off to Lyons to hold a council (1245) at which both sides made their cases. Frederick was convicted of perjury, heresy and sacrilege, deposed from all his offices and excommunicated. A new emperor was crowned in Germany, and war went into a relentless, indecisive phase, with no clearcut victory possible. When Frederick died in December, 1250 the war was still going on. He left his empire and kingdom to his son Conrad, but his illegitimate son Manfred, his favorite, was named regent in the south.

Frederick's death left chaos in Germany. The princes rose in civil war, and Conrad spent his whole reign (1250–54) trying to maintain himself. Upon his death rival claimants to the throne fought indecisively in a period called the Great Interregnum (1254–73) during which time

all semblance of order vanished. By 1273, Rudolph of Hapsburg was elected, and he began a new policy of concentrating on Germany, giving up the Hohenstaufen dreams of empire in Italy.

In the south Manfred took over the regency for his nephew Conradin, Conrad's young son and heir. The next three popes dedicated themselves to many schemes to destroy him, but he made successful alliances with the Greek ruler of Epirus in the East and the King of Aragon in the West, and extended his power into northern Italy. The papacy in desperation sought some champion to lead a holy war against the Hohenstaufen. Urban IV (1261–64) opened negotiations with Charles of Anjou, brother of St. Louis. The treaties were signed by Clement IV (1265–68). Charles agreed to pay a large down payment and a yearly tribute for the throne, and he promised to stay out of northern Italy. Charles invaded Italy in 1265 and on February 26, 1266 at Benevento, he destroyed Manfred and his army. All over Italy revolutions broke out as Guelph factions rose up against the Ghibellines. The young Conradin came into Italy in 1268 to rally his family's supporters, but he was defeated and captured at Tagiacozzo on August 23, 1268. He was beheaded the following October in Naples, and the Hohenstaufen dynasty came to an end.

Charles of Anjou and the Sicilian Vespers (1268–85)

The Hohenstaufen had been destroyed, but their dream of empire lived on. Charles thought of himself as the heir of that dream and he began to devise a scheme to unite Italy, Sicily, the Balkans and the Levant in one vast empire. He allied himself to the rulers of Constantinople, Frankish Greece and Hungary. He diverted his brother's Crusade to Tunis so as not to disturb his plans in the East. He became the ruler of Morea in Greece, purchased the crown of Jerusalem, and organized a full-scale invasion of the East. Martin IV (1281–85) was his firm ally in these schemes, though earlier popes had become almost as fearful of his pretentions as they had been of the Hohenstaufen.

Many other powers were also apprehensive. Michael VIII Palaeologus, who had restored Byzantine rule in Constantinople, knew he was the target of the invasion. He began an elaborate policy of intrigue to counterbalance Angevin power. He had accepted union with the Western Church at the Council of Lyons to neutralize the papacy. He entered negotiations with Genoa to harass the Venetian fleets that would support Charles. Above all, he entered an alliance with Pedro of Aragon, who sent a fleet to Sicilian waters to be ready in case of need. Meanwhile, Michael's secret agents were in Sicily whipping up discontent. A revolt was carefully planned by the Aragonese with Michael's help. On Easter Monday, 1282 riots broke out all over the island. Thousands of Frenchmen were killed. Pedro was crowned King of Sicily, while Charles retained his possessions on the mainland. The two Sicilies had been separated and remained so until they were reunited in 1443 by Alfonso of Aragon. Charles died in January, 1285, viewing bitterly the collapse of all his schemes. Naples went to his heir Charles II who ruled it without any significant changes until his death in 1309. Sicily, on the other hand, became embroiled in the antagonisms within the Aragonese house, and passed back and forth between rivals. The

Aragonese were always willing to sacrifice the island in their larger manoeuverings with France, but the Sicilians always protested. Invasion and civil disorder plagued the island for years to come.

The Later Crusades

The Third Crusade had failed because of the rivalries between the leaders and the lack of effective organization. Innocent III was determined that another crusade be called and that this one would be carefully controlled by the papacy. In 1201 at a tourney at Ecri in France, a "tourney of God" was preached and the chivalric nobility of France took up the cross. The leadership of the Crusade eventually fell to Boniface of Montferrat in northern Italy. A committee was sent to Venice to arrange for passage of the host to the East. Exactly what plan had been agreed-upon is not clear. Probably the leaders were thinking of going to Egypt to capture a city to exchange for Jerusalem, while the rank and file probably thought only in terms of an invasion of Syria. In any case, the committee signed a contract with Venice for shipping and provisions for some 35,000 men. April 2 in the following year was set as the date of departure, and Venice set to work to get the ships ready. In the following spring only about 12,000 of the Crusaders actually showed up in Venice, the others having already set out for the East from other ports. The government of Venice was outraged. They had invested heavily, and now there were no monies to pay for the fleet. In the meantime the Republic had been securing possessions along the Adriatic coast and in the eastern Mediterranean. The presence of so many fighters in the town suggested a way out of the dilemma. Venice offered the Crusaders the fleet and even more men and supplies, if they would help recapture the Christian city of Zara on the Dalmatian coast, which had fallen to the king of Hungary. Reluctantly the Crusaders agreed, and the host sailed to Zara, which fell in November, 1202. Innocent was furious at the misuse of the Crusade and excommunicated the leaders, but soon had to bow to necessity and left the excommunication unenforced.

In the meantime, envoys arrived at Zara from Alexius Angelus, son of the deposed *Basileus* of Byzantium, Isaac Angelus. Alexius had been in the West trying to raise some troops from his brother-in-law, Philip of Swabia, or from the Pope, to place his father back on his throne. Innocent had turned a deaf ear, not in the least interested in Hohenstaufen connections in the East, no matter how remote, but Philip had been encouraging. The leader of the Crusade, Boniface, was Philip's close friend and must have known of the situation. Venice was also aware of the opportunities that awaited anyone who fished in the troubled waters of the East. It is probable that no one faction actually planned what happened at this point, but each faction in the crusading army had some further interest in Eastern affairs than merely a desire to recapture Jerusalem. In any case, Alexius offered generous help for the Crusade and the submission to Rome of the Greek Church if the Crusaders would put him and his father on their throne. The Crusaders agreed and met him in person at Corfu in late April, 1203. From there they sailed to Constantinople, arriving on June 23. Surprised that the city did not rise up to welcome its rightful king, the host laid siege to the city in July. Abandoned by its Emperor Alexius III, who fled,

and disorganized, the city could not defend itself. Isaac was put back on the throne and Alexius, his son, was crowned as co-emperor.

Unfortunately, Alexius could in no way make good on his promises. Street fighting broke out between the Greeks and the Westerners. The Crusaders demanded their payment. The city rose up in revolution and deposed the Angeli. The Franks were expelled by the new *Basileus*, Alexius V. The Crusaders decided to take the city for themselves. In March, 1204, they signed a compact, whereby they would divide up the Byzantine empire among themselves, Venice to receive the lion's share, and they would elect a Latin emperor and a patriarch, either one or the other being a Venetian. The Crusade against the Muslims was dead. It had become a war against Byzantium. The assault began on April 9, 1204, and in four days the city had fallen. A tremendous mound of booty was collected. The churches and monasteries were plundered, and thousands of relics and holy articles were stolen. The richest prize in Christendom was systematically looted, then the empire was divided, Baldwin of Flanders was elected Emperor, and Tomasso Morosini, Patriarch. A swarm of Crusaders rushed through the empire to establish fiefs and take a fair share of the loot. An empire was established. Boniface set up a kingdom in northern Greece, and a principality was established in Morea, the Peloponnesus. But these states never gained much strength. The empire lasted only until 1261 when it was captured by Michael VIII. For a time Morea attracted adventurers from the West, but it slowly fell before the *ravanche* of the Greeks, who had set up states in Epirus, Nicaea, and Trebizond. The Crusade had proved a disaster. Byzantium never again had the strength to hold back Asiatic attacks on Europe. The Greeks came to hate the West, so that union between the two churches became virtually an impossibility. Energies were diverted from the war against the Muslims in the Levant. The movement, itself, had suffered a serious blow to its prestige. Only Venice gained. She established a far-flung network of ports to tap the trade of the whole eastern Mediterranean.

Innocent did the best he could to reap some profit from the fiasco, but not with much success. He sent preachers across Europe to arouse enthusiasm for another crusade. This time the response was bizarre and indicates the spiritual state of Europe at the time. Groups of children began to gather in France and Germany. Led by mere boys, they were determined to go off to Jerusalem to liberate the Holy Land. Frightened parents, worried authorities, even the King of France, himself, all tried to force the children to return to their homes, but some 20,000 of them were led by a boy named Nicholas, across the Alps from Germany and into Italy.

Thousands of them finally reached the sea, which did not open miraculously before them, as they had expected. The group began to break up. Some wandered off into Italy. Others stayed in Genoa. Others returned to Germany. The most unfortunate were those who went on to Marseilles where they were sold as slaves to Muslims of North Africa. The whole episode was shocking, but it did indicate the vigor still remaining in the crusading movement.

Ironically the Holy Land probably could have been captured with ease at the time. After Salah ad-Din's death a civil war had broken out between a host of petty rulers, the most important of whom was the Sultan of Egypt. The Franks in Palestine had been unable to take advantage of the situation. The Italians were merchants and they did not want war. The government had fallen into factionalism. Above all, there was no basic understanding between the colonials in the East and the Westerners, who wished to use the Crusade to further their own ecclesiastical or secular policies. The Fifth Crusade, for instance, organized by the papacy and led by the legate, Cardinal Pelagius, lay siege to the rich Egyptian city of Damietta. The Westerners were supported by the Eastern barons led by their King, John of Brienne. The Muslims offered to return Jerusalem and almost all the kingdom if the Crusaders would life the siege. Brienne wanted to accept, Pelagius refused. When the city capitulated, the Muslims again made their offer. Again Pelagius refused. Brienne returned to his kingdom in disgust. Pelagius led his troops up the Nile to attack Cairo, but they were caught in the annual floods of the river and barely escaped with their lives. All was lost.

Frederick II was able to retrieve the situation somewhat, as we have seen, by gaining Jerusalem by treaty, but the barons resented his government and rose up in a bitter civil war against him on Cyprus. The Muslims took back Jerusalem in 1244. St. Louis in 1248 led his host eastward on the Sixth Crusade to avenge the fall of the Holy City. It was the last expedition that had any chance of success. But again mismanagement and ignorance of conditions in the East led to a stalemate and though Louis went on to Palestine to fortify a castle or two there, nothing was really accomplished. Time had run out for the Crusaders. A new government had established itself in Egypt under the Mamelukes, and the Mongols had begun their invasions from the East. The Mongols were stopped at Ain Jalut (1260), and the Mamelukes took over all of Syria.

Crusades now had no chance at all in the East. St. Louis led his second crusade (called the Seventh, 1270) to Tunis, where he and most of his army died of disease. The last Frankish possessions in Palestine fell to the Muslims in 1291, and the crusades were over as military expeditions. As an ideal and as the basic principle of papal foreign policy they lived on for many years. The crusades provided the popes with an excuse to involve themselves in the foreign policies of all Christian states. It also gave them extensive revenues in taxes for expeditions that never quite materialized. The crusading ideal, however, waned steadily. The bitterness against Frederick II, the failure of the later crusades, the general decline of religious fervor, and the abandonment of attempts to colonize the East, all helped to destroy the movement, but it had not been a total loss. Mediterranean commerce had flourished. The Italian states had emerged. New products modified the monotony of medieval life. Stone castles, the use of the cross-bow, the chivalric code were introduced to revolutionize the feudal system. Above all a steady trade developed with the Near East, which in turn led to the development of banking and manufacturing. The crusades were not in themselves causes, so much as stimulants to many developments already under way when they were first launched in the 11th Century.

Medieval Spain

The Umayyad conquest of Spain in the 8th Century had been rapid and complete. Such Christians as survived fled to the mountains of the northwest in the area known as the Asturias. The Muslims organized them-

selves into rival emirates, in which a high cultural and economic civilization flourished. Spanish wines and citrus fruits, Cordovan leather, Toledo steel, and the scholars at the courts of all the emirs made Spain a worthy rival to Baghdad and Damascus. After the collapse of the Visigothic kingdom the only Christian state in Spain was Leon in the northwest. Slowly the rulers of Leon pushed their way southward until they established themselves in the heart of Spain in the land they called Castile. In the 10th Century Castile became independent with the help of neighboring Muslim emirs. In the north the county of Barcelona had developed in Charlemagne's Spanish March, and Navarre had emerged in the Western Pyrenees to become the strongest Christian state under its King Sancho the Great (970–1035). Sancho was able to conquer part of Leon and Castile, and his lands were divided among his sons at his death. Aragon was created in the north for one of them, Ramiro, while Ferdinand I (1033–65) became King of Castile and Leon. At Ferdinand's death, his lands were divided among his sons in an ancient custom that caused endless civil wars, but they were finally reunited by Alphonso VI (1072–1109), who used volunteers from Aragon, France and Burgundy to launch an attack on Toledo, which fell to him in 1085.

The emirs, alarmed at his advance, turned to the Muslims of North Africa for help. There, a fanatical sect called Almoravides had risen to power. Their leader Ibn Tashfin invaded Spain in 1086 and inflicted a crushing defeat on Alfonso at Zalaca. The Almoravides soon took over all Muslim Spain.

Aragon, meanwhile, had been established by the annexation of Navarre, and had been placed under papal protection by its king in 1095. In 1108, Castile and Aragon were joined by the marriage of their rulers, though a true union did not take place. Civil war was a constant plague for the Christian states in the 12th Century, but luckily for them the Muslims were just as disunited. During the civil wars a Burgundian noble had been made count of Portugal. His son, Alfonso Henriques, took the title of King in 1139. Thus, all Christian Spain was divided into three states by the 12th Century, Portugal in the west, Aragon in the east, and Castile in the center. All three pressed southward against the Moors, sometimes cooperating, but most often as rivals allying themselves with various Moorish emirs. Alfonso VII of Castile for a time was able to unite the Christian states, taking the title of Emperor of Spain in 1135, and pushing vigorously southward against the Moors. He devastated Andalusia and held Cadiz on the southern coast for a while. His lands were broken up at his death, however, and independent states again emerged. Aragon merged with Barcelona and was quickly taken over by Catalans that turned the country eastward and to the sea. The Moors, meanwhile, had found new strength. A new sect, the Almohades, had taken over from the Almoravides, and they invaded Spain in 1146. A crusade was preached to stop them, to no avail. Innocent III called a new crusade against them and at Las Navas de Tolosa a Christian army won a decisive victory on July 16, 1212. However, the Spanish rulers as usual fell into renewed civil wars and the opportunity to end Muslim rule in Spain was almost lost.

Ferdinand III of Castile (1217–52), however, was able to join Leon and Castile into a permanent union and to begin a systematic reconquest of the peninsula. By 1270

only Granada remained in Moorish hands. His death, however, brought to the throne an ineffective son and after him more civil wars. It was in this period that the feudal institutions of Castile were developed. The realm was ruled under a law of custom that was codified into the *Siete Partidas* and the *Fuere Real* by Alfonso X (1252–84), but the social structure of the country limited its effectiveness. The Castilian nobility, because of their constant involvement in the Moorish wars, had become the most independent in Europe. They paid no taxes, were free from arrest, and they could maintain private armies. At any time, they could renounce their allegiance to the king. Alongside this free nobility there had grown up in Castile a large number of privileged communes. To attract settlers in lands conquered from the Moors, the kings had offered generous charters to the towns, which became self-governing and a powerful force in the realm by joining together in brotherhoods (*hermanades*) to preserve their liberties. These towns were sending representatives to meetings of the noble assembly (*cortes*) as early as 1188, making this the first parliament in history. This assembly was made up of the nobles, the clergy and the burghers, and by 1307 had control over the finances of the king.

The institutions of Aragon were somewhat similar to those of Castile, but the influence of the nobility was much greater. Aragon was really composed of two states, Aragon and Catalonia, and each had its own laws and institutions. The Aragonese were involved in expansion within Spain, but the Catalans were more interested in moving out into the Mediterranean. The kings of Aragon were always torn between the two. James I (1213–76) conquered the Balearic Islands for the Catalans and Valencia for his Aragonese subjects. But the king-dom was divided at his death among three sons, one of whom, Pedro the Great (1276–85), was the king that benefitted from the Sicilian Vespers as we have seen. He and the next two kings, Alfonso III (1285–91) and James II (1291–1327), made Aragon the greatest power in the Mediterranean world, but they had to pay a heavy price for their ventures. The nobility at home were not ba-sically interested in overseas political ven-tures and they resented the heavy cost. In 1283 they rose up against the king and forced him to issue the General Privilege, which established the liberties of the *Cortes* of Aragon. The king had to respect the cus-toms of the realm. The nobility did not have to fight outside the realm and all classes had the right to sit in the *Cortes*. The burghers were not as dissatisfied with the overseas empire as the feudal nobility were and they eventually sided with the king. In fact the prosperous towns of both Castile and Aragon gave the Spanish monarchs an in-come and stability that was a fair match for the kings of England or France by the end of the 13th Century.

The City-States of Northern Italy

During their struggles with the Hohen-staufen, the states of northern Italy had gone through a profound change in their development. Unlike their counterparts in northern Europe, the Italian communes in-cluded the nobles of the *contado*. In the north the feudal aristocrat felt hemmed in by the crowded streets of the town that grew up around his castle and he fled to the country-side. The walls of the town served to keep

him out. In Italy the nobles moved into the town, built *palazzi* with tall towers, and car-ried on their incessant feuding within the confines of the town walls. Life was turbu-lent and dangerous. To control the situation an official called the *podestá* was hired by common consent to keep some degree of order. He was given a guard, his *palazzo* and a council to advise him. The burghers, as they grew stronger, in defense appointed their own protector, the *capitano del popolo*, who had his own council and who was in charge of the town's military forces. The *podestá* tended to represent the nobility in his councils, while the *capitano* represented the guilds. During the Hohenstaufen period the one became Guelph, the other, Ghibel-line. The 13th Century saw a great amount of anarchy in the towns as the factions fought bitterly in the wake of the papal and imperial armies that swept back and forth across the peninsula, but a certain pattern can be discerned. In general, the common people fought to win some voice in the gov-ernment, and control moved from the feu-dal nobility to the burghers.

Venice was originally founded by refu-gees fleeing the invasions of the 5th and 6th centuries. The small cluster of fishing vil-lages was organized under a Byzantine gov-ernor until 697 when it began to elect its own duke, or *doge*. In 1032 a council was established to elect the *doge*, and between 1172 and 1230 this developed into a highly centralized instrument with which the older aristocracy was pushed out by a rising mer-chant class that wished to dominate the state. Venice became almost a classic aristoc-racy, a state in which one class or faction ruled in its own interests, but since that in-terest served the whole state, their selfish rule was the best rule for the state and all other classes acquiesced. There was a grand council of 480 members elected from the several wards of the town. The council elected officials and passed on legislation submitted to it. Above them was a senate of 246 men, half elected at large, half the *doge* and his advisers. The senate was the legislative branch of the state, passing on all measures submitted to it by the *doge*. Six dukes acted as an inner cabinet that controlled the executive power of the state, including the *doge*. A *collegio* of the *doge* and other advisers headed the judicial branch of the state, the navies and the armies. Above the whole government were six *savii grandi* that served, one each day in the week, as prime ministers. The whole structure was an elaborate means of controlling the whole life of the community. The people had no voice in the state, but since their leaders controlled the whole commercial enterprise to the benefit of all, they had no real objection. In 1297 membership in the council was restricted to a group of the wealthier bourgeois families whose names were listed after 1315 in the *Golden Book*. In 1310 a sinister Council of Ten was established to act secretly to maintain public safety. In other words, the state had become a tight oligarchy. The result was a well-run state, well-suited for an aggressive policy of imperialistic expansion.

Florence, unlike Venice, was more a manufacturing than a commercial town. As a result society tended to be less mobile. The lower classes found it almost impossible to rise in the guilds and remained more dependent on upper-class rule. In Venice new families were always rising to the top. This was less true in Florence. Class tension was bitter, and the early history of Florence is mostly one of anarchy, but one thread runs through it all, the steady rise of the bourgeois class. By the 13th Century there were

five main classes in the town: the Guelph aristocrats, the Ghibelline aristocrats, the major guilds, the minor guilds, and the *popolo piccolo*. In 1282 a constitution was adopted that set up a *signoria* composed of six priors, one for each guild and from each city ward. The *signoria* had power over all other officials in the state. In 1293 a new official, the *Gonfaloniere della Giustizia,* was created by the institution of the Ordinances of Justice. The *Gonfaloniere* had to be a non-noble member of a guild. He had power over the priors and had a guard of 1,000 men. The priors had to be guildsmen. Nobles had to post bond to ensure their good behavior. They were barred from government and became second-class citizens. The new constitution was so extreme it was bound to lead to civil war. The Guelph faction split into the Blacks and the Whites, and the two fought bitterly for control over the town.

No matter how chaotic, the town had to prosper. The wool of Tuscany was brought to Florence where it was made into one of the finest cloths of Europe. The guilds prospered, and through them certain families became very wealthy. The Bardi, for instance, and the Peruzzi became the leading bankers in Italy, handling all the collection of papal taxes. They set up branches in all the leading cities of Europe and from these centers they dominated the finances of the whole continent. One of the banking houses that appeared on the scene in 1277 was the Medici.

Milan in north-central Italy rose to greatness primarily because of its geographic location. All the trade routes across the central Alps led to the town, just as the produce of the Lombard plain flowed into the town for shipment north. Milan had a huge population for the Middle Ages (200,000 in the 13th Century). The classes were so evenly balanced that no one faction could dominate, though the town was consistently Guelph. The history of the town was dominated by its proximity to Germany. Every expedition the emperor made from the north brought him first to Milan, and on his return, it was the last town he let go. The city had fought the emperors long and hard, and the price had been high. The first powerful official in the town was the archbishop, but by the mid-13th Century there was a *podestá* who took second place. The only means of maintaining order was to bring in an outsider who had no connections with any faction. All through the century one *condottiere* followed the other. A *condottiere* was a mercenary captain with a band of cutthroat followers that sold their services to the highest bidder. They brought a degree of order to Milan as long as they stayed in power. The city prospered. But it was just a question of time before one of these captains would decide to take over the town for himself.

Scholarship and Art

The 12th Century translators had amassed a vast amount of knowledge, often indiscriminately, rarely with a critical eye. The task for scholars in the 13th Century was to study this material, assess it and absorb it into a system consistent with traditional belief and cultural patterns. At first, the attempt was made simply to gather the knowledge together. Huge encyclopedias were the result. The *Speculum Majus* of Vincent of Beauvais, for instance, is a good example. In over 6,000 folio pages Vincent gathered together quotations from all the authors he knew on every topic conceivable.

Much of the material came from the Arabic works recently translated, and about half dealt with scientific subjects. The book is arranged in thousands of chapters, in which each subject is broken down into sub-topics in a scholastic style, and shows no originality whatever. But it does present a general view of the knowledge of his day.

The contact that Europe had made with the world at large after the 11th Century had led men to take a closer look at the world around them. This growing awareness of things as important phenomena in themselves lay behind the nominalist position in philosophy and it was reinforced by the new contact with the scientific works of the Greeks and the Arabs. Men began to examine the world much more closely, not only in its physical properties, but in the arrangements men had made to live in it. Scholasticism, to be sure, with its emphasis on abstract patterns, and realism, even the modified realism of Aquinas, tended to lead men to inner "truths" and away from external properties, so that science was still largely a matter of inspired exceptional guesses. Yet it is hard to escape the tone of practicality that colors the works of the 13th Century. If formal scholars still saw theology as the only really practical science, if many were content to accept the ideas of the ancients as intriguing mental exercises and were not interested in adding to them, there were many who were willing to experiment, to test the sonorous statements of Aristotle, to find truth for themselves.

Often the result could be bizarre. Men of science often ended up dabbling in the occult. Astrology became more important than astronomy. Frederick II conducted many mad experiments to see a living heart beat, or to measure the speed of digestion in humans. On the other hand, Arabic mathematics had obvious practical value, even if men did not see it at first. Leonardo of Pisa introduced Arabic numerals at Frederick's court in Sicily, where a group of scholars, led by the court astrologer, Michael Scot, were translating Arabic and Aristotelian scientific texts, often to satisfy the King's interest in magic. Often progress in science resulted inadvertently from philosophical and theological speculation. Many anti-Thomists, particularly the spiritual Franciscans, sought to destroy his philosophical arguments by proving his authority, Aristotle, wrong. Experiments were conducted to point out Aristotle's errors. Roger Bacon (1219–94) was a member of this group. Historians credit him with advocating the scientific, inductive method, though his idea of it was quite hazy. He did emphasize the practical application of scientific knowledge to produce machines, for example, but he was rarely read in his own day, and his later reputation was much exaggerated.

In many ways the most important works of the day were those that dealt with geography, history and political affairs. Europeans had begun to travel and when they reported what they had actually seen, they were accurate. Unfortunately, the myths and legends of the past still filled in the empty spaces of their maps with exotic creatures. In the 12th Century men had begun to describe their own lands, and in the 13th, John of Piano Carpini and William of Rubruck traveled across Asia to the Mongols and brought back fascinating descriptions. The greatest traveler of the age was Marco Polo, whose description of his journeys to Cathay published late in the 13th Century show what a careful and accurate observer he really was, though his tales were derided in his own day.

Historical writing in the Middle Ages had usually taken the form of world histories that began with the Creation and came down to the writer's own day. The 12th Century had seen added to these historical accounts of specific kings and their deeds. There were also narratives of special campaigns or crusades. All of these flourished in the 13th Century. Few could match the excellence of the *Chronicle of Two Cities* of Otto of Freising, covering events down to 1146, but many were of high quality. Suger's *Life of Louis VI* and his unfinished *Life of Louis VII* are models of biographical history. The *Life of St. Louis* by Joinville (1225–1317) is a literary masterpiece as well as an accurate incisive portrait of the man. The Crusades inspired many good histories, the *Conquest of Constantinople* of Geoffrey de Villehardouin being the finest. Of the Church historians, Matthew of Paris, whose *Chronicles* cover the years 1235–59, is by far the best.

Political theorists, curiously enough, are often, though not always, realistic observers of the world around them. In the 12th Century, for instance, John of Salisbury, a personal friend of Becket, wrote his *Policraticus (Statesman's Book)* to describe the well-ordered state in purely Platonic terms. Each part must function properly in harmony with every other part, and all parts have assigned to them specific functions. Yet in the midst of this restrained recital, the bishop lashes out at tyrants and claims that each Christian has the right to kill the tyrant and is answerable only to God for his deed. St. Thomas Aquinas in his *De Regimine Principum* expressed a view more in keeping with an age of parliaments. He feared the anarchy that would result from John's views and states that the tyrant ought to be removed, to be sure, but only by the people through their appropriate representative voice, i.e., the parliament. He also felt that it was the Church that provided the means of identifying tyranny and that kings were answerable to the pope. Dante (1265–1321) in his *De Monarchia* gives an opposite view. For him man is destined to live in peace and harmony under the rule of the emperor, who receives his power from God and is answerable only to Him.

St. Thomas Aquinas

Undoubtedly the greatest achievement of the century, of the whole age, in fact, was the work of St. Thomas Aquinas (1225–74), a Dominican friar. When the works of Aristotle first began to circulate, traditional churchmen were disturbed by the commentaries of Muslim philosophers and theologians that appeared in glosses in the margins of the texts. These and many of Aristotle's statements, themselves, seemed quite opposed to basic tenets of medieval Christianity. Some students of the *Metaphysics* were so impressed by the comments of the Muslim Averroes on the eternality of matter, the impossibility of personal salvation, and pantheism that they formed a heretical sect, led in the 13th Century by Siger of Brabant. Other scholars, however, saw the tremendous value of Aristotle and sought ways to purge his works of their seeming contradiction of the orthodox faith. Albertus Magnus (1193–1280), another Dominican, strove all through his teaching career at Cologne and Paris to reconcile man's knowledge, typified by Aristotle, and his faith, as expressed in the Church. His greatest student was Aquinas.

St. Thomas wrote many works, but the two most important were the *Summa contra Gentiles*, written for non-believers to show them that reason can lead them to religious truth and can never contradict it, and the *Summa Theologica*, which unites reason with faith, Aristotle's philosophy with Christian orthodoxy. He accepts Aristotle's suggestions that man was made by a Creator, a Prime Mover that set him in motion. Motion is the realization of potential, to become in time what one is already in essence. Thus, according to St. Thomas, man was made a creature that desires to return to God. It is his nature to seek Him and he is drawn to Him as by a magnet. To reach Him, he must use all of his faculties, the highest of which is his reason. By the correct use of reason, and here St. Thomas means the methods of scholastic logic, man can achieve a knowledge of God and of His sacraments, but he can never achieve a real union with them, for his nature is such that he cannot be one with God. But God, as a loving Deity, has offered man the means whereby he can reach Him. He has offered His sacraments, which man can perceive only through faith. By adding to what he has perceived through his reason, what he accepts through his faith, man achieves his purpose, a union with God. In his magnificent creation, St. Thomas demonstrated that the world was logical. The senses were trustworthy, for they could only announce what was true. Science ought to be encouraged for it would illuminate what was already known. Man was placed in the world to learn about it and to master it. There was no conflict between mind and body, reason and faith, science and theology.

Of course, St. Thomas had severe critics, from the very moment his works were published. His stress on knowledge offended many who preferred a more mystical approach to God. For them, the intellectual path was cold and sterile. For them, God had to be felt. The Franciscan St. Bonaventure (1221–74) believed that the search for God depended on man's will, not his reason. A bitter dispute between the two Mendicant Orders resulted. The most original writers of the next century, William Ockham and Marsiglio of Padua, joined this emphasis on will to nominalism to produce revolutionary concepts in political theory.

Gothic Style

In art the 13th Century again followed the lead of the preceding century. The elements of the Gothic style were abstracted and fully realized. The greatest cathedrals of France, Chartres, Paris, Amiens, Rheims, and others, were built at this time. The roofs were raised ever higher—that of Beauvais was so high it collapsed, windows grew larger, walls were reduced to simple pillars. Sainte-Chapelle, for instance, built by St. Louis to house the Crown of Thorns he acquired in the Orient, has no stone walls at all. It is all glass. The facades of the Gothic cathedral were a challenge to the sculptor and the makers of stained glass. Every church was covered inside and out with lovely forms that related the story of the universe. At first, highly stylized, almost abstractions, the story was told in symbols, but later in the century a certain naturalism was introduced. Again men's preoccupation with the world around them led them to see the transcendent in the actual forms of the physical world. In the end, this interest led to extreme realism and an empty photographing of the world, just as the challenge to use the walls to tell a story led to the flamboyant late Gothic style that emphasized decoration for its own sake.

XIII

THE DECLINE AND TRANSFORMATION
OF THE BYZANTINE WORLD
▼ ▼ ▼ ▼ ▼

▶ **Lavra, Mt. Athos, Greece.** This community of monks was established in the 10th Century by St. Athanasius, a monk who had lived for fifty years in a cave on the mountain. He was a friend of the Emperor Nicephorus Phocas, who was building a monastery on the mount when he was killed. The tower is 10th Century.

▶ **Mt. Athos, Greece.** Orthodox monks were in two groups, the eremites, or hermits, and the cenobites, those who lived in communities. The mountain has twenty monasteries and many solitary caves for hermits.

▶ **Mt. Athos, Greece.** Some of the monastic communities were quite large. Some are still filled with monks. The monasteries are now part of Greece, but have special autonomy. Each community sends a representative to a general council headed by a *nomarch.*

Byzantine Culture

The culture of the Eastern Empire was a combination of three elements: Roman law and institutions, the Christian church, and Hellenistic art forms. These were woven together until a distinct culture was produced. All through its history Byzantium used Roman law and institutions, and in every generation refinements and new adaptations kept them alive as a living tradition. From the time of Justinian to the end of the Empire, the emperors sponsored changes in the law.

Roman Law and Institutions

The several codifications of the laws have been analysed in other places in this book. In addition, the Emperor Leo the Wise produced the *Book of the Prefect*, which regulated the life of the guilds of the Empire. He also wrote a noteworthy book on *Tactics*. Another Emperor, Constantine Porphyrogenitus, wrote a series of monumental studies: *On Themes, On the Administration of the Empire*, and the *Book of Ceremonies*, which give a detailed view of the Empire under the Macedonians. He also wrote a *Life of Basil I*, the founder of the dynasty. All these works are of distinguished literary merit, another sign of the sophistication of the Byzantines.

The Byzantines were always interested in the plastic arts. The markets of the City offered the riches of the Orient. Byzantines lived on a luxurious scale with clothing made from the finest fabrics, decorated with jewels from all over the world. The mosaic portraits in the church of San Vitale in Ravenna of Justinian, his wife Theodora, and their court give some idea of how the well-dressed courtier looked. In general, Byzantines were well-dressed and well-housed. They went to the theatre to view ancient classics and new plays, some based on local themes and some taken from their Muslim neighbors. They bathed daily at a time when Westerners bathed only twice in a lifetime, once when they were baptized and once when their corpse was readied for burial. When the First Crusade arrived in Constantinople, the Western knights hated the Byzantines on sight, thinking them effete and artifical, while they in turn were considered barbarians. This prejudice colored the whole movement. The West never regained any trust in Byzantium.

The Christian Church

It was perhaps inevitable that their love for beautiful things led the Easterners to mosaics as a characteristic art form. Byzantine mosaics are indeed renowned, but their development is in some ways complicated. They seem to have developed out of the traditions of Hellenistic painting. Early icons were representations of Christ, the Virgin, or some saint. Soon scenes from their lives, or the depiction of miracles, became popular forms of teaching and of giving comfort. Hellenistic statuary had also been used in this way. Early Byzantine statues exist, but they did not survive the iconoclastic controversy. People favored flat icons. The acts of Christ were more conveniently painted, in local costume and scenes, than sculpted. The scenes began to depict contemporary settings, it was a small step to turn to secular themes and portraiture. The introduction of the mosaic is a means of depicting a scene in stone which is more permanent, and the skill with which artists chose small bits of stone and embedded them in plaster at appropriate angles to catch the light produced works of the highest artistry.

But a Byzantine church must be viewed as a whole to understand the role of the icon in mosaic. Byzantine churches, unlike Western cathedrals, are rather plain on the outside. Little effort is spent on decoration of the exterior. But the inside is another matter. The philosophy behind a Byzantine church is Platonic. By *mimesis* man seeks to create his own world-model taken from the ideal universe. In other words, just as there is an order in heaven where God is king, surrounded by His saints and angels, so too ought man to recreate this same order in his church on Earth. So a church replicates the heavenly order. St. Sophia in Constantinople achieves this to a marvelous degree and has become the standard example. First, the church is covered by a great dome to depict the vault of heaven. Justinian's architects solved an ancient problem to do this: How to place a circular dome on a square building. The solution was brilliant. One dome is built with an inscribed circle as its base, and another is built with a circumscribed circle as its base. The overlapping parts of the larger dome are cut off, leaving a dome held up by cornerpieces, the pendentives. The result is great spaces of wall filled with windows that allow light to stream in. The effect is exactly what the philosophy demands. On Earth there is a copy of the vault of heaven. At the top is depicted Christ in Judgment or beckoning all to come to Him. And all round are His saints in graphic mosaics, His angels, reminders of His miracles, and above all in an apse of her own, His mother, the *Theotokos*. Everyone is there in order, including the worshippers. The *basileus* sits on his earthly throne, or the bishop on his. The priests wearing their robes, the other members of the family of the bishop, and finally the laity are all present. The order in Heaven is replicated on Earth. The mood of the mosaic icon is best suited to capture this scene. These icons become jewelled "windows into heaven."

The Church had its own schools, beginning with the bishops' schools and reaching the university level. All through its history the Church produced a stream of clerics who were well-versed in Plato and Aristotle and lesser lights of philosophy. All theological disputes were carried on in terms of the application of Platonic or Aristotelian principles. The works of St. John Chrysostom, St. Gregory of Nyassa, St. John Damascene, St. Gregory of Nazianzos, and a host of others can still be read with profit, and they have been canonized for their intellectual contributions, rather than for good works.

The same educational system emphasized the literary arts as well. There was a long tradition of religious poetry, which was of high quality. The Mass of St. John Chrysostrom has remained unchanged down through the centuries and has been translated into all the languages of the Orthodox Church. It set the standard for poetic style throughout the Byzantine world.

Hellenistic Art and Literature

The third element in Byzantine culture was Hellenistic art forms, especially literature. The official language of government in the Eastern Empire began as Latin and most citizens were bilingual. But from the start Greek was the favored language. The Hellenistic world had developed the *koine*, "the common language" in which the Gospels were written. It was the language spoken in the street, but educated people could use the ancient language fluently. From the beginning there was in use a full educational program that began in grammar school, went through what we would call high school and then on into university studies. It has been said that at its height ninety per cent of the Byzantines were literate.

Byzantine literature begins as a continuation of classical forms. There was never an interruption in the flow as there was in the West, where illiteracy became common. The language was Greek, but a variety of levels of Greek, from the *koine* to Aristotelian, was used. There were changes in the grammar and morphology of the Greek used, and certainly the pronunciation became distinctive, no matter how Greek had sounded originally. Older Hellenistic themes and forms were continued and copied. In fact, Byzantine literature formed a bridge linking classical culture to their own times. The changes in the structure of the language went on and in the end a new literature began to emerge with a new emphasis on Christian themes and the new historical experiences of the Byzantines.

Secular literature ranged from popular novels, the witty biting comments of the poetess Kasia (9th Century), to biographies, geographies, and analyses of the ancient classics. Foreign themes were studied, even one so exotic as *Barlaam and Iosaph*, which includes elements taken from the life of the Buddha. Some of the most charming works are the many romances called chivalric tales. Hellenistic romances like *Daphnis and Chloe* had given pleasure to an avid audience, but it is important to note that the tone of the tale is melancholy and nostalgic. Hellenistic literature comes at the end of an age, and there is a sense of loss, of looking back. The same is true of another story that tells of a group sailing along the Dalmatian coast when suddenly they hear a booming voice cry out, "The Great God Pan is dead!" No one ever knew whose voice it was and what was the occasion, but somehow the story captures the same flavor, and it has survived to the present.

But a new mood is struck in the Byzantine romance. *Callimachus and Chrysorrhe*, *Velthandros and Chrysantsa*, *Phlorîos and Platzia Phloras*, and *Iberios and Margarona* are examples; the first is pure Byzantine, the second is an adaptation strongly influenced by Western poetic themes, the third is an adaptation of a Western work, and the last is a translation of a Western work. These are stories that are rather modern in tone. The theme is usually that the young man, always the younger son, sets out to find adventure. On his way he meets the young lady, sometimes the captive of a dragon, sometimes in bondage. The two escape and go through many trials. Eventually they make their way home and live happily ever after. In the Byzantine stories there is a basic optimism which contrasts with the world-weary tone of the Hellenistic romances.

Many chronicles written in vernacular verse have survived. Some have transmitted Eastern themes to the West, while others, like *The Chronicle of Morea*, have brought Western themes Eastward. The *Chronicle* is the story of the establishment and subsequent history of the principality of Morea in southern Greece in the wake of the Fourth Crusade (1204). A band of adventurers, largely French and Burgundian, stumbles into the chaotic conditions left behind as the

Empire loses control of this backwater. Seizing the opportunity, the French take over the whole Peloponnesus and establish a feudal principality with its capital in the town of Andravida. They quickly create a court, and set out, each vassal of the Prince, to conquer his feudal lands and build a castle. The Franks maintain good relations with the Greeks on their lands, for they hadbrought a more stable government. Morea was also an outpost of French culture where a constant stream of visitors and immigrants from France were amazed at the orderly feudalism and the level of culture they found there. The *Chronicle* itself is of fundamental importance in the development of late Byzantine Greek. It seems that in time subsequent generations born in Morea lost their facility in colloquial French. They saw in the *Chronicle* the history of their ancestors and a good story as well. A translation was made into the vernacular Greek of the day. In fact, it can be said that the *Chronicle* is the first book written in modern Greek.

There was an unbroken line of historians who were writing in the classical tradition. They are, naturally, of uneven quality, but at their best they are on a par with the classical writers. Procopius wrote excellent histories of the wars of Justinian. He also kept a *Secret History* which he arranged to have published after his death, in which he gives a racy, if not always reliable, picture of the court. Michael Psellus in the 11th Century was a very learned university professor who went into politics as so many Byzantine scholars did. His works cover the period of the final schism between the two Churches. He was active during the last days of the Macedonians and he gives insightful thumbnail sketches of the important people of his day.

Chivalric chronicles were very popular tales of adventure, often based on history, or what the audience believed to be history. A famous tale is the 11th Century *Digenes Akritas*, the story of a Warden of the Marshes whose father was Greek and his mother Saracen. It has become the Homeric epic of medieval Byzantine literature. The chronicles were recited in verse, and often provide, like the *Chronicle of Morea*, the only source for a whole period of Byzantine history, in this case the foundation of the Frankish states of Greece. The use of the chronicle not only entertained by the exciting story it told, but it kept alive the past as a kind of living history.

The work of Suidas, the *Lexicon*, has been of lasting importance. It was an analysis of grammar and philology, but also a history of the ancient literature. Most of what we know today about the ancient Greek writers comes from this encyclopedia. It is this service of keeping alive the past culture that brings us into Byzantine debt. The Emperor Justinian was an outstanding example of what Byzantine education could achieve. His uncle, Justin I, was an illiterate peasant who rose through the ranks of the army until he became Emperor. His nephew was among the most educated and sophisticated men of his day.

But there was always present a tone of artificiality in Byzantine culture. A vernacular literature did appear, written in the language of the people. But it was never easy for some educated Byzantines to shake off a reverential attitude to the literature of the past. An ominous sign were the attitudes of Michael Accominatus, who was the Archbishop of Athens when the Fourth Crusade took place. He was always in a state of shock when he reflected that his church was in the Parthenon of ancient Athens. It is said that whenever he chanted the Mass, he washed out his mouth afterwards because he felt the Greek of the Mass was so adulterated.

Another example of this awkwardness is found with Anna Comnena, daughter of Alexius I, who wrote a very valuable biography of her father. In it she gives a unique picture of the leaders of the First Crusade as an educated Byzantine saw them. What is striking is that she chooses to write in a stilted, somewhat artificial Greek, but one that would have been natural to Procopius. It is remarkable that Byzantine literature could still be written in that Greek, but that was the whole point. The bridge that linked the classical age to her day had accomplished its purpose.

A modern vernacular language had emerged and like French, Norman English, Spanish or Italian, Greek ought to have developed its own history from there. But it did not. After centuries of Ottoman rule, in an age of national revolutions the Greeks in 1821 began to establish a modern state. One thing that makes a state is a common language. But what language ought modern Greeks to have? There was at hand the living vernacular language, demotic Greek. But the intellectuals of that day chose to interpret the revolution as if it were in the manner of ancient Greeks like Pericles and Demosthenes, not the Greeks who were their contemporaries. So they had to base a new language on ancient roots, and they called it the "pure" language. Demotic Greek was rejected just as the whole Byzantine experience of the Greek people was rejected. Modern Greeks have to keep alive the illusion that they are linked to the ancient Hellenes. After all, they speak the same language. But in fact they do not, and language has become a political issue. Some

choose to use the "pure" language and others the demotic according to their philosophical orientation. Unfortunately, modern Greeks feel they have inherited from the Byzantines only that they are that bridge to the past.

Church and State

The most learned man in the history of Byzantium was Photius. Some have called this "encyopedic scholar" the most learned man of all time. He was the founder of a university in Constantinople in the 9th Century. He attracted a faculty of outstanding intellectuals like Leo the Mathematician, and started a renaissance of classical learning. He was made Patriarch and used his great learning to work out in theory and in practice a solution to the fundamental political problem that had plagued all thinking Christians, the relation between the earthly empire that rules men in this world temporarily, and the heavenly kingdom that will rule them for all eternity. The historian Eusebius had proposed a harmonious cooperation between the Emperor Constantine and the heads of God's Church on earth, and this had worked well enough, though as the Church became a powerful leader of mens' lives in this temporal world, tensions had grown. In Byzantine history, as we have seen, there was a sort of Caesaropapism that broke down as the Iconoclastic emperors attempted their reform of the Church. The monks, fearful of the secular learning of the leaders of the Church, led the people into a long resistance. It was Photius with his analysis of Platonic and Aristotelian political theory who worked out the theory of *economia*, the cooperation between Church and state based on the fact that they have the same basic goal, universal peace. It was for this reason that Photius converted the Slavic peoples to Christianity and brought them under the jurisdiction of the Patriarch of Constantinople, not only to extend the power of the Church, but to serve the interests of the state by removing its main enemies.

Later Patriarchs followed this same policy, and as the state began to disintegrate and needed help, the Church did all it could to mend the schism between the churches so that help would be forthcoming from the West. Unfortunately, the state fell to the Ottomans in 1453, but the groundwork laid by Photius made it possible for the Church to step in to provide government. The Orthodox Church had developed autocephalous churches so that in each country within the Empire there was a primate who handled affairs within his own church. These primates met in synods under the leadership of the Patriarch of Constantinople. The Ottomans used this clerical organization, for they felt it was safer a secular one would be. In this way the autocephalous churches flourished under them. Even at the parish level a local pasha gave orders to the parish priest. Today in East European countries the primates of the churches exert important political influence. The Greek War for Independence of 1821 was largely led by the Church. Byzantine study of the ancient classics went far beyond merely keeping them alive. Rather they became part of a living culture and are still exerting influence in the Eastern world.

There is a natural piety within the Slavic peoples that matched Byzantine piety and made it possible for the Church to continue its influence under materialistic totalitarian regimes. This same piety had given rise to a world-weariness from the early days of Christianity. Many Christians sought to avoid a world in which it was not worth living. They retreated into out of the way places.

Monasticism

From those days, there was always a strong monastic movement in the Byzantine Church, though its influence has often been over-stated. The solitary life has always been attractive to some, and down through the centuries in troubled times people have retreated into themselves to escape. In early Christian times many thousands of solitaries streamed to the Thebiad of Egypt and to Cappadocia in Anatolia. Their lives were often bizarre, and filled with almost insane proofs of sanctity. To bring some degree of order, St. Anthony of the Desert and St. Basil of Caesarea introduced rules, and monks were gathered into houses where prayer and work combined to bring a healthier devotion to God.

Pious women followed the same paths from the beginning. St. Scholastica, sister of St. Benedict, and St. Melania the Younger, friend of St. Jerome, founded early communities in Italy and in Jerusalem. Nunneries became as common as monasteries. They were also convenient places to place trouble-making women, as happened very often in Byzantine history.

Byzantine monasteries almost always followed the rule of St. Basil. There were two forms of the rule, the cenobitic and the eremitic. The former monks lived in monasteries where they shared all work and all prayer, while the hermits lived in isolation in caves or in the woods following their own individual practices of worship. In general, both types tended to retire from social contacts and sought lonely places on mountaintops or in deeply-wooded regions. They were often not well-educated, and were narrow-minded. Such monks had turned the Iconoclastic period into a national crisis, yet there were exceptions like those mentioned above who had established monasticism and had begun the practice of collecting manuscripts.

In the 10th Century St. Athanasius had built the monastery *Lavra* on Mount Athos. The Emperor Nicephoras Phocas was a personal friend of the saint and planned to build a monastery on the Holy Mountain. Over the years scores of monasteries were built and the monks set up a state of their own. Monks lived cenobitic lives there, but there was always a large number of hermits and the two groups often clashed. The most important of these clashes came with the Hesychist movement that disrupted the whole Eastern Church just as the Ottoman Turks were emerging in Byzantine territories. As the name suggests (*heyschia* means quiet or contemplation), the traditional life of the hermits changed into an extreme form of asceticism which began to spread through the Greek monastic world. Borrowing practices from the *fakirs* of India the Hesychists sought to achieve a vision of the Divine Light and they used extreme, often frightening exercises to train their bodies. The whole Church was offended, especially on the Holy Mountain, where attempts to control the hermits had gone on for years. A monk, Gregory Palamas, championed their cause for years. For a decade (1341–51) councils, often violent, were called to end the dispute. In the end, Greek rationalism was again victorious and the movement was condemned. But the hermits still prac-

ticed extreme forms of asceticism on the Holy Mountain. Mt. Athos survived the Ottoman conquest and today it is a part of Greece, but with a certain degree of autonomy, and it is governed by a representative synod.

The Comneni and Survival

When Alexius I Comnenus became Emperor (1081–1118), he had to face a series of threats such as few rulers have ever had to face. That he met them one after the other resolutely and successfully was a fine tribute to the man. That his solutions did not bring a permanent restoration of Byzantine power was a sign that the Empire had been mortally wounded by the period of anarchy that followed the collapse of the Macedonian Emperors. The loss of Anatolia had been the deciding factor. Long the source of gold, soldiers, and commercial wealth, the disintegration of Anatolia and its capture by the Seljuks robbed the Empire of any means of reconstituting its strength. He had to accept its loss to the Turks as an accomplished fact, but he fought desperately to meet the Norman attack across the Adriatic. He raised whatever troops he could, but more important, he enlisted the help of the Venetians.

Venice was already anxious to extend its power in the Mediterranean and to do so it had to control the Straits of Otranto and both coasts of the Adriatic, to have free access to the Mediterranean. It defeated the fleets of Robert Guiscard, whose death prevented him from launching another attack. Alexius had to give Venice wide trading advantages throughout the Empire, and Byzantine policy became very dependent on Venetian fleets. It was at this time that Byzantine fleets lost control of the Mediterranean to the Italian cities.

During the Norman wars the Patzinaks had invaded the Balkans again. Supported by the Bogomil heretics of Bulgaria, they swept to the very walls of Constantinople in 1090. There they entered into negotiations with an emir of Smyrna, Tzachas, who was eager to establish a sea empire in the Aegean. Attacked by sea and land, the City passed the winter in terror. Alexius called in the Cumans and Uzes, Turkish peoples who had crossed the steppes with the Polovtsi in the wake of the Patzinak invasion. On April 29, 1091, the Emperor and his allies met the Patzinaks and wiped out the entire tribe. Tzachas lifted the siege, and the City was saved. During the crisis the Serbs and Croats seized important Dalmatian towns. Vukan, *Zupan* of the Serbs, in particular, had struck at Byzantine border defenses. A campaign against him forced his submission for a time at least.

Alexius' work of restitution was interrupted at this point by the arrival of the First Crusade, launched as a result of complex factors, not the least of which was his own request for help during the Patzinak attack. The Western armies that began to arrive in the City were a real menace for Alexius, especially since they included some of his bitterest enemies, notably Bohemond, son of Robert Guiscard, but he tried to keep control over the situation and turn it to his advantage by exacting from all the leaders oaths of vassalage for any Byzantine lands they might free from the Turks. He gave them no little help, and the Crusade was a resounding success. Trouble soon arose, however, over Tarsus and Antioch, both former Byzantine possessions. They had been taken by Bohemond and his nephew Tancred, who refused to return them to Alexius. Bohemond threatened to use Antioch as the base for an attack on Constantinople, but constant skirmishing with the Turks made this impossible. He sailed back to Italy to raise a considerable army by spreading tales of Greek perfidy, and crossed over to Avlona in 1107. This time, the Normans were decisively defeated, and Bohemond became a vassal of Alexius and promised to return Antioch. The *Basileus* never actually got the city, but his prestige had grown among the Balkan peoples and his frontier was made secure.

Alexius had met all the crises of the early years, and the state seemed secure. However, he had been unable to strengthen the inner vitality of the government. The minor themes began to be absorbed by the greater ones under the *duces*, who absorbed military and civil authority into their own power. As military holdings disappeared the *Basileus* resorted to heavy taxes and the debasement of the coinage to raise funds for mercenaries. He also added military service to the *pronoia*, so that great feudal lords emerged, who controlled large areas, administered them and enjoyed the income in return for military service to the state. Contacts with Western feudal institutions slowly transformed the *pronoia* into an Eastern version of the fief.

Anna Comnena, the famous daughter of Alexius, made a bid for the throne when her father died, but her brother John took over instead (1118–43). She retired to write a magnificent biography of her father, the *Alexiad*. John turned out to be an outstanding ruler. A man of high moral purpose, he carried forward his father's work. His reign opened with clashes with the Hungarians, who were consolidating themselves at this time and invading to the south, and with the restless Serbs, still trying to establish a stable kingdom in the center of the Balkans. John held his own, though he could not win through to any permanent success. In Syria, the tale was different. John marched triumphantly through Cilicia, Lesser Armenia, to Antioch, which fell to him in August, 1137. Meanwhile, in Italy, he entered an alliance with Conrad III and Pisa against the growing power of Roger II in Sicily. He was preparing to pursue a rigorous role in Palestinian affairs, when he was killed by a poisoned arrow while on a hunting trip.

The new *Basileus* Manuel (1143–80) was a romantic pro-Westerner, in love with the chivalric way of life being introduced to the East by the Crusaders. His two marriages were to Western women, and he actively sought to introduce Western institutions throughout his Empire. He always admired the West, even though he was engaged in wars with the Franks throughout his reign. He laid claim to Antioch as his father had done, and he even made some suggestion of his suzerainty over Palestine. He allied himself with the kings of Jerusalem in their fights with the rising power of Zanghi and his sons. He also extended the privileges of the Italian trading communes, Venice, Genoa, and Pisa, all through the Empire.

In 1147, the Normans under Roger II attacked Corfu and Corinth, the leading silk-manufacturing centers in the Mediterranean. Many silk-weavers were carried off to Palermo. Roger had taken advantage of the bad feeling that had resulted from the Second Crusade. Louis VII and the papacy blamed the fiasco on the failure of Manuel to help them adequately. Manuel, on his part, allied himself with Conrad III, whose sister he had married, and prepared an invasion of Italy. But Conrad died, Serbian

and Hungarian uprisings broke out, and Manuel had to wait until 1155 to launch his invasion. His plan was to restore his imperial authority over all Italy. The campaign began as a great success, all the land from Ancona to Taranto fell to him, but he could not hold it. The Normans easily recaptured it. Frederick I Barbarossa, Venice and the Pope were all worried by the presence of Byzantine armies in Italy. He attempted to form an alliance with Pope Alexander III and the Lombard League against Barbarossa, who was obviously the real threat to Byzantine interests. He requested an imperial crown from the Pope, which was refused, even though he offered union of the two churches for it. In 1171, Venice opened hostilities and signed an alliance with Sicily against him. He retaliated by arresting all Venetians in the Empire and confiscating their goods. Venice began to raid the towns on the Greek coasts.

In Hungary he was able to form advantageous treaties. In Serbia, the new *Zupan*, Stephen Nemanja, was checked in his creation of a stable Serbian state, though he was eventually successful. In Syria, the *Basileus* achieved his greatest victory when he made a triumphant entry into Antioch in 1159. He was not able to keep abreast of the rapid rise of the Seljuk Sultan, Kilij Arslan of Iconium. On September 17, 1176, Manuel's army, sent to defeat the Turks, was overwhelmed by them at Myriocephalon, the worst defeat since Manzikert.

The campaigns had been very expensive, and to raise funds Manuel had increased the tax burden, as usual, to crushing proportions. Furthermore, he had to rely increasingly on the *pronoia* to raise troops. He even had to allow the mercenaries he hired to exact for themselves whatever monies they could from the people. Dissatisfaction rose everywhere and it was especially directed against the Westerners whom Manuel had brought into his capital and to whom he had given appointments in his government. When he died, in fact, he left his twelve-year-old son Alexius II (1180–83) under the regency of his second wife Marie of Antioch, who gave preferential treatment to Westerners in everything. Plots to overthrow her sprang up on all sides. The one that succeeded was the work of Manuel's cousin, Andronicus Comnenus, who had been exiled by the Emperor many times for his scandalous way of life. He had taken asylum with the Turks and Russians on many occasions, and there seemed to be no way to control him. In 1183, he marched on the City at the head of a hysterical national anti-Western army. Riots broke out in the capital in May, 1182 that led to a ghastly massacre of all the foreigners living in the City at the time. Andronicus removed all the advisers of his young relative, forcing the unhappy boy to sign his mother's death warrant with his own hand. In September, 1183 he became co-emperor and had his colleague strangled two months later. Cruel as he was, he began a rigorous reform of the government, rooting out corruption and fighting down the prerogatives of the landed military aristocracy. But his foreign policy became a disaster. The Hungarians and the Serbs rose up to avenge the murder of Marie and moved down the Dalmatian coast and through the central Balkans to Sophia. All that had been won at such cost by Manuel was lost. In the Near East things were even worse. Isaac Comnenus seized Cyprus for himself. Andronicus made an alliance with Salah ad-Din. He made concessions to the Venetians, but nothing could help him against the invasion the Normans began at Dyrrachium in 1185. They marched

unopposed across Greece and took the rich city of Salonica, which they sacked in savage reprisal for the massacres of three years before. The Normans started to march on Constantinople, where the Emperor let loose a reign of terror. Mobs rose up in fury and hacked him to death on September 12, 1185.

The Angeli and the Fourth Crusade

The new Emperor Isaac II Angelus (1185–95) was a thoroughly corrupt and incompetent man who did nothing to check the disintegration that was gathering speed. An excessive tax burden was driving the provinces to desperation. The themes were in a state of complete collapse. Local lords were squeezing out whatever imperial tax collectors left behind. Wandering mercenaries ravaged the country, and in the midst of all this, the court enjoyed a frivolous, dissolute life of luxury. The day of reckoning was near, though the Normans were defeated and had to retreat. They left Greece, but kept Cephalonia and Zante.

In Bulgaria two brothers, Petes and Asen, disgruntled because some claims they had to *pronoias* were denied by a corrupt official, organized a revolt that drew together many ethnic elements and led to the establishment of the Second Bulgarian Empire, centered in Greater Wallachia. Isaac led three major campaigns against the rebels, who had the support of the Serbs, who took advantage of the war to extend their territories. In the end, the *Basileus* had to sign a treaty that gave up Byzantine control over all their lands north of the Balkan mountains. A new archbishopric was established at Trnovo and there Asen was crowned Czar

► **Mistra, Greece.** This is an example of secular Byzantine architecture. William de Villeharduin was very fond of this castle and he added a whole wing. Eventually it passed back to the Greeks who won back the whole Peloponnesus. The mountain is close to ancient Sparta.

► **Modon, Greece.** This ancient Roman town was fortified by the Byzantines and became an important prize in the wars with Venice. It became a possession of William de Villeharduin of Morea. The ruins are Byzantine, Frankish, Turkish.

of the Bulgars. A younger brother, Kalojan, went to Constantinople as a hostage. The Third Crusade added even more danger. Frederick Barbarossa entered into negotiations with the Serbs and Bulgars as he marched eastward and by the time he had arrived at Adrianople he had decided to take Constantinople by storm. Isaac signed a treaty with him and agreed to give him supplies. But Frederick's death released Isaac, who now rushed to the Balkans to try to retrieve some authority there. He came to terms with Nemanja, recognizing his title, but he was badly beaten by the Bulgars. At that juncture, he was deposed and blinded by his brother Alexius, who seized the throne. Alexius III (1195–1203) was a power-hungry coward, who brought ruin to his country. His daughter Eudocia had been married to Nemanja's son Stephen, who now took over his father's throne. Alexius was not able to turn his relationship to his advantage, however, and Serbia entered the orbit of Rome. A war broke out with Bulgaria that led to a civil war there. Kalojan (1197–1207) finally emerged as a strong king and turned to Rome for his coronation. Innocent III sent a cardinal who consecrated the Bulgarian bishop of Trnovo and crowned the King in November, 1204. Distrust of Byzantium led Balkan kings to distant Rome which they hoped could not play any decisive role in their kingdoms.

The greatest threat to Byzantium came from the West, however. Henry VI became Emperor of Sicily and Germany, combining the Norman traditional hatred of Byzantium with his father Frederick's plan for a conquest of the Eastern Empire. His excuse was the marriage of his brother, Philip of Swabia, to Irene, a daughter of Isaac II. He intended to come East to avenge his brother's father-in-law. In desperation, Al-exius imposed a heavy tax and stripped the royal tombs to raise a payment of tribute to satisfy the Western Emperor. Henry died unexpectedly in 1197, and Byzantium won a respite. But the Fourth Crusade brought the final disaster.

Venice had long enjoyed special privileges within the Empire, but now Genoa and Pisa became rivals. If Byzantium were to fail, Venice felt able to press its advantage over the others. The leader of the Crusade launched by Innocent III with such high hopes was Boniface of Montferrat, a close friend of Philip of Swabia. It seems clear that Venetian policy and a desire to replace the deposed Isaac and his son Alexius on the throne led to the diversion of the Crusade. The attack on Byzantium was not planned, but the opportunity to dominate the Empire that was offered at Corfu by the young Alexius was too good to miss, and the Crusaders sailed to Constantinople.

The Frankish Interlude

The Crusaders had already met before their assault to sign a treaty for the division of the spoils. In accordance with its terms they elected Baldwin of Flanders Emperor and Tommaso Morosini Latin Patriarch. The lands were divided up, one quarter going to Baldwin, and of the other three-quarters, half to Venice and half to the knights of the Crusade. The Emperor was assigned Thrace and northwest Anatolia, while Venice took the best ports and islands in the Empire. Boniface of Montferrat took Salonica as his share and began to carve out a kingdom in northern Greece. The other Crusaders scurried to take over their lands, though most of them followed Boniface to Greece. The Burgundian de la Roche family established themselves at Athens and Thebes, while Guillaume de Champlitte and Geoffrey de Villehardouin created the principality of Morea in southern Greece. These were typical feudal states common in France at the time, and though they made concessions to local ways, they kept their Western form to the end.

In fact, the principality of Morea illustrates the whole period. At the inception of the Fourth Crusade, some contingents had set out directly from local ports and had not appeared at Venice. When they heard of the events that had diverted the Crusade and of the capture of Constantinople, not to be left out at the last minute, they rushed to set sail for the City. One group of adventurers stopped by chance at Kalamata in southern Greece to escape a storm. There they were approached by a local lord who offered to hire them as mercenaries. They quickly saw their opportunity and set out on their own. They never went on to Constantinople. Instead they marched through the Peloponnesus and ended up with a principality. They called in relatives and friends from France, and soon they established a state modelled after the classic feudalism of 13th Century France. Under the Villehardouin princes of Morea a court was set up in which better French was spoken than in Paris, it was said, and its procedures give a better picture of feudal usage than in the French courts themselves. More important, French culture was transported to Morea, just as classical Greek works began to be translated into Latin, and sent to the West, Aristotle's *Politics* being one of them.

The Latin Empire itself was fatally weakened by its feudal nature. It was actually a collection of separate states with no real institutions to keep them together. The Greeks were not hostile to the Franks, in fact they often welcomed them as deliverers from the anarchy of the past decades. Furthermore, a type of Byzantine feudalism had developed in the *pronoia*, which when considered a fief by the conquerors and as a form of land tenure respected by them, made it possible for the Greeks to change masters with little trouble. The Franks were very careful to respect the customs and arrangements they found on the land. The one bone of contention was the religious problem. Whenever Latin bishops tried to force union, the Greeks rebelled. When the Orthodox priests were respected, as in Morea, the Greeks became quite loyal to the Frankish regime.

The Greek nobility tended to resent the conquerors more than the lower classes and many of them fled to the unconquered lands. Many migrated to the Empire of Trebizond, where grandsons of Andronicus I, the Grand Comneni Alexius and David, had established themselves with Georgian help. Others flocked to Nicaea, where a son-in-law of Alexius III, Theodore Lascaris, had settled. Some went to Epirus in western Greece where a state emerged under the control of a cousin of the Angeli, Michael Angelus. These three states kept alive the concept of empire and became bitter rivals for the crown of *basileus*.

Baldwin was already in difficulties. The Crusaders had been tactless in dealing with the Greek nobles of Thrace, who revolted in February, 1205, and called on Kalojan for help. The Bulgar, so recently reconciled to Rome, had already offered his help to the Crusaders, who arrogantly rejected it. He became a bitter foe and sent a large army to meet Baldwin in battle. They met near Adrianople on April 14, 1205 and the result was the annihilation of the Frankish host.

Baldwin was captured and died later in prison. His brother Henry (1206–16) recoiled and turned to the task of checking the growth of the power of Lascaris at Nicaea, where the Byzantine imperial system had been carefully reconstructed. The Patriarch had gone there and in 1208 he crowned Theodore, though he had been already considered Emperor since 1204. Hostilities between him and the Latins dragged on until a truce was declared in 1214. Each state recognized the other and Nicaea became the authentic heir to Byzantine authority; Trebizond went into decline. Epirus, on the other hand, grew rapidly under Michael's brother, Theodore, who invaded Thessaly and captured Salonica in 1224. Theodore Angelus was soon calling himself emperor, and the two rivals aimed at the reconquest of Constantinople.

While the Latin Empire sank into dispirited debility under weak emperors and regents, confined as it was to the immediate land around the City, the other states within the old Empire led vigorous lives. John III Vatatzes (1222–54) began a spirited expansion of the Empire of Nicaea. He expelled the Latins from all Anatolia and he captured the principal islands of the Aegean. He even invaded Thrace and entered Adrianople. Theodore Angelus had been equally victorious, but he had been checked by John Asen II (1218–41), Emperor of Bulgaria, who aspired to the Byzantine throne himself. He defeated Theodore in battle and overran his lands. John and Vatatzes now came to terms. The Nicaean Emperor recognized the Bulgarian crown and an autocephalous Bulgarian church was established. Vatatzes was now the leading contender in the imperial race and he invaded Greece to consolidate his advantage. The Mongol invasion called him back.

The Mongols

The Mongols were one of the nomadic Turkish peoples living north of the Great Wall of China. A ferocious people, they lived in the saddle, had only a most rudimentary culture, yet were excellent warriors. Ruthless in victory, they killed untold millions of people. The Mongols were united by Timujin, the son of a minor chieftain, who fought his way to power and took the name Chingiz Khan (Great Lord). The nomads had always been a menace to the more settled peoples around them. Usually only temporarily held together by a strong leader and picking up allies on the march, the earlier Huns, Magyars, etc., had struck like lightening, only to disappear just as quickly with the death of the leader. Chingiz Khan's conquests proved to be much more permanent. Between 1208 and 1214, north China was conquered. In the same year Turkestan fell. Afghanistan, Persia, all the lands of the Khwarizmian Shahs fell in rapid order. Millions upon millions of people were killed with unspeakable cruelties. In 1233 the first encounter with a European army took place. Sabutai defeated a Russian army, destroyed the kingdom of Georgia and laid waste southern Russia.

The death of Chingiz Khan brought home all the armies. The empire was divided among his sons and nephews, under his favorite son, Ogodai. The conquests continued. China was conquered, while another army destroyed the Bulgars on the Volga and in 1237–38 all the Russian states, including Kiev, were overturned. In 1241, the invasion of Poland and Hungary began. Every army that met them was destroyed, all the main cities were sacked mercilessly. The Adriatic was reached in 1242. The Mongols settled in Russia on the Volga. They organized themselves into several Hordes, the Golden Horde being the most powerful. They exacted heavy tribute, but tended to allow the subject states wide latitude, sweeping out occasionally to chastise any threat or any failure to pay tribute.

In 1252 a Mongol army wiped out the Assassins and obliterated their stronghold Alamut. The army went on to destroy Baghdad in 1258. All Syria fell rapidly, and the Mameluks of Egypt marched out to meet them. The defeat of the Mongols at Ain Jalut in 1260 probably saved Africa and the Mediterranean from the conquest. The Mongols settled down in Persia where they founded the Il-Khanate. The conquest of China was completed by Kublai. Within seventy-five years the fabled empires of Asia had all been defeated and replaced by new states.

The Restoration of Greek Power at Byzantium

John Vatatzes was able to take immediate advantage of the Mongol conquest. The Bulgarians had been crushed and he was able to take over all their lands in Greece. In 1246 he entered Salonica and took over Thessaly. Some Greeks still rallied around the Empire of Epirus, now in the hands of Michael II, an illegitimate son of Michael I. Vatatzes signed a treaty with him to stabilize the situation in Greece. He also entered into negotiations with the pope over the question of Church union, though nothing came of them. When he died he left behind a revived, well-organized state that ensured the life of the Empire for another two centuries.

Theodore II Lascaris (1254–58) was a scholar who brought a high degree of culture to his father's state. He was an epilep-

tic, however, and he had little time for great works. His death brought his seven year old son, John IV, to the throne. Michael Palaeologis took over the regency. He was a member of an old aristocratic family and had had a distinguished career in the army. By 1258 he had been crowned co-emperor and turned to the threatening situation in Greece. Manfred, the son of Frederick II, had taken up the dream of empire that had fired Henry VI. He had allied himself with Michael II, the despot of Epirus, and with Guillaume de Villehardouin, the prince of Achaia. The decisive battle in the war that followed was fought at Pelagonia in 1259. The Frankish nobility of Greece was virtually wiped out and Guillaume was taken prisoner. Michael had emerged the winner of a delicate game and his entry into Constantinople seemed imminent. He took one more precaution, however, by allying himself with the Genoese against the Venetians. An imperial army simply walked into the undefended city on July 25, 1261 and Michael entered on August 15. The city lay in ruins, its great treasures all sold to finance the impoverished Latin Empire.

The Palaiologoi

The state that fell to Michael VIII (1259–82) was a shadow of its former glory. Cut off from its richest provinces, stripped of all its wealth, surrounded by mortal enemies, it did not seem Byzantium could survive. Yet Michael was determined that it should. He first had to counter aggressive moves that were being prepared against him in the West. He carried on a fairly successful campaign in Morea, then he modified his policies in Italy. The Genoese had not helped him, so he turned to an alliance with Venice. He also made overtures to the Pope. All his work was put to a severe test when Charles of Anjou came to power in Sicily. Charles had come to an agreement with the Latin Emperor Baldwin II to reconquer Byzantium. He had also acquired title to the Frankish states of Greece and was preparing to launch an extensive offensive against Michael when he was interrupted by his brother Louis's Crusade to Tunis.

Michael made every political alliance he could to meet the threat, even with the Tartars in Russia and the Mameluks in Egypt. His most delicate arrangements were with the Pope. He had to agree to union at the Council of Lyons (1274) for help from Gregory X. But his diplomatic manoeuverings were magnificently successful with the Sicilian Vespers of 1282. Byzantium had been saved by the genius of its Emperor.

Andronicus II (1282–1328) was an Emperor of only moderate ability, though he was eager to support a cultural revival of his shrunken state. Feudalism continued to spread, the *pronoia* becoming a hereditary fief. *Paroikoi*, non-free tenants on the *pronoia*, also became very common as life became too precarious to maintain on free holdings. At the same time, the system fell out of the government's control so that it did not produce an adequate number of soldiers. Mercenaries still were the mainstay of the government, now hard-pressed to find the cash to pay them. One of these mercenary bands was the Catalan Grand Company he invited in to fight the Turks. Unpaid, they revolted to get their money. They settled first at Gallipoli, where they ravaged the countryside, then they took the duchy of Athens.

No sooner had the country recovered from the Catalans when Andronicus began a civil war with his grandson. Andronicus

had planned to leave his crown to his son Michael X, who was crowned co-emperor in 1295. Michael died before his father and left as his heir a fun-loving wastrel, whom Andronicus refused to accept as emperor. Andronicus III (1328–41) fell under the influence of a general, John Cantacuzenos, and forced his grandfather to abdicate in 1328. Andronicus III soon died, leaving behind a young son, John V (1341–91). Cantacuzenos rose in revolt and had himself crowned John VI (1347–54) at Adrianople. He came to terms with young John and they ruled jointly until John V forced his older colleague to resign. Such dissension at so critical a time in its history was fatal for the Empire. The Ottomans had already entered the orbit of the Empire, reaching the Dardanelles by 1354. Cantacuzenos invited them across as his allies, then could not force them back.

Under Stephen Dushan (1331–55) the Serbs overthrew the Bulgarians, who had never recovered from the Mongol attacks. He pushed right down into Greece and had himself proclaimed "Czar of the Serbs and Romans." Dushan died before he could realize his dream of a Serb-Byzantine empire, but his place at Adrianople was taken by the Ottomans in 1365. The civil war continued. John V was overthrown by his son Andronicus IV (1376–79), but he regained his throne and proclaimed his younger son Manuel co-emperor. Andronicus's son, John VII, called in the Turks and took the capitol for a while. But Manuel II (1391–1425) was able to succeed his father. He made repeated trips to the West to obtain help against the Turks. A large army did come in 1396, but it was destroyed at Nicopolis. The only thing that saved the Empire at this time was the defeat of the Ottomans by Timur at Angora in 1402.

Manuel abdicated and left the throne to his son John VIII (1425–48), who attended the Council of Ferrara-Florence in 1439. The union of the churches he agreed to there was repudiated by his people, quite properly as it turned out, for the promised help never came. One last crusade was launched, to be defeated at Varna, in 1444, and no one could stop the Turks.

The Rise of Russia

Kiev, the first state of any importance in what is now Ukraine, went into decline even before the Mongol conquest. The incursions of the Polovtsi across the Ukraine had cut the rich trade routes from the south. The *appanage* system of Yaroslav had destroyed the unity of the state. In 1113 the Kievans had brought in as their prince Vladimir Monomakh of Smolensk. His reign (1113–25) and that of his son Mtislav (1125–32) are the last in Kievan history. Civil war broke out, and Rostislav of Smolensk added Kiev to his own lands. During his reign (1159–68) there was a unified state that stretched from the Baltic to the Black Sea. Another state came to greatness at Suzdal under Andrei Bogolubski, who moved the capital from Kiev to his own city of Vladimir. This tendency to establish new towns led to a strengthening of the power of the prince, for in the old towns this had been limited by popular assemblies and by a strong class of aristocratic *boyars*. In the new towns the prince was careful not to let such institutions grow. In the west, Silicia emerged as an independent state.

The Mongols conquered all these principalities except Novgorod, which remained a free commune with a representative assembly. Alexander Nevsky led the northern Russians to many victories in the 13th Century, and as Grand Prince of Vladimir he became a great patron of the Christian Church. He also worked closely with the Mongols and began the policy of becoming their most trusted servant, a policy carried on by his son Daniel, who founded Moscow.

The princes of Moscow concentrated on building the wealth of their state and on keeping the friendship of the Mongols whose special agents they had been since the time of Ivan I (1328–41), who had the right to collect the tribute from all the Russian princes for the Mongols. Ivan II (1353–59) won the right of judging disputes among them. The Russian metropolitan bishop had already moved to Moscow during the reign of Ivan I. Dimitri Donskoi (1359–89) was the first prince to defeat the Mongols. The battle of Kulikovo (1380) was a psychological turning point in the struggle with the Mongols. A civil war was put down by Vasili II (1425–62), during whose reign the Russian metropolitan declared the Russian church free from the Byzantine patriarch, whom he condemned as a traitor for accepting union with Rome. Moscow now became the home of Orthodoxy and the heir of the mission of the Orthodox Church to convert the heathen and to bring the whole world under its dominion.

In the West a large state had been established with the marriage of Jagiello of Lithuania (1377–1434) to Jadwiga of Poland. The country accepted Roman Catholicism. Tensions within the country over religion kept the vast land internally weak. Meanwhile, Ivan III came to the throne of Moscow (1462–1505). When he took over the state, Moscow was still a tiny subject state of the Mongol Horde. First he conquered

Novgorod, expelled the Hanseatic merchants, closed the popular assembly, and incorporated the state into Moscow. He continued his expansion and in 1480 threw off allegiance to the Mongols. In 1472 he married Zoe Palaeologina, a niece of the last Byzantine Emperor. He adopted the double eagle of Byzantium as his insignia and laid claim to the title of Caesar (czar). The Third Rome had risen to continue the mission of Byzantium.

The Ottomans

This Turkish tribe had entered Anatolia as mercenaries of the Seljuks and had settled at Dorylaeum around 1240. United by Osman I (1290–1326), the Osmanli or Ottomans, pushed outward, taking Nicaea by 1329. Orkhan (1326–59) was an ally of John Cantacuzenos, and his son Murad I (1359–79) captured Adrianople with well-disciplined troops led by the Janissaries, an elite corps of men stolen as children from Christian families. In 1389 at the battle of Kossovo, Murad defeated a combined Balkan army, and his extensive holdings passed to his son Bayazid I (1389–1402). Europe finally awoke to the menace of the Turk and sent a crusade that was crushed at Nicopolis in 1396. Timur the Lame (1335–1405) gave Europe a respite. Attempting to reconstitute the great Mongol empire of the 13th Century, Timur conquered all central Asia. then invaded Anatolia, where he won the battle of Angora. The Ottomans were stopped for a generation.

Murad II (1421–51) took up the conquest again, taking most of Greece. In 1444 he defeated a great Christian army at Varna. Muhammed II (1451–81) not only took Constantinople, but completed the conquest of all Anatolia, Greece, and the Balkans up to Belgrade.

The Fall of Constantinople

The last *Basileus* of Constantinople was the brother of John VIII, the Despot of Mistra Constantine XI (1448–53). After years of frivolous squabbling over who should have the empty honor of being Emperor, the moment of truth had arrived. The grand City had deteriorated into a collection of small villages within miles of walls with only a few hundred soldiers to man them. Constantine sent out desperate calls for help to the West. But the City had outlived its usefulness. It was no longer the essential defense against Asia, nor the only middleman for trade with the Orient. The history of the last two centuries had illustrated what happens to outmoded anachronisms. It is to his credit that Constantine rose to the occasion and acted in the best Byzantine tradition.

He manned the walls with a few hundred men, largely foreigners, and put up whatever defense he could against the siege of Muhammed II. For a month the walls were bombarded by rocks launched through cannon. When the walls were sufficiently weakened, the final attack came on May 29, 1453. The *Basileus* died valiantly defending his City and his body was never found. This time the miracle had not saved the City.

There is an old tradition that at the moment the Turks burst into St. Sophia, the church of the Holy Wisdom, where a crowd had gathered to pray for deliverance, the priest was raising the goblet to offer Communion to the faithful. At that moment, the wall of the church opened and the priest walked into it. It is said that when the City is restored the wall will open again and the priest will conclude the Mass, and that will be the final miracle in the long history of Byzantium.

XIV
THE END OF THE MIDDLE AGES
▼ ▼ ▼ ▼ ▼

▶ **Cathedral, Lincoln.** Begun in 1084, and after an earthquake damaged it rebuilt in 1192–1250. It is a fine example of the early English Gothic style.

◀ **Blois.** By the end of the Middle Ages France had developed a way of life, a sense of style that was distinctive. Blois combines old castles, Renaissance palaces, and now is distinctly French.

▶ **Ghetto, Toledo.** The Jews in Spain were under the special care of the bishop. The ghetto where Jews lived was always close to the cathedral. The Jews prospered and lived well until they were expelled in 1492 by a monarchy which chose to take control of its own finances.

The Collapse of
the Medieval Church

For a century after the pontificate of Innocent III all seemed to be going well for the papal monarchy. The Investiture Controversy seemed to have been won. The Pope had firm control over his Italian States. His role in Italian and European political affairs seemed decisive. Yet there were currents under the surface that boded ill for the future. Secular interests were attracting people of all classes. The bourgeoisie was becoming restless; it came to feel its way of life was increasingly restricted by the ideals of the medieval church. The peasants were encountering absorbing problems that required new secular institutions. The medieval monarchs had emerged as the focus of the lives of all their subjects, and it was to them that first loyalty was now turned. Furthermore, the reputation of the papacy had been badly tarnished by the Pope's involvement in the struggle with the Hohenstaufen. He had become a leading political figure of the Italian scene, and his position as a prince of the papal states detracted from his position as head of the Church universal. These tendencies did not mean that Europe was ready to turn away from the Church, nor that spirituality was on the wane, nor that the pope was no longer regarded as one of the focal points of the whole society, but it did mean that men were ready to turn to new forms of piety, new expressions of their spirituality. They would accept alternatives to a papal monarch, even if it meant that a new definition of the church was needed.

Thus, a crisis developed during the papal election of 1292–94, when there was no pope because dissension in the College of Cardinals was so severe, the factions so evenly balanced that no candidate could win enough votes for election. Finally a pious hermit, Pietro de Morroni, was elected as a stopgap pope. The plan was that the aged pope, who took the name Celestine V, would not have time or inclination to inaugurate new policies, and in the interim a compromise could be worked out to elect a strong candidate. Celestine, a truly holy man, had no concept whatever of the administrative duties of a pope, and as multitudes followed him around for his blessing, he allowed the business of the papal court to collapse. Overcome by the worldliness of Rome, he came to rely more and more on Cardinal Benedetto Gaetani. Finally, frightened by angelic voices calling on him to retire from the world, Celestine retired from the papacy to return to his monastic cell, an act unique in the history of the papacy, and for which Dante places him in Hell. The cardinals promptly elected Gaetani, who took the name Boniface VIII. Boniface had hoodwinked the old man. The "angelic voices" had been his; and now that he was Pope, he arrested Celestine, and threw him into prison, where he died nine months later by the order, if not the hand of Boniface, according to rumor.

This was only one of the crimes of 1294. The political maneuverings in the College had been openly corrupt. Bribery and public pressure had marked the election, and all Europe was shocked. The actions of Boniface VIII did nothing to win him support. He attacked his Colonna enemies by preaching a crusade against them. He then preached a crusade against the Ghibellines in Florence. Obviously the new Pope was simply a wily, aggressive Italian prince.

His serious troubles began however, when he opened an attack on all secular governments. In 1296 he issued the Bull *Clericis laicos,* which forbade secular governments to tax the clergy. Edward I of England immediately put pressure on his clergy and got whatever revenues he needed. Philip IV of France simply confiscated all church funds in France, cutting off their flow to Rome. Boniface had to back down, but after the Jubilee of 1300, when thousands of pilgrims went to Rome to spend great sums of money for the indulgence the Pope had offered, he felt he was in a much stronger position. In 1301 he issued *Salvator mundi* and *Asculta fili,* in which he hit at Philip's financial privileges, and warned him that kings were under the final jurisdiction of the pope. He called a council in Rome to judge the actions of the king. Philip called into session the first real meeting of the Estates General, accused the Pope of many crimes, declared his election invalid, and denounced him in a letter to the cardinals. The French clergy and nobility supported Philip.

But the council met in Rome, and during its sessions the Pope issued the famous *Unam sanctum* of 1302. He claimed supreme power over kings and the right to overthrow them if disobedient: "We declare, proclaim and define that subjection to the Roman pontiff is absolutely necessary to salvation for every human creature." Philip immediately called a meeting of his council, and repeated his formal charges against the Pope: the election had been fraudulent, he was a heretic, his private life was vicious and immoral. The King claimed the right to call a Church council to purge the Church of such a monster, and used a combination of propaganda, national feeling, and royal pressure to win the support of his council. Soldiers were sent to Italy to arrest the Pope and bring him to France for trial. They found him at Agnani, in a papal summer villa, laid violent hands on him, and imprisoned him while deciding what to do. The townspeople rose indignantly to rescue the eighty-five-year-old Pope, but he died soon after from the shock of his humiliation.

A wave of indignation swept across Europe that might very well have provided a vigorous pope with an effective tool to use in rebuilding the prestige of the office, but the cardinals elected the weak Benedict XI, who absolved the French King from any responsibility for the crime of killing Boniface. Within a year Benedict had died and, after a stalemate of many months Bertrand de Got, archbishop of Bordeaux, was elected Pope. He took the name Clement V, and decided to remain in Avignon, and not come to Italy at all. He began to work hand-in-glove with the King. He nullified Boniface's bulls, praised the King and his agents for their actions against Boniface, and became an instrument of French the king's will. This was the beginning of the "Babylonian Captivity" of the papacy, that was to last until 1377.

The seven Avignon popes have always had an evil reputation for licentious and pleasure-loving lives. Yet with all their shortcomings, they were no more or less evil than many popes of the late medieval Church. They were all Frenchmen and allowed themselves to be pliant tools of French policy. The rest of Europe began to identify the papacy itself with France, and national feeling led many to turn away from the spiritual leadership of the pope. The main problems facing the Church at this time were financial, and the popes had to resort to every conceivable expediency to raise revenues. The popes claimed immediate control over the wealth of all bishops. Special fees were demanded whenever a clergyman entered office. Rents on Church property were raised. The papacy claimed appellate jurisdiction over all ecclesiastical courts and, having forced a flow of cases to Avignon for settlement, raised the fees for court services. All Europe was angered by the emphasis the popes placed, no matter how understandably, on money matters. People were indignant at the luxurious court they maintained, at the expensive and ineffective crusades they preached against their enemies, at the general low moral tone of the Church.

Inevitably, alternatives to papal government, to the traditional Church itself, were sought. The Spiritual Franciscans, for instance, were a group of dedicated men who believed that their order had become too worldly. They demanded that it give up all its possessions and return to the original simple poverty of St. Francis. Pope John XXII (1316–34) was horrified at such an idea and excommunicated them. They answered by denying the authority of the pope, and by putting forward the general Church council as the proper voice of the universal Church. One of these *Fraticelli*, as they were called, was William Ockham who, as we have seen above, believed that knowledge of God and of absolute truth did not result from human reason, but from God's Will that men know Him. He emphasized will, rather than reason, in all aspects of life. Furthermore, he was a nominalist and believed that the individual Christian's attitudes and actions were the basic component of Christendom, and not the abstract universal Church as such. Marsiglio of Padua went even farther. He claimed in the *Defensor Pacis (The Defender of Peace)* that the best form of government was that of a monarch, who ruled through the laws of the realm and the popular will as expressed in an aristocratic government. The Church was just another human institution that served a useful purpose, but only under the control of the secular government.

Many men who were shocked at the general decay of morality within the Church felt that the problem lay with the general tone of society. They felt that men needed to build within themselves a new piety that would come from closer contact with God. Men were to live a Christ-like life, then the problems of society would disappear. The *Imitation of Christ* of Thomas á Kempis put forward this idea, as did the schools of the Brethren of the Common Life, a lay order established by Gerard Groote to teach the principles of the good Christian life. Some of these advocates of a new mysticism were later condemned of heresy, but only two men went openly into heresy. John Wycliffe (1324–84) was a teacher at Oxford when he was selected in 1374 to go to the Continent to help work out a truce between France and the papacy. When he returned he published a book, in which he claimed that the Church was vassal to the English crown for its lands in England, a popular argument in England at the time. He then began to preach against the worldliness of the Church, claiming that the pope had no greater power than a parish priest. He was condemned by the pope, but large crowds supported him and he was encouraged to launch a general attack on the whole medieval Church. He called for the creation of a National English church, in which he claimed the church was not the clergy alone, but the whole body of the faithful. He attacked monasticism, and the office of the pope. He said that God alone, not a priest, could hear a confession and absolve sin. He denied Transubstantiation, and declared that only a blameless priest could administer valid sacraments. Such ideas were clearly heretical, and he was so charged and found guilty. He finally went into retirement, and died as he was preparing to go to Rome to answer charges against him. His ideas were carried all over England by his followers, the Poor Priests or Lollards, and were an important factor in the social upheavals of the time.

Eventually, the Lollards were repressed in England, but their ideas moved to the Continent, where they spread to Bohemia. There an anti-German Czech nationalism had centered at the University of Prague, where a rector, Jan Hus, had already begun an attack on the Church. He eagerly took up Wycliffe's ideas, and claimed that each individual had the right to find religious truth for himself in the Bible. His ideas were condemned, and he was excommunicated as a heretic. He became the head of a separatist movement that was to persist for many years after his own execution at the Council of Constance (July, 1415).

There was a growing restlessness in Europe. The Church was dissolving into its constituent parts. As the cement that held society together, its decay might lead to a general breakdown of all morality, and to general chaos. Many men of good will were scandalized and apprehensive at the prospect, but they refused to go into heresy, or to overturn the traditional Church. They began to put strong pressure on the pope to return to Rome, free himself of French control, and launch a general Church reform. In Rome, however, a demagogue, Cola da Rienzi, had proclaimed a republic in 1347. Cola was eventually defeated and executed, but the city was in turmoil. The next popes were frustrated in their hopes to start Church reforms. Gregory XI (1370–78) was urged by St. Catherine of Siena to make another attempt. He tried, but was preparing to flee back to France when he died. The papacy had returned to Rome, but the election that followed Gregory's death was hectic. French cardinals **predominated, but they supported rival candidates.** The people of Rome demanded a Roman or at least an Italian pope. Finally Urban VI (1378–89) was elected, because the cardinals thought they could control him. He proved to be a determined reformer, who attacked the luxurious lives of the cardinals themselves. They soon withdrew to Anagni, where they elected Clement VII (1378–94), who returned to Avignon.

Now there were two popes, both elected by the cardinals, and each claiming to be the heir of St. Peter. The scandal was immense. All the powers of Europe lined up behind one or the other, but the prestige of the papacy was irretrievably injured. No one knew from whom dispensation ought to be sought, to whom appeals should be made. The ideas of the Lollards and Hussites began to make sense to the lower classes, while the intellectuals took up the ideas of the Spiritual Franciscans and Marsiglio of Padua. To make things worse, as each pope died a successor was named, so two lines of popes developed. By 1400 the Church verged on disintegration. In desperation, the cardinals of both popes joined forces and summoned a council to meet in Pisa in 1409. Both popes were deposed, and the cardinals eventually elected John XXIII (1410–15), who had been a pirate in his youth, and had become since then notorious for his worldliness and flair for political intrigue. The supporters of the deposed popes, Benedict IX and Gregory XII, renewed the cause of their men, so there were now three duly elected popes. The Emperor Sigismund finally summoned the Council of Constance (1414–18).

Reports claim that as many as 40,000 people gathered for this Council, at which among other decisions Jan Hus was put on trial, found guilty, and burned as a heretic. There was a great deal of difficulty in deposing the three popes, though it was finally accomplished by March, 1417. In November, Martin V (1417–31) was elected, and the schism was healed. The Council, meanwhile, had asserted its authority over popes and claimed the right to correct and depose them. Martin V was called on to institute reforms, and it was decided to summon another council in five years, and yet another seven years after that.

Martin soon showed he had no real intentions of using the council effectively. The Hussites, however, had broken out in open revolt after the death of Hus, and the Pope had to preach crusades against them. The ineffectiveness of these crusades finally led him to summon a council at Basel in 1431. Martin died, and the cardinals elected Eugenius IV (1431–47). The Council dealt with the Hussites with some success (though the movement remained alive until well after the Reformation), and began to legislate strong reform measures. The new Pope, meanwhile, had claimed jurisdiction over the Council, and in 1437 an open split developed. He demanded the Council move to Ferrara, to meet with Byzantine envoys who had come to discuss union between the Greek and Latin churches as a price for aid against the Turks. Many delegates met with the Pope, while others remained at Basel. The union with the Greeks was announced in Florence, where the Council had convened after being forced out of Ferrara by plague, though the union was rejected by the Greeks in the East and came to nothing.

Eugenius had more success with his schismatics closer at home. In 1439 he de-clared the pope supreme authority over the council, and finally under the proddings of the next Pope, Nicholas V (1447–55), the Council voted itself out of existence in 1449. The conciliar movement had failed because of its very success. Once it had healed the schisms and strengthened the papacy, there was no more need for councils. By the 15th Century, however, the medieval church had virtually failed. Europe had witnessed an unedifying spectacle of scheming, power-hungry popes sacrificing the welfare of their flocks in order to defeat their rivals. The demand for reform was stronger than ever, but the popes of the 15th Century were far more interested in the flowering of the Italian Renaissance than in reform, which did not come until the Council of Trent after the Protestant Reformation.

The Failure of Secular Government

The collapse of the Church brought about the very result that many had feared. As men lost faith in the Church, they lost faith in the moral code that had been based upon it, which no longer seemed to restrain their activities. Loyalty to the established institutions of Europe began to dissolve. Lawlessness, an eagerness to turn to violence, an unrestrained attack on society became characteristic at all levels of society. The medieval kings had overextended themselves and were unable to keep the society in control. The parliaments could do no better, for they had even fewer weapons to use. The nobility had been badly weakened by the kings, but they still held on to their privileged status. The introduction of a money economy, though, proved too much for them.

They had no way of acquiring the wealth to maintain their position. Only bankers could do this. On the other hand, the turbulence of the age was disastrous for trade, and cities went into decline. The guild system froze into immobility as those at the top refused to allow newcomers to rise, or to share dwindling profits. Kings fought each other, the nobility rampaged without restraint to gain by pillage what was unattainable by peaceful means, the cities fell into civil war. The peasants fared no better as their crops were ruined and the towns closed their gates to immigrants. The society had no leadership, yet the problems of the age were pressing and demanded drastic solutions.

The Black Death, for instance, a form of bubonic plague that was introduced from the East in 1347, swept from center to center killing off from one-fourth to one-third of the total population of Europe. Markets shrank, causing new hardship in the towns. Population remained low for at least two generations, and men began to fight over what they had rather than develop new opportunities. More important, there was a severe shortage of talent, as monasteries and towns, where there were schools and creative crafts, were devastated.

The mood of Europe was one of pessimism. Men began to feel that the world and all its institutions had failed. The Devil seemed to have come into his own. Witchcraft and devil-worship became popular. Even to the orthodox, God seemed to have abandoned the world. A stern judge, implacable and remote, God seemed far beyond the reach of men, who now needed intermediaries to reach him. Men turned more to the saints or to the Virgin to intercede for them. The sale of indulgences and relics soared. Everywhere men went on pilgrimages seeking a way of reaching God. A wave of revivalism followed in the wake of the plague. The use of the rosary was introduced and popularized. Preachers called men to repentance in apocalyptic sermons listened to by vast crowds, who responded by burning their worldly vanities in great bonfires. Hysteria seemed to grip the whole society. It was no wonder that formal institutions failed, though there always remained an undercurrent of balanced, constructive endeavor to find new solutions to the problems of the age.

England and France in the 14th and 15th Centuries

The sons of Philip IV maintained the works of their father, but were unable to carry them forward. All were plagued with money problems which led them to rely on aristocratic *parlements* that increased in power as a result; their main problems were over the succession. All three were either childless or had only daughters. Since Salic Law prevented females from taking the title, eventually a cousin, Philip of Valois, became King as Philip VI (1328–1350).

In England the throne had passed to Edward II (1307–27), a weak, extravagant man, who allowed himself to be dominated by selfish favorites. He soon fell out with the barons of the realm, who forced the King in 1310 to appoint a committee known as the Lords Ordainers to reform the government. These Ordainers proved to be a weapon that reactionary nobles used to control the King. The failures of the Scottish Wars and general famine conditions added popular grievances to the pretentions of the Ordainers, but the King found new supporters and declared war. He defeated the nobles in 1322 and for four years ruled as a tyrant.

In 1325 the Queen, Isabelle, daughter of Philip IV, went to France to arrange a treaty to settle disputes on the borders of Gascony, the last French territory under English control. There she met and became the mistress of Roger Mortimer. The two invaded England in 1326. The country rallied to their support, and the King was forced to abdicate in favor of his young son Edward, under the regency of Isabelle and Mortimer. The tyranny of the regents soon led the young King to oust them in 1330. Mortimer was executed for treason, and Isabelle retired to a nunnery.

Edward III (1327–77) was not a great King, but he was a brave warrior, who led his armies well in the war with France that occupied England throughout his reign. While he was abroad fighting, the Parliament completed its process of growth. The division into the Houses of Lords and of Commons took place, the latter soon becoming the initiating agency for all important legislation. The Parliament also gained control over military supplies, and over the king's ministers through the right to impeach (1376). The king's Council became the chief judicial arm of the government, but peers of the realm were tried by the Parliament. The English Church was freed from papal control by the statutes of Provisors (1351), that decreed that English sees had to be filled by Englishmen, and *Praemunire* (1353), that forbade all appeals to Rome as treason. The Parliament also had the right to legislate in certain economic matters. As England turned increasingly to the production of wool, manorial lords enclosed large tracts of land for pasturage, which forced serfs off the arable land. At the same time, the lords found it more profitable to free their serfs, and turn their lands over to rent-paying tenants, to hired farm-laborers, or to

sheep-growing pastureland. As a result, large numbers of ex-serfs began to wander around the countryside. Shortly afterwards the Black Death suddenly made labor scarce, and caused wages for hired hands to rise rapidly. In 1351 the Statute of Laborers was passed to freeze wages at the 1346 level, and in 1361 a measure decreed that laborers who left their jobs to seek higher wages elsewhere were to be punished by branding. Discontent continued until the demands of the peasants led to a great revolt in 1381.

The Hundred Years War

Edward III decided in 1347 to lay claim to the throne of France as a grandson of Philip IV. The French had been supporting the Scots in the north, and they had been making inroads into Gascony, the last English possession on the Continent. They also had been preying on English shipping in the Channel, which had been increasing as the wool trade with Flanders had grown in importance. All these frictions had grown in importance. The breaking point was reached when France invaded Flanders to support its Count, Louis of Nevers, against the merchants who had ousted him. Louis took reprisals against the English merchants who had supported the Flemish, and Edward took the title of King of France and declared war in November, 1337.

The Hundred Years War was a series of engagements that lasted from 1337 to 1453, but fighting was not continuous. Throughout the war, the tactical advantage was with the English, who relied mainly on archers using the deadly longbow. Most of their troops were mercenaries paid with ample funds, provided by the Parliament,

260 ▼ Chapter XIV

with whom the war was popular. The French fought mostly with feudal heavy cavalry units that were undisciplined and poorly led. The French kings were hard-pressed for cash to recruit mercenary companies, or to equip their own troops adequately.

The war opened with a phase (1337–64) during which the English won a series of victories. At Sluys the English took control of the sea, but defensive warfare was still better developed than offensive, and the French remained behind their walled cities, except on the occasion of the battle of Crecy (August 25, 1346), when English bowmen decimated the French cavalry.

The war had been exhausting for both sides, especially since the Black Death was ravaging Europe at the same time. The king's need for money to continue the war allowed the French provincial Estates and the Estates General to increase their authority. The Estates General demanded and won control over all finances voted to continue the war. The Estates elected a Council of State and forced the king to accept its advice in running the government. Finally, in 1357, the *Grande Ordonnance* was issued whereby the whole government was reformed. The king's ministers became answerable to the Estates, whose representatives now sat on the king's council. Coinage and taxes came under the control of the Estates, and they had the right to meet whenever they wished.

Civil war broke out, and all over France mercenary companies, the terror of the turbulent 14th Century, pillaged at will. In a fury, the peasants rose up in a bloody insurrection against their lords to show their anger at the king's failure to keep order in the country. Over 20,000 of them were cut down. Charles V (1364–80), by relying on competent assistants and using a shrewd diplomatic sense, was able to raise new monies, reform his army, win over English allies, rid the country of the marauding companies, and slowly push the English out of France. By 1377, when Edward III died, France had regained all her territories except for five ports: Calais, Cherbourg, Brest, Bayonne, and Bordeaux. A truce was signed in 1396.

Civil War in England and France

The war had been popular in England when it broke out, and in the early stages when English victories brought rich booty. But as the French began to reconquer their lands, the war had become unpopular. High taxes, French attacks on coastal towns, the ravages of returning veterans who had turned to banditry when they could not find employment, all added to the terror and frustration left in the wake of the Black Death. As we have seen, the English government had moved strongly towards a limited monarchy under parliamentary control, but the Parliament had fallen into the hands of the nobility. Unable to provide programs to solve the social and economic problems of the day, they were interested only in protecting their own prerogatives. As Edward III grew older and more senile in the course of his half-century reign, factions led by his sons broke out at his court. The Black Prince led one until his death, and his brother, John of Gaunt, Duke of Lancaster, led another. Their bitter squabbling continued on into the next reign, as Edward's grandson, Richard II (1377–99), still a minor, came to the throne under the regency of the Council.

The factions at court became so involved in a struggle to dominate the government that they failed to realize that the country was about to explode in a widespread peasants' revolt. The inflammatory ideas of Wycliffe had prepared the war for political and economic radicalism. The peasants and the lower middle classes felt that they were being exploited by the rich, who refused to allow them to advance. They blamed the Council for failing to take measures against the effects of the enclosures of lands, and the expulsion of the serfs. In 1381 the government tried to collect an excessive poll tax, and resentment broke out in open revolt, first in Kent and Essex, and then all over England. Peasants burned old charters and manor records, and demanded reasonable rents and higher wages. A large army of them converged on London, where the Council fled to the Tower in panic. The rebels took the city, burned the palace of the hated John of Gaunt, destroyed as many records as they could find, and killed as many lawyers and merchants as they could capture. The King alone had the courage to go out to meet their leader, Wat Tyler. While Richard was conferring with him, a band of rebels got into the Tower of London, where they killed the Archbishop of Canterbury and many members of the Council. At the conference, Tyler in turn was cut down, and the boy-king rode straight up to the rebels and promised to satisfy their grievances. Awed by his bravery, the crowds dispersed, and the rebellion ended. The promise was immediately ignored, as the frightened nobles took terrible revenge on the miserable rebels. They were cut down mercilessly all over the country, and the survivors sank into worse serfdom than ever.

Richard had been the only one to keep his head in the emergency, and when it was over he planned to take power away from the Council. In 1388 he made his bid for power, but a group of nobles led by his uncle, the Duke of Gloucester, marched on London as the "Lords Appellant," and took over the government. The King allied himself with his Lancastrian uncle, John of Gaunt, and ruled with him until 1397, when he took over on his own. For two years Richard played the tyrant. He struck out at his enemies. Gloucester was murdered. The Lords Appellant were executed or imprisoned, and his cousin Henry of Derby, John of Gaunt's son, was exiled. The King had deceived himself. He had no real military power to use against the aristocracy. When John of Gaunt died, Richard confiscated his Lancaster estates. Infuriated, the young Henry decided to return from France with an army. His chance came when the King led an expedition to Ireland. In 1399 Henry landed in Yorkshire and raised a general revolt. The King took refuge in Wales, but he was captured and deposed by the Parliament.

It was significant in English history that during this period the nobility not only gained dominance over the King, but that they were able to institutionalize it in the Parliament. In France this development did not occur. There the nobles remained free, but they never developed lasting controls over the king, not only because of the traditional lack of unity among them, but also because France was harder hit by the war than England, and was content to have a strong king heal the country's wounds.

Charles VI (1380–1422) was only twelve years old when he came to the throne of France. The regency was shared by his four uncles, the Dukes of Anjou, Burgundy, Berry, and Bourbon. The country was restless and flared up in revolts as the government tried to raise taxes. The uncles took strong action, but the King decided in 1388 to rule by himself. He soon fell under the influence of his brother Louis of Orleans, an extravagant libertine. Burgundy and Orleans were extremely hostile to each other, and when the young King suddenly went completely insane after 1392, uncle and nephew competed openly over the control of the King. In 1404 the old Duke of Burgundy died and was succeeded by his son, John the Fearless, who began to build a powerful Burgundian state. He declared war on Orleans, and had him murdered in 1407. The widow and son of the dead Duke went to war with Burgundy, and by 1413 a statemate was reached. Paris and the government were in the hands of the Orleanists, and Burgundy was loose with a powerful army. It was at this moment that England renewed the War.

The End of the War

Henry IV (1399–1413), son of John of Gaunt, had come to a shaky throne. There were other descendants of Edward III who had better claims to the throne of England than his. He was always careful to court the friendship of Parliament to keep himself in power. He also had to compensate the nobles who had helped him to win the throne. The reign began with uprisings in Scotland and Wales. The former was put down rather easily, but the latter dragged on for a decade. More important, all through his life Henry had to put down a series of rebellions within the country. The Percies, his former supporters; the Beauforts, his half-brothers; Mortimer, his cousin; all made attempts to topple him, but skillfully he parried every

thrust, carefully conserving his wealth and energy and putting them to most effective use. By the time of his death, the country was finally at peace.

Something of a wastrel in his youth, by the time he was crowned, Henry V (1413–22) accepted the responsibility of his office and became an intelligent, energetic King. Unfortunately, he was totally absorbed in renewing the war in France. He continued his father's policy towards Parliament. In 1407 the Parliament had taken total control over all money bills, and now in 1414 they asserted their right to veto any law of the realm. In 1415, Henry made a treaty with Burgundy, laid claim to the French throne, and invaded Normandy. On October 25, 1415 his army repeated the victory of Crecy on the field of Agincourt, and wiped out a French army three times its size. In two campaigns, Normandy was taken, while the Orleanists and Burgundians ravaged central France. John of Burgundy captured Paris. The Dauphin Charles fled to the south, and France now contained three governments. John was murdered by the Dauphin's henchmen on September 10, 1419. His son Philip joined forces with the English King, and the two negotiated a treaty with mad King Charles VI. Henry became regent, married Charles' daughter Katherine of Valois, and was named heir to the throne. The Dauphin was pursued across the land, but the war was still going on when Henry died in August, 1422. Charles VI died in October of the same year.

Henry VI, an infant of nine months, became King of both England and France under two regents, Humphrey of Gloucester in England and John of Bedford in France. Bedford renewed the war and laid siege to Orleans in October, 1428. The Dauphin was desperate. At this moment Jeanne d'Arc arrived to take control of the royal army. A poor peasant girl, born at Doremy around 1410–12, Jeanne had grown up during the worst of the civil war. She had withdrawn into herself and become convinced that she heard "voices" of saints that called her to the sacred mission of saving France. She set out for Orleans, where she forced the Dauphin to place her at the head of his army. The Maid of Orleans had supreme confidence in herself and she infused the army and its leaders with faith in her mission. She slipped into the besieged city in April, 1429, and led a series of inspired attacks against the English, who were forced to raise the siege. All France took heart at the news. She cajoled the reluctant Dauphin into rushing across France to be crowned as tradition demanded in the cathedral of Rheims. Her mission was accomplished, but her luck had turned. Her attack on Paris failed, and she was captured by the Burgundians, who turned her over to the English to be tried and burned as a witch. Her Dauphin, now King Charles VII of France, did nothing to save her. Jeanne's spirit, however, did not die with her. All France rose against the invaders. In 1435 Burgundy withdrew from the war, and in 1436 Paris was taken. By 1453 all France except Calais was retaken, and the war was over.

France to the End of the Century

Charles VII (1422–61) came to be known as "the Well-Served" during the second half of his reign. He turned for help to the bourgeois class to subdue his nobles and to raise the money for the enormous job that faced him. France had been ruined by the war.

Large areas had become deserts. Commerce had slipped; towns were abandoned. Yet by the time of his death, Charles had restored the country. Roads were rebuilt. Harbors and rivers were dredged. Trade began to flow again. The King drove out the mercenary companies who had turned bandit, and he made a truce with his nobility. Within a generation France had made an amazing recovery.

The monarchy, moreover, had emerged from the war much strengthened. The country had proved to be too big for any one representative institution to control. Thus the Estates General never could provide effective government, while the local Estates were able to provide essential laws and controls. To facilitate the reconstruction of the country, the King had been given almost unlimited funds, while the Estates had given up all their restrictions over him. It was easy for him to continue to collect the funds and ignore the Estates, which slowly died out. The King also had the support of the large professional army that had developed in the later part of the war. The only real check on the powers of the monarch was the system of royal *appenages,* such as Burgundy and Brittany. During the reign of Charles VI it had been the rivalries of the great dukes and their pretensions to the throne itself that had led to civil war and chaos. Of them all, the most powerful was Burgundy.

Burgundy was essentially the Middle Kingdom of late Carolingian times, but it had been reconstructed with great effort through careful marriages and annexation. When Charles the Bold (1467–77) acceded to the dukedom, he absorbed the Low Countries and acquired the imperial title. The state was wealthy because of the steady flow of trade that passed through it between

◄ Synagogue, Toledo. There were Jews in Spain who were primarily scholars in Talmudic studies, but who also played an important role in the transmission of the works of Aristotle to Western scholars. Synagogues were built in local styles.

► Towers, San Gimignano. As society in the Middle Ages broke down, there was disorder everywhere. Even in a small town in Tuscany the symbols of disorder became the style. Each family in the town built a tower for protection, then it became a race to see whhat family had the tallest tower.

the Low Countries and Italy. Its court had become the leading art center of Europe, while its first-rate army was organized under the most elaborate chivalric code of the day. During the reign of King Charles VII, Burgundy had joined with the other royal dukes in a rebellion against the bourgeois sympathies of the King. The Dauphin Louis, who hated his father, fled the court and allied himself closely with Philip the Good. The old king summed up the situation shrewdly. "My cousin of Burgundy," he said, "is nourishing the fox that will eat up his chickens." Louis XI (1461–83) came to the throne with Burgundy's blessings, but this crafty "Spider King" was to become an implacable foe. Louis was miserly and cynical. Untrustworthy as a friend, sinister as an enemy, he was almost universally hated, yet his reign was an important step in the emergence of the absolute power of the French monarchy.

As the reign began, the dukes organized themselves into a League of the Commonwealth and made yet another attempt to check the growth of the monarchy. Led by Philip's son, Charles, they besieged the King in Paris. One by one, Louis bought them off, drove wedges into their alliance, and sent his agents into their lands to raise revolts. The only one who could not be bought was Charles, who became Duke in 1467. The rebellion turned into a war between the two that was marked by the gallant fighting of the Duke and the sly diplomatic intrigue of the King. Charles was distracted by his desire for a royal title from the German emperor, and during an attack on the Swiss, he was killed at Nancy in January, 1477. His plans fell with him, for he left only a young daughter, Mary, who married Maximillian, the son of Emperor Frederick III. Louis immediately absorbed most of the duchy of

Burgundy, and arranged a marriage between his son Charles and Mary's daughter Margaret that was to bring the rest to France as her dowry.

Louis had already acquired all of the other *appenages* except Brittany. When he died, France was well on its way to becoming one of the new types of monarchies characteristic of the Renaissance. Charles VIII (1483–98) completed the process. He broke his engagement to Margaret, losing her eastern Burgundian lands to the Hapsburgs, and married Anne, heiress to Brittany. France was finally united. The monarchy was absolute. The economic recovery from the war had brought vast wealth, and France was ready to take a leading role in European affairs.

The War of the Roses

The reign of Henry VI began a period of civil war in England that closely paralleled the Orleanist-Burgundian rivalries of the reign of Charles VI of France. During Henry's minority, the government was in the hands of intriguing quarreling nobles, who sacrificed the interests of the country to gain personal power. Even after Henry reached his majority, his dislike of violence and the periodic madness he inherited from his French grandfather prevented him from checking his corrupt advisors. The war went badly in France, and discontent with the government spread across England. The Parliament cut off their grants to the crown. The nobility, meanwhile, had profited from the war. Plunder from France and the income from the new wool industry had given them the cash to hire private armies, with which they had freed themselves from all royal restrictions on their feudal prerogatives. All semblance of order collapsed when civil war broke out after King Henry VI went completely mad in 1453.

The Queen, Margaret of Anjou, claimed the regency as the head of a faction of Lancastrian supporters of the King. Richard of York, descended from Richard II's son Lionel, led another faction and claimed the regency for himself. Parliament favored him and for a while (1453–54) recognized him as regent. War between the two factions broke out, named the War of the Roses for the emblems of the two contending houses, the red rose of Lancaster and the white rose of York. It was a bitter struggle between factions of the barons of England for personal power. They assassinated and betrayed each other, and kept the kingdom in turmoil; but they never made an attempt to transform the government, or to antagonize the Parliament and the middle classes. The country on the whole remained neutral, and survived the madness almost intact.

Richard, with the support of Richard Neville, Earl of Warwick, the "Kingmaker," had some initial success. But he was slain by Margaret's forces at Wakefield in December 1460. Warwick led Edward, the young Duke of York, to London, and crowned him as King after deposing and later imprisoning the pathetic Henry VI. Edward IV (1461–83) soon proved ungrateful to the "Kingmaker" and formed a faction of his own. With the help of Louis XI of France, Warwick overthrew Edward and put Henry back on the throne in 1470. But no one wanted the madman as King, and when Edward returned from exile, he easily defeated and killed Warwick. Henry was secretly murdered, and the Yorkists were in power. Edward became an absolute King, ruling through his council and summoning Parliament only when he needed money. He was ingenious in devising new ways of squeezing taxes out of his people, which caused widespread resentment, and he took away from the Commons the right of initiating legislation. Law now became the will of the sovereign. He also introduced the technique of forcing through the Parliament bills of attainder against his enemies that convicted them of treason without trial.

Edward made an unpopular marriage with Elizabeth Woodville, the widow of a lesser Lancastrian baron. The Yorkists were repelled by the pretentions of the Woodvilles and rallied behind the King's brother, Richard, to oppose the Queen. When Edward died, the crown passed to his thirteen-year-old son Edward V (1483). Richard usurped the throne and had himself crowned as Richard III (1483–85). The young King and his brother were declared illegitimate, imprisoned, and murdered. The country was outraged. Richard was accused of the crime, and though he apparently attempted to ally himself with the middle classes and give England a strong rule, his reputation as a villain and murderer led to a revolt of the barons against him. Henry Tudor, Earl of Richmond, with a vague claim of descent from John of Gaunt, landed in Wales in 1485, rallied some support, and met and killed Richard at Bosworth Field. As Henry VII he then married Edward IV's daughter Elizabeth, uniting Yorkist and Lancastrian factions. The new dynasty, the Tudors, ushered in a new era in English history. The confusions and civil wars of the Middle Ages were replaced by the efficiency of an absolute monarchy, popular because it brought peace and prosperity. Unlike France, England retained its representative institutions, however, for their very efficiency made them effective tools of the absolute monarch.

The Empire and its Neighbors

The medieval German empire might well have disappeared with the collapse of the Hohenstaufen, but the chaos of the Great Interregnum (1256–73) had convinced the majority of the German nobles that an emperor was necessary to keep some degree of order. Of course, it was understood that he would in no way limit the independence of the great magnates of the empire. Rudolph of Hapsburg (1273–91) was elected precisely because he understood his new role so well. He gave up all imperial claims in Italy, and in Germany he acted merely as an arbitrator between contending princes. He was far more successful in building the fortunes of his family. At first Hapsburg aspirations were countered by claims of other rival princely families and by the Diet of Germany, that passed a decree in 1320 that the election of an emperor was exclusively the responsibility of the Diet. The role of the emperor was further restricted by the promulgation of the Golden Bull of 1356, that set the number of electors at seven great princes, three of them ecclesiastical (the archbishops of Mainz, Trier, and Cologne) and four secular (the count Palatine of the Rhine, the duke of Saxony, the margrave of Brandenburg, and the king of Bohemia). The princes were forbidden to alienate or divide their lands, and they were given almost complete sovereignty over them. Since the empire had become a political impossibility, it was hoped to stabilize Germany by encouraging the growth of large stable states within the imperial framework.

The emperors of the 15th Century, mostly Hapsburgs, were largely ineffective. All semblance of central government disappeared. In the western part of the empire, holdings continued to disintegrate into smaller and smaller competing states, while in the east the Wittelsbachs, in central Germany the Wettins in Saxony and the Hohenzollerns in Brandenburg, were building the nuclei of future strong states.

In other words, just as modern states began to emerge from the debris of feudalism, the Empire began to disintegrate into its feudal parts. Germany came out of the Middle Ages disunited, and had to wait for centuries to achieve unity, and that only by conquest.

A positive act of value came with the marriage of Maximillian (1493–1519) to Mary of Burgundy, which took place in 1477. Through his marriage he added Upper and Lower Burgundy, the Low Countries, and Franche Comte to his Austrian lands. He made a treaty in 1491 with Ladislas, King of Bohemia and Hungary, which stipulated that these lands would go to him if Ladislas died without heirs. Finally, in 1494 he arranged the marriage of his son Philip to Joanna, the mad daughter of Ferdinand and Isabella, and heiress of Spain, Sicily, Naples, and the New World. By the end of the century, the Hapsburgs dominated the known world.

The Swiss and the Hanseatic Leagues

The one glaring failure in the spread of Hapsburg power was their loss of Switzerland, the original homeland of the family. In the western Alps there had gathered a tough, freedom-loving people who had already in the 13th Century shown resistance to Hapsburg domination. When Rudolph of

Hapsburg was elected Emperor, the cantons of Uri, Schweitz, and Unterwalden united in a compact to protect themselves, and a border warfare broke out. In 1315 the Swiss defeated a Hapsburg coalition at Morgarten and became almost independent. Their league grew as the leading commercial centers of Upper Germany joined it. At Sempach in 1386 the Swiss again defeated the Hapsburgs, this time for good. The cantons were self-governing and never developed a central administrative system, though they were almost the only example of medieval republics that were able to survive and become stronger. Their armies became famous and fought in all the Italian and French wars of the 15th Century.

Another medieval league that did not fare so well was the Hanse. Trading centers began to develop along the Baltic coast as early as the 11th Century. During the 13th Century the towns were working together closely to develop the trade of the area and by the 14th Century a formal league had been established to maintain a monopoly of the traffic in northern goods. Towns stretching from Lubeck on the Danish peninsula to Novgorod in Russia joined until there were some 70 or 80 members. There was no central administration, and the league acted only by cooperation to achieve ends of mutual interest. For a time the Hanse dominated all the trade of northern Europe, but its wealth was never as great as that of the Italian or even the Rhenish towns. By the 15th Century, Novgorod had fallen to the Grand Duke of Moscow, southern German towns found a way to bypass the Hanse, and new banking houses had begun a new era in the economic development of Europe. The Hanseatic League had no part in this, and it slowly declined until it broke up during the 16th Century.

Spain and Portugal

The history of Castile and Aragon in the 14th and early 15th Centuries was largely one of civil war. Rebellion, pretenders, disputed successions kept the Christian states in turmoil, while the Moors held on feebly in Granada. The country was largely Catholic, but a sizable and productive Jewish population, and a Moorish state on the borders, led Spanish rulers to adopt a policy of religious toleration at least until the fall of Granada in 1492. The nobles and towns were all-powerful throughout the period, and kings were involved in dynastic struggles for personal power. They antagonized their nobles with attempts to rule Sicily and Italy after 1309. The situation was reversed when Isabella became Queen of Castile in 1474 and Ferdinand, her husband, King of Aragon in 1479. Many factions in Spain had opposed their marriage in 1469, and Louis XI of France had lodged a strong protest, but a general desire for peace and an end to the political anarchy was in their favor. After the centuries of occupation by various invaders, the only common history in the land was the perpetual crusade, the only common feeling among all the inhabitants of the peninsula was Catholicism, and the only universal institution was the Inquisition. These are the ingredients that the Catholic kings used to forge a unified state. Slowly all classes fell under the domination of the king. Town charters were revoked. Feudal privileges were curtailed, but the nobility was placated by freedom from taxation. The rest of the country had to pay ruinous taxes on purchases, which discouraged the growth of trade and industry. The country became increasingly a homogeneous, Catholic people anxious to display their loyalty to the Catholic king so as to avoid his Inquisition. Moslems and Jews were even less fortunate, and they were finally expelled in 1492 with ruinous consequences for the culture and economy of Spain.

Portugal, meanwhile, was establishing its independence on the Atlantic coast. In the 14th Century Portuguese kings had resisted all attempts of Castile to annex their territories, and they had entered into commercial contracts with England to export wine. In 1415 during the reign of John I (1385–1433) Portugal began her overseas expansion with the conquest of Ceuta in Morocco. John's son, Henry the Navigator, fired by missionary zeal, built an observatory, opened a school of navigation, and began directing a series of spectacular voyages down the African coast. The Madeiras were discovered in 1418, the Azores in 1427, and in 1434 Portuguese ships reached the Guinea Coast. Wealth producing wines and slaves began to flow into Portugal, and voyages were sent out to find new sources of wealth. In 1486 Diaz rounded the Cape of Good Hope, and in 1497 Vasco da Gama reached India. The state was ruled by an absolute government, but the regime was popular because of the great prosperity of the country. After the arrival of da Gama in India, Portugal established an empire in the East Indies, while Spain moved across the Atlantic. The scene had shifted away from the traditional centers of the Middle Ages.

The Italian City-States

In northern Europe, as we have seen, the 14th and 15th Centuries witnessed the collapse of medieval institutions. The old ways of doing things just did not seem to work any more, and many people were disheartened at the failure. But life was changing under the impact of new economic activity. There were vital forces at work that posed profound challenges to the more acute and sensitive elements in the society. They became impatient with traditional patterns, which were changing too slowly to provide the new structure that was needed, and they turned to Italy to learn and adapt the institutions that had been emerging there in the late Middle Ages.

The city-states of Italy had become involved in a way of life that was quite different from that of the medieval North. Contacts with the Mediterranean East had introduced new economic, political, and intellectual activity which had to be adapted to the institutions that had survived into the Middle Ages. The result had been a great amount of social tension, as classes moved in and out of power, and states expanded or contracted. Caught between the two most typical medieval institutions, the Church and the Empire, the Italian states had to keep up a constant struggle to preserve their own way of life. It is no wonder, then, that by the 14th Century people in all the towns were ready to find security and peace under strong despots. The constant need to keep down the internal disorders tended to make the despotism a hereditary office, and strong ruling families emerged all over Italy. Sometimes the family was elected to the office, often they usurped the power. In Florence the Medici bribed their way to dominance within the bourgeois class, and the Visconti of Milan began as imperial vicars. In any case, these despots imposed their stamp on Italy, and created a political system that answered many of the problems of the age. All Europe came to learn.

Venice had become a mercantile aristocracy by the 14th Century. Her fortunes lay obviously on the sea, and throughout the century she kept up a bitter rivalry with Genoa until she won control over the Levantine trade. By the end of the century, however, Venice was already planning an expansion into the Italian mainland. To build and maintain her fleets, she needed wood and other supplies. In 1308 Venice attempted and failed to annex Ferrara. Until the end of the War of Chioggra (1378–80), Venice was preoccupied with her maritime war with Genoa and could only follow a defensive policy on the mainland. After 1402 she went on the offensive. Padua and Verona were annexed. A war with Milan (1425–32) brought her certain Lombard towns. By a war with Ferrara in 1482–84 she reached the limits of her expansion. The war in the east did not go so well. All through the 15th Century Venice fought a losing battle with the Turks, eventually losing all her possessions.

Venice made no changes in her government during this period. The oligarchy still functioned. The total integration of the social and economic life still ensured efficiency and prosperity. The subject states were treated fairly, though they were expected to contribute to the wealth of Venice. The Serene Republic had achieved stability, wealth, and peace. The price was the absence of individual liberty, a price men are often ready to pay for prosperity.

Florence had been able to maintain its republican Ordinances of Justice into the 14th Century, although the city was wracked by savage civil war. The attack of Emperor Louis VII was fought off, but Florence was forced to bring in Walter of Brienne as *capitano del popolo* to keep order. He proved to be such a tyrant that he was overthrown, and the towns never again experimented with so absolute a monarch. Social tension kept increasing as the Guelph party, the *popolo grasso*, increased its power over the *popolo minuto*. In 1378 Salvestro de Medici led a revolt of the *Ciompi*, the lower working class. The revolt accomplished little, and foreign war proved distracting for a time. Pisa was conquered in 1406, and Florence dominated all of Tuscany, which led to more wars with Milan.

The solution to the Florentine political problem was found in the Medici family. Members of the new nobility, the Medici had sympathy for the objectives of the greater guilds and the Guelph aristocracy, but they also understood the problems of the poor and offered attractive programs of reform. The result was that Medici rule became an absolute despotism, even though the republican institutions were scrupulously preserved. The Medici ruled through an effective political machine, that always elected their men to office. By keeping complete control over all power in the state, the Medici put down civil strife and were able to lead Florence to the height of her power in Tuscany and Italy.

The family came to power with Giovanni de Medici, but it was his son Cosimo who began the despotism in 1434, when he was given the title *Pater Patriae*. He was able to form an alliance with Milan and Naples which maintained a balance of power in Italy. He was also instrumental in making Florence the cultural and artistic center of the Renaissance. His greatest *coup* was the lavish scale upon which he played host to the Council of Florence in 1439. By the time of his death in 1464, he had established the family as the popular and benevolent despots of the city. His son Piero (1464–69) continued the family's popularity, which was put to a severe test in the reign of Lorenzo the Magnificent (1469–92). In 1478 the Pazzi, an rival aristocratic family, attempted to assassinate Lorenzo and overthrow the family. Lorenzo escaped, and the city exploded in a demonstration of loyalty to the Medici. Lorenzo now formed a great coalition against the papacy that stabilized Italian affairs until the invasion of Charles VIII of France. At home Lorenzo set up a popular Council of Seventy to run the affairs of the city, seeing to it, of course, that its members were good friends of the Medici. Florence, like Venice, had found internal peace and prosperity under a despotism that consolidated all the forces of the community into a homogeneous unity.

Milan also followed the same pattern. The town had been the leader in the 13th Century in Italian resistance to the emperor. Internally, the city fell into civil war as the great noble families fought each other for control. In 1287 the people elected Matteo Visconti *capitano del popolo*. In 1294 he secured his appointment as imperial vicar, which was confirmed by Henry VII in 1311. Later he took the title of General Lord of Milan. He began to bring the Lombard towns under Milanese rule. His son, Archbishop Giovanni Visconti, was able to extend Milanese rule even over Genoa (1353), but at his death in 1354, his three nephews went to war over the lordship. Bernarbo emerged the victor (1354–85), but his atrociously cruel regime was ended by his murder by Gian Galeazzo, his nephew. Gian Galeazzo (1378–1402) was an almost perfect example of the despots of the age. Opportunistic, cruel and crafty, a true Machiavellian, he dominated Italy until his death.

He purchased the title of Duke of Milan from the emperor, and began to form a grand coalition of all the North Italian states. Padua, Pisa, Bologna, Siena, even states as far south as Perugia were brought into his state. At home, he worked closely with the merchant class. He systematized the tax structure, reformed the administrative system, built a canal from Milan to Pavia, and turned Milan into the best-ruled state in Europe. His nemesis was the determined resistance of Florence and Venice, which undid much of his work during the reigns of his infamous sons Gran Maria (1402–12) and Filippo Maria (1402–47). The state again dissolved into civil war. The lesson was obvious. When the government was strong, even though despotic, the state prospered, even if not free. Freedom meant anarchy. One of the *condottieri* that rose in this period was Francesco Sforza, who forced a marriage with Bianca, the daughter of Filippo Maria. In 1447 a republic was proclaimed, and Sforza became the commander of its troops in the war with Venice. In 1450 he made himself Duke. He made an elaborate system of alliances and continued the interrupted good rule of Gian Galeazzo. His son Galeazzo (1466–76) was a tyrant who was assassinated by a group of would-be republicans,, but his son Gian Galeazzo became Duke under the regency of his mother, Bona of Savoy. In 1479 Galeazzo's brother Ludovico took over the regency of his nephew, after whose death he announced his purchase of the ducal title from Emperor Maximillian. During the squabbles over the regency, Ludovico had appealed to Charles VIII for help. The invasion that followed put an end to the age of the despots.

The Renaissance

It was clear that a new way of life had emerged in Italy. Merchants and bankers had become deeply involved with the goods of this world, while the despots had become absorbed in a politics of reality. Individual self-made men were typical of the age, and dynamism became the characteristic of social behavior. The moral and ethical system of the Middle Ages no longer seemed to have relevance. Restrictions on credit, individualism, the emphasis on universal, eternal institutions made the emerging classes of the period uneasy. Men had to accept the ideals of the former age and feel guilty for their new way of life, or they had to abandon them and create new ones. The Renaissance was the creation of a new system of attitudes that were closer to the realities of 15th Century life. At the same time, the new men of Italy took pride in their new way of life. They hired artists and scholars to glorify it and present it in as beautiful a way as possible. Finally, there was an uneasiness underlying their arrogance. They were self-made men, without legitimate claims to power. By becoming cultivated gentlemen, they made up for their lack of aristocratic lineage.

It is customary to view the emergence of the new morality in the transition from Dante, who died in 1321, through Petrarch, born in 1304, to Boccaccio, born in 1313. Dante presented the finest summation of the medieval ideals. Men were involved in this world only to prepare for life in the next. Human love, for instance, taught man the love of God, who had placed on earth the Church and the Empire to give men a foretaste of eternal heaven. When men were living harmoniously under one emperor and in one faith, they would have achieved happiness. Dante was confident, sure of his faith, and his *Divine Comedy* reflected this mood.

Petrarch was a man caught in a moral dilemma. An active Renaissance type man, deeply involved in politics, wealthy, courted by popes and kings, carnal and pleasure-loving, yet he was plagued with a medieval conscience. He was never happy within himself, though his disturbance never led him to sacrifice his way of life for his outmoded ideals. Neither did he have the courage or strength to abandon them. The only redeeming quality of this hypocritical and vain man was his sincere love of learning, though even this took the form of a worship of the classics of the Greco-Roman world. He was sincerely concerned with gaining knowledge about man and life in this world, and he was a talented writer, whose style had a profound impact throughout Europe.

With Boccaccio a new world had come into being. A member of the middle class and trained for a career in law, he never lost contact with the very real world around him, nor was his Latin so good that he abandoned his native Italian in his books. His great work was the *Decameron*, a marvelous window into the world of the 14th Century. Here the new life had emerged triumphant. Men were motivated by *virtu*, manliness. Life was a challenge and its prize went to those who had the courage to grasp it. The heroes of the book were the typical opportunists of the day, the seducers, the men of versatility and imagination. The villains were the seduced, the duped husbands, the losers. Chance had become the operating force of the universe and the future was what you made it. God always helped those who had already helped themselves.

The emphasis on individual desires and their satisfaction could easily have led to bestiality in Italy. In fact, there was a great deal of shocking cruelty. But on the whole, Italians were saved by an almost innate love of style. The memory of Roman civilization had never died in Italy. It was not enough that one love. One had to live in a manner that excited wonder, that stimulated artistic response. Articles were not to be merely utilitarian. They also had to be beautiful. Thus, the Renaissance produced a way of life, a means of artistic expression that has remained one of the most exciting in the history of Western man.

First, the Renaissance tried to find an ideal to emulate and found it in the life of the Roman Empire. Men seemed to have lived lives then that were far closer to the Renaissance types than during the Middle Ages. The Romans and Greeks had understood man as the men of the Renaissance understood him, as God's most perfect creature placed on this earth to accept the challenge of life and to take command with verve and style. The humanism of the Classical Age fascinated them. Those who specialized in uncovering this rich literature became known as Humanists, and they became the arbiters of good taste. A mad search for classical texts preoccupied men of learning throughout the Renaissance, not because the contents were not known, but because the wealthy aristocrats of the age wanted the reputation for good taste and discrimination that went with being a patron of scholars. In an age when the pretensions of self-made despots were vulnerable, Humanists could topple a tyrant with ridicule. A more serious aim of the Humanist movement was the study of the classics to learn more details about the actual world in which men lived. Greek was studied, acade-

mies were formed, and the knowledge began to circulate. If the movement was originally aristocratic and restricted, translations and the printing press soon brought the new knowledge to an ever-widening audience.

The artists of the age never became as detached from everyday life as the Humanists tended to become. Usually from the lower classes, the artists were really artisans, who were hired to do specific jobs. Their learned their techniques from actual experience and though they learned from the ancients and borrowed themes, they were involved in creating original forms of expression. The architect, for instance, may have learned from his study of the ancient ruins so common in Italy, but his churches were churches, just as his *pallazzi* were exactly what they were supposed to be, armed fortresses. The sculptors also learned from the past, but they invented anew the method of casting bronze statues, nor did their work have the calm, unreal quality of the Greco-Roman ideal types. On the contrary, Renaissance sculpture is vibrantly alive. In painting, the artists were perhaps the most inventive, since no easel painting had survived from the ancient world. The painters were preoccupied with representing this world as it appeared to man. Very often the themes were religious or classical, but the spirit was always contemporary. Man, his inner emotional life, his attitude toward this world around him, these were the real themes of Renaissance painting, and to express them all the techniques necessary to depict a three-dimensional world on a two-dimensional surface were developed. Realism was achieved by an understanding of the rules of perspective and color. This realism satisfied the vanity and pride of the art patrons, just as did the exquisite artifacts of the period. But psychological insight, so unfamiliar in the ancient world, was also the goal of the artist.

Finally, the art of living was also studied by the Renaissance. The idea of the gentleman, who could express with precision and style his every thought, was perhaps the greatest invention of the age. States were studied in the same way. The emergence of the national state was suggested in the history of the Italian states, and it was in Italy that sovereignty, international diplomacy, and balance of power make their first appearance.

The Renaissance in the North

The mood of the 14th and 15th Centuries in northern Europe was one almost of despair. Social institutions had failed, and man was left adrift. Many men could not believe what had happened. They kept trying to revive the medieval world. Chivalry became a travesty of its original form. Court dress became as exaggerated as court procedure. Other men gave up in despair. The world had failed, there was no hope. In panic they turned to bizarre religious practices and a preoccupation with death and dying.

Yet under the surface new forces were at work. The political experience of the Italian states brought to the north a new sense of the national state. New monarchs arose, the Tudors in England, Louis IX in France, Ferdinand in Spain, who put the king forward as the guarantee of internal peace. The stronger he became, the more he consolidated the realm under his sovereignty, the more secure all his subjects became. Medieval particularism and freedom were sacrificed to destroy the anarchy that accompanied them.

The North also retained a deep sense of piety. When the pagan Humanism of Italy came to the North, it took on a deeply Christian tone. There scholars and mystics studied the past not to imitate, but to learn. The desire for reform was as profound as the need. But to reform the Church and society one had to know their original form. Men learned Greek and Hebrew to become better acquainted with the early Church and the ideals of Christian society. They hoped to be able to recreate them. The Renaissance in the North was more contemplative, more introspective, and finally more productive than the more brilliant rebirth of paganism in the south.

PORTRAITS
▼ ▼ ▼ ▼ ▼

Homer

There is nothing known with certainty about Homer. The ancients believed he really lived and that he had composed both the *Iliad* and the *Odyssey*. Probably around 700 B.C. someone drew together many tales of the Mycenaean period and gave them a poetic form. It is difficult to avoid a unity of tone, especially in the *Iliad,* that reflects a single sensibility. In the ancient world the two works would take the place the Bible holds for the Western world. Not only are gods presented in their many forms, but their activities within the unity of a universe set the models for men, who either follow suit or rebel and go off on their own. The whole range of human life, its morality, its standards are drawn from Homer.

The subtitle of the *Iliad* is *The Wrath of Achilles.* A war has broken out between Troy (Ilium) and the other Greek states of the Mycenaean world. Whatever the real reasons, the poet chooses to blame the war on the activities of the young son of Priam, King of Troy. Paris was visiting the court of Menelaus, King of Sparta, when he fell in love with Helen, wife of Menelaus. The two ran off to Troy, leaving the husband seeking revenge and the return of his wife. He called upon his brother Agamemnon, King of Mycenae, and husband of Helen's sister Klytemnestra. One by one all the great kings are drawn into the war and an expedition sets out for Troy.

When the *Iliad* opens the kings have been besieging Troy for ten years. They are tired of the war, tempers are running high. Achilles, the champion of the Hellenic cause, is sulking in his tent, hence the title of the work. It seems that after a successful raid against the Trojans much loot is taken and Achilles receives as his share the beautiful Briseis. But Agamemnon, leader of the host, claims her as his own and Achilles has to give her up, and now he is in a fury. The reason for his fury is clear enough. Men have short lives and then they are soon forgotten. The only thing that survives a man is his fame. So long as men remember his great deeds, a man still lives. The host has stolen Achilles' chance at immortality by demeaning him. The fury sets off a chain of events that illustrate the moral code of the military society. Homer's poetry describes in touching detail the day to day values that set the standard for the ancient world. At one point, Helen loses her composure. She looks out from the city's walls at the ships that have carried a whole host to bring her back to her husband and she grieves at the suffering she has caused. But a group of aged men, too old to fight, have gathered in the cool of the evening to gossip and, chattering like cicadas, they comment on her beauty and don't blame her for the war.

What better reason to go to war than to serve beauty, even a terrible beauty?

The Trojan hero of the tale is Hector, who is happily married and has an infant son. When Achilles refuses to fight, his dearest friend fights in his place and is killed. Now Achilles has a more seemly cause for anger. He challenges Hector to a duel. In a touching scene, Hector says farewell to his wife and infant son, and meets Achilles in battle and is killed. The victor dishonors the body of valiant Hector, but when King Priam comes to beg permission to bury the body of his son, Achilles remembers his own aged father and relents. These scenes from the *Iliad* set the standard poetic language for the emerging Greek code of conduct. All educated men of both the Greek and Roman worlds accepted the way of life illustrated in the *Iliad* as the norm for human excellence.

Socrates

One day Socrates was walking along the walls of Athens. He loved nature and the countryside, but rarely left the city and the atmosphere of city living. He saw the handsome young student Phaedrus walking along outside the walls and seemingly in deep thought. He was intrigued so he called to him. The youth explained that he had just heard a lecture by the popular Sophist Lysias on the subject of *eros*. Rhetoric was very important to Athenians for in their democracy each citizen had to plead his cause in the assemblies and in the courts by himself. Sophists specialized in teaching rhetoric, and Lysias was renowned. Socrates eagerly joined the young man to discuss the lectures form and also its subject, *eros*. The

two wandered along the banks of the Ilissus River and found a shady spot where they discussed the art of rhetoric and the meaning of *eros*.

The structure of this late dialogue of Plato, the *Phaedrus*, arises in the very setting itself. The world of nature is extolled, not only in the appearance of the natural world but in its very nature. Plato's vision of reality unfolds. Behind the world of appearance there is a world of ideal reality that ought to and indeed does regulate the activities of men. In the discussion that follows the soul is described as a regulating agency that directs the activities of all men. Every man has a soul and therefore knows the good life that is instinctive to men. There is a mechanism in men that indicates the good life. In Greek that mechanism was called *eros*. By nature man knows the good and the beautiful by *eros*, love. In Greek the two are the same word: *kalos*. So man is attracted to the good and the beautiful by *eros*. The point is that man knows what is the good by his nature. It is not a question of one man's opinion about the beautiful. There is a kind of mystical realization of the good, just as there is about the beautiful.

Plato wrote another dialogue about *eros*, the *Symposium*, in which he outlines essentially the same ideas, but the setting allows him to stress the different kinds of love that exist. Socrates always distinguishes between those who are the "victims" of passion and those who are true lovers. In the *Symposium* Plato introduces us to Alcibiades, the most renowned young man of his day. He was brought up by the famous Pericles, who introduced him into Athenian politics. In the *Symposium*, when he enters the room the whole group including Socrates himself is struck by his physical beauty. He spoke with a lisp, which everyone found charming, as if the flaw made him more endearingly beautiful. Everyone "fell in love" with him. But look at his career. He was ambitious and deserted the Athenian cause and went over to the Spartans. Then, back with the Athenians, he led the fleets in the invasion of Sicily. He got involved in a drunken prank and desecrated the Hermes. Charged with impiety he fled to the Persians. Eventually, after years of half-hearted attempts to get back into the political scene, he was murdered by assassins sent by the Athenian government of the Thirty Tyrants. So what good did *eros* do for Alcibiades? According to Socrates, *eros* should lead the lover and the beloved to the good life, which is innate to men who follow the guidance of their souls' predilection for what is the proper life for men. The life of Alcibiades reminds us of Sophocles' advice at the end of the *Oedipus Tyrannus* not to call a man's life a happy one until he has crossed over into death.

Herodotus and Thucydides

The ancient world saw Herodotus as the "father of history." But the modern world tends to think more highly of Thucydides. His *Peloponnesian War* (431–403 B.C.) has modern traits after all. He understands the role economic factors play in history. He appreciates the effect of differences in the psychologies of peoples. He paints a picture of the coming of the war as the unfolding of a destined pattern. We already know the end, so there is the illusion of completeness. But the historian is making comments on what he sees as a story and whether or not he is aware of it he has formed a bias. All through his history he recreates in speech after speech what he considers the appropriate words to express the mood that the historian feels ought to be there. Today this type of history is almost obligatory. "How true to life" is a common if left-handed compliment. Thucydides has a point of view which is clear. His heros speak like heros and the effect is "true to life."

But Herodotus (484–420 B.C.) is a better historian. For his history of the *Persian War* he visited many lands and described what he saw there. He heard many stories and took them all as he heard them. The reader can take or leave them as he wills. Sometimes you do know what the historian believes, but even then he allows you as the reader to come to your own conclusions.

The styles of the two historians are very much with us today. The one recreates the past from his understanding of it and paints a picture that will amuse and educate. The other just puts forward the past as he comes across it, through literary sources or personal observation. He allows the reader to come to his own conclusions. He needs an audience that can think along with him.

The argument goes on. To some Thucydides amuses but is a propagandist after all. To others Herodotus is a *naif* believer in old wives' tales. The trick is to combine the two, measure one's audience and write just a little beyond them.

Aristotle

Aristotle (384–322 B.C.) was born in Stegira in Macedonia into a medical family. He came to study with Plato at his Academy when he was seventeen or eighteen, but he studied with him for only twenty years, until Plato died. In those days the relationship between teacher and student was considered a lifelong one, just as Jesus, as rabbi, was teacher to his disciples (*discipilus* or "pupil" in Latin). Aristotle's stay with his teacher was a short one and he was taunted as a drop-out later. He left the Academy in a huff, because he was piqued when he was not chosen to follow his master and become its head. He wandered from place to place looking for the right one in which to open a school of his own. For a time he was hired by Philip of Macedon to tutor the young Alexander. Someone has said that never was so great a teacher wasted on so great a student. At least the boy developed a lifelong love and respect for learning.

At last Aristotle came to Athens where he opened the Lyceum, a university of higher learning. Like the Academy and other schools of the day, the Lyceum was peripatetic in that teachers delivered lectures as they and the students walked back and forth sharing a lecture in a give and take fashion. It is still not clear whether the books of Aristotle are lecture notes taken down by students in this fashion or notes Aristotle used to give his lectures.

One thing is certain: the Lyceum was a graduate center. Students travelled widely, gathering information of all kinds, which was collected at the center. When Aristotle had enough to compose a work, he published the work under his name. The students, for example, gathered together materials to write the constitutions of over 140 city-states (only one of which remains, *The Constitution of Athens).* From this material he seems to have composed the *Politics.*

The range of the writing of Aristotle is staggering—*Metaphysics, Physics, Organon, On the Heavens, On the Soul, On Motion,* etc. He understood the nature of fossils and their significance. His study of the shellfish of the eastern Mediterranean is still the standard work on the subject. All his works were of fundamental importance, but two were of crucial significance for the non-specialist—the *Politics* and the *Poetics.*

Down through the years his *Politics* has had an enormous influence when it was in circulation and when it was "lost" for periods of time. The reason for this influence is probably because Aristotle sees the state as a natural phenomenon. He sees the family as a natural group necessary for the human race, for a human cannot fend for himself at birth, but must rely on a family. Another necessity for the family arises from the nature of man himself. Man is a rational creature by nature. His rationality makes it possible for him always to imagine goals for himself beyond his capacity to realize them. He must have a society around him. It follows that he also is a social animal by his very nature.

From the family there grows a group of families that becomes a village, and a group of villages that becomes a *polis* (a city-state). Thus out from man's nature by definition there develops a society which then follows a historical pattern of growth.

Aristotle analyses the growth of Athens as a *polis.* It begins as a monarchy in which one man rules the society for the good of all. In time he needs the help of an aristocracy of agrarian landowners. The landowners tend to think of their own good, while the monarch must think of the good of all. This leads to conflict, and in time monarchy disappears all over the Hellenic world. The aristocracy puts an end to internal strife, and peaceful conditions lead to overpopulation. The remedy is colonization. And every Hellenic state sends out people to carry the name of the mother state overseas. Ships have to be built. New products are acquired. Money and writing are introduced, and eventually a new class emerges that grows in importance. The old aristocracy becomes an oligarchy, because it no longer seeks to serve the good of all the people, just as the new commercial class follows suit. Class war breaks out between the oligarchies, with no class strong enough to take control of the whole society. Tyrants arise who organize the masses to control the oligarchies by introducing democratic elements in the courts and in the *ecclesia* (the popular assembly). But the tyrants serve only their own interests in the end. The people take over their own government and for a short while Athens, at least, was a democracy. But people become impatient with the slowness of government, and certainly they must always blame bad news on someone, so soon democracy disintegrates into ochlocracy, mob rule. Soon Greece is ripe for invasion.

In outline Aristotle sees this pattern as the natural one for the system of the *polis*. Monarchy leads to aristocracy, to oligarchy, to tyranny, to democracy, and to mob rule. And he asks how many forms of government are possible? There is the rule of one man, of some men, and of all men. There also are good governments and bad governments. A good government has as its end the welfare of all. A monarchy is the rule of one man who aims at the welfare of all. An aristocracy is the rule of some men in the interests of all. And democracy is the rule of all men in the interest of all. These are the good governments. Tyranny is the rule of one man who rules in his own interest. Oligarchy is the rule of a particular class, serving its own interest, while ochlocracy is the mob who rules without reason at all. From Aristotle's point of view again nature works out in practice what reason already knows.

Aristotle's insight that the state is natural to man has had decisive influence. He himself tended to be conservative. "The middle way is the better way," and "Nothing in excess" sum up his philosophy.

The Hellenes were the first people to consider aesthetics a branch of philosophy. For them art was always didactic, never "art for art's sake." Art was a vehicle for the teaching of life and its values. This explains certain aspects of Hellenic art. In sculpture, for example, there is little modelling as we know it. There is no attempt at portraiture. There is no question that had the artists wanted to they could have made true portraits, but that was not their aim. A statue is supposed to portray the essence of its subject, whether it is a beautiful woman, an athlete, or a god. The maidens carrying their burdens in a sacred procession on the Porch of the Erechtheion are a perfect example. They seem to be moving. The statue shows what the subject is supposed to look like. It is a model from which we learn what life is.

The Parthenon on the Acropolis of Athens is an excellent example of the same thing in architecture. When one examines the building, one finds that there are almost no straight lines in it. The sculptures of the metope lean out. The columns are slightly bulged. The lines along the rows of columns are not true. What has happened is that the builders were quite aware of what we call optical illusions. From a distance, if the lines were true, the building would look wrong. But by bulging the columns, by slanting the sculptures of the metopes and the rows of columns, they made the building look perfect. The whole effect is an illusion, effected by the application of reason to correct the physical world. Life, itself, is the triumph of reason over matter. A well-ordered life is precisely that and art teaches the same moral principles as philosophy does.

In his *Poetics*, Aristotle suggests the same basic morality as he does in his *Politics*. He tells us that attending a tragedy we learn profound truths about life. He chooses to illustrate this by an analysis of Sophocles' play *Oedipus the King*. As we go into the performance, we already know the plot. There are no surprises. We know that Oedipus was the son of the King and Queen of Thebes. A prophecy had foretold that they would produce a son who would kill his father and bed his mother, the two most horrible crimes possible to the Hellenes. Today one wonders at the role of intention in crime. The ancients were more interested in how a man confronts his destiny. Does he meet it in a manly way? Life is short and is controlled by destiny, so it was irrelevant to the ancients that Oedipus did not choose to commit the crimes. Being cast in the role of the sinner, how did he act? A sin disturbs the equilibrium of the world, its *stasis*. The sinner must be sought out and made aware of his sin so that he can atone and restore equilibrium to the world. There is collective guilt for crime. When one man sins all mankind is held responsible. So we know that the father decided when the baby was born to expose him to be eaten by wild animals. He tried to do good and avoid the crime. There was a shepherd working for the King of Thebes who had become friendly with a shepherd of the King of Corinth. His Queen had lost her baby, so when the first shepherd was given Oedipus to expose, he gave the baby instead to his fellow shepherd for the Queen of Corinth to raise as her own, and to ease her pain. Who would know the difference? So they all try to do good. But Fate controls man's destiny.

And Oedipus grows to manhood. He has always had a sense that there is something wrong within him. He cannot make peace within himself. Freud will make much of this search by every man to find his true identity. So he decides to go to the shrine of Apollo at Delphi to find who he really is. When he reaches the spot where the three roads meet, one that goes to Delphi, another to Orchonemos (an ancient shrine), and the third to Thebes, he encounters an old man with an escort. A fight breaks out and Oedipus without knowing him kills the King of Thebes, his father. When he gets to the town he finds he is a hero, because he has killed the sphinx who was ravaging the countryside. He does not realize the old man he had killed was the King, for one of the escort, ashamed to admit they had been routed by one man, had told everyone that the king had been set upon by a whole band of ruffians. So no one sees Oedipus as the killer. Oedipus marries the widow, and becomes a good king and a good husband. Everyone in the story has tried to do good as he sees it, but our lives are played out in accordance with a higher justice.

The play by Sophocles that Aristotle analyses opens at this point. A plague has struck the town and Oedipus, being a good king, does everything he can to save his people. But it is learned that the plague has been caused by the sin a man in the town has committed. Bit by bit it becomes clear that Oedipus is the sinner, but not before his mother has killed herself, not before he has cursed himself and finally not before he has plucked out his own eyes in horror at what he has done.

But Aristotle believes there is therapeutic value in witnessing the tragedy. There is a "fatal flaw" in Oedipus' character.

He is so sure he is a good king, that he could never be guilty of such crimes. The Hellenes called this arrogance *hybris*. We are all capable of feeling it, so that we can sympathize with Oedipus, we can feel his pain. And those of us who can feel the pain of committing the sin, can also feel the catharsis, the cleansing that comes with the atonement. As Aristotle expresses it, we come out of the theater better people than we were when we entered. We have learned a great lesson in the art of living.

Aristotle lived a long life at Athens, but he was always considered an outsider, wearing elegant Macedonian dress and living in high style. At the end he seems to have accepted Alexander the Great's demand that he be accepted as a god by the Greek city-states. When Alexander died all Macedonian garrisons were ousted from Greece. Aristotle was threatened with a charge of impiety and he left Athens, he said, to save the Athenians from committing the same crime twice against philosophy.

Alexander the Great

Alexander (356–323 B.C.) inherited from his father an ability to lead men and a skill at war-making. From his mother, who was a priestess, a mystic and a woman capable of great emotional upheaval, he developed a basically unstable personality. The two sides of his character made him unpredictable and a mystery to most men. He always attracted men of deep devotion and self-sacrifice. From the very beginning of his meteoric career he was considered almost divine by his followers. There were the usual signs of supernatural phenomena surrounding his birth, and the excessive love between him and his mother were also the bases of legendary tales. Certainly he was ready to take on the role of god-king that his experience at the oasis of Siwah seems to have suggested to him. Yet he was capable of extreme paroxysms of rage. One night during a bout of drinking, he became enraged at his foster-brother Kleitos, who was expressing scorn for Alexander's pretensions to dress like a Persian *basileus* and play the role of a god-king. Alexander picked up a lance and threw it across the room, and pierced through him to the wall. Then he lapsed into paroxysms of grief that went on for days. It was no wonder that his men came to believe he was divine. They followed him literally to the ends of the earth.

His death at thirty-three years of age cut short his career and gave it a kind of unreality. It was filled with nothing but success. He had freed the old Greek states of Asia Minor. He had brought under his control the Persian Empire that stretched from Egypt to northern India. He laid out the trade routes on land and sea that would become tradition for ages to come. He was a great builder of cities, the most important of which, Alexandria in Egypt, was to become the cultural capital of the Hellenistic world. He had brought into one world many peoples, speaking many tongues, following many cultural patterns. They all shared one basic acceptance of a basic way of life natural to man.

But what if he had lived long enough to have to cope with the problems that his very successes had begun to pose? Would he still be considered "the Great"? There are many arguments about how aware he was of the philosophical significance of his accomplishments—did he understand the Stoic and Cynical implications of the world his conquests had created? But one thing is certain: He came at a crucial moment in history and his life itself sums up the tenor of the age. It is appropriate that it be called the Age of Alexander.

Euclid of Alexandria

When Alexander the Great died, the chief generals of his army became his heirs (the *Diadochoi)*, and they divided up his newly-established empire among themselves. Egypt fell to Ptolomy I. After 306 B.C., perhaps under the influence of Alexander's restless quest for knowledge, Ptolomy opened a university in honor of the Muses, the *Museum.* It was a graduate center like the Lyceum of Aristotle, and Ptolomy invited many scholars from all over the Hellenistic world to come there to teach. Ironically, this is the same center destroyed when Julius Caesar invaded Cleopatra's Egypt.

Among those who came to teach was Euclid. We know nothing of his origins, nor of his teachers, but at the center he is known to have written many works on mathematics, especially his renowned *Elements* (*Stoichia),* which from the time it first appeared was considered a classic in the field, a reputation it still enjoys. Though it was not the first attempt to organize geometry into a deductive form, it quickly superceded those that preceded it.

It is fundamental in the development of Greek thought that it is always assumed that what we call the universe (the *sympan* of the Greeks, the whole) is a systematic phenomenon capable of being understood by men through logic. In every field Greek men of thought were always attempting to reduce the visible world to a collection of transcendent principles that constituted a world of higher reality. Men had access to that reality through logic and was recognized as knowledge as opposed to opinion.

In his *Elements* Euclid reduces what was known as geometry to a deductive system. He distinguishes what he considered postulates, statements to be taken as assumed, as opposed to theorems that need proof to be accepted. He also works out how definitions should be formulated.

Euclid took five geometric postulates as a basis for his deductive treatment of what we now call Euclidean geometry. One postulate, called the parallel postulate, stood in sharp contrast to the others because of its complexity; it did not express a self-evident truth about physical space as was then required of geometric postulates. Euclid was keenly aware of this, but part of his extraordinary achievement was to recognize that such a statement was needed to support the most complex of his geometric deductions and to boldly take it as a postulate after attempts to deduce it from simpler statements were unsuccessful.

Euclid's contemporaries and successors considered the taking of such a complex statement as a postulate a blemish on an otherwise magnificent work. The parallel postulate problem that arose was to free Euclid from this blemish by either deducing the parallel postulate from Euclid's other postulates, or replacing it with an equivalent postulate which was simple and self-evident. The problem attracted many scholars from many lands. Some attempts to solve it were ingenious, but all were unsuccessful. It took more than twenty-two hundred years for Euclid to be vindicated in his judgment. In the early 19th Century it was shown that the parallel postulate could not be replaced by an equivalent but simpler postulate and non-Euclidean geometry, and with this modern attitudes about the nature of mathematical proof were born. Euclid's seed had brought a rich mathematical harvest.

We are told that when Euclid was approached by Ptolomy to find some easier way to learn geometry than reading the *Elements*, he replied, "There is no royal road to geometry." Even more telling, especially in today's world, when once a student asked him what use there was in studying geometry, he is said to have told his slave to give the student an *obol* (the smallest Athenian coin) "since he must make gain of what he learns."

The best tribute to Greek mathematics is the inscription that was written over the entrance to Plato's Academy were the words: "Enter not those who have no knowledge of geometry." The Greeks believed that the virtue of man (his *arete*, his characteristic uniqueness) was his ability to reason. By being reasonable he was merely living the life that was natural to him.

Hannibal

Hamilcar Barca was the general who led Carthaginian armies in the First Punic War (264–241 B.C.). He had never agreed with the policy of suing for peace with Rome. Accordingly, when his government did so and he was sent to Spain to further Carthaginian power there, he is said to have taken his two young sons, Hannibal and Hasdrubal, into the temple of Baal to swear eternal hatred for the Romans.

The two boys inherited their father's command and they headed two armies in Spain. Hannibal attacked the city of Saguntum, which was south of the Ebro River which marked the border of Carthaginian territory. There were Roman troops in Spain to ensure that Carthage would not gain too much strength. These were under the command of two aristocratic but ineffective brothers, Publius and Gnaeus Scipio. They were despatched to the aid of Saguntum.

Hannibal's strategy for the Second War with Rome was to break up the alliance system Rome had used to unite Italy. His hope was that by using Galia Cispina, the Po River system, as a base his troops could exert enough pressure on the allies to isolate Rome at the center. The strategy depended on the weakness of a Roman alliance system, a failure of the nerve of the Roman people, and the capability of Hannibal as a general. Hannibal went on the offensive as soon as war broke out. He crossed the Rhone, and crossed the Alps by a high pass. He fought Alpine tribes and led his army over trails that had to be blasted into roads. We are told the builders poured vinegar into holes that froze and expanded overnight and exploded in the day. He lost all his war elephants (leading scientists some centuries later to assume early fossils uncovered in the Alps to be the bones of Hannibal's elephants), and most of his horses, but he came across the Alps with an army that met and defeated Publius' army that lay in waiting for it.

A series of brilliant battles followed, culminating in the battle of Cannae (216 B.C.). This battle was a copy of Alexander's battle of Issus, where in 333 B.C. the Persian King Darius was routed. The plan was to lead the stronger Roman army into the weak center that would give way while the cavalry wings were sweeping across the rear of the Roman infantry. At a crucial moment the Carthaginian army stopped its retreat and reinforced by reserves became an anvil against which the charging cavalry hit the rear of the Roman army. The result was a slaughter until the dead bodies lay so deep the Carthaginians could not reach the living to kill them. The Romans never forgot Cannae.

But Hannibal was caught in a web of his own making. The Roman people never lost courage, and the alliance system, with a few exceptions, held. The younger Scipio, who came to be called *Africanus* after he celebrated a triumph when Carthage lost the war, invaded Africa and forced Carthage to recall Hannibal from Italy to defend the state. After years of war he had accomplished nothing. He was feared in Carthage so his efforts were not supported by the state and it was a relief when his troops were recalled to come more closely under the control of the state.

The battle of Zama (202 B.C.) settled the issue. The two greatest generals of their day met in a ferocious battle, but when mercenary troops deserted to the Romans Hannibal's front collapsed and he barely escaped with his life. In the ensuing negotiations Rome asked for his head and an ungrateful country planned to give him up. He escaped eastward, became involved in petty politics, but Rome was remorseless. She attacked and attacked to force his capture, and he fled from place to place. Finally, as his home was surrounded by Roman troops, he took poison and ended a frustrated, defiant life.

Julius Caesar

An aristocrat of aristocrats, Julius Caesar traced his lineage back to the goddess Venus. After an adolescence active even by standards for a Roman aristocratic youth, his first appearance in a political setting came as he delivered the eulogy at the funeral of an aunt, who was the widow of Marius. The funeral took place while Sulla was still in power and the young Caesar showed courage in willing to be identified with Marius. Like him, from that time he identified with the political program of the *Populares*, the Populist party set up by the Gracchi brothers.

When he approached Pompey and Crassus to make known his decision to enter a serious political career his political bent was still Populist. These three men formed a political alliance called the Triumvirate because all three were determined to keep alive the Republic and to work within the bounds of its institutions. Caesar's contribution was through the control of a large vote in the Roman assemblies through his family connections and his large number of clients. It was no accident that when he alone remained of the three, his reform of the Republic focused power more and more in the hands of one man, Caesar, who believed the reason the Republic was faulty was because too much power was held by men who were not under constitutional control. He felt he could place himself under the constitutional control of the government.

In the meantime he went to Gaul where he gathered together the strongest army of the day. He acted almost like a king, making war and peace as he saw fit. Eventually his activities drew criticism and he was recalled to Rome to stand trial for malfeasance. Instead he invaded with his army, took the city, and set up a program of reform. He met Pompey and defeated him at Pharsalus (48 B.C.), then pursued him to Egypt. Pompey was killed by the young

King Ptolomy's supporters. Attacked by them, Caesar escaped by diving fully-clothed into the sea and swimming out to the famous Pharos, the lighthouse. For a man already into his fifties, this was a real physical feat. It was during this disorder that the library of Alexandria caught fire and was destroyed, a great disaster for the collection was the greatest in the world at that time.

The affair between Cleopatra and Caesar produced by her claim a son, Caesar's only son. Whatever the details, Caesar left her as soon as he was ready to continue his business in Rome. It is significant that Mark Antony was with Caesar at the time, yet did not learn an important lesson. When he himself became involved with Cleopatra years later, he did not do likewise. Antony proved he was the perfect number two man, and not number one. He sought the pomp and glory that he thought made Caesar great, and he just transferred to Cleopatra his allegiance as her number two man. Unfortunately, she lacked the strength to be number one. The end was disaster for them both.

The group who set out to assassinate Caesar saw only that he seemed to be emerging as a king. The plot was the worst-kept secret in Rome. Everyone knew of it except Caesar, who would not listen to gossip. On the Ides of March he did not feel well enough to go to the Senate. But the conspirators came to him and told him someone would appeal that day to his sense of clemency. So he decided to go. His wife had had bad dreams of blood and she begged him not to go. As he left his house a man who had been warning Caesar to beware of the Ides of March was there and Caesar called to him that the day had come

without mischief. The man called back, The day has come, but it has not gone yet.

By a stroke of irony they fell upon him at the foot of Pompey's statue set up in the entrance of a theatre Pompey had built and which was being used by the Senate while a new Senate chamber was being constructed. Caesar fought off his attackers until he saw Brutus, a special protege and the son of a woman with whom he had had an affair. Slipping into Greek, Caesar mentioned his name, and spent his last moments arranging the folds of his toga so that his body would be decently covered as he died. The only group who had the courage to claim the body and carry it home was the Jews of Rome, who saw a friend in Caesar since he was an enemy of Pompey, who had placed on the throne of Judea Herod, an Idumean convert to Judaism.

Cicero

Cicero (106–43 B.C.) was a provincial who came to Rome as "a new man." He was educated in Athens and Rome, and his fortunes rose quickly in Rome as he began to specialize in defending provincials against the arrogant exploitation by the old aristocratic families of upperclass Rome. He was not only the greatest orator of his day, but he also became the most important authority on the government of the Republic. In a series of important studies he gave definitive analyses of the origins and development of its institutions. He carried on a correspondence with the principal politicians of the day. His descriptions of the civil wars that flourished in his time are a basic source for the history of the period. He had, to be sure, strong prejudices; often his is the only voice available today, and his prejudices often distort history.

In a sense he was always considered by many to be an outsider. Only occasionally was he a man of action, as when he ran for the consulship in 63 B.C. against Catiline. When he lost, Catiline planned an invasion of the city and an assassination of Cicero and others. Cicero walked into the Senate that day to be confronted by the picture of Catiline surrounded by a crowd of Senators. He was the man of the hour and gloated. Then Cicero began to describe Catiline's conspiracy. "How long, how long will you try our patience, O Catiline?" By the time Cicero finished, one by one the Senators left his side and Catiline was sitting all alone. He fled the city and was killed in battle soon after. Cicero was not a man for decisive action. His way was to use words and convince rather than to kill. This could be dangerous in an era of violence.

When it became clear that Octavian was Caesar's heir, Cicero offered his friendship and support, hoping to bring the young man into the ranks of the Senatorial aristocracy. When the Second Triumvirate was set up between Octavian, Mark Antony and Lepidus, taking the roles of Caesar, Pompey and Crassus, Cicero made a serious mistake in judgment. He miscalculated the character of Octavian and his control over him. He delivered a series of orations which have come to be called the Second Philippics in imitation of the speeches Demosthenes gave to warn the Greeks about the true intentions of Philip of Macedon who was about to fall on Greece "like a wolf dressed in sheep's clothing." Cicero wanted to warn the Roman people of Mark Antony's true intentions as he sought to pick up Caesar's career. Antony never forgave Cicero, nor did his wife Fulvia.

When the Second Triumvirate returned from Greece after having defeated the assassin of Caesar at the Battle of Philippi, they came together to decide how to begin their rule. They decided to eliminate all their enemies. Each put the names of his enemies onto a list. Of course, Antony put Cicero's name first on the list. It shows much about Octavian's character that he did nothing to protect his mentor. When Cicero's head was severed from his body Fulvia rushed forward to nail the tongue of this man of words to his skull, so he would never again be able to speak.

St. Augustine

He was born in 354 in Tageste, near the ancient Carthage. His life illustrates the path a gifted provincial took to achieve a successful career in late Roman times, and also within the emerging hierarchy of the Roman Church. Son of a peasant, who was determined his son would get somewhere, he was given the education of a rhetorician that led him into the life of a teacher. Perhaps this was due also to his mother, who was a dedicated Christian and a mother who had had enormous ambitions for her son.

In his *Confessions*, an extraordinary work of utter sincerity, he tells of his youthful life of peccadillos, including a son born out of wedlock, the usual wining, gambling, and time wasting. But more important, for he always showed a high intelligence, was a delving into the various forms of Gnosticism, current in this time of intellectual ferment. Gnosticism comes from the Greek word "to know." It can refer to a special intuitive immediate knowledge of God, or the wholeness that is the universe, or in his time to the knowledge of how the real universe operates. It raised the contrast between spirit and matter. The proper life for man is the life of the spirit, and matter becomes the world of evil.

Mani was the founder of a Gnostic religion in the Sassanid Persian Empire of the 3rd Century. His followers formed this religion, and for many years it rivalled Christianity as the most popular religion of the day. St. Augustine was a Manichean during his early manhood. Though in his forties he became a Christian, he always reflected the Gnostic dualism of the Manicheans.

According to them, there are two forces in this world from the beginning of time. The one is a God, the good, constructive force, and the other is the Devil, dealer in evil in the world. Since the Devil is constantly at work, he is always delving in evil. It is his nature. God, the source of good in this world, is always active too. In fact, St. Augustine in his *City of God* works out a whole philosophy of history based on this idea. From the beginning of time the two forces, God and the Devil, are at work in the world of men, each following his true nature. The history of the world is the bringing of mankind under the control of these forces. Kingdoms come and go, each bringing knowledge to more and more men, until the Roman Empire made it possible for the whole world to know God and at the same time the Devil. Now the final battle is possible. Now that all men now have the knowledge of good and evil and can choose the one or the other, the great battle between the hosts of God and those of the Devil can take place. The end is foreknown and the temporal world can come to an end and the world of eternity can begin.

By putting forward this cosmic theory of history, St. Augustine explains why it was

right that, having brought the world under one empire and making it possible for all men to know Christ, Rome's role in history was completed and like all states in the past it was destined to fall. The occasion for the book was the Visigothic taking and sacking Rome in 410. The Christians were accused of being responsible by making the tradional gods angry by the introduction of a new god who claimed to be the only god.

The morality of the *Confessions* and the political philosophy of the *City of God* not only dominated the medieval world, but through the adaptation of Calvinists still exerts a continuous influence.

Justinian and Theodora

Justinian became co-emperor with his uncle Justin (518 A.D.). Justin was an uneducated peasant who made his way up through the army ranks until he was chosen Emperor. Justinian, in contrast, went through the school system in Constantinople and became one of the most sophisticated men of his age.

He dreamed of reestablishing the Roman Empire, the Eastern part and the Western part. To accomplish this he sent armies to the West under Belisarius and Narses that destroyed the Vandal, the Visigothic, and the Ostrogothic empires. The armies bogged down in the end, and though it can be said they accomplished their tasks, they did not bring a true integration into one empire. The Visigoths converted to Roman Catholicism and began to unite Spain. The Vandal territories were invaded by Berber tribesmen and, worst of all, Lombard invaders crossed the Alps and began a conquest of Italy that was more destructive than the earlier Germanic invasions. Justinian had had a dream, but could not bring it to reality.

Theodora was the daughter, according to Procopius who relates the fact in his *Secret History* as a scandal, of a bear-keeper in the arena in the City. Her first appearance was with her mother when they asked for charity from the crowds in the Hippodrome. She became an actress and prostitute, and travelled widely in the Middle East. She met Justinian at a party where she was a courtesan to entertain the guests. He fell in love with this extraordinary lady on sight, and she became a most autocratic empress when he married her. Such marriages were very common in Byzantine history.

When Justinian met opposition in his attempts to bring about better relations between the various patriarchates of the Christian churches and the *Nike* riots broke out and threatened his throne, he was ready to flee the City, but Theodora refused to run. "Now that I have learned to wear the royal purple, let it become my shroud," she declared and forced her husband to stand firm and go on the offensive. She saved the day and Justinian's throne.

She was also keen on social reform and opened a school for wayward girls, such as she had been. Scandal was amused to point out the girls did everything they could to escape back to the streets, but Theodora became a great lady and led a brilliant court.

Basil I, the Macedonian

The father of Basil I was an Armenian who had settled in Adrianople, capital of Macedonia, hence the name of the dynasty. His mother seems to have been Slavic, but the family spoke Armenian as their native tongue. Basil was one of the Armenians carried off by Krum, Czar of the Bulgars. On his release the seventeen year old future Emperor entered the service of the *Strategos* of the theme as a groom, and made his way to the capitol with an introduction to a friend of the Emperor Michael III.

The groom was an unusually competent wrestler and was noticed by the Emperor. He was sent as a minor official to the Peloponnesus, where he became the favorite of a "virtuous" rich widow, Danieles, who had a factory which produced silk. With her support he returned to the capital and entered the immediate entourage of the Emperor. They soon became friends and Basil ruthlessly eliminated all who stood in his way. He became co-emperor and after a drinking bout he murdered his friend and became sole Emperor (867–886). An illiterate of peasant origins was able to climb his way to ultimate power. His dynasty became one of the most literate in Byzantine history, and illustrates its social freedom.

It is difficult to explain this social freedom. Justinian married a courtesan, and later Macedonian emperors married women who had won beauty contests so that the most beautiful girl in the empire would become empress. Time after time the emperor was a man who had fought his way to the throne. Others had concocted schemes in the beds of empresses and had murdered their way to the throne. One can speculate. However, there was an upward thrust in Byzantine society. Dynasties had loyal supporters but that loyalty depended on being sifted through a greedy court that benefitted from them. The outcome was a way of life that depended on intrigue and eventually corruption. To this day in countries that are the heirs of Byzantium the same philosophy prevails that one needs a friend at court. It is important to know the right people and to have someone to intercede on one's behalf.

Charlemagne

Charlemagne came to his throne as a Germanic king (768–814). As head of the King's *comitatus* he had loyal counts who provided government at the local level. Inadequate as it was, it was enough to maintain an obedience to the customs of the Franks and even to local usage. In an era when reading and writing were disappearing no one expected any more from government. The King was responsible for the defense and expansion of the whole realm. Again much depended on local armies, but when the King summoned his counts they came under the King's leadership, as when he invaded Spain to keep at bay the Moors or as when he went to war with the Saxons. The war went on for thirty years and cost the Saxons 30,000 casualties. In the end Saxony was Christianized and absorbed into the Frankish kingdom.

Charlemagne was himself a lusty man with several illegitimate children. He himself seems to have been illegitimate. His claim to the throne was under a cloud and he invaded Italy to seek out a nephew, son of his legitimately-born brother.

During the invasion he visited Rome to renew his father's donation of central Italy to the Bishop of Rome. Rome had loomed large in his imagination. He was quite familiar with the traditions of the Roman Empire. Byzantines still called themselves Romans and to be exact Eastern Romans. The Western Empire had failed after Justinian's attempt to revivify it. He was in contact with Harun al-Rashid, the fabled Caliph of the Abbâsid Empire, who sent him a menagerie including an elephant which was shown all over the kingdom. It is no wonder that he came to think of himself as an Emperor.

In the manner of a Roman Emperor he began to involve himself in the religious needs of his people. He presided over Synods that established orthodoxy in religion, even though he himself had only a hazy idea of such matters. In fact, it was at one of these synods that he forced the adoption of the *filioque* in the Creed. This caused no end of trouble for the Church and the ultimate schism between the Roman and Orthodox Churches. In the original Creed adopted at Nicaea it states that the Holy Spirit proceeds from the Father. In Spain the phrase "and the Son" was inserted. This seemed to disturb the original Trinity and it was rejected by the Popes, but Charlemagne liked it and he insisted on it. He even tried to get involved with the Iconoclastic controversy. Not understanding in the slightest the Aristotelian overtones, he acted like an Emperor. He declared illegal the attacks on icons while at the same time he dismissed the defense of icons.

So it comes as no surprise that when he visited Rome and attended the Christmas service in the church of St. John Lateran he was not exactly displeased when the Pope suddenly produced a crown and declared him a patrician of Rome and Emperor. The only doubt the new Emperor had was the implication in the fact that the Pope had crowned him after all.

Charlemagne took the stance that there was no other legal Emperor of Rome but he. But to call oneself Emperor is a far cry from being one. He himself could hardly sign his name. How was it possible to govern a substantial empire in an age when only some bishops were literate? He invited a flock of monks from England to come to establish schools and he insisted that his nobility send their sons to learn a Latin curriculum. The emergence of Latin minuscule (small letters) was one result. The Carolingian Renaissance, as this attempt to revive learning has been called, in the end failed. The momentum of the society was too strongly going in the opposite direction. Charlemagne has become merely a man of legend as a result. Though some men called him a new Alexander, it was at best a dream of those who remembered the past. Alexander symbolized an era that was about to bring a rebirth of Hellenism, known as Hellenistic. At best Charlemagne spells the end to a long tradition.

Gregory VII and Henry IV

Gregory VII (1073–85) was named Hildebrand before his elevation to the papacy, and as Hildebrand his name is connected to the most important reform movement in the medieval Church. It was a series of reforms that freed the Church from any secular control and made it possible for it to wield the sword that God had put into the hands of the pope to help govern men in this world. But to achieve this desirable end Gregory did not always follow honorable means. In his struggle with Henry IV, Holy Roman Emperor, he followed a policy of clever political realism to achieve his ends.

The struggle was over the question of who ought to give a bishop his pallium, the symbol of his power as bishop. Whoever gave the pallium had the first loyalty of the bishop. The emperor had done so since the time of Constantine. But now the pope, who over the years assumed control over all the bishops of the Church, demanded their first loyalty. In the end the Pope excommunicated the Emperor and absolved all his subjects from obedience to him. In this way the Pope raised a revolt all over Germany, for the dukes of Germany were developing a German feudalism that would limit the powers of the Emperor.

In desperation Henry gambled on an extravagant move. It was winter, and the Pope had gone to spend the Christmas season with the Countess Mathilda of Canossa. Henry crossed the Alps, appeared barefoot before her castle, declared he was penitent and knelt there in the snow asking the Pope to forgive him. Gregory was in a quandary. As Pope, as any priest for that matter, he could not refuse to hear Henry's confession. He let him kneel in the snow for four days but in the end he had to absolve Henry and lift the excommunication.

Gleefully Henry rushed back to Germany and told the leaders of the revolt that the Pope had abandoned them. The revolt went on, for there were deep causes for it, but the Pope lost control over it. Eventually, Henry, with the full support of the German clergy and nobility, invaded Italy, took Rome, and chased Gregory out of the city. Gregory made contact with Norman warriors who had invaded Italy and were attacking Muslims and Byzantine holdings there. They eagerly decided to return the Pope to his city. They took Rome by storm and destroyed the whole city as neither Visigoths nor Vandals had done.

The Pope invited them to return with as many Norman mercenaries as they could induce to come. The number of Normans in Italy increased, and the establishment of the Kingdom of the Two Sicilies was the eventual result.

The struggle between these two led to years of civil war in Germany which helped the feudal duchies weaken imperial central government. Just as feudalism was bowing before strong centralized monarchies in England and France, it was being introduced into Germany.

The Pope lost ground just as his arch-enemy the Emperor had. National churches began to imitate the German example. Increasingly the papacy had to face the threat of heresy and other alternative religious communities. Above all, there developed a general loss of piety. It became clear that if the pope entered the secular political world as a king, then increasingly he would be treated like a king.

Innocent III and Boniface VIII

The strongest pope in the history of the Church is Innocent III (1198–1216). He dominated the politics of Europe in the manner the reform-minded popes of the 11th Century had envisioned. Apart from the politics of earthly kingdoms, he could support all causes that were righteous in spite of local political considerations. He forced the kings of Europe to take up the Third Crusade. In domestic matters he prevailed on Philip Augustus not to divorce his wife (of course, the lady spent the rest of her life in prison). His greatest triumph was the Fourth Lateran Council which spelled out the structure of the medieval Church as the greatest government in the medieval world. The secret of his success was not to make claims beyond his power to execute them.

Of course, he had failures. His selection of Frederick II as legitimate Emperor of Germany was a mistake. The failure of the Third Crusade and the loss of his control over the Fourth Crusade were monumental errors. But overall his establishment of the best and most efficient government the world had seen until then was a victory.

Boniface VIII came to power a century later (1294–1303). He made great pronouncements about papal power and the limitations of secular power before it. In *Unam Sanctum* he makes the strongest claim to papal jurisdiction ever made in the history of the Church. Since there is only one universal Church of God and since the pope is the head of that Church, it follows that all secular governments if they would be Christian must come under the authority and jurisdiction of that supreme head, the pope.

In answer England cut off all revenues from church lands and fees to Rome. In France Philip IV called the first meeting of the *Estates General* in France to act as a court to try the Pope on charges of heresy and other crimes. The court found him guilty, and soldiers were sent off to arrest the Pope and to bring him to France for punishment. It was summer and the Pope was on his estate in Anagni, south of Rome. The French soldiers seized the Pope and began to lead him off when the citizens of the town in horror at the scene rose up to rescue the old man. When he died as a result of the injuries he had suffered, it was a shocking statement of how far the prestige of the Church had fallen. A king had ordered the killing of a pope!

At first glance, the moral is light: Do not bite off more than you can chew. But the incident is much more indicative of how the whole society had gone through profound change so that secular interests had far outdistanced the religious ones. The Reformation was just a step away.

Salah ad-Din

Salah ad-Din became famous in the West at the time of the Third Crusade (1189–92). He was the enemy worthy of King Richard of England and Philip Augustus of France. In the East he was known for his reuniting of the Muslim world to evict the Western Crusaders. One day Salah ad-Din's sister was on a journey to join her brother. Franks attacked her caravan and took her captive. In a fury Salah ad-Din vowed to take revenge with his own sword and he declared that the war against the Frank had now become a *jihad*, a holy war to protect God's people. After the battle of Hattin, in which almost all the Frankish army was killed, Salah ad-Din with his own hand struck off the head of the offender against his sister's honor, and closed Jerusalem to all Christians.

Salah ad-Din was the paragon of Eastern chivalry. Some historians suggest that the chivalric order in the West had Eastern roots. Nothing stands in starker contrast than the taking of the Church of the Holy Sepulchre during the First Crusade and the taking of the same church during the Third Crusade. As the knights of the First Crusade fought their way to the church on the spot where Christ's tomb was supposed to be, crowds of women and children had taken refuge in the church hopefully protected by the Christian humanity of the Crusaders. In vain, for the Crusaders killed inside the church until the horses walked hock-deep in blood. When the same church was taken by Salah ad-Din he did not allow anyone to desecrate the church. All the Christians within the city became hostages and could be ransomed by their families. Salah ad-Din himself ransomed hundreds as an act of charity, his brother and his courtiers did likewise. At the same time the papal legate was caught sneaking out of the city in disguise. In his packs lay all the treasury of the church in Jerusalem, enough to ransom all the captives. Salah ad-Din derisively allowed the Christian leader to take his wealth and leave Jerusalem as an object lesson.

These stories illustrate what had become evident. The West despised Byzantium for its civilized style of life, which it considered effete, and it fought the Muslims as infidels. Even in Spain where Christians lived side by side with Jews and Muslims and learned to share their lifestyles, there was some sort of cultural blindness that led Christians to assume a superiority. Throughout the rest of the emergence of the Western world we see this idea getting stronger and stronger.

Frederick II, "Stupor Mundi"

"Wonder of the World" was what he was called by his contemporaries and he was just that. He came to the throne of the Holy Roman Empire as a youngster (1215–1250) with the sponsorship of Innocent III after much devious maneuvering, and he became perhaps the greatest enemy of the Church in all history. A freethinker in an age of faith, at his court in Palermo he gathered an assembly of the most original minds of his time, whether Muslim, Christian, or heretical.

He had an insatiable curiosity, sometimes cruel. One time he became interested in the motions of the heart and lungs. He selected healthy prisoners and had skilled surgeons try to open them up quickly enough to catch the living organs at work. He failed, but not for not trying.

He is said to have remarked, "The world has been fooled by three great impostors, Moses, Christ, and Muhammed," yet he was still interested in knowing what language was spoken in Heaven. To find out he had a group of new-born babes put into the care of deaf-mutes to be reared. The idea was that whatever language they would speak would be the natural language spoken in Heaven. Unfortunately the children all died of neglect before they spoke at all. Such was his mind. But he also was interested in ornithology and wrote a book on how to hunt with birds which is still in print.

He had promised to launch a crusade, but had to delay while pope after pope accused him of bad faith. On one occasion a council was called to investigate the matter. In desperation he ordered the sinking of the ship that was carrying the bishops to the council. In the end he went on the crusade, negotiated a ceasefire and free access to the holy places in Jerusalem. Needless to say the pope rejected the treaty. One went on crusades to conquer the heathen, not to negotiate with him.

In his day he caused havoc. After his death his Empire fell to pieces almost immediately. He caused irreparable damage to the Empire in Germany. One wonders how far afield a freethinker ought to wander?

St. Francis of Assisi

The saint was born in the town of Assisi (1182–1226), where his father was a prosperous merchant who expected his son to take up the family tradition and enter a career as a businessman. Instead, after an adolescence as a rich man's son, Francis suddenly appeared in the town square, stripped off all his clothes, and vowed to live a life of poverty.

He led a group of companions — sparrows he called them—who lived in the forest begging each day just enough food for that day, lest they not have faith that God would provide for the next day. He preached a life of ideal poverty and sanctity. There was a strain of pantheism in all his teaching. He would not put out Brother Fire lest he hurt him, wrote a *Canticle to the Sun* that is pagan in its tone, and worshipped Lady Poverty. In many ways his attitude was a reaction against the emerging town life and bourgeois values that were arising in his day.

Eventually Francis led his scrawny band to Rome to receive the Pope's blessing and formal recognition of the order. The group was met by derision and scandal that they would waste the Pope's time. But Francis persevered and waited. When word was brought to the Pope, Innocent III agreed to see them. It seems the night before the Pope had had a strange dream. He saw the church of St. John Lateran, the cathedral church of the Pope as Bishop of Rome, collapsing when suddenly a strange man stood and prevented the collapse. When Francis was led into the room, Innocent cried out that that was the man in the dream. The order was established with the Pope's blessing.

Francis went on the Fifth Crusade and wandered off across the desert to convert the heathen. He met the sultan, who listened with attention to all Francis preached and then escorted him back across the lines. The Muslims always respected madmen. Even while still alive Francis found that men cannot do without wealth and died an unhappy man, even as members of his order turned toward lives of comfort and learning, which the saint also despised. Eventually the Franciscans declared the worship of poverty a heresy. They still remain an order devoted to learning.

Giotto

Giotto (1266–1336) was a student of Cimabue who began his career as a painter in the Byzantine style. His paintings are large, colorful, and at first glance have the look of Byzantine icons. But they have lost their Eastern look. The Byzantine icon was essentially flat, a "window into Eternity." In Cimabue the mother and child are already of this world, even though still in the older medieval style. There is an attempt to give a lifelike expression to the mouth, the eyes. Color is used to give a suggestion of shadow, suggesting a three-dimensional world.

His student's work breaks through into a fully three-dimensional world. Of course, Giotto has no real knowledge of anatomy. He cloaks his figures in shapeless robes to give them the illusion of proper anatomy. But he does have the ability to create the illusion of a three-dimensional world by the use of perspective. His paintings are at the beginning of a whole tradition of mathematical perspectives which

will end with accurate laws of perspective that will make it possible to draw on a two-dimensional surface a world that has the appearance of being three-dimensional. Of course, it is but an illusionary world and contemporary artists will eventually reject that illusion precisely because it is an illusion.

But why have artists beginning with Giotto attempted to capture this illusionary world? Because by the end of the middle ages attention was beginning to focus on this world as opposed to the eternal, changeless world of eternity. As this day to day world became more important in itself, men began to see beauty in it. Just as men became interested in the sonnet as a controlled expression of one man's statement about this world, so lyrical painting became important as a man's own statement about this world. The individual himself became important and what he had to say about the world became important as well.

Eleanor of Aquitaine

In the march of the Capetian monarchs to power the marriage of Louis VII to Eleanor, duchess and heiress to rich Aquitaine, was a crucial step. By this marriage the lands under royal control doubled, and it was the culmination of the efforts of the Abbot Suger of St. Denis to further the Capetian cause.

The two youngsters went on the Second Crusade as if it were a honeymoon. The highlight of the journey for Eleanor was a visit to her uncle Raymond, Count of Antioch, which was considered the most fashionable French court overseas. The visit became a matter of public scandal, and though it is still not clear what actually happened, as soon as he returned to France Louis divorced her, thereby losing control of Aquitaine. She was too important an heiress to remain unmarried for long, and soon she was married to Henry Plantagenet, heir to the throne of England through his mother Mathilda, granddaughter of William the Conqueror. This was one of the stormiest marriages of all time. When he became King of England, Henry II controlled more feudal lands in France than Louis did, and the two became archenemies.

Eleanor bore several children, two of whom became kings of England, Richard *Coeur de Lion* and John Lackland (who in 1215 was forced to accept Magna Carta). Henry II was an innovative King and embarked on a long program of reform to strengthen the monarchy against the pretensions of feudal vassals. He did not trust any of his sons and refused to share his power with them. In turn they plotted with Henry's vassals to dethrone him. Eleanor became deeply involved in these plots and was imprisoned for many years to keep her out of the way. The sons also plotted with Louis, and after his death with his son Philip Augustus. Henry died a bitter old man betrayed by his sons.

When Richard became King of England he barely spoke the language. He spent almost the whole of his reign in France, and used England as a source of revenue from taxes on the wool trade. His fame rests on his physical exploits. He was indeed a mighty warrior. He set out on the Third Crusade, a grand adventure, but the Crusade did not go so well. He had trouble in Sicily. Then he sailed off to Cyprus to rescue his new bride, Berengaria, who had landed there in a storm and was now being held for ransom. By the time he got to the Holy Land

Salah ad-Din was in full control and the Crusade accomplished little.

The most bizarre upset of the adventure was that Richard decided to quit the Crusade and ride across Europe to his lands in Normandy and England. On his way he fell into the hands of the Duke of Austria, who informed John, Richard's brother and regent, of the capture. John offered to pay the Duke to keep Richard in a secure place. Eleanor, now an aged dowager, was determined to find her beloved son. A romantic tale, probably not true, describes how she sent the minstrel Blondel, a favorite of Richard, to tour the castles of Austria. In each Blondel sang a particular song they had sung together until Richard answered and the secret was out.

The Duke set an enormous ransom, three times the total royal income from England. Eleanor went from vassal to vassal across the rough roads of England, cajoling and threatening, until the whole sum was collected and Richard was released. It was all in vain, however, for as soon as Richard was released he heard a rumor that ancient treasure had been discovered on the lands of one of his vassals. By feudal law Richard had a right to a share of the treasure. He demanded his share, and attacked the vassal's castle. In the fight he was struck in the eye by a stray arrow and died in agony. Richard had expelled the Jews from England because he had built up enormous debts to them and found expulsion a handy way to get rid of the debts. Now his greed had cost him his life. The final irony was that there was no real treasure at all.

Dante, Petrarch, Boccaccio

It comes as a surprise to most when they remember that all three lives overlap. Dante died in 1321 when Petrarch was already seventeen and Boccaccio was a boy of eight. The surprise comes because Dante epitomizes the world of the Middle Ages. His *Divine Comedy* tells the tale of a man who midway through his journey of life loses his way in a shadowy forest and misses the straight path. His discovery of the true path leads him from Hell, through Purgatory into Heaven, and along the way he finds all those who have lived in their appropriate places. It reflects the calm acceptance of the world as laid out by Divine Providence. We still speak reflectively of that serenity that marks a time when there was no doubt, no questioning that God was in His proper place, and all men were sure they had access to Him.

But the world of Boccaccio has another spirit. The people in it are all involved in a world of their own making. Divine Providence has given way to Fortune's wheel. This world is ruled by luck. No matter where he starts a man must make his own way and the best one can say is that, "God helps those who help themselves." It is a far cry from Dante's realm. It is the world of the Renaissance, of self-made men who create their own morality. In spite of the pride man can take in a world of his own making, it is also a lonely world. When man is on his own he also is often by himself. It is not easy to live in a world in which everyone lives in a world of his own making. What holds the several worlds together?

Petrarch was a man caught in the middle. Petrarch was the most successful intellectual of his day. Popes and kings sought his opinions. He made large amounts of money. But he was always bewailing his misfortunes. "In sorrow was I born. In sorrow do I live. In sorrow will I die." It is difficult to see why he took this attitude. He once wrote a letter to a friend in which he described a walk up a small mountain that lay outside the town. He had asked what the view was like from the top, and no one knew. No one had ever bothered to climb it. So Petrarch—in good Renaissance style—started to climb. This was the new spirit of adventure, the spirit of enterprise. And he started out. Soon he began to feel the heat, but on he went. He got tired, so he stopped to rest. He took out a copy of St. Augustine's *Confessions*—this man of the Renaissance—and read a while. Then he went on until he reached the top. He was tired, angry with himself that he had bothered to make the climb. The view was mediocre at best. Then he went down. Enough adventure for the day. But the letter tells us much of Petrarch. He sets out, but somehow he falters midway. He always desired to learn Greek, but he never did, though he carried a copy of Homer around his neck as a talisman.

He was still at heart a medieval man, conservative, basically a formalist, like the sonnets he wrote. He was not ready to leave the world of shared common values and common destinies. Especially he had the conscience of the Middle Ages. He still believed in the values of the past and was not ready to substitute man-made values for God's values. He was truly the man in the middle and his confusion is contagious. All seems to be going well, all is positive, it's great to be alive, then suddenly we are reminded of the transient quality of a man-made world and we are plunged into doubt and even despair. Dante seems passé and Boccaccio seems *naif*. Petrarch's mood seems to fit the world of todays men.

Jeanne d'Arc

The figure of Jeanne d'Arc raises a traditional question in the study of history: Does the man create the circumstances, or the circumstances the man? France was in a state of crisis at this late date in the Hundred Years War. The King was a weak, befuddled, and cowardly crownless figure. The English and Burgundians had ravished the land. At that moment the young, strange girl appeared to offer hope and divine intervention to help the cause of the French people. Her career as a soldier was not particularly gifted nor was it long, but all people saw in her someone who was in contact with divinity, either God as the French saw it, or the Devil as the English saw it.

The lifting of the siege of Orleans in 1429 seemed to prove that God was on her side and the dash to Rheims to obtain the crown for her worthless King had a quality of the miraculous. Of course, she was used by the real leaders of the French, but to such good purpose that her inspiration led to French victory. When she was captured, tortured and burnt to death as a witch she had served her purpose. No one came to her rescue, certainly not her ungrateful monarch whom she had made King. And the question remains, at moments of historic importance is it just a matter of fortune, as Macchiavelli thought, or was it Jeanne who arranged and directed events to a happy conclusion? One thing is clear, that her efforts focused a people who were on the brink of achieving a national consciousness.

EPILOGUE
▼ ▼ ▼ ▼ ▼

Among all the ancient peoples the Greeks were the first to reject a mythological view of the universe. Instead, they tried to find some rational explanation of man, the world, and his place in it. In fact, this desire for logical explanations led the Greeks at all times to find satisfaction in the attempt to bring order out of chaos. All aspects of life came to be seen as one part of one basic harmony. This harmony, itself, was the universe, and law was nothing else but the rhythm that could be felt throughout it. Man was drawn to that harmony by some inner compulsion. In his famous Funeral Oration, Pericles tries to sum up what it meant to be an Athenian, but what in a broad sense was probably true of all Greeks to some degree. He speaks of a people who had versatility, who combined a love of activity and a love of learning. He describes the willingness of a citizen to join into his *polis*, his state, to offer to it his best. Of course, man receives in return a sense of achievement, of belonging, of having significance. "Men make the best citizens when character can count on the highest rewards." In other words, men are good when goodness is rewarded. A practical statement, but Pericles also says, "We are lovers of beauty."

Love among the Greeks was a force that impelled a person toward that which was lovable, the beautiful, the good. This is why man turned to the universal harmony. By definition it was natural, perfect, and complete. It could be seen in Fate or Destiny,

the inevitable fitness of all things as they are; in the gods; in the laws of the state. A Greek submitted himself to this order wherever he found it. He was part of a *polis* and obeyed its laws and officials. He accepted the dictates of the gods, who had superior power, as was right. Above all, the Greeks believed in a basic balance that held together the whole universe and all its parts. This phenomenon was called *stasis*. Every man felt his own activity was part of it. In fact, it gave focus to his life. If any man tried to do otherwise, if he refused to be part of the whole, if even without willing it himself he suddenly found himself outside the harmony, then he was in a state of sin.

For the Greeks, then, sin was being out of harmony. The result was guilt, but guilt as a vague feeling of things not being quite right, a restlessness that pursued man until he again found his place and returned to harmony. The whole was so delicately balanced that even one man's sin forced the whole system out of balance. All men suffered at one man's sin and continued to do so until the sin was expiated, and then all would fall back into place again.

Thus, man exists as a single part of a harmonious whole. His life has meaning only because he is that part. But he is not merely an automatic robot. No, man understands the situation and through the use of his reason and his love of the good he strives always to achieve his proper place. "An uncriticized life is scarcely worth living at all," Socrates once said, and this sums up the Greek's love of logic, enquiry, and knowledge as paths to the good life.

Surely this analysis of what the Greek Stoics held to be the ideal community for man must have some special meaning for us today. People now have a deep sense of loss —of the family, of the community, of order in our lives. Everything seems upside-down. Men of little merit receive the best rewards. Emphasis on the ephemeral is more respected than the truly worthwhile. Good citizenship is sacrificed in a mad scramble for the material stuff of life. Crime is considered our main concern, yet it is felt little can be done about it. As St. Augustine once said, "Who will watch the guardians?" These are symptoms of a basic malaise. Our society is ill and as at so many times in the past needs a doctor. Too often the role is filled by the dictator, who by intuitive insight finds solutions to all problems. Their name is legion in today's world in spite of their growing power to do harm. History, if read acutely, offers guidance to a more trustworthy solution.

By the 2nd Century, Rome had created a world state that expressed a world-view held by Stoics, Christians, Jews, salvationist cult members, and others. Men always had a set of ideals they believed were the elements of the good life, and in no other time have so many men shared so widely the same vision and never have so many men been able to live out in their daily lives these same ideals. What better definition of happiness than this: to live in practice the ideal life that all men consider the appropriate life for man. This idea must have led Edward Gibbon in his *Decline and Fall of the Roman Empire* to declare in a much-quoted passage that the age of the Antonine emperors was the happiest time mankind has ever known. He points out that everywhere all classes of people lived under "the immense majesty of the Roman peace." Peace did not mean merely the cessation of war, but rather it meant that under Rome men could concentrate on those things that are appropriate to the art of living well. To live well takes skill, self-control, a community in which the skill is to be used. All men live, but just as a good mariner must practice well the skill of the mariner, so too must men live skillfully the good life. It follows that the attitude men have toward each other is an indication of how happy they are. Tolerance becomes a significant index of happiness. Romans believed they were a people chosen by Destiny to show mankind by their own example the art of living well.

Officially, the Roman government for a long time in its imperial history was really tolerant of all kinds of religions and races. The Roman people were not always as tolerant as their government, but by and large so long as the state did not feel threatened, so long as it did not feel there were any alternative viable forms of government, it took a very broad point of view.

But there came a time in Roman history when the government suddenly became very intolerant of Christians. Under the Emperor Diocletian (303 A.D.), for instance, certain edicts were passed which were probably the most intolerant ever seen. Just to be a Christian was already to be guilty of a crime, and it became synonymous with sedition. The Emperor's attitude was that to be a Christian meant that one had chosen not to be a Roman, not to be a loyal citizen. The Roman state had come to see in the Christian Church a threat. The Roman Christian movement offered an alternative to despotism, even though benign. The Christian state had become a state within the state and the government lost control over it. One is reminded of the attitude of most recent governments toward what they considered a Communist conspiracy to work underground for the overthrow of the official government.

The Roman government went to war with the Christian Church. The Christian bishops proved to be dedicated leaders in this war and they led their flocks to acts of great courage and self-sacrifice. They proved to be better Romans in the traditional sense than those who oppressed them. In the end they won the respect of the people and finally the government, which gave in and compromised in the edicts of toleration of 311 and 313 A.D. The "blood of the martyrs" had nourished the Church and it survived.

In the medieval world, people were as a rule very intolerant. This reflected the same basic rule of behavior described above. In his daily life the common man felt deeply threatened. Sickness and war were constant. The very facts of life themselves imposed a terrible gloomy weight on people. Moreover, the Greek view of life that in this world there is some kind of homogeneous scheme of things in which every individual has a part to play had become the predominant Christian view of life. The scheme had to operate properly so that all might benefit. But if it did not, or worse still if there was no scheme at all, all would be lost. The heretic, the non-believer, the apostate were thought to represent a threat to the whole order and were absolutely not to be tolerated. If they succeeded the whole scheme would fail.

But in Byzantine history we see yet another variation of the same pattern. Contrary to many popular misconceptions, the Byzantines were by and large a tolerant people. Exceptions occured in religious disputes, but people of all races and nationalities were welcomed in Byzantium.

The Byzantine people were absolutely sure that the Christian view of the world was true. They felt as had the ancients that they were a people chosen by God to have a special mission. They were working for God, they were spreading His word, they were expanding His power. The emperor was almost a vice-regent of God on earth. There was a very strong commitment to an expansionist state that was going toward the proper end for mankind and there was nothing that was going to stop it. They were absolutely convinced of this. After all, did not God intervene time after time to convince them of it? When the city of Constantinople was under severe attack, the Virgin would appear on the walls, or some saint would appear. St. Demetrius was always coming in to save Salonika, St. George was on the walls of the city in the nick of time to save it. From their point of view, this was absolute proof of their cause, of their sense of mission and success that was bound to happen. But, as no one could expect, as the state began to shake, the confidence of the people failed, and it became increasingly difficult to maintain this sense of destiny, and intolerance began to creep in.

During the Fourth Crusade (1204), for instance, Byzantines began to show signs of intolerance and withdrawal from the sophistication on which tolerance had always been based. The state was in chaos as centralized government began to fail and feudal aristocrats began to take control at the local level. The organizers of the Crusade were attracted by this development, and instead of going to the Holy Land they attacked and took Constantinople. They set up a Latin Empire that introduced Western feudal institutions. The man in the street welcomed the new government as deliverers from a corrupt and inefficient one.

Individual Western lords began to claim their share of the conquest. One contingent went West and moved into Greece. In Salonika they found that the people had been badly mistreated by the late government, and they were perfectly willing to accept the Crusaders' new state. Everything was going well until the papal legates who had come with the Crusaders attempted to impose a reunion of the Western and Byzantine Churches, apart since the schism of 1054. They thought that the Crusade would be an opportunity to bring the two Churches together, even by force if necessary. The tactlessness of the Westerners caused the people to bridle. They would not take union under force. In fact, they did not want union with the Western Church at all! A political leadership from the West they would accept. A religious leadership they would not. Why not? Because all that was left to these people to give them any sense of security was their Church. It had become identified with a way of life for them and any interference whatever, no matter how small or simple the interference was, they now saw as a terrible threat to whatever was left to them of security.

Again, it is clear that whenever people feel secure, safe, that they are not threatened, then they somehow feel that they can afford to be tolerant of others. In today's world a special kind of insecurity has developed, for there is a new kind of threat that people feel, an inner threat. With the growth of individualism as a philosophy of life, man is more and more disconnected from those institutions that used to offer him a sense of community. He must rely more and more on himself to find the ideals for the good life. Some men, the artist, the teacher,

the doctor welcome this self-reliance, this aloneness, for it allows them to develop by choice the discipline, the dedication, the unity of purpose that the Roman world idealized as necessary elements of the good life.

But most men today feel a center of emptiness within themselves, a loneliness. They feel this leaves them vulnerable. They see threats all around them. The sense that man is part of a community has been largely replaced by a world of materialism, for one can be sure at least of the evidence of his senses. In such a world the capitalistic way of life becomes appropriate. Our society has become one of producers and consumers of material things, and money, the way of acquiring these things, has become the measure of success in life.

Men have turned to materialistic ways of filling their lives. But man cannot love a machine. He has cut himself off from the deepest part of his being. To feel connected and secure has taken on a new intensity. The security of being able to trust one's fellow man, tolerance in other words, diminishes. In a capitalistic world, how can one be tolerant of one's competitors? The best one can hope for is a Hobbesian world in which everyone tolerates everyone else so long as each stays out of the other's way. This is hardly the way to build a trusting community.

Surely, here is a situation in which we can put history to good use. The 2nd Century found a solution to a problem that plagues us today. We can learn from their experience. This is not to suggest that history "repeats itself." When we have a problem to solve, we can learn from those in the past who have encountered the same problem and who lived through a solution. We can pick and choose from the different solutions attempted in the past, and if we are careful of our analyses and of how we apply our own solution, history can be what it ought to be: an extension of man's capacity and need to go forward. The test of the quality of a culture is its willingness and capacity to do this, but nowhere were the Romans more correct than when they advised: *Fastine lente,* make haste slowly.

INDEX